Democratic Empire

Also by Jim Cullen

The Civil War in Popular Culture: A Reusable Past (1995)

The Art of Democracy: A Concise History of Popular Culture in the United States (1996)

Born in the U.S.A.: Bruce Springsteen and the American Tradition (1997)

Popular Culture in American History (2001; Editor)

Restless in the Promised Land: Catholics and the American Dream (2001)

The American Dream: A Short History of an Idea That Shaped a Nation (2003)

The Fieldston Guide to American History for Cynical Beginners: Impractical Lessons for Everyday Life (2005)

The Civil War Era: An Anthology of Sources (2005; Editor, with Lyde Cullen Sizer)

Imperfect Presidents: Tales of Misadventure and Triumph (2007)

Essaying the Past: How to Read, Write, and Think About History (2009)

Sensing the Past: Hollywood Stars and Historical Visions (2013)

A Short History of the Modern Media (2014)

Democratic Empire

The United States Since 1945

Jim Cullen

WILEY Blackwell

Registered Office
John Wiley & Sons, Ltd, The Atrium, Southern Gate, Chichester, West Sussex, PO19 8SQ, UK

Editorial Offices
350 Main Street, Malden, MA 02148-5020, USA
9600 Garsington Road, Oxford, OX4 2DQ, UK
The Atrium, Southern Gate, Chichester, West Sussex, PO19 8SQ, UK

For details of our global editorial offices, for customer services, and for information about how to apply for permission to reuse the copyright material in this book please see our website at www.wiley.com/wiley-blackwell.

Library of Congress Cataloging-in-Publication Data

Names: Cullen, Jim, 1962– author.
Title: Democratic empire : the United States since 1945 / Jim Cullen.
Description: Chichester, UK ; Malden, MA : John Wiley & Sons, 2016. |
    Includes bibliographical references and index.
Identifiers: LCCN 2015043946 (print) | LCCN 2015049973 (ebook) |
    ISBN 9781119027355 (cloth) | ISBN 9781119027348 (pbk.) |
    ISBN 9781119027461 (pdf) | ISBN 9781119027362 (epub)
Subjects: LCSH: United States–History–1945– | United States–Social conditions–1945– |
    United States–Politics and government–1945–1989. | United States–Politics and
    government–1989–
Classification: LCC E741 .C84 2016 (print) | LCC E741 (ebook) | DDC 973.92–dc23
LC record available at http://lccn.loc.gov/2015043946

A catalogue record for this book is available from the British Library.

Cover image: © GraphicaArtis/Corbis

Set in 10/12pt Galliard by SPi Global, Pondicherry, India
Printed and bound in Malaysia by Vivar Printing Sdn Bhd

1   2017

For William Norman
Who hears, and makes, the life of American music

Contents

"We were all brought up to want things and maybe the world isn't big enough for all that wanting. I don't know."

—Henry "Rabbit" Angstrom, protagonist of John Updike's *Rabbit Redux*, 1971

Acknowledgments

The textbook is a specific genre of historical writing—it's a different enterprise than producing a work of original scholarship, for example, and it's one intended more for the needs of the diploma-minded student than the pleasure-minded general reader (however much one might strive to entertain). Writing a textbook feels a little like making an album of cover versions of your favorite songs: there's stuff you know you *have* to do, stuff people are *hoping* to get, and it's your job to be both familiar and (a little bit) novel at the same time in reinterpreting songs that are already out there. The accent in this book, as my musical analogy suggests, is a cultural one. But whatever the subfield in question—political history, social history, women's history—my first word of thanks must be to the generations of scholars on whose shoulders I stand, and here I want to name my mentors at Brown University who decisively shaped my vision of US history: Bill McLoughlin, Jim Patterson, Jack Thomas, and (especially) Mari Jo Buhle, who accepted me into Brown's American Civilization doctoral program. Other figures are acknowledged in my short bibliographies and footnotes at the end of this book. Still others are part of the rich loam that has and will germinate future works of history. I hope my work may yet settle into a layer of such sediment.

I'd also like to thank my longtime editor, Peter Coveney, who reacted to my pitch for a book about the 1970s and 1980s by suggesting something considerably more ambitious. This is the fifth book (not counting subsequent editions) that I've produced in the Wiley publishing stable; this particular one was aided by a series of kind of competent staffers, among them editorial assistant Ashley McPhee, project editor Julia Kirk, copy editor Aravind Kannankara, and production editor Vimali Joseph. Thanks also to marketing manager Leah Alaani.

This book was finished during a stay as a "Thinker in Residence" at Deakin University, with campuses in various locations in the state of Victoria, Australia, in the summer (well, actually, in the Australian winter) of 2015. My deep thanks to Cassandra Atherton, who organized the trip, her husband Glenn Moore of Latrobe University, and the staff, faculty, and students of Deakin who made my trip so memorable. The Ethical Culture Fieldston School has been my professional home for the last 15 years, and I'm grateful for the good company of my students and colleagues and the administration there. Of particular note has been the exceptionally valuable role of music teacher William Norman, who performed a series of roles here that ranged from fact-checking to providing excellent interpretative advice. The dedication of this volume to him is a necessarily insufficient gesture of gratitude.

A word in memoriam: I lost my beloved friend of 33 years, Gordon Sterling, while writing this book. He embodied what was best in our national life: optimism, decency and curiosity of an instinctively egalitarian kind.

Lyde, Jay, Grayson, Ryland, and Nancy: you're with me always—even at Starbucks, where most of this book was written at its Dobbs Ferry and Ardsley, New York locations. I thank God for you, and for Grande Coffees, among other blessings.

—Jim Cullen
Hastings-on-Hudson, New York
January, 2016

Prelude: The Imperial Logic of the American Dream

YOU ARE A CHILD OF EMPIRE. You probably don't think of yourself that way, for some understandable reasons. So it's worth considering those reasons before explaining why it's helpful in terms of your past—and your future—to understand yourself as such.

One reason you don't think of yourself as a child of empire is that relatively few people go around talking in this way about the place where you live. You are an American; more specifically, you are a resident of the United States ("America" being a term to describe terrain that rightfully stretches from Canada to Chile, even if common usage suggests otherwise), and you probably think of yourself as living in a democracy. In fact, that's not true. A democracy is a society in which all citizens—a term that connotes a set of legal rights including those of property, voting, and other privileges—have a say in making government decisions. The proverbial case is that of ancient Athens. Of course, the actual number of *citizens* in Athens (as opposed to slaves, women, or mere residents, none of whom could claim citizen status) was relatively small. Given the restricted number of people involved, Athenian democracy was a practical possibility: citizens could literally make their voices heard.

The United States, by contrast, is a *republic*, a geographically large political entity in which representatives get chosen by citizens—more precisely, a subset of citizens eligible to vote that does not include children, for example—who then make laws that apply collectively. The number of people in the US population who enjoyed such a status at the time of the American Revolution was much larger than in ancient Athens, even if it was still relatively small. (The whole question of who actually *had* representation was of course one of the major *reasons* for that revolution.) In the centuries that followed, the proportion of citizens grew steadily, and by the middle of the twentieth century it might have almost seemed that *inhabitant* was virtually the same thing as *citizen* (*voter* was always another story). Not only was that untrue, but a great many people who actually *were* citizens found themselves systematically deprived of their rights, as even a cursory look at women's history, immigration history, or that of US race relations makes clear.

And yet, for all this, the United States continues to be commonly described, by natives and observers alike, as a democracy. While this is not factually true, it does make sense in cultural terms, if not in political or social ones. Whether as a matter of folkways, foodways, or the popular media, the United States has always been notable for the degree to which a panoply of voices and visions have shaped its society and customs, and the fluidity of its cultural margins and center. It is one of the great ironies of American history, for example, that the period covered in this book, a period that marked the apex of US power and affluence, was decisively influenced by the legacy of its most oppressed people: American slaves. That's why there's some logic in designating the nation as democratic in spirit if not always, or even often, in reality.

In any case, the terms "democracy" or "republic" are hardly synonymous with "empire." In popular imagination, empire is sometimes thought of in terms of a dictator presiding unilaterally over a vast domain, such as Chinggis Khan or Napoleon Bonaparte figuratively straddling continents. There's some truth to that, though even the most powerful dictators are usually subject to more powerful cultural, if not legal, constraints than is sometimes supposed. But in fact any number of governments can form the basis of an empire. Ancient Athens was both a democracy *and* an empire. Julius Caesar and his successors presided over a multiethnic and multilingual imperial domain that covered three continents, but the Roman Empire began as a kingdom and thrived as a militarily aggressive republic long before he came along.

Perhaps by this point you're wondering just what I mean by the word "empire." I'll take my definition from the online version of that quintessentially American source, the Merriam-Webster dictionary:

> **1 a** (1) : a major political unit having a territory of great extent or a number of territories or peoples under a single sovereign authority; *especially* : one having an emperor as chief of state (2) : the territory of such a political unit
> **b** : something resembling a political empire; *especially* : an extensive territory or enterprise under single domination or control

By any historical global standard, the continental United States, stretching thousands of miles from the Atlantic to the Pacific Oceans, is a "major political unit having a territory of great extent." That "unit" is also under a "single sovereign authority," which happens to be the US Constitution. The expansion of that sovereign authority over the continent is something that happened over the course of centuries, as Native American peoples were expelled, displaced, or absorbed by the descendants of Europeans, particularly those from the British Isles. Even before that process was complete, the United States had acquired overseas territories and military bases, which now circle the globe. Americans do not have an emperor, but they do have a president who wields considerable power—and, in the realm of foreign affairs, that power now verges on unilateral. And while not all this territory is governed by the Constitution, the US government nevertheless exercises considerable economic and/or military power far beyond its territorial boundaries. Empires have always exercised power over so-called client states, which are often more convenient to rule indirectly than by formal conquest or control.

By way of illustration, consider the different-but-related status of Hawaii (a set of islands that collectively comprise a state in the Union); the US military installation at Guantanamo Bay in Cuba (which the United States has held for over a century, even though Cuba was never part of the United States and, indeed, despite the two nations being sworn enemies for much of the twentieth century); and Japan (a conquered but now independent and powerful ally bound to the United States by strong military and economic ties). All these, and others, have been important constituent parts of what can legitimately be called the American Empire.

Another reason why this phrase might not roll off your tongue: you haven't been brought up to think of "empire" as a nice word. You think of empires as unhappy places where people are forced to live in ways not of their own choosing. You understand there are people who make precisely this claim about US behavior abroad, even at home, and have done so for some time. But insofar as you think such people have a point, you're likely to think of the situations they describe as a temporary, an exceptional—or, perhaps most often—a regrettable situation, not really reflecting US principles. The people most likely to invoke the American Empire wish to make the point that the American government is scarcely any different from European empires of the nineteenth century (or any others, for that matter). This is to say that the United States is hypocritical, violating the terms of its own creation, in which ideals such as "all men are created equal" and "life, liberty, and the pursuit of happiness" are considered sacred—more sacred, at this point, than the Christian faith that underwrote them. Americans think of themselves as exceptional, these critics say. In fact, they're just like every other empire that falsely trumpets its own virtue.

These critics are correct. The United States is not exceptional in terms of the nature of its government, its rapid territorial acquisition, its global influence, or its tendency to think of itself as uniquely virtuous. That said, while empires are—by definition—aggressive and self-serving in the ways they amass power, they have their uses, even for many of those who are involuntarily subject to them. Empires impose order, and while order can be tyrannical, it can also be convenient, and necessary too, for many forms of a desirable life, whether defined in terms of domestic tranquility, the movement of goods across borders, the protection of minority rights, or the creation of durable works of art.

The other point to be made here—and one that's most relevant to the matter at hand—is that while empires may not be unique in their behavior, they tend to have distinctive accents. Their power always depends on a substantial degree of brute force, and force that is always applied internally as well as externally. But the success of empires, whether defined in terms of size, longevity, or influence, always rests on other factors—sometimes it's a culture, the way it was for the Greeks (adapted and extended by the Romans); other times it's religion, as in the Islamic empires of the seventh through seventeenth centuries; yet other times it's a personality, such as Alexander the Great, though these tend not to last long. Very often, of course, successful empires exhibit all these features, among others.

But one thing all empires must do is come up with a way to distribute power. There is always concentration at the top. As a practical matter, however, power must be divided somewhat, whether geographically (such as among states), among heirs in a political dynasty, literally or figuratively (we've had both in the United States, from the Adams family through the Bush family), or into a set of government functions (such as the three branches of government in the US Constitution). Distributing power is also a way of rewarding friends and punishing enemies.

Depending on their circumstances or values, there can be wide variations in the way empires distribute power. A lot of this will depend on the nature of the power they have, and a lot of that, in turn, will depend on how much control they have over their neighbors. The typical engine of empires is conquest: an army as an investment of time, money, and life, marshaled in the promise of gain that amounts to taking stuff away from other people. The leaders of successful empires keep their promises to reward their soldiers, and a share of the proceeds gets directed toward those who deliver the goods.

That said, the long-term stability of an empire will very often rest on its ability to distribute resources widely—not universally, mind you, but relatively so. Things such as terror or religious fervor can also work, though it's hard to keep a population in a state of psychological intensity for long periods of time. In general, providing a segment of people (sometimes sorted by race, class, or other markers) with a basic sense of safety and a workable livelihood will reduce the incentive of such people to join resistance movements that will always develop. Over time, the number of people enjoying imperial privileges is likely to grow. So it is, for example, that Roman citizenship was gradually extended to all Italians, foreigners from remote provinces willing to serve in the army, and eventually all free inhabitants of the empire. The Roman Dream, as it were.

Which brings us to the case of the United States. As I've said, the United States is not unique in any of the terms I've been discussing. But there is one *quantitative* factor so significant that it has become a *qualitative* one, and that is the relatively wide distribution of the fruits of empire. Simply put, there has never been anywhere on earth at any time when so many people have had so much.

Before going any further, I need to qualify this assertion about American abundance. First of all, saying so many people have so much *doesn't* mean everybody has enough. Discrimination and bad luck have always been facts of life. And even those who have "enough" defined in a narrow sense (sufficient calories to live on, however empty; shelter to speak of, however dangerous; sources of comfort or pleasure, however limited or self-destructive) does not mean that many, or even most, Americans live what most would call a decent life.

If you're reading this book, the chances are that you *do* have a decent life. But the chances are also that you hardly think of yourself a child of empire. It seems too grand a term to describe the rather ordinary circumstances of your existence, even if they happen to be comfortable. There's something a little comical about such a description, similar to the once-proverbial parental demand that a child eat his or her peas because there are starving children in Africa. Insofar as it's true, it's also irrelevant (those peas on your plate will never make it to Africa).

But I'm here to tell you that, in some important sense, considering yourself a child of empire is accurate, and it is relevant. From the very beginning of the colonial era, the settlers of what became the United States were, in the words of the title of a classic work of history, a people of plenty. "Take foure of the best kingdomes in Christendom and put them all together, they may in no way compare with this countrie either for commodities or goodnesse of soile," the deputy governor of the Colony of Virginia, Thomas Dale, said, not entirely exaggerating, in 1611.[1] Even unquestionably oppressed slaves enjoyed a standard of living higher than their counterparts elsewhere in the Americas, as historians of slavery routinely acknowledge.[2] The reality of relative plenty continued into the twentieth century. In 1948, the government of the Soviet Union screened the 1940 Hollywood film *The Grapes of Wrath* to illustrate to Russian public the failures of US capitalism. But government censors had to pull the movie from circulation when it became clear that Russian audiences were amazed that these impoverished Americans nevertheless owned cars.[3] Televisions, cellphones, Internet connections: even unacceptably poor Americans enjoy the fruits of US technology and consumer culture in ways that would have dazzled kings of earlier generations.

One implication you should *not* draw from the presence of widespread prosperity across American history is any special virtue in the ruling elites that have run this country in the last 400 years. The conditions I'm describing were as much the result of a series of pre-existing conditions—moderate climate, good soil, a bounty of natural resources, relatively weak challengers for the relatively capacious and lightly populated land—than any human design. When Thomas Jefferson famously proclaimed that all men are created equal, and that they were entitled to life, liberty, and the pursuit of happiness, he did not present these notions as aspirations. Instead, he presented them as facts, as "self-evident" truths conferred by what he called "Nature's God." To the degree that there *was* any human design on the part of the nation's founders—and there certainly was some—the relatively wide distribution of resources was a form of enlightened self-interest in charting a path of least resistance in gaining the allegiance of a populace that was not always unified. To cite perhaps the most important example: the emancipation of four million slaves in 1865 represented more an economic imperative and the triumph of one imperial elite over another than the inevitable triumph of a just cause, the inspiring prose of Abraham Lincoln notwithstanding.

Emancipation occurred just as the Industrial Revolution, which laid the foundations for modern American consumer capitalism, made the pursuit of happiness here seem more plausible to millions of people around the world. This form of capitalism also made it plausible to believe that material prosperity would engender conditions conducive to psychic prosperity as well. Note, however, that "plausible" does not mean "certain," or even "likely." Nor does it deny the possibility that someone could say, with at least as much credibility, that the reality of life, liberty, and happiness are far from self-evident—and that happiness is not actually the most worthy goal in life. Actually, many people in the United States *have* said such things in any number of ways in the last few centuries. Doing so is part of the polyglot literary tradition, which stretches from Anne Bradstreet to Herman Melville to Malcolm X and beyond. And these figures had some very good reasons for saying so as a matter of personal experience or observation.

But the key point—actually it's the premise on which this book rests—is that enough people have believed in the grand promises of the Declaration of Independence to make the United States more or less governable since 1776. In a sense, *this* is what's self-evident, for if large numbers of people did *not* subscribe to that myth (a term I use to describe a proposition that is widely believed but not empirically confirmable), the Union would not have survived. Amid some widely expressed doubts, and amid well-founded suspicions that the nation's abundance was being squandered, unfairly distributed, or simply evaporating, a critical consensus on the viability of the myth managed to hold sway. Elections could proceed and decisions could be made precisely because the legitimacy of national hopes were taken for granted. It was always a matter of *how*, not *if*, they could be realized.[4]

In modern times, we've given a name to these promises, placing them in a conceptual umbrella that we call the "American Dream." Though the term only came into widespread use in the 1930s, Americans of earlier centuries would have understood that it functioned as shorthand for what a great many of them had always believed was there for the taking—the reality of abundance; the real possibility of gaining, augmenting, or redistributing it; and the sense of satisfaction that would follow from its flow.

It's significant that the term "American Dream" first entered common parlance during the Great Depression, because it was during these years that the promises of national life went under their widest and deepest reappraisal, as the nation's collective confidence was shaken to its core. But as many studies of the decade have attested, the nation came out of the 1930s with widespread reaffirmations of the American Dream. There are two basic reasons for this. The first is that the US government and economy were able to stabilize internally, to at least some degree as a result of the statecraft of Franklin Delano Roosevelt, who sanded down the most destructive edges of industrial capitalism and successfully reassured electoral majorities of Americans that their fears about the death of the American Dream would prove unfounded. The other is that the most obvious alternatives to it—represented on the Left by Stalin's Soviet Union and the Right by Hitler's Germany—were decidedly less appealing. Actually, these two reasons converged in the military buildup that the United States began in the late 1930s, which bolstered the nation's capacity to contend with its imperial rivals and, in the process, stimulated the economy even more effectively than Roosevelt's New Deal did. A reinvigorated American Dream trumped the collectivist fantasies of Communists and Nazis.

It was a third rival, imperial Japan, who finally provoked a cautious, even skeptical, United States into World War II. A generation earlier, the nation had intervened in World War I and emerged from it as the only other major power stronger than it had been at the start of the war. Despite such success, the

United States, unlike Japan, reverted to a longstanding tendency to avoid direct involvement in overseas affairs. But when the nation finally did commit to war in 1941, the results were, from an imperial standpoint, spectacularly successful. The United States risked the least and gained the most from World War II, fighting on two fronts simultaneously and steamrolling arguably superior military talent under the sheer weight of its immense industrial capacity (and extending lifelines to its British, Soviet, and Chinese allies in the process). When the war ended with the dropping of two atomic bombs in 1945, the United States was unquestionably the world's greatest military and economic power, even if it also had gathering rivals preparing to challenge it.

World War II was also a watershed event in the domestic history of the United States. Despite fears of a return to the economic conditions of the Great Depression, it soon became clear that the promises of the American Dream were more shimmering and alluring than ever. Again, the *realities* of national life were, in a great many cases, different. And across the nation there were forces mobilizing to thwart the great expectations that were rising in the land. But the potency of hope was simply too great to be denied. That potency was powerful in what it could achieve; it was dangerous in what it could upend; it was risky in the disappointment it could engender. But neither friend nor foe could anticipate, much less control, the force of the American Dream as it surged to high tide.

This is the point where our story begins. In the three-quarters of a century since World War II, US power was like an alternating current that surged through the body politic. That power affected people in different ways, and generated different outcomes. It was sometimes channeled in specific directions; in others, it was impeded (consider the role of the semiconductor as fact and metaphor); and in still others it was suppressed or denied in ways that generated friction (a source of electricity in its own right). In a very important sense, the *perception* of power was often more significant than the reality. What people *believed* was possible, what they *feared* and what they *hoped*, are the keys to understanding American culture since World War II.

This book will look at those perceptions, fears, and hopes in the context of the facts of American life as they are known. These facts include financial resources (measured in terms such gold reserves and annual GDP), technological innovations (here I'll note that virtually all modern electronics, from computers through cell phones, run on alternating current), and sociological changes (e.g., the rise and fall of birth and divorce rates). However, that elusive but pervasive thing we call *culture*—discussed here primarily in terms of the mass media, the fine arts, and the intellectual currents that coursed through academe and journalistic circles—will be central to what the book purports to chronicle, which is to provide a framework through which recent US history can be understood.

This story is, perhaps inevitably, one of declension: the American empire was so powerful in 1945 largely because its rivals were by comparison so weak. That was bound to change, in part because shrewd US politicians understood that rebuilding former enemies was good policy. But it is also hard not to sense a more immutable, if dimly understood, rhythm of history at work. Empires rise and fall. That's certain. And yet, their peculiar trajectory can only begin to be understood in retrospect. In any case, individual lives always unfold somewhat independently of national fates. Those lives unfold in a particular context that demarcates any number of possibilities and limits. That's why trying to understand that context makes some sense, and why in particular it makes some sense to do so relatively early in one's life. We study the past in the hope that history is not necessarily destiny: we hope for the capacity to plot our own futures. This hope may be an illusion, but it's a sustaining one, and one that can have positive consequences even if our aspirations go unrealized. In any case, a desire to dream your own destiny—and, more crucially, the notion that you can plausibly do so on these shores—is nothing if not characteristically American.

Notes

1   Dale quoted in David Potter, *People of Plenty: Economic Abundance and the American Character* (1956; Chicago: University of Chicago Press), 78.
2   The relative mildness of slavery in North America compared to elsewhere in the hemisphere has been widely discussed. For an overview, see Peter Kolchin, *American Slavery, 1619–1877*, revised edition (1993; New York: Hill & Wang, 2003), esp. 133–168, Ch. 4.
3   Jim Cullen, *The American Dream: A Short History of an Idea that Shaped a Nation* (New York: Oxford University Press, 2003), 150.
4   Garry Wills makes this point in *Nixon Agonistes: The Crisis of the Self-Made Man* (1970; New York: Houghton Mifflin, 2002), 453.

Part I
The Postwar Decades

1

Victory and Anxiety
World War and Cold War, 1945–1962

Figure 1.1   CHE BELLO! Residents of New York City's Little Italy neighborhood greeting the news of Japanese surrender in August 1945. The victory of the United States and its allies in World War II left the nation in a position of unparalleled global supremacy that defined its expectations for decades to come. (Source: Library of Congress Prints and Photographs Division Washington, DC, 20540, USA, http://hdl.loc.gov/loc.pnp/cph.3c35620)

Democratic Empire: The United States Since 1945, First Edition. Jim Cullen.
© 2017 Jim Cullen. Published 2017 by John Wiley & Sons, Inc.

Colony to Colonizer: American Rise to Globalism

Awesome

In recent decades, the word has been a slang expression of approval. "That was an awesome game." "Those are awesome shoes." "She's really an awesome person."[1] Rarely do those who use the term consider its literal meaning: that which inspires amazement, even fear, in its overwhelming power. "Awe" generally (including aw*ful* as well as awes*ome*) has often had religious connotations; Moses coming down from Mount Sinai with the Ten Commandments, or the earth-shaking grief of God as Jesus died on the cross: these were events that evoked awe for those who experienced them. Earthly phenomena can be awesome too. A volcanic eruption or a tornado is an awesome experience. So is the miracle of birth.

Here's something else that's awesome: US military power. With bases that circle the globe, soldiers who are the best equipped and trained in the world, and cutting-edge technology that is continually updated, the president of the United States can, at a moment's notice, wreak terrifying havoc on just about any location on this planet, and by having his orders executed at the touch of a button that directs a drone. And that doesn't even take into account bombs that are capable of destroying all life on earth, or any number of weapons systems of which most of us are blissfully ignorant. There are of course any number of practical inhibitions on the ability to exercise this power, and any number of ways determined enemies are currently plotting their ways around it (the technical term for this is "asymmetrical warfare"), something that has been accomplished with notable success in Vietnam, Afghanistan, and New York's World Trade Center, among other places in the last 75 years. But neither friend nor foe can doubt the immensity of the destructive power that the United States currently has at its disposal.

This awesome capacity, which has been used for good as well as evil, has been a fact of global life since World War II. Actually, in relative terms, English North Americans were powerful from their beginnings. Despite the tenuousness of colonial settlements on the eastern seaboard in the early decades of the seventeenth century, New Englanders were able to defeat Native peoples in the Pequot War of the 1630s, less than a decade after Massachusetts was founded. Colonial Virginians prevailed over the Powhatan Indians in 1622 and 1644, and English settlers generally prevailed in wars against Indians that stretched over the next century and half. There was no question that the British Empire was vastly more powerful than the colonists who went to war for their independence in 1776, and yet the Americans were able to win it anyway (with French, Spanish, and Dutch help). For most of the nineteenth century, US security was guaranteed by the British Navy, which effectively enforced the Monroe Doctrine of 1823 that warned European powers against reasserting themselves in the western hemisphere (that's because Britain had a shared interest in keeping rivals out). Such insulation allowed the nation to assert its dominion over the rest of the North American continent in wars with Mexico and various indigenous peoples. Even when the United States was wracked by a fierce Civil War, England and France, though tempted, thought better of intervening to bolster their respective positions in North America. When the Civil War ended, the US Army was the largest on the face of the earth. Foreign governments sent military experts to observe that war closely: they understood that they were witnessing the future of armed conflict in innovations such as the Gatling gun (an early machine gun) and trench warfare.

After 1865, the US Army and Navy shriveled to the point of insignificance. Here's a paradox: for a nation of its size, the United States has been able to get away with an absurdly small military and *still* throw its weight around. Rarely has a nation been so fortunate in its enemies. When the United States finally did collide with a European power—Spain in 1898—it won decisively in a matter of months despite an embarrassingly clumsy mobilization. Victory in that war accelerated a trend toward acquiring overseas possessions that had begun with Alaska in 1867 and now extended to the Philippines. By the time of the outbreak of World War I in 1914, the United States had reached the point of becoming a prominent second-tier power, behind Britain and Germany.

Enjoying oceans of protection from Great Power politics, the American people reacted to World War I with deep skepticism about intervention, notwithstanding a profitable trading relationship with Europe that resulted in a vast transfer of wealth to US advantage. After hesitating early in the war, Germany resumed attacks on Atlantic shipping to prevent US aid to England and France. American public opinion changed dramatically, and the United States went to war in 1917. The German high command gambled that the Americans would not be able to mobilize fast enough to stop a last-chance German offensive against Paris. Though plausible, that bet was a losing one: American troops arrived in force in 1918, re-energizing allies who flattened the Germans in a matter of months. Once again, the nation benefited from the weakness of others, this time the financially and militarily devastated European empires. President Woodrow Wilson and his supporters hoped that the United States would now assume a position of global leadership. But the deep grooves of public opinion, suspicious of what this might entail, rejected the League of Nations and the vision of international engagement that it represented, and Congress voted accordingly. The nation turned inward again, in large measure because it could afford to, for another generation.

Wages of War: Triumph over Germany and Japan

World War II proved to be a turning point in the nation's relationship with the world. At first, it didn't seem it would be. Over the course of the 1930s, volatile European powers—the Germans now under Nazi rule; the Soviet Union under the Communist Joseph Stalin; the British and French avoiding conflict with either while trying to prop up their sagging empires—lurched toward disaster. Meanwhile, in the Pacific, the Japanese empire expanded across the Pacific, eating into northern and eastern China and threatening European interests, many of them petroleum-based, in Southeast Asia. None of this was enough to budge American public opinion, which strongly supported the Neutrality Acts passed by Congress in the second half of the 1930s, designed to handcuff the desire of internationalists—notably President Franklin Delano Roosevelt—from acting on their concern that the Nazi and Japanese regimes represented a bona fide threat to the United States.

Yet, by 1939, when Germany invaded Poland and triggered World War II in Europe, even the most committed of the so-called isolationists recognized the value of bolstering US defenses. In the first 2 years of the new decade, the US government stepped up building up its military capacity—reinstituting the draft, for example—and spending money on weapons. It certainly helped that rearmament also helped stimulate an economy that had never fully recovered from the Great Depression of the 1930s. With some difficulty, President Roosevelt managed to sell Congress on a program known as Lend-Lease—military aid to US allies in the form of loans or the transfer of assets such as naval bases—because it seemed cheaper and easier to have American allies do most of the heavy lifting. Meanwhile, more high-minded advocates of internationalism advocated greater engagement, most famously *Time* magazine editor Henry Luce, who in a February 1941 article exhorted his fellow citizens to embrace the coming "American Century."[2]

The United States finally did enter World War II after the Japanese attack on Pearl Harbor in December 1941, years after the other principal combatants had attacked each other in the Atlantic and the Pacific. There is of course much to be said about this. For our purposes, what's notable here is not simply that the United States prevailed in fighting across two oceans simultaneously, but the *way* it prevailed: by simply overwhelming its opponents with its sheer—yes, awesome—power. That power rested on a number of foundations. One of them was an impregnable geographic position (the Japanese managed to drop a total of four virtually harmless bombs into the woods of Oregon, the only ones ever to land on mainland soil during the war).[3] Another was the size and competence of its armed forces, mobilized from a wide cross-section of society, that was notably well-fed, literate, and confident.

The most decisive aspect of US power, however, was an economic base that staggered its opponents. Germany and Japan could boast of considerable productive prowess, all the more impressive for an ability to function under tremendous pressure from encroaching enemies. And German as well as Japanese soldiers were typically at least the equal of any the United States sent into battle. (Many observers consider the army with which Germany invaded Soviet Union, an ally it turned on in 1941, the finest the world has ever seen.) But neither the Japanese nor the Germans could withstand the seemingly bottomless ability of the United States to supply not only itself, but its allies, with whatever it took to win. By 1943, most informed leaders of both Germany and Japan knew they were doomed simply because they could not compete with the seemingly bottomless US capacity for war-making.

Numbers alone tell a vivid story. For example, the United States absorbed what initially seemed like a crippling blow at Pearl Harbor, where hundreds of aircraft were damaged in a single day. And yet, within months, American contractors were building more planes every *day* than were lost in that attack, which had been planned for many years.[4] A Liberty ship, used to carry cargo, took 355 days to build in 1941. Within a year, production time was cut to 56 days, and in one case a mere 2 weeks. (The construction quality was not as good, but US capacity was great enough for such assets to be considered disposable, an observation that was made of other kinds of US war production, such as tanks.[5]) The impact of this power may well have been even more dramatic in its impact on US allies. There is little question that the Soviets bore the brunt of the Nazi war machine, and that Soviet blood was indispensable to eventual victory. But the Soviets could not have prevailed without the 13 million pairs of boots, 5 million tons of food, 2,000 locomotives, 11,000 freight carriages, and 540,000 tons of rails—more than the Soviets laid between 1928 and 1939—that Americans provided, among other supplies, in 4 years of Lend-Lease, to say nothing of what it provided to Britain, China, and other allies. In 1939, the United States was a negligible factor in the international arms market; by 1944, it was producing 40% of the world's weapons. And by 1947, the nation was producing almost half of the manufactured goods in the world.[6]

War sometimes destroys economies. In the case of the United States, however, World War II proved wondrous, with a glow that lasted decades. Stanford University historian David Kennedy has aptly summarized its transformative power:

> At the end of the Depression decade [1939], nearly half of all white families and almost 90 percent of black families still lived in poverty. One in seven workers remained unemployed. By war's end unemployment was negligible. In the ensuing quarter century the American economy would create some 20 million new jobs, more than half of them filled by women. Within less than a generation of the war's end, the middle class, defined as families with annual incomes between three and ten thousand dollars, more than doubled. By 1960 the middle class included almost two-thirds of all Americans, most of whom owned their own homes, unprecedented achievements for any modern society.[7]

This is not to say that World War II can account for all of this, or that it had a positive economic outcome for everyone, or that its rewards were evenly distributed. Prosperity may have alleviated evils such as racism, for example, but it hardly eradicated them in a society where discrimination had always been a fact of life, and would remain a fact of life. During the war, millions of African Americans left the rural, segregated South to find jobs in Northern cities. They found those jobs—and they found ongoing segregation, sometimes repressive enough to spark violence in cities such as Detroit and St. Louis, which experienced bloody race riots. Perhaps even more than the actual opportunities generated by the war, it was the rising sense of expectations that marked the war years in domestic life.

Indeed, it was precisely this sense of hope that led African Americans and other minorities to fight, not only to defeat Hitler and the nightmarish vision he represented, but also to resist Hitlers at home. Foreigners also understood the appeal of the American way of life, and that its realization was directly correlated with one's proximity to America itself. It's no wonder that defeated German soldiers vastly preferred to surrender to Americans than the Soviets, not only as a matter of survival prospects, but also as a matter of what life was likely to be like after the war. Nowhere was the coming economic divide more obvious than in territories partitioned between the two major powers at the end of the conflict. The comparison between a Soviet-dominated East Germany and US-dominated West Germany, or a Soviet-controlled North Korea and a US-controlled South Korea, proved to be object lessons in what communism and capitalism had to offer. It was no contest.

American international economic dominance was codified at the Bretton Woods Conference of 1944. It was at this gathering of 44 allied nations in a New Hampshire hotel that the parameters of a United States–centric global economic order was established, one that included the General Agreement of Tariffs and Trade (GATT), the World Bank, and the International Monetary Fund (IMF). The dollar in effect became the international currency, replacing the British pound sterling. While the world economy has changed substantially since that time, and the relative position of the United States has slipped significantly, world markets still play by these American-made rules.

But the greatest demonstration of American might in World War II was technological. It was a single act, performed on August 6, 1945: the dropping of the atomic bomb. If this was not awesome, nothing on earth ever was. While some critics argued it was too terrible a weapon to be deployed even against a hated enemy, there was relatively little domestic opposition to its use at Hiroshima, and, when surrender was not immediately forthcoming, at Nagasaki 3 days later. Military planners were acutely aware that less than 5% of Japanese soldiers had ever surrendered in battle, and that the planned invasion of Japan would involve millions of soldiers and hundreds of thousands of casualties. Though his decision was criticized at the time and ever since—almost 100,000 people died instantly at Hiroshima—President Harry Truman, who took office upon the death of Roosevelt that spring, never doubted his responsibility to end the war as quickly and decisively as he could.[8]

The atomic bomb was only the most visible, and terrifying, manifestation of US technological might during and following World War II. But it was during the latter part of the war that the American government began developing another technology that would also have a dramatic impact on the shape of the postwar world: computers. To a significant degree, the US innovation in this field was related to policy surrounding the bomb.[9]

For most of US history, the word "computers" did not refer to things; they referred to people, many of them women, who did the math of everyday commercial life—managing payrolls, budgets, and the like. They were assisted by a series of tools such as the slide rule, commonplace before the invention of calculators. The 1924 creation of International Business Machines (IBM) under the leadership of executive Thomas J. Watson became one of the greatest success stories of corporate capitalism. Over the course of the next generation, IBM led the way in the development of increasingly elaborate devices that could perform ever more complex calculations. These early computers were often enormous pieces of engineering, with lots of sensitive moving parts that occupied large rooms and required delicate management.

It was during World War II, however, that a decisive new chapter in the history began, and here the US government, not private corporations, proved pivotal. Computers were vital to the processes of code-making and breaking, as well as for performing ballistics calculations for artillery. Wartime use of computer technology was an important part of the Manhattan Project, from which the atomic bomb emerged. But it was the implications of atomic warfare even more than the bombs themselves that proved particularly significant for the future. Of particular concern was the ability to act decisively and responsibly in the event of a future nuclear war. In 1946, the US government created the Research and Development (RAND) Corporation, which grappled with such problems. It was followed in 1958 by the Advanced Research Projects Agency, or ARPA. (The agency was renamed the Defense Advanced Research Projects Agency, or DARPA, in 1969.) So it was that the US government's quest to maintain its newly acquired military supremacy laid down the tracks for what would become one of the most powerful tools of every civilian life in the twenty-first century: the Internet.

But all this was too far into the future to be perceived in anything but the dimmest of ways. In 1945, virtually all Americans were entirely focused on victory over Germany (in May) and Japan (in August). The end of the war was met with widespread ecstasy in the United States, symbolized by Albert Eisenstaedt's famous photograph of two young strangers, a sailor and a nurse, kissing in New York's Times Square. But—and this is one of the great paradoxes of the war—its end was at least as sobering as it was celebratory. That's not only because of the terrible human cost paid by the some 400,000 combat and other deaths sustained in the war, and the loved ones they left behind.[10] It's also because the *way* the war ended was unmistakably ominous; it took no great feat of imagination to think that atomic weapons would only get more powerful, and that the enemies of the United States would soon acquire them, as indeed they did. And those enemies asserted themselves more quickly than most Americans anticipated.

First Frost: Dawn of the Cold War

Certainly, many Americans did see trouble coming even before the war had ended. Relations between the United States and the Soviet Union had never been very good. The Communist-led Union of Soviet Socialist Republics (USSR) was explicitly dedicated to the overthrow of capitalism not only in Russia, but in the rest of the world as well, and the US government was part of a coalition that had unsuccessfully tried to aid the enemies of the Soviets in the civil war that followed the Russian Revolution of 1917. The American government refused to recognize the legitimacy of the Soviets until 1933, and ties were lukewarm at best before the Germans violated the Nazi–Soviet pact of

1939 by invading 2 years later. For a brief period in the early 1940s, the United States and USSR cooperated effectively, but there were mutual suspicions even when relations were strongest. Stalin believed that the repeated delays in what became the D-Day landing in Europe in 1944 were designed to bleed his countrymen dry; American policymakers worried that Stalin intended to impose his will on Eastern Europe, as he did, ruthlessly, in the aftermath of the war. The acrimony between the two nations was more than a matter of traditional Great Power competition; it was also rooted in ideology. Though the Soviets' stated intention to spread revolution around the globe was more posturing than reality, it set up a series of satellite states governed by a set of doctrinaire communist parties, stretching from Korea to Poland. A combination of legitimate security concerns, a historic tendency toward expansion, and an increasingly paranoid dictator made the USSR difficult to manage, much less control.

Tensions were increasingly obvious when Roosevelt, Stalin and the British prime minister Winston Churchill met in the Soviet seaside town of Yalta in 1944. The strain was even greater in the following year at a meeting convened to make more postwar plans in the German town of Potsdam, where Harry Truman, who acceded to the presidency following the death of Roosevelt in April 1945, took a harder line with Stalin. (Truman did not reveal that he had the atomic bomb ready to go, but Stalin's spies had already informed him.) As the Soviets moved with increasing decisiveness to solidify their grip on Eastern Europe in early 1946, Churchill famously proclaimed that an "Iron Curtain" was now dividing the two sides in what came to be known as the Cold War.

In the second half of the 1940s, the Americans and Soviets played a carefully calibrated game of chicken in which they staked out as much literal or figurative territory as they could without precipitating armed conflict. When it looked like communists might come to power in Greece and Turkey in 1947, the Truman administration gave aid to their enemies to keep this from happening. In 1948, the Soviets demonstrated their displeasure with the Americans by closing the highway leading to the old German capital of Berlin, which had sectors of control assigned to both the United States and Soviets, but which was located deep in the heart of Soviet-controlled East Germany. Truman responded to the road closure with an 11-month-long airlift to keep the city supplied; the Soviets reopened the road in 1949.

Besides such reactive measures, the American government was also formulating a broader anticommunist strategy known as "containment," a term coined by US diplomat George Kennan in a 5,000-word message transmitted from Moscow in 1946 that came to be known as the Long Telegram. Kennan argued that much of Soviet aggression was less a function of communist ideology than an expression of centuries of Russian expansionism, a problem best dealt with by selectively applying pressure at key geographic points in order to discourage the Soviets from their instinctive desire to control more territory. Although his ideas would prove to be highly influential, Kennan was among those who came to regret the way the United States practiced containment in the decades that followed, because it tended to lead the United States to back regimes, however abhorrent, that took anticommunist positions. This approach would reap bitter rewards in Vietnam, for example.

But not all US policy was mindless in this regard; indeed, the Truman administration met the Soviet challenge with notable enlightened self-interest as well. Responding to reports of severe privation in Europe—and concerned that it would lead some Europeans to embrace radical solutions—a massive international aid program, the Marshall Plan, named after former World War II commander and then-current secretary of state George Marshall, was announced in 1948. The Marshall Plan helped Western Europe get back on its feet, and in so doing helped re-establish a market for American goods. The Soviets and their allies were invited to participate, but Stalin, sensing a trap, refused to allow it. Truman further bolstered the US position by creating a series of military alliances around the globe, most notably the North Atlantic Treaty Organization (NATO) in 1949. The Marshall Plan and NATO were termed the "two halves of the walnut" in American foreign policy in the Cold War era. He also authorized a re-expansion of the military outlined in a famous 1950 National Security Council report known as NSC-68, an important blueprint of US strategy. Even though the American military infrastructure shrank after the war ended, it was clear that the United States would not demilitarize in the way it had after previous wars. The national defense budget for 1947 was a hefty $13 billion higher than the last prewar budget of 1940.[11]

Stalin had resources of his own, among them an immense army that he kept poised on the perimeter of the Soviet empire. The most important postwar military asset he acquired was the atomic bomb, ending the US monopoly in 1949. While the United States would generally have more powerful and sophisticated weapons at any given time in the next 40 years, the Soviets would acquire sufficient nuclear power to assure a state of deterrence known as mutually assured destruction (MAD).

It was MAD more than any other factor that prevented the Cold War from ever becoming a hot one. Instead, the two sides asserted their interests through a series of proxy fights, overthrowing governments they considered hostile to their interests. As indicated, this had already started before the Soviets acquired nuclear bomb technology, in the form of US interventions in Greece and Turkey, as well as Soviet interventions in Poland and Czechoslovakia during the late 1940s. But MAD both raised the stakes and engendered caution. So when the Americans intervened in Guatemala to put a friendlier regime in power in 1954, for or the Soviets acted similarly in Hungary in 1956, each side implicitly recognized the other's sphere of influence, hesitating to resist too strongly for fear of triggering a nuclear catastrophe.

Along with the loss of nuclear monopoly, the other serious blow that the United States sustained in 1949 was the communist takeover of China. Again, this was a foreseeable turn of events. China had been wracked by civil war since the 1920s, and the bloody contest of wills waged by the Nationalists led by Chiang Kai-Shek and Communists led by Mao Zedong was suspended, not ended, when Japan invaded in 1931. Once the Japanese were expelled in 1945, the two sides resumed fighting. The United States supported the Chiang regime, which it knew was corrupt but hoped to reform, yet was unable to broker a deal between Chiang and Mao, who drove the Nationalists onto the island of Taiwan (which the United States improbably insisted until 1972 was the location of the legitimate Chinese government).

So it was that, by 1950, the United States was confronted with *two* major communist adversaries. The severity of this challenge became apparent that year, when Stalin gave his blessing for North Korea to invade South Korea. Caught off guard, the United States scrambled to put together a force in the name of the recently formed United Nations, winning approval for a multinational force to prevent the unification of Korea under communist influence. (The Americans were able to do this because the Soviets, who normally would have vetoed such a move, had temporarily boycotted the UN over its refusal to recognize the communist Chinese regime.) The UN counterattack that followed was successful—a little *too* successful. When the army under the command of American general Douglas MacArthur approached the Chinese border with North Korea, a huge Chinese force overran UN forces and pushed them all the way back down again. By mid-1951, a rough equilibrium was established near the location of the original partition at the end of World War II. But it would take 2 years of wrangling over the fate of prisoners of war before a truce was finally declared. It has remained in place—which is to say that the United States technically remains at war with North Korea—to this day. The Korean War was unpopular with the American public, which, while never expressing strong opposition to it (the way it would in Vietnam), tended to view the conflict as remote and fruitless, one that grimly clarified the high price of the Cold War and the burden that the nation shouldered as a self-appointed global policeman.

Seeing Red: The Cold War at Home

It would be hard to overstate just how frustrated many Americans were with the state of the world by the early 1950s. The nation had banded together and won a gargantuan battle against Germany and Japan, only to confront a new set of enemies that seemed equally dangerous. To make matters worse, the Soviet acquisition of the atomic bomb (by 1964, China joined the club, which by then included England and France) meant that the world could end at any moment. How could this state of affairs have come to pass? And who was to blame? Angry citizens—and the politicians who sought to tap that anger—looked hard for culprits. Perhaps not surprisingly, they found enemies within.

Although it might sometimes seem so, empires never speak with one voice. At times of crisis—such as the onset of financial calamity, for example, or the outbreak of a war—consensus may exist for a leader to focus the energies of a people in a particular direction. That certainly happened in a number of countries in the case of the Great Depression and World War II. But such unity is the exception rather than the rule. There are always alternating currents at work, even if they fall short of sparking civil war. This is true even in dictatorships; factions always compete for a leader's attention or jockey for position to literally or figuratively inherit a throne. In a nation such as the United States, alternative visions for society have long been organized and legitimated through political parties that compete for the electorate's support. Those parties, and the politicians who lead them, may use any number of tactics to win votes. Some are principled; some are not. Most often they're a blend of the two.

One of the more dramatic internal disputes on foreign policy in the early Cold War era took place between Truman and MacArthur, the general who had accepted the surrender of the Japanese, governed occupied Japan, and who led the UN forces in Korea. Truman and MacArthur disagreed on a number of points, principal among them the danger of Chinese intervention in the conflict (MacArthur underestimated it). Truman ultimately relieved MacArthur of his command, a deeply unpopular decision that led to talk of MacArthur for president. But the legacy of their conflict was a reaffirmation of civilian control of the military, a deeply ingrained value in American political culture, but also one that strengthened the imperial power of the presidency.

Other conflicts were not so easy to resolve. By the early 1950s, a significant number of Americans were convinced that the communists could never have achieved such gains abroad without significant assistance from foreign agents and traitors operating within the United States. This was not an irrational idea; Stalin and other communist leaders had repeatedly asserted their intention to create worldwide revolution, even if that was usually more bluster than reality. There really *was* a Communist Party in the United States (albeit one riddled with American informers).

Actually, fears of domestic communist subversion long predated World War II. The Red Scare, a major crackdown involving harassment, arrests, and expulsion of communists and other radicals, followed in the wake of World War I. From the 1920s until the 1970s, the Federal Bureau of Investigation (FBI) was headed by the reactionary J. Edgar Hoover, who often showed more interest in prosecuting political radicalism than organized crime. In 1938, Congress created the House Committee on Un-American Activities (HUAC), chaired by Texas Congressman Martin Dies (it was also known as the Dies Committee), to investigate subversive activities by fascists or communists. Once the United States and the Soviet Union became allies against Nazi Germany, hostility toward communism receded somewhat, though it never entirely disappeared.

With the advent of the Cold War, however, domestic anticommunism feelings intensified again. Beginning in the late 1940s, the Truman administration began requiring loyalty oaths to be taken by federal employees—the FBI, which handled this work, almost doubled in size[12]—and a number of professional organizations required background checks for their members. In 1947, HUAC generated national headlines when it began investigating political affiliations in the film industry, demanding that actors, writers, and other filmmakers reveal whether or not they had ever been communists, and to name any others they knew to have been. The so-called Hollywood Ten refused to cooperate with the investigation, and were cited for contempt by Congress, making it impossible for them to find work in the industry (a few screenwriters later escaped such "blacklisting" by writing under false names).

The actual number of people who lost their jobs in these investigations—called witch-hunts by their detractors, and memorialized most vividly by playwright Arthur Miller,[13] whose 1953 play *The Crucible* turned the 1692 Salem Witch Trials into an allegory of the investigations—was not especially large. In New York City, for example 321 schoolteachers and 58 college professors were fired, a tiny fraction of the work force.[14] But fear over accusations, whether true, false, or misleading, generated enormous anxiety and resonated outward far more than these figures would suggest.

Again, part of what made all of this complicated is that, while fears of communist subversion were very often exaggerated, they were never quite total nonsense. In 1950, a highly placed State Department official, Alger Hiss, was caught lying about his former communist ties in a case prosecuted by future president Richard Nixon, who became a national figure as a result of it. One of the most controversial legal cases of the early 1950s was the trial, conviction, and 1953 execution of Julius and Ethel Rosenberg, who were accused of passing atomic secrets to the Soviets during World War II. Their guilt was long in question, though that of Julius has since been established, while that of his wife appears likely. Whether or not they deserved to be executed is another question.

In this climate, anyone who advocated policies that remotely resembled those of the Soviets—or who had anything but the harshest of words for the Soviets—was often considered suspicious. Actually, this dynamic was in place long before the Cold War; it was one reason why Democratic Party officials demanded that Roosevelt replace his third-term vice president, Henry Wallace, with the more anti-Soviet Truman in 1944. Wallace remained active and relatively well-disposed toward the Soviets for the rest of the decade, though he and his supporters came to be seen as increasingly irrelevant (at best).

Some members of the opposition Republican Party saw political opportunity in casting suspicions on government officials—even when reasons for doing so where dubious if not outright lies. Among the most notorious was US senator Joseph McCarthy of Wisconsin. McCarthy, first elected in 1946, had made little national impact before a famous speech he delivered in Wheeling, West Virginia, to mark Lincoln's birthday in 1950. The tone of the speech was as notable as its content. Back in 1944, McCarthy explained:

> … there was within the Soviet orbit 180 million people. Lined up on the anti-totalitarian side there were in the world at that time roughly 1.625 billion people. Today, only six years later, there are 800 million people under the absolute domination of Soviet Russia—an increase of over 400 percent. On our side, the figure has shrunk to around 500 million. In other words, in less than six years the odds have changed from 9 to 1 in our favor to 8 to 5 against us. This indicates the swiftness of the tempo of communist victories and American defeats in the Cold War. As one of our outstanding historical figures once said, "When a great democracy is destroyed, it will not be because of enemies from without but rather because of enemies from within."

Seemingly impressive statistics aside, there are multiple problems with this statement, among them the mangled "quotation" from Abraham Lincoln (ironically, McCarthy appears to be alluding to an 1837 speech Lincoln gave about the dangers of demagoguery) to the misleading measure of power by population alone. But reasoning like this, such as it was, had a visceral appeal to a great many people. So did McCarthy's assertion that he had evidence of 205 communists in the State Department. McCarthy subsequently changed the number (57, 81, 10), but as far as his supporters were concerned, what difference did it make? If there was even *one* communist (and could you really doubt not only the possibility, but the *likelihood* of that?), the man had a point.

This fear of subversion from within was powerful because it resonated with other anxieties in postwar life. Among the most important of these was sexual. Fear and persecution of homosexuals had been widespread in the first half of the twentieth century, but it took on a new intensity in the 1950s, particularly with reference to McCarthyism, a phenomenon that historians have dubbed "the lavender scare." "The homosexual is likely to seek his own kind because the pressures are such that he feels uncomfortable unless he is with his own kind," a US Senate report stated in 1950. "Under these circumstances, if a homosexual attains a position in government where he can influence the hiring of personnel, it is almost inevitable that he will attempt to place other homosexuals in government jobs."[15] (Ironically, McCarthy's prominent aide Roy Cohn was a closeted gay man, as reputedly was McCarthy himself.) Same-sex identity was considered a form of mental illness, and it was widely assumed that a gay person could be easily black-mailed, since revealing such an identity was assumed to be a fate worse than death. This in turn justified even greater bias against such people.

Over the course of the next 4 years, a political phenomenon that came to be known as McCarthyism dominated US politics. McCarthy made ever more outrageous attacks on suspected communists, culminating in a highly implausible assertion that the US Army was riddled with them. A shrewd attorney for the army, Joseph Welch, rehearsed and delivered a stinging attack on McCarthy in a hearing broadcast on the new medium of television. "Have you no decency, sir?" he asked in understated outrage. This marked the beginning of the end for McCarthy, who was censured by his colleagues in 1954 and succumbed to alcoholism 2 years later. But the memory of his tactics, and an occasional tendency to resort to them, have remained features of American politics ever since.

Anxiety about the state of the postwar world was not limited to political or legal discourse. In terms of its public impact, the most important document about life in the nuclear age was John Hersey's "Hiroshima," an account of the atom bomb's impact on that city first published in *The New Yorker* in August 1946. (The article took up the entire issue of that magazine; it was published later that year in book form.) In spare language, Hersey traced the lives of six people, graphically describing the terrible impact of the explosion. ("The eyebrows of some were burned off and skin hung from their faces and hands. Others, because of pain, held their arms up as if carrying something. Some were vomiting as they walked.")[16] For the most part, however, popular culture of the time addressed postwar international questions in oblique or symbolic ways. Attempts to address them directly, as in the 1949 film *I Married a Communist*, tended to fall flat, artistically as well as commercially. Far more successful was the 1954 film *On the Waterfront*, starring Marlon Brando as an ex-boxer who reluctantly concludes he must blow the whistle on corrupt friends (a plot line that was widely assumed to mean naming communists). Director Elia Kazan cooperated with HUAC and was vilified by segments of the film community for the rest of his life.

One of the more telling indicators of popular sentiment was a genre of film that achieved new prominence in these years: science fiction movies. The 1954 film *Them!*, for example, tells the story of gigantic irradiated ants that terrorize Alamogordo, New Mexico. The setting is no accident: Alamogordo was the site of nuclear testing in the 1940s. The 1956 film *Invasion of the Body Snatchers*, in which "pods" replicate the residents of a California town, replacing them in unnervingly emotionless form, was more thematically complex, but widely regarded as an allegory of communist brainwashing.[17]

There was also an important religious dimension to the Cold War. By the 1950s, the great wave of immigration earlier in the century had subsided, and the forces of assimilation promoted both inter-ethnic marriages—in the aftermath of the Holocaust, one heard less talk of the Italian or Polish "race," for example—and religious tolerance. In 1955, theologian Will Herberg published *Protestant–Catholic–Jew*, a sociological study arguing that a pluralistic (if somewhat diluted) religious culture characterized the American society of the 1950s. But the crucial backdrop for this pluralism—the indispensable enemy that made it possible—was, in the common phrase of the time, "godless communism." It was in the 1950s that the phrase "In God We Trust" began appearing on US coins, and the phrase "under God" was added to the pledge of allegiance recited by American school-children. Even those who did not consider themselves especially religious still found themselves saturated in such a sensibility, as reflected in President Eisenhower's unintentionally hilarious 1952 affirmation of religious commitment: "Our form of government has no sense unless it is founded in a deeply felt religious faith, and I don't care what it is." One of the greatest evangelical preachers in American history, Billy Graham, rose to prominence in the 1950s with a striking blend of piety, patriotism, and a penchant for sidestepping party politics (he would minister to a half-century of US presidents from both parties).

To some degree, the intensity surrounding the Cold War abated a bit in the mid-1950s, partly the result of Eisenhower's leadership. The former commander of allied forces in Europe during World War II, Eisenhower—or "Ike," as he was affectionately known—was courted by Democrats and Republicans alike as a presidential candidate in 1952. Eisenhower chose the latter, but he also made it clear that he planned to govern as a centrist with little interest in rolling back the major reforms of FDR's New Deal.

At times, Eisenhower also struck a moderate stance in foreign policy; his campaign pledge to "go to Korea" if elected was popular with voters, and his credibility as a military leader made it possible to make conciliatory gestures without seeming weak, an important factor in the truce that was reached in

1953. He had little to say about McCarthyism, correctly calculating that McCarthy would self-immolate. In 1955, Eisenhower also participated in the first of a series of presidential "summit" conferences with his counterpart in the Soviet Union, Nikita Khrushchev, who ascended to power after Stalin's death and who denounced some of Stalin's excesses. The Eisenhower/Khrushchev conference, held in Geneva, Switzerland, did not achieve all that much in terms of nuclear disarmament, in part because Eisenhower insisted on the United States' right to conduct surveillance flights over the Soviet Union and to have on-site inspection of military installations. Still, the "Spirit of Geneva" raised some hopes that the Cold War was moderating.

Playing with Dominoes: Cold War Hot Spots

In most other ways, however, the Cold War seemed as cold as ever. Indeed, just as he inherited aspects of his predecessors' approaches in domestic policy, so too did Eisenhower take his cue from Truman's foreign policy, though he did make a linguistic innovation. Asked by a reporter in 1954 about the United States' strategic position in Indochina—a region that included Vietnam, Laos, and Cambodia, all of which were wracked by civil war—Eisenhower explained why the United States could not stand idly by while communist insurgencies sought control of those governments. "You have broader considerations that would follow under what you would call the 'falling domino' principle. You have a row of dominoes set up, you knock over the first one, and what will happen to the last one is the certainty that it will go over very quickly."[18] In a sense, Eisenhower was simply paraphrasing what had been known as "the Truman Doctrine"—that the United States would aid any government trying to fend off communists. But it was Ike who coined the term "Domino Theory," a metaphor that would shape US foreign policy for a generation with fateful consequences.

President Eisenhower may have been a typical American in his conception of US foreign policy, but there were some aspects of it that he conducted in a distinctive way. His secretary of state, John Foster Dulles, was a hardline Cold Warrior who frightened some of his contemporaries in his willingness to push the Soviets and Chinese to the brink. The cost-conscious Eisenhower tried to limit the growth of conventional forces; as a result, his so-called New Look policy viewed atomic weapons as both economical and practical instruments of foreign policy.

It was also on Eisenhower's watch that the United States made fateful decisions to intervene in the domestic affairs of other governments. Truman had tried to *prevent* communists from coming to power in Turkey and Greece; Eisenhower was the first postwar president to succeed in *overthrowing* regimes he feared might go that way. The first such case was Iran, where the prominent Iranian politician Mohammed Mossaddeq was appointed premier in 1951. By this point, Iran was a major international oil exporter, and Great Britain well as the United States had important financial interests there. When Mossaddeq indicated that he wished to nationalize the petroleum business and expel foreigners, the CIA and Britain's MI6 intelligence agency engineered his overthrow in 1953, restoring a monarchy that itself had been overthrown a decade earlier. The new young king, Shah Reza Pahlevi, became a staunch anticommunist, a stalwart US ally, and an oppressive ruler over his own people for the next quarter-century (until *he* was overthrown, a story we'll get to later).

The CIA also played an important role in the overthrow of the democratically elected government of Guatemala in 1954. Here, the issue was land reform, which in effect meant redistributing economic resources to poor people and, again, reducing the power of foreign business interests—notably the United Fruit Company, a US-based corporation. The government of Prime Minister Jacobo Arbenz had concerned the Truman administration as early as 1950, which secretly armed his opponents. But Arbenz loyalists discovered the plot and prevented its realization. Eisenhower put the CIA to work, setting the stage for a 1954 armed invasion that resulted in the overthrow of Arbenz in favor of Carlos Castillo Armas, who, similar to the Shah, redirected Guatemalan politics and foreign policy until his assassination in 1957. Guatemala, like other Latin American nations, would undergo decades of internal instability rooted, though never entirely, in Cold War issues.

However morally dubious, US interventions in Iran and Guatemala achieved their objectives, at least in the short term. In other cases, however, the Eisenhower administration made moves that, however understandable or even necessary they may have seemed at the time, caused long-term problems. A good example was Vietnam. A French colony since the mid-nineteenth century and occupied by the Japanese during World War II, the Vietnamese waged a long struggle for independence that culminated in a victory over the French at the Battle of Dien Bien Phu in 1954. Because the US government was afraid of communist influence, the Truman and Eisenhower administrations provided money and weapons to the French. After the war, the country was subdivided, much like Korea, into two sections. A 1956 conference was planned to organize elections to decide the future of Vietnam, but when it became clear that the communists under the North Vietnamese leader Ho Chi Minh would prevail, the Eisenhower administration refused to participate, giving its backing to the strongly anticommunist Ngo Dinh Diem of South Vietnam, who would prove to be an unsteady ally before his assassination in 1963. From the 1950s until the 1970s, Vietnam would become one of the most frustrating problems in US foreign policy.

But few Americans were paying attention to Vietnam in the early postwar era. Far more obvious were some embarrassing moments with the Soviet Union. In 1957, the USSR launched Sputnik, the first satellite launched into the earth's orbit, demonstrating what was widely perceived as Soviet technological superiority in what came to be known as the Space Race. Sputnik was followed by further Soviet demonstrations of technological prowess (e.g. sending a dog into space) and American flubs (the first US rocket launch a couple months later went down in flames). Besides the possible military implications—did this mean the Soviets could fire atomic weapons directly into the United States?—Sputnik generated an enormous amount of handwringing about the apparently poor state of American education, particularly in science and technology. "Why Johnny can't read" became a buzz-phrase of the time; the infusion of federal aid into education that followed was one of a number of ways in which domestic welfare programs were implemented, and justified, as military measures (more on this in Chapter 2).[19] This was just one more indication of the way events abroad shaped Americans' perceptions of themselves at home.

In fact, Soviet technological superiority was more illusory than real. The Eisenhower administration knew this—knew far more about the Soviets than it was willing to say—because of a key technological asset of its own: the U-2 spy plane, which could fly undetected at high altitudes and take photographs that could be enlarged to the point where it would be possible to read a newspaper headline shot from 10 miles above the earth. Such reconnaissance made it clear that the Soviets were not nearly as dangerous as they appeared, something the US Defense Department and its many commercial suppliers did not want to become common knowledge, lest it become more difficult to persuade the American public that further military investment was necessary, leading to the loss of their lucrative contracts.[20] Despite a belief in its invulnerability to detection, U-2 pilot Francis Gary Powers was shot down over the Soviet Union in May 1960. After the Eisenhower administration disavowed any suggestion that the missing aircraft was on a spying mission, Khrushchev responded by putting Powers on television with the wreckage of the plane and its cameras. He also cancelled a planned summit meeting between himself and the US president. Eisenhower was caught in a lie, which hurt his prestige abroad. On the other hand, Ike was much less obsessed with losing face than many of his Cold War peers.[21]

Cold War Showdown: Cuba

The final (partial) Eisenhower fiasco, one that carried into the ensuing Kennedy administration, occurred in Cuba. Ever since the Spanish–American War, Cuba had been an unofficial US colony. A major US naval base was established at Guantanamo Bay, and Americans largely controlled the Cuban government, often insisting on corrupt rulers who would do its bidding (this included organized crime figures who helped make Cuba a favored tourist destination). But, in 1959, change finally came to Cuba when a revolution led by the charismatic Fidel Castro took over the country. Castro's politics were initially unclear, but when it became increasingly obvious that he was tilting toward the Soviet Union, which eagerly extended aid, the Eisenhower administration decided that Castro—who governed an island a mere 90 miles from the US mainland—must go. An invasion to be led primarily by mercenary Cuban refugees was planned for the spring of 1961. Eisenhower left office before it came to fruition, but the newly elected John F. Kennedy decided to proceed—sort of. When the Cuban exiles landed at the Bay of Pigs in April 1961, Kennedy decided not to include air support, which would make US fingerprints on the operation all too obvious. But withholding that support allowed Castro's Cubans to crush the invasion, further enhancing his image as a dragon slayer. Kennedy accepted the blame for the bungled operation, which was a public relations as well as a military disaster. But he remained committed—some would say obsessed—with Castro, authorizing dozens of unsuccessful assassination plots against him in 1961–1963.[22]

Similar to Eisenhower, Kennedy was a World War II veteran (Eisenhower had been the commander of US armed forces in Europe; Kennedy had been a junior naval officer in the Pacific, decorated for his valor in combat), but they had differing styles in foreign policy. While Eisenhower played the role of a wise, even avuncular figure, Kennedy's persona was based on masculine vitality, even swagger. On his way out of office, Eisenhower gave a famous farewell speech in which he warned his fellow Americans against the danger of what he called "the military–industrial complex," whose economic and political influence had the potential to subvert the democratic process. Kennedy, by contrast, tended to strike the pose of the hardline Cold Warrior with a firm technocratic grip on that military–industrial complex. In his famous 1961 inaugural address, he pledged to "let every nation know, whether it wishes us well or ill, that we shall pay any price, bear any burden, meet any hardship, support any friend, oppose any foe, in order to assure the survival and the success of liberty." One example of his commitment to this vision was the creation of the so-called Green Berets, special forces trained for undercover operations. Another was waging a secret CIA war in Laos against a communist insurgency there, one that would continue into the 1970s.

Kennedy was capable of restraint. The status of Berlin was a constant irritant in Cold War relations, and one that became especially problematic for the Soviets, given the tendency of the residents of East Berlin (and other Soviet bloc nations) to defect to Western Europe through West Berlin. When, in exasperation over this and other aspects of US conduct, Khrushchev authorized the construction of a concrete wall to separate the two sides of the city, Kennedy resisted calls to respond militarily, recognizing the Soviets' right to close their zone. But he did give a celebrated speech in the city 2 years later, famously proclaiming "I am a Berliner" and responding to the prospect of Soviet aggression by saying, "Let them come to Berlin."

But it was Cuba that remained the primary front in the Cold War during the Kennedy years. The Bay of Pigs proved to be the prologue for a much more serious confrontation—the most serious one of all.

By some reckonings, the roots of the crisis were in Vienna, where Kennedy and Khrushchev met in June 1961. Kennedy, who spent much of his adult life in pain and far more time than he ever disclosed on painkillers, was substantially medicated in his discussions with Khrushchev,[23] which apparently contributed to the Soviet premier's perception that the American president was a lightweight—and in any case contributed to his sense of frustration with the United States, as negotiations between the two powers on Berlin and other matters made little progress. (Indeed, it was in the aftermath of the conference that the Berlin Wall was erected.) Later that year, Khrushchev began sending increasing numbers of military personnel to Cuba. He also began sending missiles capable of carrying atomic weapons to the US mainland. When American U-2 flights began documenting these developments in late 1962, the stage was set for the Cuban Missile Crisis.

Kennedy responded to the Soviet challenge by assembling an executive committee ("Ex-Comm"), which solicited opinions and weighed options over a 2-week period in October 1962. At one end of the spectrum was the option of doing nothing—the Soviets already had the capacity to launch missiles into the United States, after all—but this was rejected primarily because of the *perception* of weakness that would follow from Soviet Union's completion of its missile installation. At the other end was a full-bore invasion of the island, rejected because of the likelihood that it would result in World War III in the form of nuclear annihilation. Airstrikes were also considered and rejected. Kennedy ultimately decided on a blockade of Soviet supply ships to Cuba—the less threatening term "quarantine" was used—and after a very tense moment of confrontation, the Soviets turned back. But this did nothing about what was already in progress on the island, tension that was intensified still further when a US spy plane was shot down, something both sides decided not to disclose for fear of taking the crisis beyond the point of no return.

Amid this moment of high drama, Khrushchev transmitted two diplomatic cables to Kennedy. The first was conciliatory, offering to remove the missiles and permit inspections. The second, which arrived as the Ex-Comm was still analyzing the first, struck a more bellicose tone. After much deliberation, Kennedy decided to ignore the second and respond publicly to the first. At the same time, he delegated his brother, Attorney General Robert Kennedy, to secretly propose to the Soviet ambassador in Washington an option raised in the second cable, and one the administration had been considering all along: an offer to remove largely obsolete US missiles based in Turkey as a gesture of reciprocation, something that Kennedy said could not be done unilaterally but which he pledged to do in cooperation with NATO allies. (The missiles would be replaced by ones based on submarines, a key tactical advantage in mobility that the United States would enjoy for the rest of the Cold War.) Ultimately, this became the formula for a resolution of the crisis. Khrushchev, whose impetuous behavior was largely responsible for the confrontation, lost face in the eyes of his allies—Castro was furious with him—and weakened his position at home; he would be replaced by Leonid Brezhnev the following year. Kennedy, who was at least as lucky as he was skillful, crowed. "I cut his balls off," he said in his private mode of macho bravado.[24]

Although the Cold War would last for another 27 years, the Cuban Missile Crisis was a turning point in the struggle. In its aftermath, both sides realized they had narrowly averted a catastrophe and took steps to limit future escalation. One was the installation of the so-called telephone "hotlines," so that the two leaders could speak to each other directly in the event of a crisis. Another was the signing of the 1963 Nuclear Test Ban treaty, which prohibited underground atomic detonations, an important component of weapons testing. While the arms race would continue, an important precedent had been set, principally in terms of establishing ongoing dialogue as a plausible approach to superpower relations, which would result in more substantial arms control agreements in the 1970s and 1980s.

For most Americans in the 1960s, the outcome of the Cuban Missile Crisis was an affirmation of American global supremacy: when push came to shove, the United States won (again). Many interpreted the outcome as an affirmation of Kennedy in particular; after the bungled Bay of Pigs, it appeared he had grown in office, applying a carefully calibrated combination of firmness and flexibility in his approach—a combination that George Kennan had called for in formulating his own approach to the Cold War. In the decades to come, the United States would struggle to strike this balance in places such as Vietnam, Laos, Indonesia, Bolivia, and Chile. Its record would prove mixed at best.

But most Americans weren't really aware of what went on in these places. And this, in a sense, is actually an affirmation of US foreign policy. Empires don't simply afford security to their citizens: they afford them the luxury of not having to care about what happens beyond their borders. While there were certainly principled voices that raised objections or articulated high standards of international conduct, most Americans were content to let their leaders act as they saw fit in foreign policy, as long their actions did not blatantly violate stated national ideals, damage the nation's collective self-image, or threaten tranquility at home. Americans sometimes liked to think of themselves as different or better than previous great powers in this regard. But they were fairly typical imperialists in this regard.

What made the second half of the twentieth century different is that the shadow of nuclear war made it impossible to feel entirely secure. By the early 1960s, however, there were indications that Americans were willing to grapple with their fears more directly than they had in the previous decade. The 1959 Hollywood film *On the Beach*, based on a novel of the same name by British writer Nevil Shute, depicted a group of Australians awaiting the arrival of fatal radiation in the aftermath of a nuclear holocaust. *Fail Safe*, a 1962 novel by Eugene Burdick and Harvey Wheeler, and made into a 1964 film of the same name, dramatized how miscalculation by Americans and Soviets could result in the destruction of entire cities. But the most striking statement on the subject was a film released earlier that year: Stanley Kubrick's *Dr. Strangelove, or: How I Learned to Stop Worrying and Love the Bomb*, a black comedy about Armageddon that featured Peter Sellers in a trio of roles, most notably that of the title character, a former Nazi who explains the logic (if that's what it is) of nuclear war. Somewhat improbably, *Dr. Strangelove* proved to be the most successful and durable of these films, its grim message paradoxically evoking (perhaps fatalistic) laughter.[25]

Indeed, it may well be that the powerlessness of any given individual in the face of the nuclear threat—a powerlessness that paralleled the inevitable mortality of each individual life—engendered a desire simply not to think about it too much. However inevitable a nuclear war may have seemed, the risk seemed relatively low on any given day (except during the Cuban Missile Crisis). In the meantime, the road appeared to be open for Americans to savor the fruits from the victory in World War II, and to pursue—on an entirely new scale—the alluring promise of the American Dream.

The Man in the Gray Flannel Suit (1955/1956)

The stereotypical image of post–World War II life in the United States centered on a nuclear family—husband, wife, children—nestled happily in a suburban house in which dad works in an office, mom works at home, and the kids are all right. This was the archetype conveyed in many television shows of the postwar years. The reality, as we now know, was often more complicated. But a great many Americans at the time understood that the reality was often more complicated back then, too. The success of *The Man in the Gray Flannel Suit*, a highly popular novel and movie that has faded in collective memory, makes that clear.

Actually, there was a rich sociological discourse in the United States about work and family life in the 1950s, much of which expressed concern about its perceived soullessness. Works of scholarship such as David Riesman, Nathan Glazer, and Reuel Denney's *The Lonely Crowd* (1950) and William Whyte's *The Organization Man* (1956) depicted an American landscape of conformity and domestic isolation, alarm bells that were insistent precisely because corporate capitalism and suburbanization

Figure 1.2 OFF THE PAGE: Gregory Peck walks off the cover of the celebrated 1955 novel *The Man in the Gray Flannel Suit* to address the audience in the trailer for the film, released the following year. The story follows the struggle of Tom Rath (played by Peck), his wife Betsy (Jennifer Jones), and their family's effort to establish a sense of stability in the corporate and suburban worlds of the 1950s (1956, directed by Nunnally Johnson, and produced by Twentieth Century Fox Film Corporation).

seemed like such powerful, even unstoppable, forces. It was in this milieu that novelist Sloan Wilson published *The Man in the Gray Flannel Suit* in 1955, which was made into a major Hollywood movie starring Gregory Peck the following year.

Peck plays Tom Rath, a mid-level Manhattan executive with a wife (Jennifer Jones) and three kids in suburban Westport, Connecticut. Though the family has a relatively high standard of living, a sense of malaise afflicts the Raths. They're stretched financially, and the proceeds from a family will they've been counting on have proven disappointing. Rath's wife Betsy nudges her husband to be more aggressive in seeking a higher-paying job. But she's also concerned more generally that her husband has lost his way ever since he returned from World War II, where he served on both the European and Pacific fronts. As she says in one particularly brutal line in the movie, "You've lost all guts and all of a sudden I'm ashamed."

Tom Rath, as it turns out, is a man with secrets. We seem him suffering from what we would now call post-traumatic stress disorder (PTSD) in flashbacks that show him having particularly brutal experiences, which include stabbing a wounded German soldier to death. We also learn that, though he was married at the time, he had an affair with an Italian woman whom he discovers bore him a son. Such experiences engender a faint sense of estrangement from his children by his wife, who appear to routinely ignore or disobey him (one comic subtheme involves a nanny who is far more terrifying to them than their father ever is).

Despite these challenges, a significant opportunity comes Tom's way when he lands a job with a publicity firm led by a renowned businessman Ralph Hopkins (played by Fredric March in the film). Tom is now making more money, and the Raths are able to move into the large house his grandmother bequeathed him, though there are legal problems with her estate. Tom reminds Hopkins of the son he lost in the war, and tries to mentor him. But office politics makes this difficult, and it becomes clear as the story proceeds that Hopkins has paid a high personal price for his professional success. Tom gradually realizes that he's going to have to be honest with himself—and Betsy—if he's ever really going to get his life back in order. And that will involve reckoning with difficult truths.

For decades after its publication/release, the phrase "man in the gray flannel suit" became a catchphrase, shorthand for the combination of postwar affluence and ennui that seemed pervasive in the second half of the twentieth century. The advent of feminism, the decline of traditional corporate capitalism, and the growing diversity of the US population, even in the suburbs, have made the story seem dated. But American couples, and American families, continue to struggle in their quest to balance their personal and professional lives and to put past challenges behind them. Gray flannel will never entirely go out of fashion.

Suggested Further Reading

The transition from relative isolation to international engagement is a subject that has been widely discussed by historians. Among the most important works are Stephen Ambrose, *Rise to Globalism: American Foreign Policy Since 1938*, 9th ed. with Douglas Brinkley (1971; New York: Penguin, 2010); Michael Sherry, *In the Shadow of War: The United States Since the 1930s* (New Haven: Yale University Press, 1995); and Christopher McKnight Nichols, *Promise and Peril: America at the Dawn of the Global Age* (Cambridge, MA: Harvard University Press, 2011).

The transformation of the nation's economy and culture is discussed extensively in James Sparrow, *Warfare State: World War II Americans and the Age of Big Government* (New York: Oxford University Press, 2011). John Morton Blum captures the domestic side in *V Was For Victory: Politics and American Culture During World War II* (New York: Harcourt, Brace Jovanovich, 1976).

Though he has critics who find his perspective too conservative, the current preeminent historian of the Cold War is John Lewis Gaddis. See *Strategies of Containment: A Critical Appraisal of American National Security Policy During the Cold War* (1982; New York: Oxford University Press, 2005). Gaddis has also written an elegant brief overview, *The Cold War: A New History* (New York: Penguin, 2005).

For an excellent one-volume treatment of McCarthyism, see Robert Griffith, *The Politics of Fear: Joseph R. McCarthy and the Senate* (1970; Amherst, MA: University of Massachusetts Press, 1987). See also Ellen Schrecker, *Many Are the Crimes: McCarthyism in America* (Princeton: Princeton University Press, 1999). Schrecker has also edited a useful anthology, *The Age of McCarthyism: A Brief History with Documents* (1994; New York: Bedford, 2002).

Notes

1 It appears "awesome" as slang has origins in the California surfer culture of the 1960s. Two decades later, it appears to have migrated into a decidedly different sub-culture, appearing in *The Preppy Handbook*, edited by Lisa Birnbach (New York: Workman Publishing, 1980), 218.

2 The text of Luce's piece can be found at http://www.informationclearinghouse. info/article6139.htm (November 5, 2014).

3 David M. Kennedy, *Freedom From Fear: The American People in Depression and War* (New York: Oxford University Press, 1999), 746.

4 John Patrick Diggins, *The Proud Decades: America in War and Peace* (New York: Norton, 1991), 5; Godfrey Hodgson, *American in Our Time: From World War II to Nixon, What Happened and Why* (New York: Doubleday, 1976), 19.

5 Blum, 113.

6 John Keegan, *The Second World War* (New York: Oxford University Press, 1989), 218–219.

7 Kennedy, 857.

8 Diggins, 48–49.

9 The information in the following paragraphs tracing the emergence of computer technology comes from Jim Cullen, *A Short History of the Modern Media* (Malden, MA: Wiley-Blackwell, 2014), 243–245.

10   Joshua B. Freeman, *American Empire: The Rise of a Global Power/The Democratic Revolution at Home, 1945–2000* (New York: Penguin, 2012), 50.

11   Alan Wolfe, *America's Impasse: The Rise and Fall of the Politics of Growth* (Boston: South End Press, 1981), 14.

12   Freeman, 92.

13   Miller, who was called before HUAC, answered questions about his own past, but refused for furnish information about others.

14   Diggins, 166.

15   *Employment of Homosexuals and Other Perverts in Government Interim Report* (1950) in *The United States Since 1945: A Documentary Reader*, edited by Robert P. Ingalls and David K. Johnson (Malden, MA: Blackwell, 2009), 39.

16   John Hersey, *Hiroshima* (1946; New York: Vintage, 1989), 29.

17   Peter Biskind, *Seeing Is Believing: How I Learned to Stop Worrying and Love the Fifties* (New York: Pantheon, 1983), esp. 137–144; Stuart Samuels, "The Age of Conspiracy and Conformity: Invasion of the Body Snatchers," in *American History/American Film: Interpreting the Hollywood Image*, edited by John E. O'Connor and Martin A. Jackson (New York: Ungar/Continuum, 1988), 203–217.

18   Dwight Eisenhower, Press Conference, April 7, 1954 in Ingalls & Johnson, 88–89.

19   Information cited in last paragraph and the next one draws on Freeman, 165.

20   To some extent, this strategy backfired in 1960, when Democratic presidential candidate John Kennedy claimed that a "missile gap" had opened up to the disadvantage of the United States on Eisenhower's watch. Eisenhower fumed at this characterization, but did not feel it was politic to challenge it, much to chagrin of Republican candidate Richard Nixon.

21   Garry Wills, *Nixon Agonistes: The Crisis of the Self-Made Man* (1970; Boston: Houghton Mifflin, 2002), 134.

22   James Patterson, *Grand Expectations: The United States, 1945–1974* (New York: Oxford University Press, 1997), 498.

23   Richard Reeves, *President Kennedy: Portrait of Power* (New York: Simon & Schuster, 1994), 158ff.

24   Patterson, 504; Michael Beschloss, *The Crisis Years: Kennedy and Khrushchev, 1960–1963* (New York: HarperCollins, 1991), 542–544.

25   Rick Perlstein usefully contextualizes *Dr. Strangelove* in *Before the Storm: Barry Goldwater and the Making of the American Consensus* (2001; New York: Nation Books, 2009), 284–286.

2

Conformity and Rebellion
American Culture and Politics, 1945–1963

Figure 2.1   HOMEWARD BOUND: Homer Parrish (Harold Russell), Fred Derry (Dana Andrews) and Al Stephenson (Frederic March), all World War II veterans, share a plane back to the fictional Midwestern town of Boone City in the 1946 film *The Best Years of Our Lives*. Though war's end brought relief and hope to many, it was also a time of uncertainty, even despair, for veterans and their families trying to rebuild their lives (1946, directed by William Wyler, and produced by The Samuel Goldwyn Company).

Democratic Empire: The United States Since 1945, First Edition. Jim Cullen.
© 2017 Jim Cullen. Published 2017 by John Wiley & Sons, Inc.

Best Worst Time: Early Postwar Years

NINETEEN FORTY-SIX is a landmark year in US film history, a year that dramatized just how dominant a role movies played in the everyday life of Americans. About 75% of the able-bodied national audience went to a theater at least once a week—and a great many went multiple times, not only to see a feature film, but also cartoons, newsreels, and other "shorts" that made moviegoing so appealing.[1] It was also in 1946 that a number of films were released that are now widely viewed as classics: the John Ford Western *My Darling Clementine*; the Howard Hawks film noir touchstone *The Big Sleep*; and, though it wasn't a big box office success, the subsequently much beloved Frank Capra favorite *It's a Wonderful Life*.

The movie that won the Academy Award for Best Picture in 1946, however, was William Wyler's *The Best Years of Our Lives*. Much admired at the time and ever since by critics, it has not persisted quite as powerfully in the nation's collective imagination as those other movies, which are now standard fare for movie buffs. *The Best Years of Our Lives* can be easily compared with *It's a Wonderful Life*, in that both films took a hard look at postwar realities before affirming that life is about more than making money (though they also suggest you can do that too). However, *It's a Wonderful Life* has a mythic resonance that only partially obscures its painful honesty about family and small-town living that lurks below its surface sentimentality (and haunts you long after the movie is over).[2]

As a snapshot of its moment, though, *The Best Years of Our Lives* has no peer. The film traces the lives of three veterans—a soldier, a sailor, and a pilot—who become friends after a plane ride back to their fictive hometown of Boone City (some film footage was shot in Cincinnati). The soldier (Fredric March) is a banker with a wife and two children struggling to overcome his cynicism as he adjusts to civilian life. The sailor, who lost his hands in combat—the disabled Harold Russell won an Academy Award for Best Supporting Actor for his performance—has trouble believing that his fiancé (Cathy O'Donnell) really wants to marry him. And the pilot (Dana Andrews), who was decorated for valor in combat, comes home to a wayward wife (Virginia Mayo) and encounters difficulty in finding a job. He also finds himself drawn to the grown daughter of March's character (Teresa Wright). In a moment of desperation, he decides to leave Boone City for good and heads to the airport for the first flight out. While he waits, he wanders silently amid a vast field of partially disassembled B-17 bombers: symbolically, he too is a disposable relic. But the pilot gets shaken out of his melancholy reverie by an edgy junk dealer. After a somewhat hostile exchange between the two, the junk dealer explains that he is stripping the planes for metal to be used in prefabricated housing. The pilot asks for a job—the turning point in his fortunes, and in the resolution of the story.

In multiple ways—including a title that was meant to be at least partially ironic—*The Best Years of Our Lives* opens a window into the uncertainties of American life as World War II ended. The long shadow of the atomic bomb looms over the returned veterans, suggested when the soldier hears his son explain its devastation for a school project he's doing. Domestically, there were widespread worries that the war's end—and the huge outlays of government spending that had powered the economy—would lead to a return to economic depression, a concern voiced by an unlikeable, but by no means stupid, minor character. While the end of the war brought with it many happy family reunions, it also resulted in a doubling of the prewar divorce rate (the pilot's wife leaves him after bitterly observing that she has given up the best years of her life).[3] President Harry Truman and the liberals in Congress were disappointed by their failure to pass a Full Employment bill in 1945, a law that would have theoretically helped the pilot; its failure was an indication that Franklin Delano Roosevelt's New Deal was truly over (a more modest Employment Act was passed in 1946).

There were other tensions of the time not captured in the film. Wartime price controls, managed by the federal government's Office of Price Administration, ended in 1947, another indication of the New Deal reaching its limit. Long-pent-up labor demands held in check by the war also exploded in a wave of strikes in 1946, which abated when the normally labor-friendly Truman threatened striking rail workers with being drafted into the army. Women who had entered the workforce in large numbers were thrown out of jobs. And the outbreak of the Cold War engendered resentments that sparked accusations and suspicion about the dangers of communism at home and abroad. Victory over the Germans and Japanese were widely celebrated in 1945. There was a national hangover in 1946.

Boom! The Postwar Economy Explodes

For all its melancholy air, *The Best Years of Our Lives* also captured another important and durable truth: the very resources that provided the raw material for weapons in wartime also furnished the raw material for prosperity in peacetime. Swords were turned into plowshares—along with the forging of new and more powerful swords. For all the immensity of the resources it committed to World War II, the United States finished the war with its national territory intact and vast stores of gold in its vaults. An empire at the zenith of its power could now turn the vast productive capacity it had unleashed for military purposes and direct it toward achieving civilian ends.

To a great extent, however, that empire would not provide for those civilian ends unless they *also* conferred military benefits. Take, for example, the creation of the nation's interstate highway system. Its funding was signed into law by President Dwight Eisenhower in 1956, at least in part to allow rapid transit for troops and supplies in the event of an invasion or other emergency. Another example is the creation of the Internet, which originated in the US Defense Department during the war years and whose early uses focused on government communication in the event of a nuclear war. Today, interstate highways and the Internet are thoroughly integrated into the fabric of civilian life; we think of them as emblems of domestic tranquility. But their very reason for existence was disruption: they came into existence as tools of war that have also become artifacts of peace.

Actually, the real measure of United States' greatness after World War II was that the nation did *not* have to allocate a large proportion of it resources for military use. Defense spending as a percentage of total US expenditures fell from 83% in 1945 to 38% in 1947.[4] Of course, 38% is still a lot, and that proportion would continue to decline. But in terms of the old expression, the government could afford to spend freely on guns *and* butter. It's important to reiterate that the existence of wealth does not mean it is distributed evenly (in 1947, a third of US homes had no running water, 40% had no flush toilets, and 60% had no central heating),[5] or that wealth is the best or only measure of domestic tranquility, which is always elusive. But there's probably never been a society with as much pure promise as the United States in the late 1940s, a perception that was perhaps even more important than reality for the have-nots in terms of their hopes for the future.

At the same time, the optimism of Americans at war's end was perhaps a bit more tempered than it would be later on. Historian James T. Patterson has described the nuanced quality of the American Dream in arrestingly plain terms: "This was not a dream of rags to riches; few sensible citizens had ever imagined that. Nor did it imagine the abolition of privileges and special distinctions: Americans at the time, as earlier, tolerated open and unapologetic rankings in schools, in the military, in job descriptions. Rather, it defined a belief that hard work would enable a person to rise in society and that children would do better in life than parents. The United States was indeed the land of opportunity and high expectations."[6]

The raw materials for opportunity and higher expectations in American life were apparent by the numbers. With 7% of the world's population in the late 1940s, the United States possessed 42% of its income and accounted for half of its manufacturing output. American workers produced 43% of the world's electricity, 57% of steel, 62% of oil, and 80% of cars. The caloric intake of Americans was double that of Western Europeans. Such resources, which had been mobilized for wartime purposes, were now being redirected to the civilian economy, where Americans had accumulated US$100 billion in savings that could now be spent on consumer goods.[7]

Among those best poised to take advantage of the emerging postwar world were US military veterans. In 1944, Congress passed one of the most powerful pieces of welfare legislation in American history, the GI Bill. The law gave returning veterans a comprehensive package of benefits, including up to 4 years of college tuition *with* living expenses, employment assistance, and easy terms for loans on a house or business. The home mortgage provision financed 20% of all the single-family homes built between 1946 and 1966, and the GI Bill generally accounted for 15% of the federal budget, spending that rippled outward into the economy generally.[8] Victorious soldiers have always been awarded the spoils of victory in one form or another, but never had any society offered such wide, deep, and systematic benefits, even if racism and sexism led to discrimination against entire categories of people.[9] Nor would this one ever again.

The mobility promised by these developments was literal as well as figurative. Americans have always been a relatively restless people, blessed with a vast nation of open spaces. From the 1940s to the 1970s, roughly 20% of the US population relocated to a new home in any given year.[10] In the postwar years, most of that movement was away from the provinces and toward metropolises (though, as we'll see, much of that was to the *edge* of metropolises).

The other major feature of the postwar landscape in the early postwar years was a surprising—and not entirely explained—demographic expansion known as the Baby Boom, a surge in births that stretched from 1946 to 1964. In these years, 76.4 million children were born, comprising 40% of the 1964 US population.[11] "Boomers," as they were known, were a pig in the national python that would dominate national cultural life for the next half-century. They would also be a fact of significant economic consequence, as entire industries, from toys to housing, would spring up to profit from their growing needs and expansive desires.

Indeed, there are few more obvious characteristics of postwar society than the pervasive spread of consumer culture into virtually every crevice of American life. From the very beginning, Americans have been notable for their appetite for small luxuries—they were inveterate importers of pricey tea and sugar in the colonial era, for example—and the first half of the twentieth century had been notable for the introduction of a cornucopia of new technological gadgets, from cars to vacuum cleaners. But it was in the postwar decades that a wide array of new gadgets entered the marketplace, among them the electric clothes dryer, the Polaroid instant camera, and the 45-rpm as well as 33-rpm record player. A variety of formerly exotic products entered the mainstream, among them frozen foods, Styrofoam containers, and vinyl floor coverings. Meanwhile, older innovations became truly pervasive. By 1956, 96% of US households owned refrigerators, 86.7% owned washing machines, and 73% owned cars.[12]

Cars in particular were crucial not just to the postwar economy, but to postwar society generally. This is true for a number of reasons. First, the automobile industry was an engine of the US economy in its own right. It employed hundreds of thousands of workers in manufacturing, sales, and related industries. The auto industry was also a bastion of the modern labor movement, which peaked in the 1950s, when approximately 35% of US workers belonged to unions. Moreover, the proliferation of cars in US society spurred the development of new industries that included chain hotels, motels—shorthand for motor hotel—and fast food restaurants, the most notable of which, McDonald's, was first franchised in 1955 and grew rapidly as the result of easy parking, takeout, and the consistency of its cuisine. (The very first McDonald's was founded before the war in California, ground zero for so many of the postwar developments described here.) The expansion of car culture was possible because the cost of fuel was, in both absolute and relative terms, cheap. In 1949, a gallon of gasoline cost 27 cents, and in real terms the price kept falling until 1972. Mileage per gallon in cars actually went down in these years; the United States had long been an oil exporter, but the fact that it started becoming increasingly reliant on foreign producers did not seem problematic—yet.[13]

Because cars were big-ticket consumer items, and could not often be paid for in cash, they also fueled the growth of the credit industry. Indeed, over the course of the twentieth century, General Motors became less an automobile manufacturer than a lender for car buyers. The first modern credit card, Diner's Club, was issued in 1950, soon followed by BankAmericard (later Visa), MasterCard, and individual store charge cards. The US tax code allowed consumers to deduct the interest on credit cards from their taxes until 1986. Claims for such deductions rose from 3% of tax returns in 1950 to more than 10 times that by 1960.[14]

Rising Suburbs: Life on the Crabgrass Frontier

The most important engine of the domestic economy in these years was the housing industry. The country came out of the war with a ferocious housing shortage; it was addressed in a way that transformed the national experience: the ascent of the suburb.

Suburbs were not new in 1945. Their origins can be traced back to the eighteenth century, when the British residential district of Clapham, about 5 miles from London Bridge, began serving as a refuge from city life. By 1900, such residential enclaves had taken on what we now regard as the prototypical elements of the suburb: low-density communities dependent on urban commerce but dominated by single-family houses in park-like settings.[15]

Early American suburbs were tethered to cities by public transportation: ferries (such as the boat traffic that connected Brooklyn to Manhattan), rails (such as the Main Line that connected Philadelphia to Bucks County), or streetcars (first drawn by horses, later by cable, as in those that stitched together greater Cleveland, Miami, and Los Angeles, among other cities). By the 1920s, suburbanization was well underway in the United States.

But World War II marked a turning point for a variety of reasons. Some of these are owing to long-term trends, such as the steadily increasing rate of car ownership, which promoted urban sprawl unlike the radial pattern of earlier (rail-based) suburban development. This was of course made possible by the growth of the Interstate Highway System, which points back to the reality of suburbanization as inextricable from the creation of a permanent military state. That's not only because the GI Bill created a huge government entitlement that allowed millions of families to get loans for houses for which they otherwise would not qualify. It's also because the growing defense establishment created jobs that could support families in metropolitan regions such as those along Boston's Route 128 or Washington, DC's Beltway. Dads—and a growing number of moms—went to work for companies that made weapons systems (or the drycleaners and restaurants to which those company employees flocked after work). The paychecks from those jobs covered the cost of pillowcases in bedrooms and swing sets in backyards.

Nor is the notion that the nation's housing stock was built on a war foundation merely metaphorical. The most important figures in the postwar residential market cut their teeth in war production, applying military construction techniques for civilian uses. Henry J. Kaiser, the industrialist who churned out aircraft carriers and other naval vessels in huge numbers during the war, built tract housing in Southern California after the war was over. The team of Abraham Levitt and his sons William and Alfred, who were contracted by US Navy to construct housing, used mass production methods for the Long Island development they dubbed Levittown as well as similar projects in New Jersey and Pennsylvania. They built nearly identical homes in a few standard variations, typically 750 square feet (about a third of the average house size today), and sold them for as little as US$6,990, washing machine included. A mere 10% of that amount was required as a down payment, and since interest on the loan could be deducted from one's taxes, home ownership was often cheaper than renting. A housing boom to go along with the baby boom was born.[16]

Nothing in American history was quite like it. Of the 13 million homes built in the United States between 1948 and 1958, 11 million were suburban. One-fourth of *all* homes standing in 1960 had been built in the previous 10 years, and some 83% of all population growth in the nation was in suburbs. By 1970, there were more people in suburbs than in cities or on farms. A 1949 article in the *New York Times* captures the stunning impact of the transformation on Long Island: "A potato patch of 1945 may now have 500 small houses, exactly or nearly exactly alike, marching across it in parade ground alignment.... Shopping centers have sprung up where billboards and hedges used to line the roads. Small communities that were established before the war have spread out to cover adjoining areas. Garages, filling stations, stores of all sorts, movie houses, taverns, and small industrial plants have sprung up almost overnight." The United States had become a suburban nation.[17]

This represented a geographic transformation, an economic transformation, and a demographic transformation, among other kinds. But perhaps most striking was the degree to which suburbia represented a cultural shift in the tenor of national life, as inner cities became hollowed out and suburbs became more populous, though urban downtowns remained a locus of employment. One of the reasons why this change seemed so powerful to contemporaries was the way suburbia interfaced with some of the other developments of the time. Two, as already indicated, were the proliferation of the automobile and the Baby Boom, both of which were highly conducive to young families living in detached houses. As with most societies at most times and places, Americans had always placed a large emphasis on family life. But family life of the mid-twentieth century had some distinct contours, among them the primacy of the nuclear family, a tendency described as "togetherness." After the spike right after the war, divorce rates came down sharply; so did the average age of marriage, which dipped from the mid-20s to 22 for men and 20 in women. In the 1950s, 90% of Americans were married at some point in their lives. "It's not a matter of 'want' or 'like to' or choice," one woman explained. "Why talk about things that are as natural and routine as breathing?" Another woman, asked why she hoped to marry and have children, responded with a similar rhetorical question: "Why do you put on your pants in the morning?" She was presumably responding to a man; women didn't often wear pants at the time.[18]

Another distinctive facet of suburban culture was the prominence, if not necessarily the predominance, of the single male breadwinner. Never before, or since, did so many families have the *option* of a woman in the role of full-time homemaker: economic pressures typically necessitated wage-earning for both spouses. That's not to say the stay-at-home mother was always experienced as an attractive option; in fact, there were strong social pressures that made it difficult for women to establish professional careers, and undercut them when they did. The prevalence of a culture of domestic togetherness was never simply an ideology foisted on women, however; for many, it represented a goal, whether achieved or not.

Suburbia was also well suited for the great media revolution of mid-century: the arrival of television. As with so many other developments of the time, its roots go back to decades earlier; the first successful attempts at broadcasting sound and image took place in the 1920s, a time when radio was dominant. The first television stations and networks began broadcasting during the war years, when the television set was an exotic gadget to own. But, by the decade's end, the industry was poised for an explosion.

The spread of television was amazing. In 1948, when the industry was in its infancy, 172,000 homes had a television set. About 4 years later, that number had jumped to 15.3 million. By 1955, 75% of households had one; by 1960, that figure had reached 90%.[19] No single event can be truly considered as the decisive one, but a series of developments in the early 1950s typically mark the moments in the nation's collective memory when television truly arrived, among them the arrival of coast-to-coast broadcasting, beginning in 1951. (Because the ability to record shows was primitive, most shows were live, creating complications with time zones.) Until this point, less than half of US homes had television sets. Within a few years, most did. This is particularly notable, given that a television set was a big-ticket item, perhaps akin to buying a high-quality computer today.

Another major reason for television's explosion was the growing appeal of television shows, such as the wildly popular *I Love Lucy* (1951–1957), which prompted consumers to take the plunge. *Today*, a multi-hour program of news and conversation, made its debut in 1952, and has continued its run to the present, as has its companion piece *The Tonight Show*, which began in 1954. By the mid-1950s, television was not simply a presence, but a bona fide phenomenon.

It was also increasingly a factor in breaking news—and increasingly tangled in politics itself. The early 1950s were a time of high anxiety over the Cold War and a moment when many politicians addressed—or exploited—fears about communist subversion within the country. As with the film industry, a number of television performers were accused, usually with flimsy evidence, of harboring communist sympathies. But for the first of a number of times, television also became an instrument for combating false claims. In 1951, the famed radio broadcaster Edward R. Murrow took his radio show *Hear It Now* to television, where it became *See it Now*. Murrow's coverage of the controversial Wisconsin senator Joseph McCarthy did much to expose the nation to his bullying political style, one that was fully unmasked during the 1954 congressional hearings, after which public opinion turned decisively against him.

Television was the most pervasive medium in the annals of the American media, and yet, paradoxically, it was also among the most private. For most of its history, popular culture was a public experience—something you went *to*: the movies, the ballgame, the dance hall, etc. But even more than radio (which by this point was migrating to cars), television was something you experienced at home. As such, it became of vessel of domestic ideology. Some of the most popular shows of the era had suburban settings: *The Adventures of Ozzie and Harriet* (1952–1966), *Father Knows Best* (1954–1960), and *Leave it to Beaver* (1957–1963), among others. The later years of *I Love Lucy* featured a plot line in which the main characters relocated from New York City to suburban Connecticut.

These shows, many of which are lodged deeply in collective memory, etched a lasting perception of 1950s life as highly traditional in matters such as gender roles. This perception resonated outward in other directions as well, reflected in rising religious observance among Catholic, Jewish, and Protestant families. Much of this focused less on doctrine than the ritualistic and social dimensions of religious experience—communions, bar mitzvahs, weddings, and wakes structured the routines of social interaction and the trajectory of an individual's lifespan.

Restless in the Promised Land: Suburbia's Critics

The appeal of suburbia was self-evident: a huge segment of the US population voted with its feet (or, perhaps more accurately, with its wheels). But from a very early point, suburbia was also a target of much criticism. Skeptics charged that the very thing that made the suburbs attractive—their distance from the sometimes gritty realities of urban life—fostered suffocating insulation, as well as racial segregation and urban impoverishment. They also argued that, in its massmanufactured housing stock and rampant consumerism, suburbia engendered conformity that similarly strangled the individualism that had been a cherished national trait. While some of these charges were misguided, if not exaggerated, they often contained more than a grain of truth.

Some of the sharpest critiques of suburbia came from those who knew it intimately. Perhaps the most incisive came from the realm of literature, especially a series of male writers—Philip Roth, Richard Yates, John Updike—who made their mark in the mid-century. In *Goodbye Columbus* (1959) and other books, Roth portrayed suburbia as a haven for upwardly mobile Jews who could not quite escape the weight of the past, whether that of the big city or the old country from which their ancestors came. Yates portrayed suburbia as literally deadening in his ironically titled novel *Revolutionary Road* (1961), as a young couple tries, but fails, to break out of their Connecticut home and make a new life for themselves in France. In Updike's body of work, which, similar to Roth's, spanned a half-century, suburbia was perhaps more alluring, but a place where secrets (most of them sexual) festered below a placid surface. This sense of secrecy also animated the work of Updike's contemporary John Cheever. In his 1954 story "The Country Husband," Cheever, a short story writer who gave many of his stories suburban settings, described a husband who survives a plane crash, only to return to a stultifying existence that leads to self-destructive acts. In one way or another, all these writers depicted one of the great luxuries of US international pre-eminence: the luxury not to think about unpleasant things that happen far away. In the words of Harry ("Rabbit") Angstrom, the protagonist of four novels that Updike published each decade between 1960 and 1990, "I don't *think* about politics. That's one of my Goddam precious American rights."[20] Angstrom, we're meant to understand, can be a jerk, and the outside world (in his case, the Vietnam War) intrudes into his domestic life in the 1960s in a way that it did not in the 1950s, when he was spared deployment in the Korean War. But here he is only saying what millions of Americans certainly felt in the postwar decades.

Men were not the only ones to struggle with a nagging sense of alienation with suburban life; if anything, women felt it even more acutely. Betty Friedan is widely considered a founding mother of modern feminism for her 1963 book *The Feminine Mystique,* in which she famously described "the problem with no name." Friedan was a housewife in the New York metropolitan area at the time (though her background was Midwestern and Jewish, and she was a veteran journalist with a strong affinity for labor politics). "Each suburban wife struggles with it alone," Friedan explained of that problem. "As she made the beds, shopped for groceries, matched slipcover material, ate peanut butter sandwiches with her children, chauffeured Cub Scouts and Brownies, lay beside her husband at night, she was afraid to ask even of herself the silent question—'Is this all?'"[21] Friedan, like millions of other women, would decide the answer was "no." But it would take many of them a few more years to act on that conclusion.

Not all attacks on suburbia were made from the inside, however—or were entirely fair. It has become fairly standard in this context to cite the work of folk singer Malvina Reynolds, who wrote the song "Little Boxes," a biting critique of the suburbs, for folk musician Pete Seeger in 1962. Reynolds, who hailed from San Francisco and was 62 when the song became a hit, described the suburbs—and the people who inhabited them—as "ticky-tacky" (a phrase that became slang for tinny suburban values). Suburbanites, she asserted, went to similar schools, held similar jobs, had similar values, "and they all look just the same." There was more than a whiff of elitism in this put-down, as indeed there was in much of the folk music scene from which Reynolds emerged at the time. Satirist Tom Lehrer, who could be similarly biting in his own songs, described "Little Boxes" as "the most sanctimonious song ever written."[22]

Reynolds's attack on suburbia may have been broad, but it captured the general thrust of a critique advanced by some of the most prominent social scientists of the time. These writers were particularly concerned about the way the mass affluence that followed World War II was channeled into mass conformity in public no less than private life. Among the first to sound this alarm were sociologist David Riesman and his colleagues Reuel Denney and Nathan Glazer, whose 1950 book *The Lonely Crowd* was widely influential. Riesman and company distinguished between three major social types: the tradition-directed person, typically found in pre-modern societies, whose life is shaped by long-established conventions; the inner-directed person, who works toward self-identified goals; and the outer-directed person, whose sense of self-worth is shaped by the perceptions of others. *The Lonely Crowd* argued that all three could be found in the United States, and that all three had advantages and disadvantages. But there was an unmistakable lament that the inner-directed type, which had been a major force in shaping the restless dynamism of American society, was giving way to outer-directedness. Published as suburbanization accelerated, *The Lonely Crowd* seemed to anticipate the direction the country was taking, and remained a fixture of public discourse for a generation.

Two other major social thinkers of the era focused their attention on the world of work, specifically that of the modern urban corporation, where so many suburbanites were employed. In his 1956 book *The Organization Man*, William H. Whyte described, in a manner that paralleled that of *The Lonely Crowd*, the displacement of the "Protestant (work) Ethic" with what he called the "Social Ethic," in which the primary value of an individual is defined by his relationship to the groups with which he is affiliated. Whyte's criticism of the Social Ethic was relatively moderate—"I call for individualism *within* organization life,"[23] he explained—but the tenor of his indictment was clear. In *White Collar* (1951) and *The Power Elite* (1956), the more sharply critical C. Wright Mills described a systematically organized ruling elite—what would soon be termed "the Establishment"—designed to resist challenges from outsiders.

These writers focused on what they perceived as a gullible, even anesthetized, American public dangerously susceptible to mass persuasion. Some of this was a matter of professional-class skepticism toward American capitalism generally—journalist and social critic Vance Packard caused a sensation with his 1957 book *The Hidden Persuaders*, which called attention to the techniques of subliminal advertising, and much of it took the form of hostility toward American popular culture. A divide between elite and mass taste, which had become increasingly obvious by the turn of the century, was at its peak in the early postwar era. (Many intellectuals had even less patience for so-called middlebrow culture, which sought to popularize history, philosophy, and other subjects in more digestible form, typified in the mild fare purveyed by the Book of the Month Club, which was quite successful in these years.) In part, elite disdain for pop culture was rooted in recent memory, when charismatic politicians seduced the masses with images and symbols that reflected dangerous totalitarian tendencies.

In part, it also reflected the imperatives of some American intellectuals, who justified their existence by articulating cultural alternatives to the status quo.

That status quo was powerful. To be sure, there were social conflicts in American life; some, such as those involving foreign policy, have already been indicated. Others, such as those involving race relations, are yet to be discussed. Such divisions were certainly experienced acutely by Americans who were alive at the time. But when compared to earlier and later periods of American history, the 1950s appear, in retrospect at least, to be a time of remarkable stability, even placidity, for significant segments of the American public. Mass affluence partly explains this; so does a communist threat that fostered a sense of unity and patriotism.

Some observers at the time viewed these developments through a longer-term lens. They explained that the hallmarks of the period—a belief in the efficacy of market capitalism; strong property rights (especially home ownership); a discrete measure of government intervention in the economy (as often as not to benefit business as it was to protect individuals)—were a matter of common agreement throughout American history generally. This was a point made most forcefully by figures such as historian Arthur Schlesinger Jr. in *The Vital Center* (1949), as did political scientist Louis Hartz, who articulated the concept of American Exceptionalism in his 1955 book *The Liberal Tradition in America* to help explain why the nation had escaped the totalitarian solutions of communism on the Left and fascism on the Right, as well as sociologist Daniel Bell in his masterwork *The End of Ideology* (1960). Historian Richard Hofstadter, in his classic books *The American Political Tradition* (1948) and *The Age of Reform* (1955), became a leading figure in describing, not always approvingly, what came to be called "the culture of consensus."

Though Hofstadter portrayed the wider sweep of American history, some aspects of the culture of consensus were distinctive to the postwar decades. American capitalism of the period, for instance, was, to a great degree, corporate, substantially less entrepreneurial or finance-driven than it was before or would be later. Americans of the time placed more faith in institutions—not only those of commerce, but also government, religion, education, and the family—than those of other periods of their history. Even those people whose job it was to challenge conventional wisdom were often inclined to go along with it. That included at least as many intellectuals dependent on outside funding for their research as did those who questioned the existing social order.[24]

Ironically, the very moment when concern about conformity was most intense was also the moment when sophisticated marketers began to discern—and actively exploit—market segments and pitch their products to specific constituencies. While such practices could be crass, if not insidious, they gave the lie to the notion of American society as one of mass conformity.[25]

Moreover, American artists and intellectuals did more than complain about the mediocrity they saw around them: they also generated powerful work that helped some Americans imagine a different, and hopefully better, world. The postwar decades were important in US history—as well as in the history of the Western world—for the way they marked the culmination of a cultural movement known as Modernism. American Modernism in particular was pivotal in the middle decades of the century, because the United States became a haven for a great many European artists and intellectuals who were forced to flee Europe and found a new home, literally and figuratively, on these shores. (For some, this home was not always comfortable, but that friction could also prove creative.)

Modernism, which first became discernible as a discrete artistic movement in the early twentieth century, is too large and complex a phenomenon to be done justice here. But in its broadest formulation, it emphasized the power of subjective and interior experience. It did so at a time when advances in science and technology (especially quantum physics) made earlier values—such as a sense of moral uplift in early-nineteenth-century Romanticism, or the goal of objectively describing reality in late-nineteenth-century Realism—seem obsolete. So it was that the primacy of narrative in literature gave way to subjective points of view and fractured storylines, evident in the works of poets such as Ezra Pound or novelists such as William Faulkner, whose works sometimes required multiple readings in order to even begin to understand what they were saying. In music, Modernist composers placed less emphasis on melody and more on other elements such as time signatures and harmony—or, as often as not, dissonance. Some composers, notably Austrian Arnold Schoenberg, essentially created a new musical language that involved using all 12 notes of a scale and giving them equal weight in a piece of music. One of Schoenberg's students, the American John Cage, stretched such experimentation into entirely new directions in terms of what kinds of sound actually constitute music; his famous 1952 composition *4'33"* calls on musicians to do nothing and audiences to consider the surprisingly specific and changing sound of "silence."

Perhaps no form of art was more vivid in illustrating the impact of Modernism than painting. For most of human history, the goal of painting was to mimic reality as closely as possible. With the advent of photography, however, the ability to do so began to seem increasingly beside the point. This was evident in terms of the suggestive images rendered by Impressionist and Post-Impressionist artists such as the French painter Claude Monet and Dutch artist Vincent Van Gogh in the late nineteenth century, as well as the early-twentieth-century forays of Spaniard Pablo Picasso or Frenchman Georges Braque in representing three-dimensional objects in two-dimensional space, a movement known as Cubism. In the first half of the twentieth century, American Modernist painters such as Georgia O'Keefe and Charles Sheeler introduced comparable elements of abstraction in their work, even as they depicted landscapes (natural in the case of O'Keefe, industrial in the case of Sheeler) that were startling in their precision. With the coming of the postwar era, however, Modernism became even bolder. The transition is nicely illustrated between the expressive, symbolic paintings of the Midwest regionalist painter Thomas Hart Benton, and those of his student Jackson Pollock. By the late 1940s, Pollock had dispensed with realism entirely in favor of the so-called action painting, in which paint is spontaneously splashed, drizzled, or smeared on canvas.[26]

Free Movement: Early Civil Rights Struggles

Artists were not the only ones seeking, and finding, alternatives to mainstream American life in the 1950s. Working within the realm of lived rather than creative experience, a number of minority communities began pushing back against their marginalization in the US society, one that long preceded the postwar period. Important in their own right, these resistance movements proved important in their impact on national life as a whole, often establishing patterns, language, and behavior that would resonate for decades to come.

By far the biggest challenge to the status quo came in the realm of race relations. As was so often true in other domains, World War II proved catalytic. The defeat of racist regimes in Germany and Japan, which had systematically brutalized people on the basis of ethnicity and/or religion, invited troubling questions about the degree of difference between the practices of those empires and that of the United States, where segregation had been the law of the land for most of American history, officially legitimated on a federal basis in the *Plessy v. Ferguson* Supreme Court decision of 1896, which made the concept of "separate but equal" a legal basis for segregating the races in public spaces. It was a foreign observer, the Swedish sociologist Gunnar Myrdal, who noted the disparity between American ideals and realities in his two-volume 1944 study *An American Dilemma*. But African Americans were perfectly capable of framing the problem succinctly themselves. "I spent four years in the Army to free a bunch of Dutchmen and Frenchmen, and I'm hanged if I'm going to let the Alabama version of the Germans kick me around when I get home," one soldier said in 1945. "No sireee-bob! I went into the army a nigger; I'm comin' out a *man*."[27]

The challenges would nevertheless be considerable. The United States of 1945 was an apartheid state comparable to South Africa. As with South Africa, this was not simply a black-and-white affair. For example, Native Americans, dispossessed of their lands and forced to assimilate whether they wished to or not, were considered citizens, but often denied the right to vote. Their numbers, from many millions prior to 1492, had dipped to 200,000 by 1900, and were only gradually starting to rise again; most were mired in poverty.

The crosscurrents of race were particularly notable for Asian Americans. Their numbers had largely been frozen for decades. The Chinese were legally barred from entering the country in 1882, a ban only lifted in 1943 in acknowledgment of the US alliance with China in World War II. Between the late 1940s and early 1950s, Indians, Filipinos, Koreans, and Japanese were also permitted to immigrate—the outbreak of the Korean War in 1950 was pivotal in clarifying the desire to express solidarity with people fighting communism—though subject to quotas that kept their numbers small. Many of those who did emigrate to the United States were the so-called war brides who were the spouses of American soldiers, or adopted children who found a stateside home amid upheaval in their native lands. Asians were not as obviously subjected to the kinds of discrimination that affected African Americans, though they were sometimes lumped with them and almost always regarded as outsiders. Over time, however, they were increasingly regarded as a "model minority," admired for (and, at times, condescended to) in their propensity to assimilate. By 1970, over a quarter of Chinese Americans had college degrees, compared with less than 12% of whites.[28]

Latin Americans were something of a special case. This is not only because of their numbers—in part a reflection of the truism that the ancestors of many had not really crossed any borders but had borders cross them—but also because of US dependence on a transient and cheap labor force for agriculture in its southwestern states. In 1942, the US government made an agreement with that of Mexico whereby Mexican *braceros*, workers under government contract, could reside in the United States as guest workers. By 1960, there were almost half a million such workers in the country, making up about a quarter of the nation's migrant labor force. Yet, Mexicans (who comprised the majority of Latinos in the United States) and other Latin Americans were tolerated at best; when demand for their services receded, they were routinely deported—almost 4 million between 1950 and 1955 alone.[29] Those that remained behind, whether part of the *bracero* program or not, were demeaned with terms such as "wetback" and harassed as undesirables. The situation was somewhat different for the explosion of Puerto Ricans—over a million of whom arrived in the United States by 1960[30]—because they were natives of a US territory. But they were hardly regarded as equals by most Euro-Americans (nor were immigrants from the Dominican Republic, who also began arriving in large numbers in the wake of a right-wing coup against the democratically elected Juan Bosch in 1963). Meanwhile, prosperous Cubans fled Castro's revolution and flooded into Miami, effectively creating a national triangle of migration from which Latinos would penetrate the US interior in decades to come.

Migration was also a major story for African Americans, though in their case it was largely internal. To some degree, this was an old story by 1945, because they had been leaving the Southern countryside for Northern cities since the turn of the century. So while the proportion of African Americans in the US population as a whole hovered in the neighborhood of 10% for most of the twentieth century,[31] its distribution changed dramatically. World War II quickened the pace of that change. In 1940, about three-quarters of African Americans lived in the South. By the 1970s, less than half did,[32] with those in the Midwest and Northeast highly concentrated in industrial cities such as Chicago, Detroit, Boston, and New York. Many came for jobs during World War II and never left.

Not that they found city life easy. It was widely understood that, while the Jim Crow South was vicious in its avowed racism and legal oppression, the North posed challenges of its own. There was an old saying among African Americans that white Southerners didn't care if you got too close, as long as you didn't get too big, whereas white Northerners didn't care if you got too big as long as you didn't get too close. But, by definition, cities are places where people are close. As a result, sparks flew: there were race riots in New York, Detroit, and Los Angeles in 1943 (the last focused on Mexicans and others wearing Zoot suits, dramatic outfits that featured long loose jackets with padded shoulders and tapered pants). From the standpoint of later history, what might be most interesting about this violence against people of color was not so much the garden-variety racism that spawned it, but the fact that these racial minorities were in a position to fight back, whether literally or as a matter of pointing out hypocrisies that were becoming harder to ignore.

They did so amid signs of change for the better. In 1948, President Truman issued an executive order desegregating the armed forces, a move that engendered much resistance and resentment among whites but was grudgingly accepted. (Indeed, the military achieved meaningful racial integration long before other sectors of US society did.) A key event in the history of American sports occurred the previous year when Jackie Robinson became the first African American to play Major League Baseball. Althea Gibson became the first female to break the color bar in the professional tennis circuit in 1949. The National Basketball Association had African American players from its start in 1949, but its teams had unwritten quotas limiting their number. It would be decades before most professional sports teams in baseball, basketball, and football were integrated, and even later before racial minorities were hired for management positions.

The most dramatic change in race relations occurred in the realm of education. In 1954, the Supreme Court of the United States ruled in *Brown v. Board of Education* that the doctrine of separate but equal was unconstitutional. Though the ruling seemed to most Americans a thunderbolt out of the blue, the case against segregation had been building slowly for many years, thanks to the painstaking legal strategy adopted by the National Association for the Advancement of Colored People (NAACP), founded in 1909 to combat racism though judicial means. Giants of the legal profession such as Charles Hamilton Houston and Thurgood Marshall (later appointed to the Supreme Court himself) were pivotal in building the case against segregation. By the time *Brown* reached the court, its chief justice, Earl Warren, an Eisenhower appointee, worked behind the scenes to make sure the ruling was unanimous. This disappointed Eisenhower, who, while clear he would enforce the court's decision even if he did not endorse it, regarded *Brown* as moving too far too fast. He described appointing Warren as "the biggest damn-fool mistake I ever made."[33]

Public reaction to *Brown* was muted at first. But when the court followed it up with *Brown II* in 1955, asserting that school systems should act "with all deliberate speed" to desegregate, opposition began to mount. Some actually came from African Americans, more specifically from that segment of the African American population that did not see integration as a self-evident good (one that would become more prominent in years to come). In a letter to a Florida newspaper, the African American writer Zora Neale Hurston, an anthropologist and novelist widely regarded as leading figure in the Harlem Renaissance of the 1920s, wondered, "How much satisfaction can I get from a court order for somebody to associate with me who does not wish me to be near them?"[34] Most opposition to school segregation came from whites, however, in what came to be known in Virginia as "massive resistance." Some took the form of quiet action, such as the founding of private schools whose (often unstated) reason for existence was avoiding the consequences of the *Brown* decision. Some was a matter of "respectable" dissent, such as White Citizens Councils, which made their case through legalistic language. ("This unwarranted exercise of power by the court, contrary to the Constitution, is creating chaos and confusion in the States principally affected," read a declaration by a group of 19 US Senators in 1956, using language typical of such groups).[35] And some opposition was brutal, such as that of the Ku Klux Klan, which mobilized in response to the ruling.

It was against the backdrop of the *Brown* decision that one of the most infamous acts of violence of the time generated national attention: the murder of 14-year-old Emmett Till. Till, an African American youth from Chicago, was visiting Mississippi relatives when he allegedly whistled at/spoke to/touched a white woman at a crossroads store (accounts differ on this). When the store owner learned of the encounter, he and his half-brother went to the house where Till was staying, took Till away to a barn, beat him, and gouged out one of his eyes before shooting him through the head and throwing his weighted body into a nearby river, where it was found 3 days later. Till's mother insisted that his mutilated body be viewed by mourners in Chicago, and his great-uncle identified Till's attackers in open court, an act of great courage, given the dangers of reprisal. But the enormous press attention that the case got made little difference: an all-white male jury acquitted the suspects. The following year, protected against conviction by the double jeopardy defense, they publicly admitted to a magazine reporter, in return for cash, that they had killed Emmett Till. The case was nevertheless important in shaping the will of a generation of subsequent civil rights leaders.[36]

Indeed, the pace of civil rights activity intensified in the second half of the 1950s. In December 1955, the Women's Political Council of Montgomery (WPC), Alabama, began a boycott against the public bus company, protesting against its policy of racial segregation on the public transit system, after Rosa Parks, an African American seamstress, was arrested for refusing to give up her seat in the African American section of the bus once it became crowded with passengers. Parks was a member of the local NAACP chapter, which worked with WPC on the boycott. One had been in the works months earlier with a case involving a pregnant teenager named Claudette Colvin, but organizers decided to hold off, considering the questions that were likely to arise given Colvin's youth and (single) marital status.

Another figure who emerged in the Montgomery Bus Boycott was a young Baptist minister who had recently arrived in the city. His name was Martin Luther King, Jr. King, who came from a prominent African American family in Atlanta, had received seminary training in Pennsylvania and a doctorate in systematic theology from Boston University before returning to the South. Initially reluctant about getting involved, he ended up as the spokesman for Montgomery Bus Boycott, which lasted for 13 months. Intense national attention and economic pressure finally led the city to capitulate to the demands for a racially integrated bus system in what became one of the great victories of the budding civil rights movement.

King's notoriety was not simply a matter of his impressive personal bearing and organizational skill: it was, first and foremost, the moral vision that infused both. At the center of that vision was his Christian faith—he was the *Reverend* Martin Luther King, Jr., a fact that the secular-minded tend to overlook. At the core of King's religious conviction was a Christ-like devotion to non-violence, and a willingness to suffer for the greater good. There were multiple streams that fed into King's non-violent philosophy, among them the writings of Henry David Thoreau, Mohandas Karamchand Gandhi (whose struggle against British colonialism furnished an instructive precedent), and a series of religious philosophers, prominent among them the American theologian Reinhold Niebuhr, whose tragic vision of life and recognition of the evils that inhered in even the most altruistic of efforts never lessened the necessity of striving for a better world. King fused these multiple strands of thought into a broad-based movement that spawned a powerful new organization, the Southern Christian Leadership Conference (SCLC). The SCLC, in turn, sponsored other efforts, among them the formation of the Student Nonviolent Coordinating Committee (SNCC—pronounced "snick"), led by gifted organizers such as Ella Baker and Septima Clark, who trained a generation of activists.

Meanwhile, the civil rights tide continued to rise. In 1957, racist elements in the city of Little Rock, Arkansas, refused to obey a court order to integrate the city's high schools. Arkansas governor Orval Faubus, not a diehard segregationist but seeking to avoid their wrath, declined to enforce the ruling and mobilized the Arkansas National Guard to prevent it, and angry mobs formed to bar the nine African American students from entering the school. A photograph documenting the bravery of one such student, Elizabeth Eckford, mercilessly heckled as she tried and failed to enter the school, has become an icon of the civil rights movement. President Eisenhower, reluctant to intervene but concluding that he could not allow such flagrant defiance of federal law, sent the US Army to Little Rock to restore order and integrate the school. Troops remained there for months. Faubus was rewarded for his racism with re-election in 1958 and for two more terms after that.

But this didn't stem the flow of protests. On February 1, 1960, a group of four first-year African American students at the University of North Carolina Agricultural and Technical State University—Joseph McNeil, Franklin McCain, Ezell Blair, Jr., and David Richmond—occupied the lunch counter at a local Woolworth store in protest of its whites-only section and refused to leave until they were served. Within days, hundreds of other people joined the A&T Four, as they were known, and demonstrations spread to a series of other Southern cities. Young women were pivotal in these protests, including Ruby Doris Smith, who worked to desegregate Atlanta lunch counters, and Diane Nash, a Fisk University student and founding member of SNCC who would go on to play a pivotal role in many subsequent civil rights battles around the country. Though these young protesters were often subject to abuse, Woolworth stores and other targets of protest backed down. King praised the lunch-counter sit-ins in typically eloquent language: "In sitting down at the lunch counters, they are in reality standing up for the best in the American Dream."[37]

The civil rights movement had a long way to go by 1960. But it was one of the signal events of the 1950s, and its impact resonated far beyond the realm of race relations, as important as that was in its own right. Its language, symbols, and logic would inspire and inform every substantial social movement that followed it—not only those on the Left (feminists, Chicanos, gays), but also those on the Right (anti-abortion activists, Affirmative Action opponents, even gun rights advocates). All these people would speak a language of equality, of organized protest, and profess non-violence as their primary means of securing protection. Indeed, their very legitimacy often depended on their ability to convince their fellow Americans that their cause was comparably worthy to that of African Americans of the 1950s.

Big Bangs: 1950s Youth Culture

The civil rights movement was also an important backdrop for many of the artistic and cultural currents of the postwar years. Perhaps the most potent means of expressing hope and frustration in these years was musical. By the time of World War II, African American music, especially jazz, had long been the dominant idiom in popular music in the United States (and even abroad). In the 1920s and 1930s, it had been the preeminent expression of youth culture, represented most vividly by big bands and the subgenre of swing. Beginning in the 1940s, however, a new form of jazz emerged on the scene: bop. Performed in small ensembles and marked by complex chordal structures and patterns of improvisation, bop was a significantly less catchy idiom than other forms of jazz, though its cerebral style could be exhilarating for those who could appreciate the work of its most gifted practitioners, among them Dizzy Gillespie, Charlie Parker, John Coltrane, and Miles Davis (whose 1959 album *Kind of Blue*, in a subsequent variant known as "cool" jazz, has quietly become one of the best-selling jazz records of all time). These musicians reflected the quickening current of impatience in African American life, an unwillingness to simply accept the rules of the game as dictated by white audiences and the marketplace. This independence, even incipient separatism, would be a crucial countercurrent in African American culture from the 1940s on.

It would also ripple outward in multiple directions. Among the people most besotted with jazz in general and bop in particular were a group of writers known as the Beats, whose improvisational literary style imitated that of their musical heroes. Beat culture was also notable for its experiments with drugs, sexuality, and Eastern mysticism. It was bi-coastal, anchored in New York and San Francisco—Jack Kerouac's 1957 road novel *On the Road* made the connection between them legendary. Other important Beat figures included Allen Ginsberg, whose 1956 poem "Howl" became a literary manifesto of alienation, and William S. Burroughs, whose *The Naked Lunch* (1959) was the subject of a celebrated obscenity trial in Boston for its language and graphic description of drug use and sex acts (a ban on the book was overturned). Novelist Norman Mailer was not a Beat writer himself, but his 1957 magazine article "The White Negro" vividly captured the appeal of the Beats and the degree to which their "hipster" culture was rooted in the ethos of jazz.

Gay Americans sought to articulate and experience an alternative lifestyle for themselves in what were, in many respects, difficult times. Beat writers, many of them gay, were important figures in this regard. But gay life also took a turn toward social activism in the founding of organizations such as the Mattachine Society (1950), which promoted the interests of gay men, and the Daughters of Bilitis (1955), a lesbian organization named after the fictional companion of ancient Greek poet Sappho. Both groups had local chapters in multiple cities.

Rebellion spread into more conventional channels as well, also reaching many heterosexual white suburban young people impatient with the smug pieties of postwar life. The work of sexologists Alfred Kinsey and his wife Clara produced a series of works documenting the degree to which Americans diverged from widely presumed sexual norms. More vivid expressions of cultural restlessness could be found in the prose of short story writer and novelist J. D. Salinger, who struck literary gold with his 1951 novel *The Catcher in the Rye*. His protagonist Holden Caulfield, obsessed with "phoniness," heralded a new generation: restless, skeptical, but animated by an idealism that would prod American society toward change.

Other forms of youth culture protest were more overt. There was a good deal of concern in 1950s media discourse about the rise of juvenile delinquency, which was sometimes attributed to the spoiled children of an affluent society (though crime rates were nowhere near what they would be later). But this culture of delinquency was at least as much alluring as it was alarming, romanticized in a series of Hollywood movies. In the 1953 film *The Wild One*, a biker movie featuring the rising star Marlon Brando, a young woman asks, "What are you rebelling against?" Brando's character famously replies, "Whaddaya got?" This live-fast-die-young ethos was mythologized in the 1955 film *Rebel without a Cause*, starring the legendary James Dean—legendary in part because the promising young 24-year-old actor died in a car crash shortly after the film's release. A third film, *The Blackboard Jungle* (1955), set in a tough inner-city high school, was notable for featuring the song "Rock Around the Clock," which became a youth anthem and helped set the stage for the coming musical revolution.

That revolution was known as rock and roll (an African American slang term for sexual intercourse). While a number of genres in slave music were important to the creation of rock and roll, its foundation is the post–Civil War idiom of the blues. The blues was rock's cornerstone, whether the basis of saying so is musical scales with flattened fifths and sevenths, an AAB lyrical pattern, or the themes of the lyrics. Gospel, another late-nineteenth-century African American genre, was also important, particularly in terms of a call-and-response vocal pattern. And jazz provided a model of improvisation that was widely adopted, particularly by keyboard players and guitarists. A series of social, technological, and economic factors were also important. The Great Migration of African Americans to the North was one. It brought African American people into new environments that subtly altered their music (the blues, for example, took on an edgier tone with electric guitars, necessary to be heard amid the din of nightclubs).

The Great Migration also brought African Americans into closer contact with Latinos and *their* cultures. Indeed, Latin music is one of the less recognized vectors in shaping mainstream popular music. It did so from a diverse base of musical subcultures in Latin America, among them Afro-Cuban music, dance styles such as the mambo and tango, and guitarron-based music from Northern Mexico.

This sense of mixing was intensified by the spread of radio; it allowed people in formerly isolated communities to feel they were part of a broad and diverse national musical culture. The growing postwar record industry adapted to meet the demand for African American artists in regional markets such as Cincinnati and Chicago. The music that emerged from these markets was known by the term "race records," reflecting the segregated character of US society at the time.

By the late 1940s and early 1950s, the emerging style of rhythm and blues—more danceable than traditional blues—made stars of a range of artists, among them Ruth Brown, Lloyd Price, and Hank Ballard and the Midnighters, whose 1954 profane hit song "Work with Me Annie" (followed later in the same year by "Annie Had a Baby") is considered a forerunner of rock and roll. Meanwhile, a once parallel country music tradition was converging with this musical culture. Jimmie Rodgers had pioneered this convergence back in the 1920s; now Hank Williams and Tennessee Ernie Ford drew on African American traditions in forging their own musical styles. Ford's huge 1955 hit "Sixteen Tons," about an indebted coal miner, draws on blues traditions in both its style and themes.

The locus of country music had long been Nashville, Tennessee. It was the other end of that state, in the city of Memphis, on the Mississippi River delta, that provided the seedbed for rock and roll. It was there that Sam Phillips, a native Alabamian and former disk jockey, founded a small record company called Sun Records. Phillips signed a number of Memphis acts to his label, among them a group of prison inmates dubbed the Prisonaires, who had a local 1953 hit with "Just Walkin' in the Rain." Phillips was an exceptionally astute judge of talent. Over the course of the next few years, he signed a series of artists who would go on to have successful careers, among them bluesman Howlin' Wolf, country star Johnny Cash, and rhythm and blues artist Ike Turner, husband of the great Tina Turner and writer of "Rocket 88," a song about a car that some historians consider the first rock and roll record.

What Phillips really wanted, as the now legendary story goes, was to "find a white boy with the Negro sound and the Negro feel." He found that boy—or, perhaps more accurately, his secretary Marion Keisker found that boy, who

Phillips coached to success over a period of months—in Elvis Presley. The son of a truck driver, Presley, who had been born in 1935 in nearby Tupelo, Mississippi, was considered "white trash," and as such mingled with African Americans more than "respectable" whites of his time did. The family moved to Memphis when Presley was 13 years old and lived in welfare housing; after his graduation from high school, he got a job as a truck driver, and quickly out-earned his father (who had spent time in jail for writing bad checks). In 1953, Presley walked into Sun, hoping to make a record for his beloved mother, which in effect became his audition. In 1954–1955, he made a string of songs now collectively known as the Sun Sessions, which revolutionized popular music. And, in 1956, Presley went to New York to begin a recording career, completing his transformation into one of the most commercially successful celebrities of all time.

Presley was dubbed "the King of Rock and Roll," but he hardly invented it. His fellow Sun label artist Jerry Lee Lewis had more raw talent, and was a spectacular showman. So were many gifted African American songwriters and performers, among them Chuck Berry and Little Richard (Penniman), who could never hope to achieve Presley's stature, given the intensity of American racism.

Indeed, it's important to remember the immense challenge that rock and roll posed to the established cultural order. In church pulpits, high school auditoriums, and newspaper editorial pages, it was excoriated as evil incarnate. Rock records were banned, investigations were launched, and protectors of public order warned that such music raised the awful possibility of racial miscegenation. Much of the angst surrounding rock focused on the young, who lavished their disposable income on a variety of products, principal among them the new vinyl (no longer shellac) records they played on their cutting-edge hi-fi record machines, which could now change the disks automatically.

The rise of rock and roll is a story worth relating in relative detail because it represents what might be termed the great paradox of the American empire: that the characteristic cultural expression of the moment when US power and influence reached its height was decisively shaped by the most oppressed people in the nation's history. This seems oddly fitting. There was never a moment in the previous three centuries when the making of what became the United States was not a matter of brutality, exploitation, and denial. And yet, no place on earth had ever honored individual aspiration so insistently. This had almost always been a matter of hypocrisy. But in the decades following World War II, such hypocrisy became harder to take precisely because it no longer seemed essential to the national experience. Indeed, even many of those with an investment in maintaining such exclusion were beginning to wonder if it was worth it. By 1960, the United States had reached a state of extraordinary hope. There are few things more exciting in a society. Or more dangerous.

CULTURE WATCH: *A Raisin in the Sun* (1959)

Hope, the great American poet Emily Dickinson once wrote, is like a bird with feathers that perches in one's soul.

> *And sings the tune without the words—*
> *And never stops—at all—*

One reason why Dickinson's poem is so haunting is the way it suggests that hope can be an unsettling burden: the possibility that things really might get better can make the way they *are* seem all the more intolerable. The power of hope as a goad to action as well as a source of pain is central in *A Raisin in the Sun*, a play by Lorraine Hansberry (1930–1965) that both captures a specific historical moment and resonates across American history.

A Raisin in the Sun depicts a few weeks in the life of the Younger family, which lives in a crowded, run-down apartment on Chicago's African American South Side. All the major characters yearn for a better life, though in different ways: Walter Younger, a limousine driver, hopes to open a liquor store; his sister, Beneatha Younger, wants to go to medical school; Walter's wife, Ruth, a domestic worker, would love a bigger apartment, as would their son Travis, who sleeps on the couch. The matriarch of the Younger clan, Mama, who is also a housemaid, wants her family to be honorably happy, something her late hard-working husband lived—and died—for before the play begins. The pending arrival of her husband's US$10,000 life insurance settlement is the engine that drives the plot. What will Mama do with the money? She tries to do a number of things, one of which involves buying a new house. The problem is that the only one she can afford is in a white neighborhood. And the people who live there are, to put it mildly, not happy about it. The pivotal question as the play reaches a climax is how the Youngers are going to handle this challenge.

The plot of *A Raisin in the Sun* is rooted in Hansberry's childhood. Her father successfully sued a neighborhood association that adopted contractual codes to prevent minorities from moving into the white Chicago neighborhood of Woodlawn in the case of *Hansberry v. Lee* (1940), which went all the way to the US Supreme Court. Such racial "covenants," as they were known, became illegal after the passage of the Civil Rights Act of 1968.

Premiering on Broadway in 1959, *A Raisin in the Sun* was a play of its moment—and ahead of its time. It captured the rising tide of expectation amid the reality of oppression that characterized African American life in the 1950s. But its textured portrayal of family life also anticipated feminism, anti-colonialism, and the always fraught politics of hair: Beneatha takes the advice of her Nigerian suitor and decides to cut it and wear it naturally, decisions that are subjects of much comment. (The topic would continue to resonate a half-century later in the work of Nigerian writer Chimamanda Ngozi Adiche

Figure 2.2 DOMESTIC STRUGGLE: Lena ("Mama") Younger, played here by Claudia McNeil, expresses frustration in a scene from the 1961 film version of Lorraine Hanesberry's 1959 play *A Raisin in the Sun.* Mama's desire to buy her family a home catalyzes the plot of the story—and dramatizes the racism that the Youngers, and by extension all African American families, had to contend with at the dawn of the civil rights movement (directed by Daniel Petrie, and produced by Columbia Pictures Corporation). Photo courtesy of Columbia Pictures/Photofest.

in her celebrated 2013 novel *Americanah.*) One topic it does not broach is homosexuality; a series of letters that Hansberry wrote anonymously indicated that she was a closeted lesbian.

A Raisin in the Sun was made into a highly regarded 1961 film starring Sidney Poitier, and has been remade many times, including as a 1975 musical, a 1988 television film, and in a series of twenty-first-century revivals. Tragically, Hansberry died of cancer in 1965, cutting short a brilliant career. Another one of her writings, *To Be Young, Gifted, and Black* (1969), was adapted into a play by her husband after her death, and it became the inspiration for a classic song by jazz singer Nina Simone.

The title for *A Raisin in the Sun* came from another American poet who also thought long and hard about hope: Langston Hughes. In his 1951 "Harlem," Hughes, a legendary figure of the Harlem Renaissance, poses the question, "What Happens to a Dream Deferred?" Perhaps, he suggests, it will wither like a raisin in the sun. Then again, it might explode. At that point, the foundering of hope ceases to be a personal problem and becomes a societal one. A successful society does not simply keep hope alive—it turns more than a few dreams into reality. The price for not doing so can be higher than any insurance policy can pay.

Suggested Further Reading

John Patrick Diggins offers a compelling overview of this period in *The Proud Decades: America in War and Peace, 1941–1960* (New York: Norton, 1988). Journalist David Halberstam renders a readable treatment of the era in *The Fifties* (New York: Villard, 1993).
    The standard history of suburbia remains Kenneth T. Jackson's *Crabgrass Frontier: The Suburbanization of the United States* (New York: Oxford University Press, 1985). Loren Baritz surveys the logic of suburban values in *The Good Life: The Meaning of Success for the American Middle Class* (1982; New York: Harper & Row, 1989). Lizabeth Cohen limns postwar consumer culture in *A Consumer's Republic: The Politics of Mass Consumption in Postwar America* (New York: Knopf, 2003).
    Important works of cultural history in the period include Richard Pells, *The Liberal Mind in a Conservative Age: American Intellectuals in the 1940s and 1950s* (New York: Harper & Row, 1985); W. T. Lhamon, Jr., *Deliberate Speed: The Origins of a Cultural Style in the 1950s* (Washington, D.C.: Smithsonian Institution Press, 1990), and the essay collection *Recasting America: Culture and Politics in the Age of the Cold War* (Chicago: University of Chicago Press, 1989).
    The literature of the civil rights movement is vast. For an introductory overview, see Bruce J. Dierenfield, *The Civil Rights Movement*, revised ed. (2004; New York: Routledge, 2013). Glenn Altschuler contextualizes rock and roll in the mid-twentieth century in *All Shook Up: How Rock & Roll Changed America* (New York: Oxford University Press, 2003). Useful books on other ethnic groups in the postwar society include Juan Gonzales, *Harvest of Empire: A History of Latinos in America*, revised ed. (2000; New York: Penguin, 2011); Shelley Sang-Hee Lee, *A New History of Asian America* (New York: Routledge, 2014); and Melani McAlister, *Epic Encounters: Culture, Media & U.S. Interests in the Middle East Since 1945*, second ed. (2001; Berkeley: University of California Press, 2005).

Notes

1   Robert Sklar, *Movie-Made America: A Cultural History of American Movies* (1975; New York: Vintage, 1994), 269.
2   For an especially insightful analysis of *It's a Wonderful Life*, see Robert Ray, *A Certain Tendency of the Hollywood Cinema, 1930–1980* (Princeton: Princeton University Press, 1985), 179–215. See also Jim Cullen, *Restless in the Promised Land: Catholics and the American Dream* (Madison, Wisconsin: Sheed & Ward, 2001), 109–113, 131–134.
3   James Patterson, *Grand Expectations: The United States, 1945–1974* (New York: Oxford University Press, 1997), 14.
4   Joshua Freeman, *American Empire: The Rise of a Global Power, The Democratic Revolution at Home, 1945–2000* (New York: Penguin, 2012), 51.
5   Patterson, 62.
6   Patterson, 65.
7   Patterson, 61–62; Diggins, 185.
8   Freeman, 33–34.
9   On the limits for the GI Bill for women and African Americans, see Cohen, 137–146 and 167–173.
10 Freeman, 11; Patterson, 66.

11   Patterson, 77.

12   Patterson, 70; Diggins, 186.

13   Freeman, 139.

14   Freeman, 124, 383.

15   This paragraph and the next draw from Jim Cullen, *The American Dream: A Short History of an Idea that Shaped a Nation* (New York: Oxford University Press, 2003), 146.

16   Cullen, 150–152; http://www.census.gov/const/C25Ann/sftotalmedavgsqft.pdf (3/25/14).

17   Patterson, 333; "The Growth of Suburbia," *The New York Times*, June 30, 1949, in *The United States Since 1945: A Documentary Reader*, edited by Robert P. Ingalls and David K Johnson (Malden, MA: Wiley-Blackwell, 2009), 45–46.

18   Patterson, 360–361.

19   Patterson, 348.

20   John Updike, *Rabbit Redux*, in *The Rabbit Novels, Vol. I* (1971; New York: Ballantine, 2003), 38.

21   Betty Friedan, *The Feminine Mystique* (1963; New York: Norton, 2001), 57.

22   Christopher Hitchens, "Suburbs of Our Discontent," *The Atlantic*, December 2008; http://www.theatlantic.com/magazine/archive/2008/12/suburbs-of-our-discontent/307131 (accessed March 16, 2014).

23   William H. Whyte, *The Organization Man* (New York: Simon & Schuster, 1956), 11.

24   For more on this point, see Terence Ball, "The Politics of Social Science in Postwar America," in *Recasting America*, 76–92.

25   Cohen, Chapter 7.

26   For more on the Benton/Pollock relationship and its implications, see Erica Doss, "The Art of Cultural Politics: From Regionalism to Abstract Expressionism," in May, *Recasting America*, 195–220.

27   Cullen, 117.

28   Patterson, 375–378. Sang-Hee Lee, 238, 248–251, 260.

29   Patterson, 379–380.

30   Gonzales, 81.

31   There's a table charting the proportion of African Americans relative to the US population as a whole at http://en.wikipedia.org/wiki/African_American#cite_note-39. Most of the numbers are based on US Census figures; numbers from years 1920 to 2000 are based on US Census figures as given by the *Time Almanac* of 2005, p. 377.

32   Patterson, 380.

33   Diggins, 281.

34   Werner Sollors, "Of Mules and Mares: Quadrupeds All?" *American Quarterly* 42:2 (June 1990): 171.

35   "The Southern Manifesto" (Declaration by 19 US Senators, March 12, 1956) in Ingalls & Johnson, 65.

36   Freeman, 152–153; John Dittmer, *Local People: The Struggle for Civil Rights in Mississippi* (Urbana/Champaign: University of Illinois Press, 1995), 57–58.

37   Martin Luther King, Jr., "The Time for Freedom Has Come," in *A Testament of Hope: The Essential Writings and Speeches of Martin Luther King, Jr.* (San Francisco: Harper San Francisco, 1986), 161. King used similar language 2 years later in his famous "Letter from a Birmingham Jail": "when these disinherited children of God sat down at lunch counters they were in reality standing up for the best in the American Dream" (302).

Part II
The Long 1960s

3

Confidence and Agitation
The American Empire at High Tide, 1960–1965

Figure 3.1 NIK AND DICK SHOW: US Vice President Richard Nixon (right) debates Soviet Premier Nikita Khrushchev during their famous "Kitchen Debate" in July 1959. Their argument about the relative quality of life between the two superpowers demonstrated the intensity of the Cold War deep into the heart of everyday life in the mid-twentieth century. © Glasshouse Images / Alamy.

Democratic Empire: The United States Since 1945, First Edition. Jim Cullen.
© 2017 Jim Cullen. Published 2017 by John Wiley & Sons, Inc.

Dishing: The Kitchen Debate as Domestic Squabble

THE COLD WAR wasn't only fought with (military) weapons.

July 24, 1959, found US Vice President Richard Nixon in Moscow, the guest of Soviet Premier Nikita Khrushchev. In late 1958, the two superpowers had agreed to host cultural exhibitions in each other's nations as part of an effort to foster mutual understanding. The Soviet exhibit opened in New York in June 1959; the American exhibit followed in the Soviet capital the next month. Nixon gave the media entourage surrounding "Nik and Dick" a tour of a simulated typical American house selling for $14,000 (no starter home, but no mansion, either). "I want to show you this kitchen," the vice president told the premier. "It is like those of our houses in California." Nixon pointed to a dishwasher.

"We have such things," Khrushchev replied through his translator.

"This is our newest model," Nixon continued. "This is the kind which is built in thousands of units for direct installations in the houses. In America, we like to make life easier for women." (Men apparently did not run dishwashers.)

"Your capitalistic attitude toward women does not occur under communism," Khrushchev answered. His tone and gestures suggested both cheerful bluster and genuine irritation—a characteristic combination for him. When Nixon explained that a World War II veteran making $3 an hour could get a mortgage allowing his family to live in the house for 25–30 years, Khrushchev asserted that, unlike Soviet houses, flimsy American ones don't last. Nixon denied this, but also said that most Americans wouldn't want to remain in the same kitchen for more than 20 years: "The American system is designed to take advantage of new inventions and techniques."[1]

The strained geniality of their passive–aggressive banter continued as the two men made their way to a television recording studio, where their exchanges were recorded on video, using new color technology, for posterity. Khrushchev appeared a bit confused about what it meant to tape their conversation, and demanded that his remarks be broadcast to the American people. Nixon pledged they would, and hoped *his* remarks would be heard by the Soviet people. The two heartily shook hands to seal the deal.[2]

According to William Safire, who later worked for Nixon but was in Moscow that day as a press agent for the company that built the house, the vice president eventually steered the topic of competition to weapons. "Would it not be better to compete in the relative merit of washing machines than in the strength of rockets?" he asked Khrushchev.

"Yes, but your generals say we must compete in rockets," the premier responded. "We are strong and we can beat you."

"In this day and age to argue who is stronger completely misses the point," Nixon said. "With modern weapons, it just does not make sense. If war comes, we both lose."[3]

As with a great many things associated with Richard Nixon, this seemingly conciliatory remark was disingenuous. Though he was implying that an arms race was destructive for the United States no less than the Soviet Union, the US government remained as committed as ever to deploying new military technology around the world and seeking an edge over the Soviets, running the very risk of nuclear war he claimed the United States was trying to avoid. During the very month that Nixon journeyed to Moscow, specially trained US forces arrived in the Southeast Asian nation of Laos, followed by air support, to train anti-communist Laotian troops to resist the pro-Soviet Pathet Lao, a revolutionary left-wing movement there. It was also in the summer of 1959 that protesters in the emerging nation of Congo were overthrowing the colonial rule of Belgium; within months, the CIA would be secretly working on the assassination of its new leader, Patrice Lumumba, who had accepted Soviet aid. He would be dead by the time Nixon left office in January 1961. So it was that the United States extended its instinctive opposition to all things communist, and cast its lot with colonial powers.

But as a piece of geopolitical theater, the "Kitchen Debate," as it became known, was a public relations triumph for the United States in general, and for Richard Nixon in particular. It generated international headlines and raised Nixon's stature with the American people at a time when he was preparing to run for president. Though he occupied a lower government position than Khrushchev, Nixon appeared statesmanlike. In part that's because he avoided crude assertions of American military might. Instead, he rested his case on what was widely known as "the American Way of Life": an implicit claim of superiority resting not simply on consumerism—though that was certainly a part of it— but also on the quality and dignity of everyday existence for ordinary Americans. In this regard, Nixon, who had based much of his political career on an unassuming image that involved a simple cloth coat for his wife and a puppy for his daughters, was an apt messenger. Not everyone bought his argument, literally or figuratively; then, as now, people tended to view such matters through a preconceived political lens. But it was nevertheless powerful at home and abroad.

In another sense, however, Nixon was an ironic poster child for the American Way of Life, because he could be cringe-inducing when he wasn't simply infuriating. The whole cloth coat/puppy dog business dated back to a notorious 1952 speech when Nixon narrowly avoided being dumped from the Republican ticket by President Eisenhower for alleged campaign finance improprieties,[4] accusations he managed to sidestep by confessing that his dog, Checkers, was the gift of a supporter, but one—critics be damned!—he refused to give back. (The speech generated lots of support from TV viewers, but political professionals were appalled by his craven performance.) Nixon may have seemed statesmanlike with Khrushchev, but a trip he made to Latin America in 1958 had provoked riots in Venezuela, where he was pelted with eggs. Such a reception couldn't be blamed on Nixon, exactly; there was widespread anger in Latin America over US policy generally. But Nixon lacked the stature to ward off such humiliation. That's exactly why his performance in the Kitchen Debate is so significant: when it came to touting the American Way of Life, even a dweeb could be cool.

American Prince: JFK

By 1960, however, a growing restlessness was stirring in the American people, as indeed it was through much of the world, especially among the young. Some of this restlessness was a wish for a little more excitement after the staid Eisenhower years. And some was a yearning that there be more to life than either superpower jockeying *or* safe domesticity. The very successes of the postwar years in providing tens of millions of Americans with a modicum of comfort were generating higher hopes; Betty Friedan's melancholy question from *The Feminine Mystique*— "Is this all?"—reflected this restlessness, and quickened it.

This is why histories of the 1960s typically do not begin with Richard Nixon. Instead, they often begin with his opponent in the 1960 presidential election: John F. Kennedy of Massachusetts. In fact, Nixon and Kennedy had a lot in common: both were World War II Navy veterans and religious outsiders— Nixon Quaker, Kennedy Catholic. They both arrived in Congress in 1946. Both had reputations as staunch anti-communists (Nixon prosecuted them; Kennedy had nice things to say about his fellow Catholic, Joseph McCarthy). And both were seen as rising stars. The two were actually friends. In terms of their public image, however, the contrast was stark. Nixon came across as earnest and hardworking. But Kennedy (or JFK, as he was known) was almost impossibly glamorous: handsome, witty, and endowed with evident social graces— along with a wife, Jacqueline Bouvier Kennedy, who was the very personifica-tion of style. Nixon was the heir apparent in the Republican Party, even if there was limited enthusiasm for him; Kennedy was an upstart who wrested the Democratic nomination away from established elders such as Senate Majority Leader Lyndon Johnson and Eisenhower's two-time opponent Adlai Stevenson. Kennedy, in fact, was more driven and vulnerable, politically and otherwise, than it appeared. And Nixon, who always seemed like a loser to a great many people, proved surprisingly, if annoyingly, resilient.

The presidential election of 1960 is often considered a turning point in American history for a number of reasons. One is that it really was the first modern campaign in which television, which had been used for advertising and conventions in the elections of 1952 and 1956, became a major factor in both reporting and influencing the outcome. This was certainly the case in the first presidential debates ever held, which were broadcast on television. In the first debate in particular, Kennedy was widely perceived to have won because he *looked* better than Nixon. That said, the contest proved to be extraordinarily close, and it is widely believed that Kennedy's razor-thin margin was a product of electoral fraud practiced by Chicago Mayor Richard Daley, who reputedly dumped ballots in the Chicago River.[5] Nixon himself believed he had been cheated, even if he also believed it would be pointless to contest the outcome (it would make him look like even more of a loser). He emerged from that contest with a conviction that he would never allow himself to be outmaneuvered again, one that would have fateful consequences for him a dozen years later.

Historians differ in their assessment of Kennedy as a politician and statesman. His champions portray him as an intelligent man who made mistakes (such as allowing the Bay of Pigs invasion to go forward) but who kept a level head (such as in the Cuban Missile Crisis) and showed real signs of growth in office. Such people believe it likely he planned to get the United States out of the increasingly messy situation in Vietnam. Kennedy moved slowly, but deliberately, toward the emerging liberal economic orthodoxy of the 1960s, as well as toward embracing the civil rights movement, something he did amid considerable resistance from the segregationist wing of the Democratic Party.

Kennedy's critics emphasize how little he actually accomplished. Most of his legislative initiatives were met with widespread resistance, and some (such as the civil rights bill he championed) were never passed on his watch. These people also note that there were sordid aspects of Kennedy's life that were largely kept hidden from the public, among them a compulsive sex drive and health problems that might have raised questions about his fitness for office, were they widely known. The Kennedy administration also abused its power in ways that included using the Internal Revenue Service to investigate perceived enemies and approving Federal Bureau of Investigation wiretaps into the private life Martin Luther King, Jr., in part because it appears the FBI chief J. Edgar Hoover was in a position to blackmail the Kennedy brothers about their sexual escapades.[6] But none of this was publicly disclosed in Kennedy's lifetime.

The real significance of the 1960 presidential election, and the Kennedy presidency generally, was cultural. At 43, he was the youngest man ever to be elected president, and as a youthful man with a wife and young children, his ascent seemed to signal a generational shift in American culture. After the relatively bland Eisenhower years, the White House became a showcase for artists and intellectuals, presided over by Jackie Kennedy, whose elegant tastes were reflected in her couture and urbanity (it was she who dubbed the Kennedy years "Camelot," an allusion to the legendary court of King Arthur).

Kennedy himself was deeply aware of his cultural impact, and exploited it to maximum advantage. This was obvious, for example, in his much celebrated inaugural address of 1961: "Let the word go forth from this time and place, to friend and foe alike, that the torch has been passed to a new generation of Americans. ... Let every nation know, whether it wishes us well or ill, that we shall pay any price, bear any burden, meet any hardship, support any friend, oppose any foe, to assure the survival and the success of liberty. This much we pledge—and more." The speech was vintage Kennedy in two respects. The first was its obvious idealism. The most famous line of the address—"my fellow Americans: ask not what your country can do for you, ask what you can do for your country"—inspired millions for decades to come. But the speech was also notable for an assertiveness, even aggression, that reflected the imperatives of the Cold War, as well as the vein of braggadocio in Kennedy's persona. The two sides of that persona were also captured in two new foreign policy programs frequently linked to the Kennedy administration: the Peace Corps, which sent humanitarian volunteers to developing nations, and the Green Berets, special forces that undertook undercover military operations in locales that ranged from Cuba to Laos.[7]

Grand Expectations: The Birth of "the Sixties"

While JFK clearly *tapped* a quickening voice of yearning, of expectation, he certainly did not *create* it. Indeed, in terms of making a long-term impact, its real locus was elsewhere—and in multiple locations elsewhere. It's worth repeating that much of this energy was generational, a by-product of the first Baby Boomers coming of age. (The term "teenager" originated in the 1940s, and had become commonplace by the 1950s.[8]) Between 1946 and 1970, the number of Americans in college quadrupled, from 2 million to 8 million,[9] creating a critical mass of young people with opportunities for channeling their idealism into action. In 1946, one out of eight people who were 18–24 years old was in college or graduate school; by 1960, that figure was one in four, and by 1970 one in three. For the first time anywhere on earth, there were more college students than there were farmers.[10]

The most famous manifestation of an emergent youthful idealism was the founding of Students for a Democratic Society at the University of Michigan at Ann Arbor in 1962. "We are people of this generation, bred in at least modest comfort, housed now in universities, looking uncomfortably to the world we inherit," reads the famous opening of the organization's manifesto, the Port Huron Statement. "Freedom and equality for each individual, government of, by, and for the people—these American values we found good, principles by which we could live as men." And yet, the Cold War and civil rights movement had made these people aware that they could no longer remain complacent about violations of national ideals. Committing to an ethic of participatory democracy, SDS called for the pursuit of a *truly* American way of life beyond mere survival or the pursuit of wealth, one rooted in the founding ideals of the nation. Though buffeted by external hostility and internal division, the organization would play a pivotal role in the social movements in the years that followed.

Not all the idealism and activism of the early 1960s was that of young people. Socialist Michael Harrington was 34 years old when his book *The Other America: Poverty in the United States* was published in 1962. Harrington's book was a notable achievement in a number of respects. First, it documented the breadth and depth of poverty in an affluent nation to a degree that a great many Americans found shocking. Second, Harrington helped explain *why* it was shocking: poverty was in effect an experience of invisible segregation, in which the poor were hidden from view, in part because they could appear superficially prosperous (clothing was cheaper than it had been), but also because the poor were concentrated in communities—communities which, contrary to popular perception, were more likely to be rural white ones in places such as Appalachia than urban African American ones such as Hough in Cleveland—that were separate from the rest of society. The experiences of the poor were far more than a matter of material deprivation: "Poverty in the United States is a culture, an institution, a way of life."[11] Finally, *The Other America* was written with a clarity and urgency that attracted attention, including from President Kennedy.

In 1961, Kennedy had acted on a campaign pledge to resurrect a Depression-era Food Stamp Program offering surplus food to the poor; the following year, in part spurred by Harrington, he expanded the pilot program.

Overcoming: The Civil Rights Movement Crests

The most crucial manifestation of idealism in the early 1960s, however, came not from comfortable people, mostly white, yearning for change, but from oppressed ones, mostly black, who were actually turning thought into action.

The most decisive engine of change in the United States in the 1960s came from civil rights activists, who in the early years of the decade extended the gains secured by the Montgomery Bus Boycott of 1955–1956 and lunch-counter demonstrations of 1960. Perhaps the most dramatic of these campaigns were the Freedom Rides of 1961 and subsequent years, in which extraordinarily courageous college students rode racially integrated Greyhound and Trailways buses into segregated Southern communities, where they were met by angry mobs. Trained in non-violence, the students absorbed whatever blows these racists rained down upon them and were often sent to jail, supposedly for their own safety. The Freedom Rides generated intense media coverage—footage of bloodied students in places such as Anniston, Alabama, were highly dramatic— and prodded the Kennedy Justice Department to demand that state and local law enforcement do their jobs in protecting the rights of US citizens. In waging the moral equivalent of war, the Freedom Riders stand with the greatest heroes of American history. Among them were Diane Nash and Ruby Doris Smith (later Robinson), both of whom had been active in lunch-counter sit-ins, as was future Congressman John Lewis of Georgia.

Another front of the civil rights struggle was higher education. In 1953, two African American women, Polly Anne Myers and Autherine Lucy, sued the University of Alabama's graduate school for denying their admission on the basis of race. The university claimed that Myers, unmarried and pregnant, was actually denied for not meeting the prevailing moral code at the university. Lucy pressed her case, which was affirmed by the Supreme Court in *Lucy v. Adams* (1955), only to be expelled by the university because it said it could not guarantee her safety—mobs threw rocks and eggs at her. (She eventually earned a master's degree in elementary education from the university—in 1992.)[12] The Supreme Court ruled for Lucy narrowly, not asserting that the university was required to admit all qualified applicants. That quest was resumed in 1963, when two undergraduates, Vivian Malone and James Hood, walked past an array of state troopers flanking the avowed segregationist Alabama governor George Wallace—more on him shortly—to register for classes under the protection of federal marshals dispatched from the White House. A similar encounter in the previous year by undergraduate James Meredith at the University of Mississippi led to a riot before order was restored by federal troops. Meredith, who was part Choctaw Indian, graduated with a degree in political science.

(There is another chapter in the Meredith saga, to be discussed in more detail in Chapter 4. He ultimately became a Republican, running for office unsuccessfully a number of times before working as an adviser to conservative Republican senator Jesse Helms of North Carolina.)

Other civil rights activism was less spectacular in its execution but proved no less important in terms of advancing African American equality. Among the most important of these campaigns was the struggle to increase voter registration in deep-South states such as Mississippi, where generations of African Americans had been intimidated and/or actively barred from participating in the democratic process. This was work every bit as dangerous as Freedom Rides, but painstakingly slow. Perhaps the most important figure in this regard is Bob Moses, an SNCC organizer who spent much of the early 1960s involved in this work. In 1964, he helped lead Freedom Summer, a voting registration project in Mississippi, joined by others, among them Dorie Ladner, Fannie Lou Hamer, and three young white men—James Earl Chaney, Andrew Goodman, and Michael Schwerner—who would be murdered for their work on the project.

A variety of civil rights organizations were active, and sometimes competed, for leadership in the movement. Martin Luther King, Jr.'s Southern Christian Leadership Conference had become a major force in African American activism, jostling among (and sometimes vying with) more established organizations such as the NAACP and the Congress of Racial Equality (CORE), which had been founded during World War II and had organized Freedom Rides. So had SNCC, which had begun as a spinoff of SCLC but achieved a life of its own under the leadership of the extraordinarily gifted organizer Ella Baker. Also pivotal was SCLC's Septima Poinsette Clark, who ran Citizenship Schools that trained a generation of activists in the techniques of non-violence.

Civil rights campaigns weren't always successful. In 1962, King and his allies were stymied in Albany, Georgia, largely due to the opposition of the wily police chief Laurie Pritchett. Pritchett made mass arrests during segregation protests, but dispersed protesters to prevent jails from filling up, foiling a tactic that civil rights activists liked to use to force law-enforcement's hands.[13] There were also internal frictions; Baker and Clark often had to put up with the unselfconscious sexism of King and other African American male leaders. As Clark wryly remarked, "This country was built up by women keeping their mouths shut."[14] The day was coming when fewer women would.

Such frustrations notwithstanding, it was the victories that gained lasting attention. A series of events in 1963 in particular solidified King's reputation as the premier figure in the civil rights movement. The first of these took place in Birmingham, Alabama, that spring, where the SCLC had organized protests in one of the most deeply racist cities in the nation. The chief of police in Birmingham, Eugene "Bull" Connor, was a good deal less subtle in his methods than Pritchett, and indeed his brutality was one of the reasons why King targeted the city, where hundreds of protesters, King among them, were thrown in jail. While in prison, King produced one of the most important documents to come out of the civil rights movement, his "Letter from Birmingham City Jail."

The letter was addressed to eight white liberal clergymen who had published a letter of their own criticizing him for precipitating civil disturbances, calling on King and his followers to be patient and to pursue their grievances through the courts. King's response was that the time for patience was over. "I have almost reached the regrettable conclusion that the Negro's great stumbling block in the stride toward freedom is not the White Citizen's Councilor or Ku Klux Klanner, but the white moderate who is more devoted to 'order' than justice," he explained.[15]

In the short term, however, it was overt hatred that posed the more immediate problem. Bull Connor had thrown so many protesters in jail that the SCLC was running low on manpower. So organizers made the controversial decision to turn to children, 2,000 of whom where also thrown in jail. Connor also used attack dogs and high-pressure hoses to disperse crowds, and did so with glee. "I want to see the dogs work," he said. "I want to see the niggers run." But, as organizers had hoped, Connor and his allies overplayed their hand. Once again, media coverage of the protests angered, and—in the context of the Cold War and the surging tide of anti-colonialism in Africa and Asia—embarrassed a great many Americans. There was also pressure, as there often was during the civil rights movement, from business interests, which increasingly regarded integration as easier to manage than massive resistance.[16] And so white Birmingham capitulated: legal segregation of public facilities ended. This was a great victory for the movement in general and King in particular. It was also one that ratcheted up the intensity of expectations. "There go my people," he would say at the time, quoting Gandhi. "I must catch them, for I am their leader."[17] As events would show, this would be increasingly difficult for him to do.

For the moment, though, King and his allies pressed their advantage. They spent the months following Birmingham preparing for the March on Washington, a huge demonstration for jobs—this economic component of the movement is sometimes overlooked—that was held at the Lincoln Memorial on August 28, 1963. Two decades earlier, the African American labor leader A. Philip Randolph had planned a similar march, but was dissuaded by the Roosevelt administration, which made concessions, among them the creation of the Fair Employment Practices Commission in 1941 (it never amounted to much). Now Randolph was at it again, teaming up with Bayard Rustin, a gay man whose civil rights activism dated back to the 1940s and had been highly influential with SNCC. Randolph, Rustin, and others put together a robust collection of speakers and performers for what became the most memorable public demonstration in American history. This time it was President Kennedy who tried to dissuade organizers from proceeding, but they rejected these suggestions and pushed ahead, bringing about one of the highlights of the civil rights movement. The most memorable event of all was King's speech, "I Have a Dream," now widely recognized as among the most electrifying addresses in US history. "I still have a dream," King said, as he headed toward its rousing climax. "It is a dream deeply rooted in the American Dream, that one day this nation will rise up and live out the true meaning of its creed—we hold these truths to be self-evident, that all men are created equal." The address ended with a rousing repetition of the phrase "let freedom ring" in a series of geographic locations that stretched from "the prodigious hilltops of New Hampshire" to the "the curvaceous slopes of California."

Voices: Popular Culture of the Early 1960s

The deep musicality of "I Have a Dream"—and the deep musicality of King's unforgettable voice—points to an important cultural reality of the civil rights movement: the centrality of song. This was something that King understood; indeed, before giving the speech, he asked the legendary gospel singer Mahalia Jackson to sing the famous Negro spiritual "I've Bee 'Buked and I've Been Scorned."[18] Traditional spiritual-influenced songs such as "Keep Your Eyes on the Prize" and "We Shall Overcome" were staples of the African American protest movement. As such, this folk music stream was part of a broader one in American life that had attained an unusual degree of prominence in the nation's popular culture by the early 1960s. White as well as African American folk music had undergone a period of rediscovery during the Great Depression, when troubadours such as Woody Guthrie and Leadbelly had attracted large audiences, as did more mainstream singers such as Burl Ives. By definition, folk music has a democratic tilt: it's the music of ordinary people, passed anonymously down through generations, though, during the twentieth century, individual performers could become famous for their recordings of such songs. Many of these artists had left-wing political affiliations, which became problematic during the early years of the Cold War, when folk music went into relative eclipse, even if acts such as the Weavers persisted and remained popular straight through the late 1940s and early 1950s.[19]

However, by the dawn of the 1960s, folk music was more prominent than ever. Artists such as the Kingston Trio, Buffy Sainte-Marie, and Joan Baez found national followings, especially on college campuses, where folk was considered both more respectable and more authentic than rock and roll. Folk music was also an important inspiration for performers who not only played old songs, but also wrote new ones. Among the most important in this category was the young Bob Dylan, a Minnesota native who migrated to New York in 1961 and made a name for himself on the Greenwich Village folk music scene. Dylan's early albums, notably *The Freewheelin' Bob Dylan* (1963), are notable for their fusion of idealistic impatience, apparent in classic songs such as "Blowin' in the Wind." African American performers were also drawing on traditional music currents in now-classic songs such as Sam Cooke's gorgeous "A Change Is Gonna Come" (1964) and The Impressions' "People Get Ready," written by Curtis Mayfield (1965). One of the most protean voices of the era was that of James Brown, whose exacting musical standards and performing charisma made him one of the most influential musicians of the 1960s, particularly in the later half of the decade as he tapped, and then reinvented, the gospel traditions of his youth.

Part of the reason the music from the first half of the 1960s is remembered so affectionately by so many people, even by people who didn't live through the decade, is the sense it was perceived as *integrated*, in the broadest sense of the term—not simply African American and white, but also traditional and modern, local and national. Rock and roll was also international: in the early 1960s, a series of British acts—led by the Beatles and followed by the Rolling Stones, the Who, the Kinks, and other groups—fused local English styles with the blues and other African American genres they had absorbed as adolescents into a compelling new synthesis. In Detroit, musician and entrepreneur Berry Gordy tapped the talents of the local music scene and forged a compelling musical assembly line known as Motown Records. Gordy sought to package African American music for white audiences, apparent in the efforts he made to train, dress, and present acts such as the Supremes, and Martha and the Vandellas (whose 1964 hit "Dancing in the Streets" was something of a civil rights anthem). But, even at its most avowedly commercial, the music of such figures as Stevie Wonder and Smokey Robinson and the Miracles were notable for the way that they brought their (African) ancestry alive in new and compelling ways.

Other media were less able to ride these currents with the same energy and grace. Some of this is a matter of timing; it typically takes longer to write a book than a song, for example. And some of it is a matter of money: it's cheaper to record a song than it is to produce a movie, and as such there's less of a risk in terms of indifference or controversy. About the only civil rights novel of any consequence to make an impact in the 1960s was Harper Lee's *To Kill a Mockingbird* (1962), which was set in the 1930s but had clear racial implications in its plot line involving an African American man wrongly accused of rape. About the only African American actor to have any commercial profile in Hollywood at the time was Sidney Poitier, who appeared in the 1961 film version of Loraine Hansberry's 1959 play *A Raisin in the Sun*, about a struggling working-class family on the South Side of Chicago (see sidebar for Chapter 2). Poitier won an Academy Award for Best Actor for his work in *Lilies of the Field* (1963), about an African American man who finds himself reluctantly drawn into aiding a group of nuns on an Arizona commune.

Countercurrents: Civil Rights Skeptics

One reason why it wasn't necessarily easy to see, much less ride, the wave of impatient optimism that characterized so much of the culture of the early 1960s was that there were also important countercurrents at work—countercurrents that would prove increasingly powerful as the decade wore on. Not all these countercurrents were external. Even as the civil rights and other movements were making their most dramatic gains, some African Americans were reaching the conclusion that it was too little, too late.

Actually, there were reasons to do so even in the movement's moments of triumph. Birmingham had been the first time that an SCLC protest had been marked by African American protesters breaking with King's non-violent mandate.[20] This, of course, was understandable, given the ferocity of the attacks on them, and the hatred directed at African American activists generally, as indicated by the assassination a few weeks later of Medgar Evers, an NAACP organizer who had worked to desegregate the University of Mississippi and to register African American voters in the state. (It would be over 30 years before his killer was convicted of the crime.) About 2 weeks after the March on Washington in August 1963, a bomb exploded at a Baptist church in Birmingham, killing four young girls. If some Americans were feeling moved, or simply shamed, into recognizing the need for racial equality, others were digging in their heels.

But the challenges in achieving racial integration were also complicated by the fact that some African Americans were beginning to question whether integration, as it was widely understood, was really worth it in the first place. In the words of the great African American writer James Baldwin, author of the classic 1963 critique of race relations *The Fire Next Time*, "Do I really want to be integrated into a burning house?"[21] Actually, some had been wondering about this for some time, but were now achieving a new level of notoriety. Perhaps the most important of these figures was Malcolm X. Born Malcolm Little, in Omaha, Nebraska, in 1925, he had spent much of his adolescence and young adulthood involved in drugs and prostitution. He also had a colorful life-style—fully engaged in a swing jazz culture in the 1930s; wearing Zoot suits in the 1940s—and was secretly bisexual.[22] Sent to prison for robbery in 1946, he experienced a religious conversion to an African American nationalist form of the Muslim faith, the Nation of Islam (NOI), led by the Reverend Elijah Mohammed out of Detroit. Upon his release from prison in 1952, Little, now Malcolm X, rose rapidly through the ranks in the organization and was sent to run an important mosque in New York City's Harlem. By the late 1950s, he had developed a major personal following, even as he faithfully evangelized the teachings of Elijah Mohammed, a mix of conservative personal morality, ener-getic business enterprise, and a strong belief that the irredeemable depth of white racism required the political and social separation of the races—in his famously ominous words, "by any means necessary." This was optimism of a sort: members of the NOI believed the moment had arrived for African Americans to assert their own autonomy, and that the means to do so were actu-ally in reach. As such, they were as much a part of a culture of rising expectations *and* an alternative to the surging appeal of racial integration.

Malcolm X rose to national attention in 1957 when, following an incident of police brutality, he mobilized thousands of African Americans to march down 125th Street to a Harlem police precinct to protest the beatings of three NOI members and to demand the release of one in need of medical treatment. In the face of this show of strength, the police reluctantly did so. In the words of one officer, "No one man should have that much power."[23] (Perhaps he meant no *African American* man should have that much power.) In 1959, Malcolm was a charismatic subject of a famous five-part television documentary, *The Hate that Hate Produced*. In the years that that followed, he remained an important point of reference in the civil rights movement, the far end of a spectrum whose other side was represented by King and non-violence. Neither man had much regard for the tactics of the other.

It's important to emphasize, however, that the power of Malcolm X— or, as he also referred to himself, Malcolm Shabazz or Malik el-Shabazz— was mostly a matter of his ideas rather than his actions, which were alluring in the seeming directness with which he advocated an eye-for-an-eye approach to social justice. Some leaders of the civil rights movement were avowedly skeptical of Malcolm's skepticism, however. "What did he ever do?" asked Thurgood Marshall, who argued the *Brown v. Board* case before the Supreme Court. "Name one concrete thing he ever did."[24] (Marshall was no great fan of King, either, once describing him as "a boy on a man's errand.")[25] While Malcolm denounced events such as the "Farce on Washington" as excessively accommodationist, people such as Bayard Rustin replied by asking, "We know the disease, physician, but what is the cure? What is your program and how do you intend to put it into effect?" Not only were the answers unclear, but Malcolm also made some strange bedfellows, as in his disconcertingly civil relationship with George Lincoln Rockwell, the leader of the American Nazi Party, which shared the NOI's desire for racial separation.[26]

But part of Malcolm X's power was his capacity for growth; his ideas were never fixed and, over the course of the early 1960s, he steadily struck out an independent path. Increasingly alienated by the financial and sexual corruption of Elijah Mohammed, he broke with the NOI, which turned on him with ferocity in both its rhetoric and a string of death threats. In 1964, Malcolm embarked on a pilgrimage to Mecca, where exposure to more mainstream Islamic currents made him aware of its multiracial dimensions. He also strengthened his ties to African and other anti-colonial movements around the world, which was an increasingly important dimension of the civil rights movement generally. But while his views became more nuanced, Malcolm remained every inch the radical. This was apparent in his famous speech "The Ballot or the Bullet," delivered in the spring of 1964. "Historically, revolutions are bloody," he explained. "Oh, yes, they are. They haven't never had a blood-less revolution, or a non-violent revolution. That doesn't happen even in Hollywood. You don't have a revolution in which you love your enemy, and you don't have a revolution in which you are begging the system of exploitation to integrate you into it."[27] And yet, *The Autobiography of Malcolm X*, published in 1965, remains a quintessentially American tale of reinvention, one that brims with affection for the characters of his early life in places such as Boston and Harlem—his best friend, Shorty; a lost love, Laura; his early mentor, West Indian Archie— who emerge from these pages with the vivid clarity of the best fiction. The book was written with the help of Alex Haley (later to become famous for the multi-generational slavery saga *Roots*, published in 1976 and made into a television miniseries the following year), and adapted into an unforgettable 1992 film directed by Spike Lee. Malcolm's career was cut short by his assassination in

February 1965, but his martyrdom only enhanced his influence. Indeed, it seems safe to say that he became a far more important figure in death than he ever was in life.

Considered in the context of his moment, though, Malcolm X typified an intensification of a civil rights movement whose impact was rippling far beyond specific victories in Montgomery or Birmingham. And its momentum was building. In the third in a string of triumphs following Birmingham and the March on Washington, King was named the recipient of the Nobel Peace Prize in 1964, an honor that emphasized the global impact of his work and invited comparisons with freedom struggles in places such as South Africa, where the young Nelson Mandela and nine other members of the African National Congress were being prosecuted in the notorious Rivonia Trial of 1963–1964.

The growing pressure for racial equality was also felt by a cautious Kennedy administration, which risked irrelevance or worse if it continued to practice the politics of caution. Still, there was a long way to go. Despite advocating one, a civil rights bill made little headway on Kennedy's watch, reflecting the limits of his political muscle. They also reflected the entrenched power of white supremacy in institutions such as the United States Senate, where skepticism if not outright hostility continued to run strong.

But critiques of the civil rights movement were both more widespread and more articulate than those of garden-variety racists. In 1960, an organization calling itself Young Americans for Freedom—a kind of right-wing equivalent of SDS—issued its own manifesto, the Sharon Statement, affirming a vision of liberty rooted in limited government and free markets. (The name of the document refers to Sharon, Connecticut, site of the home of William F. Buckley, founder of the Conservative magazine *The National Review*, launched in 1954.) It was also in 1960 that a celebrated book, *The Conscience of a Conservative*, became the bible of a new movement. Its author, Arizona senator Barry Goldwater (it was actually ghostwritten by Buckley's brother-in-law L. Brent Bozell, Jr.), represented a new type of white critic of the civil rights movement, one who sidestepped the crude racism of the Ku Klux Klan or even their more respectable counterpart, White Citizens Councils. Rather, Goldwater—who, in fact, had credentials as a racial integrator of public institutions in Arizona—opposed what he considered pernicious Big Government mandates that he believed interfered with personal liberty and undermined genuine racial cooperation. His views would become increasingly important in a Republican Party trying to make inroads in the South, where it had been weak, if not non-existent, since the Civil War. And they would help Goldwater capture the GOP presidential nomination in 1964.

It was also in 1964 that another group of people—women activists within the civil rights movement—articulated their own concerns about the movement's direction. In their 1965 statement entitled "Sex and Caste: A Kind of Memo," SNCC members Mary King and Casey Hayden (wife of SDS founder Tom Hayden) asserted that "The woman in SNCC is often in the same position as that token Negro hired in a corporation. The management thinks that it has done its bit."[28] Noting that women were treated dismissively even as they did some of the most important work, King and Hayden called for further discussion of the status of women in the movement.

Lone Star Rising: The LBJ Moment

These alternating currents, as important at they were at the time—and as decisive as they would become—were nevertheless less obvious in the early 1960s than they would be later. Mainstream social reform experienced an unexpected jolt from one of the truly shocking events in American history: the assassination of President Kennedy in Dallas on November 22, 1963. The reasons for Kennedy's murder continue to be debated. He certainly had made any number of enemies, ranging from Fidel Castro (whom the CIA had repeatedly tried to kill) to organized crime figures who alternately seem to have backed the Kennedys and were investigated by a crusading Robert Kennedy before and during his time as attorney general. Consensus opinion remains centered around the idea that a lone gunman, Lee Harvey Oswald, acted on his own (though suspicions surround the fact that Oswald spent time in the Soviet Union). Oswald was shot by a Dallas nightclub owner before he could be fully interrogated, so his story died with him.

The most relevant question for our purposes, though, is why Kennedy had been in Dallas in the first place in November 1963: to strengthen his position amid a growing divide in the Democratic Party between its old segregationist wing, based in the South, and its more urban liberal wing, rooted in the North. These tensions date back to the very origins of the Democratic Party in the 1830s, and were difficult even for as gifted a politician as Franklin Delano Roosevelt to finesse in the 1930s. Kennedy had hoped to bolster his weak flank by going to Texas. Now, in the wake of his death, a new president would grapple with the growing sectional and ideological divergences in a society swept up in a wave of grand expectations.

Few men were better prepared for the job than Lyndon Johnson. Born in the hill country of East Texas in 1908, he came of age during the New Deal, for which he worked in the National Youth Administration, creating educational and job opportunities for young people. After serving six terms in the House of Representatives, he went on to two terms in the US Senate, where he became the youngest man ever to attain the position of Majority Leader. Johnson was a man of prodigious political gifts. These included a knack for getting people to mentor him (among them the powerful Speaker of the House Sam Rayburn of Texas and Senator Richard Russell of Georgia), an intuitive grasp of the motivations of others, and a tireless capacity to wheel and deal to get what he wanted—techniques that inspired fear, admiration, and awe for those subjected to what became known as "the Johnson Treatment." Johnson was also a man who would resort to almost any way to win (his ironic nickname "Landslide Lyndon" referred to the razor-thin margin through which he won his Senate seat, under dubious circumstances, in 1948). His credibility with the Southern wing of the Democratic Party allowed him to steer the Civil Rights Act of 1957 through Congress. This was a largely toothless piece of legislation, but the first civil rights law since Reconstruction, and one that signaled Johnson's arrival as a mainstream national figure. After initially hesitating, he pursued the 1960 Democratic nomination, which he lost to Kennedy. But JFK, recognizing his own political weakness and Johnson's strengths (in Texas in particular), brought him on board as the vice presidential nominee. Johnson languished in the job, held at arm's length by the administration's leading figures, notably Robert Kennedy, who held him in contempt as a tactless buffoon. A government investigation into financial improprieties by one of his closest aides was about to become public as Johnson accompanied Kennedy to Texas on that fence-mending trip. But that was all forgotten when Johnson was suddenly thrust into the presidency.

Awakened from a depressive torpor, Johnson—widely referred to as LBJ—took the reins with fierce energy and purpose. He recognized that, in the wake of Kennedy's death, a stunned and saddened country would be disposed toward some kind of legacy in his name, and that Congress, which was largely Democratic, would likely follow his lead. (Not that he ever left much to chance; in characteristically crude language, he told aides that "You got to learn to mount this Congress like you mount a woman.")[29] Johnson skillfully positioned the passage of a civil rights bill as an act of homage to the martyred Kennedy, and it became law on July 2, 1964. A landmark act, it made the segregation of all public facilities illegal, effectively destroying the foundation of Jim Crow.

But the Civil Rights Act was only one facet of an extraordinary set of initiatives that demonstrated Johnson's—and much of the country's—growing belief that the government really could solve age-old social problems. Johnson expressed this optimism with what seems in retrospect like typical confidence: "Hell, we're the richest country in the world, the most powerful. We can do it all." In his State of the Union address in January 1964, he announced a War on Poverty, a package of proposals designed to improve the lives of poor people. The law that was passed that August, known as the Economic Opportunity Act of 1964, created the Office of Economic Opportunity (OEO), headed by JFK's brother-in-law Sargent Shriver, who had run the Peace Corps during the Kennedy Administration. The centerpiece of the OEO was the Community Action Program (CAP), which offered and allocated money to local agencies and sought "maximum feasible participation" from the poor themselves in an effort to end poverty entirely. The new agency also launched a series of other initiatives, among them the creation of the Job Corps (an employment program for young people); Volunteers In Service to America, or VISTA (a domestic version of the Peace Corps); and the Neighborhood Youth Corps (an urban, non-residential version). The Great Society, Johnson explained, rested on a premise of "abundance and beauty for all, a society of success without squalor, beauty without barrenness, works of genius without the wretchedness of poverty." As one historian later explained, "The rhetoric was incredible. Still more incredible: it seemed reasonable."[30]

The War on Poverty and the Civil Rights Act were followed by a barrage of other programs designed to improve the everyday lives of Americans from all walks of life. Indeed, the very breadth of LBJ's vision was very much the point of it—he wanted to give something to everyone, and indeed knew that *unless* he did it would be difficult to help those most in need. The key phrase that LBJ introduced to capture his vision of American politics, "The Great Society," was first used at commencement addresses in Ohio and Michigan in the spring of 1964 and became forever associated with his administration.

Building on the momentum of his re-election in 1964 (a matter to be taken up in more detail momentarily), Johnson in 1965 rammed through Congress an almost bewildering array of new programs and bureaucracies that rivaled Franklin Roosevelt's New Deal in its heyday. Many remain standing despite subsequent attempts to dismantle them, among them the National Endowment of the Arts, the National Endowment of the Humanities, and Head Start. But two achievements in particular stand out. The first was the creation of Medicare, a health insurance program for the elderly that, along with Social Security, has probably improved the quality of life for more Americans than any entitlement in American history. The law that created Medicare also created Medicaid, which funds medical care for the poor, something of an afterthought at the time but which proved to be quite consequential, and costly, in its own right.[31] Johnson touted the program in a 1965 speech that captured the optimism and determination of the moment. "In this town, and a thousand other towns like it, there are men and women in pain who will now find ease," he said in Independence, Missouri, where he had gone to visit former president Harry Truman, who had unsuccessfully sought to pass a similar law in the late 1940s. "There are those, alone in suffering, who will now hear the sound of some approaching footsteps coming to help. There are those fearing the terrible darkness of despairing poverty—despite their long years of labor and expectation—who will now look up to see the light of hope and realization."[32] The rhetoric may have been inflated, but in the last half-century hundreds of millions of Americans have benefited from Medicaid and Medicare.

Johnson's other durable achievement was the Voting Rights Act of 1965. This law outlawed many of the techniques segregationists had used to prevent African Americans from voting, such as literacy tests and poll taxes. The Voting Rights Act proved to be extraordinarily effective. At the time of its passing, 90% of African American adults in the Deep South had not registered to vote, and there were only a few hundred African American elected officials. After 20 years, African Americans voted at the same level of whites—in some cases, at an even higher rate than whites—and there were nearly 6,000 African American elected officials.[33] Similar to much of the Great Society, it too remains on the books, though the Supreme Court weakened some of its key provisions in 2014.

In the 1960s, however, the nation's highest court was expanding civil rights, not curtailing them, and did so independently of Johnson—an important indication that his Great Society was as much a *reflection* of the times as it was a *cause* of social change. Still under the leadership of Earl Warren, who had pushed through the *Brown v. Board of Education* decision in 1954, the Supreme Court issued a series of rulings that fundamentally reshaped the rights of individuals on a broad front. Among them: *Baker v. Carr* (1962), which made it easier for states to redraw their voting districts and ensure fair elections; *Gideon v. Wainwright* (1963), which expanded the constitutional rights of alleged criminals; *New York Times v. Sullivan* (1964), which protected journalists against libel charges; and *Griswold v. Connecticut* (1965), which invoked the right to privacy in striking down a law that prohibited individuals from using contraceptive devices. The Supreme Court also made a series of rulings pertaining more specifically to the civil rights movement, including *Loving v. Virginia* (1967), which struck down laws preventing interracial marriages, and some rulings designed to speed up school desegregation. By the time Warren stepped down in 1969, there was a widespread sense that the Supreme Court had moved into greater alignment with contemporary American realities.

Of course, not everyone agreed with these decisions, and some were widely perceived as going too far. Among the most prominent in this regard was *Engel v. Vitale* (1962), in which the court ruled that the recitation of a voluntary non-denominational school prayer in a public school assembly setting violated the First Amendment's separation of church and state. Associate Justice Potter Stewart's solitary dissent spoke for many: "I cannot see how an 'official religion' is established by letting those who want to say a prayer say it."[34] By the decade's end, many Americans felt that the court had become excessively protective of criminal suspects in rulings such as *Miranda v. Arizona*, which introduced the phrase "You have the right to remain silent" into popular discourse. They also objected to the way the *Griswold* decision paved the way for *Roe v. Wade* (1973), which legalized abortion under certain circumstances.

In short, even at liberalism's very highest tide in 1964–1965, alternating currents were flowing powerfully below the surface, ready to pull them back. Nobody grasped this reality better than Lyndon Johnson. It was Johnson's acute understanding of the undertow pulling to his right—his certainty that he must act quickly—that helps explain his almost incredible success in passing so much Great Society legislation.

In reading a list of his legislative accomplishments, you might get the idea— as many people at the time did, as did certainly his skeptics—that Johnson was the very essence of the Big Government liberal. But the truth was always more complicated, not only because of his origins (LBJ had essentially come of age among Southerners whose hatred of Big Government was in no small measure a function of its racial implications), but also because an element of calculation always accompanied even his most genuine altruistic impulses. It's worth noting, for example, that Johnson's very first political move—months before the passing of any War on Poverty legislation—was a major tax cut. The bill he signed was mostly designed to help the rich and corporations, and it was accompanied by herculean efforts to get the annual budget spending under the important symbolic line of $100 billion. As with the civil rights bill, Johnson advocated these fiscal measures in terms of fulfilling Kennedy's wishes. But, as with that bill, it was Johnson's pragmatic vigor that was widely seen as the reason it actually got done.

In a similarly pragmatic fashion, the War on Poverty was never promoted in terms of welfare for the poor—indeed, the very word "welfare" had long since taken on toxic political overtones. Not by accident was the name of the bill and the agency that Johnson shepherded into law cast in terms of economic opportunity: the idea was to give the poor the resources to take responsibility for their own lives. Equality of *opportunity*, not equality of *condition*, continued to be the governing logic of American life, and LBJ was careful to cast his policies in such terms. That governing logic was never a matter of re-dividing the pie. Instead, it was premised on the pie getting larger: no one should have to be deprived of anything for anyone else to get more. This was the American Way.

Indeed, the Great Society got the degree of acceptance it did because there was a widespread perception that the United States could literally afford it. Never was the nation as broadly prosperous as it was in the 1960s. In the first half that decade, the average annual growth rate of the national economy was 5.3%. That's more than double that of most years since the economic crash of 2008. Over the course of the decade, the poverty rate declined from 22% in 1960 to 12% in 1970, in no small measure because of Great Society policies.[35]

Finally, and perhaps most importantly, Johnson had witnessed what happened to American liberals in the 1940s and 1950s—not simply that anyone advocating economic redistribution of any kind was smeared as communist, but also that anything less than the most vigorous resistance to the Soviet Union and Red China was regarded as unpatriotic. In short, Johnson had to protect his right flank. "Don't pay any attention to what the little shits on the campuses do," he said. "The great beast is the reactionary elements in this country."[36]

Flanking Maneuver: Johnson in Vietnam

Fatefully, Johnson decided that the best way to protect his right flank was in the realm of foreign policy. The place where he decided to stake his ground was Vietnam. This was, he knew, a risky position. But he felt it a necessary one.

Johnson had been dealt a weak hand. For years, the United States had been trying to prop up the weak, corrupt regime of Ngo Dinh Diem, which was having trouble maintaining its legitimacy in South Vietnam, even without the opposition of the communist North Vietnamese. When Diem was assassinated by his own officers in November 1963, President Kennedy faced an important fork in the road: double down in backing South Vietnam or seek some kind of negotiated settlement with the communists. He died before reaching a decision. Johnson felt he had little choice but to stand firm.

But he was not content to leave it at that. Johnson's opponent in the presidential election of 1964—which he wanted, badly, to win by a decisive margin and establish his legitimacy beyond that of Kennedy's successor—was Barry Goldwater. Goldwater was well known as a staunch anti-communist. In one of his more memorable statements of unbending political principle (and there were many), Goldwater asserted in his acceptance speech at the Republican National Convention in July 1964 that "extremism in the pursuit of liberty is no vice." Goldwater's partisans were apt to say, "In your heart, you know he's right." His critics would reply, "In your guts, you know he's nuts." Democrats seized on the perception that Goldwater was dangerously confrontational in his willingness to resort to nuclear war. They exploited this perception in a notorious campaign television commercial known as the "Daisy Ad," in which a young child plucks a flower while an ominous voiceover ticks down to a missile launch. Amid images of a mushroom cloud, viewers hear Johnson's voice: "These are the stakes! To make a world in which all of God's children can live, or to go into the dark. We must either love each other, or we must die."

Yet, even as Johnson was painting Goldwater as an extremist, he was orchestrating a military escalation in Vietnam that would demonstrate his own toughness. On August 2, 1964, a US Navy destroyer, the USS *Maddox*, engaged a series of North Vietnamese vessels in the Gulf of Tonkin, off the coast of North Vietnam. It was believed that North Vietnamese vessels attacked again 2 days later, but this has never been documented (radar data was murky). Johnson was less interested in clarifying what happened—"For all I know, our Navy was shooting at whales out there," he later told his aide Bill Moyers[37]—than demonstrating his resolve, and so he went to Congress and asked for authorization to respond to the alleged attacks without an actual declaration of war. The Gulf of Tonkin Resolution, as it was known, sailed through the House of Representatives unanimously, and by an 88–2 margin in the Senate. The two senators who voted against the resolution, Wayne Morse of Oregon and Ernest Gruening of Alaska, protested that it violated the Constitution in not having Congress declare war. Johnson sought to follow the precedent of President Truman in Korea, who had acted without congressional approval to conduct a "police action," a precedent that would be cited by later presidents. The United States has not actually fought a Constitutionally legitimate war since World War II.

Because Goldwater had staked out a position so far on the right, Johnson was able to present the Gulf of Tonkin Resolution as a responsible position in the center, effectively inoculating himself against attacks that he was soft on communism. The humming US economy and his evident success in achieving his legislative objectives gave him a commanding position in the presidential election of 1964, which he won by a truly commanding margin, 61% to 38% in the popular vote and a crushing 486-52 in the Electoral College. Goldwater took only the five Deep South states—a tremor of changes to come—and his native Arizona. Democrats also made strong gains in the House and Senate, where they enjoyed a veto-proof margin of 68-32. Republican defeat was so overwhelming that some observers believed the party had been condemned to oblivion. But reports of its death would prove greatly exaggerated.

Johnson continued his dual political strategy into 1965. On the one hand, he pressed his credentials as an anti-communist by sharply escalating the United

States' presence in Vietnam, which reached 184,000 troops by the end of that year.[38] He also extended the larger strategy of containment to two other nations. In 1965, 14,000 US Marines landed in the Dominican Republic to prevent the left-leaning, democratically elected Juan Bosch from ousting the military coup that had disposed him from power.[39] (The United States had invaded the country in 1903, and occupied it from 1916 to 1924 to prevent financial and political instability.) It was also in 1965 that the CIA indirectly participated in a shadowy mass murder of communists in Indonesia, where it had conducted operations in the late 1950s. Johnson's militarism was checked by a desire not to allow foreign policy to distract him from his domestic objectives, and more importantly by never going so far as to provoke direct retaliation from the Chinese or the Soviets, who conducted their own foreign policy on a similarly indirect basis that typically involved funding and arming junior partners. In the 1960s, China and the USSR were increasingly competing with each other for influence, including in North Vietnam, and their growing hostility, which would culminate in a brief secret war in 1969, was an important, if not widely recognized, facet of the geopolitical landscape in the second half of the twentieth century. That hostility gave Johnson, as well as his successor, Richard Nixon, considerable room to maneuver in foreign polity.

Fissures: Democratic Fault Lines

Johnson continued pressing his advantage in domestic policy as the Vietnam War escalated, introducing the second wave of Great Society legislation that would culminate in the Voting Rights Act in 1965. Yet, even as he capitalized on the weakness of the opponents on his right, Johnson knew that his support for the civil rights movement would have long-term implications for refashioning a Democratic Party that had long been segregationist. One of the most famous remarks of his presidency reputedly occurred when he signed the Voting Rights Act. "We just delivered the South to the Republican Party for a long time to come," a melancholy LBJ said, according to his aide Moyers.[40] It was one of the most prescient lines ever uttered by an American politician.

The wing of the Democratic Party that Johnson was leaving behind was not going down without a fight. Indeed, in some important respects, the most serious challenger that Johnson faced in 1964 was not Barry Goldwater. It was his fellow Democrat, George Wallace. No understanding of the 1960s can really be complete without an understanding of who Wallace was, what he represented, and why what was happening on the American right in the 1960s was at least as important was what was happening on the left.

Wallace, a native of Alabama, began his career in the state legislature, where he was considered a moderately liberal Democrat. The core of his political identity was populist: a former bantamweight boxer, Wallace considered himself a fighter for the common people. In 1958, he made his first bid for governor with the support of the local NAACP. But his Democratic primary opponent,

Attorney General John Patterson, was backed by the Ku Klux Klan, and defeated him handily. Wallace knew why. "John Patterson out-niggered me," he was said to have explained. "And boys, I'm not going to be out-niggered again." Wallace was true to his word. Elected to the governorship in 1962, he issued his famous "segregation now, segregation tomorrow, segregation forever" motto. Unlike most politicians of his kind, however, Wallace nursed national political aspirations, and announced his intention to run for president months before Kennedy's assassination. He disavowed racism as the core of his identity. Wallace routinely responded to reporters' query to this effect by pointing out the hypocrisy of the white liberal establishment—a term usually increasingly used by the left but one he invoked no less effectively. Why, he wondered, did liberal Congressmen send their children to private schools even as they insisted on what working-class whites would have to do? (Middle-class and wealthy whites were voting with their feet; there had been 17 non-Catholic private schools in neighboring Mississippi in the 1963–1964 school year; by 1970, that number had jumped to 155, all of whom got a tax break in the process of white flight from public schools.)[41] "We're not talking about race," he asserted. "We're talking about local democratic institutions."[42]

Whatever he was talking about, Wallace struck a nerve. Johnson himself described Wallace as "a runty little bastard, and just about the most dangerous person around." Despite being small in the way of money or organization, he generated huge crowds, capturing 34% of the vote in the Wisconsin Democratic primary, 30% in Indiana, and a whopping 43% in Maryland—none of these the Heart of Dixie. Though his appeal faded by the summer of 1964, Wallace had clearly identified a rising political force in the land. And he would remain a force to be reckoned with for the rest of the decade and beyond. His most eminent biographer called him "the most influential loser in twentieth-century American politics."[43]

For the moment, however, mainstream liberalism was able to sideline, if not soundly defeat, most of its conservative challenges by the middle of the 1960s. Yet, even as it did so, challenges from another direction—by no means invisible, but not as obviously threatening—were gathering steam. The rising expectations of the left were not simply giving way to impatience, but also actions that directly challenged some of the basic assumptions, and power, of people who saw themselves as the good guys. (Most of them were indeed guys, which was part of the problem.)

This revolt of the left was the direct result of the tactics and assumptions inherent in mainstream liberalism itself. Take the War on Poverty. The Community Action Programs sponsored by the OEO explicitly pledged a commitment to "maximum feasible participation." Community organizers such as the radical leftist Saul Alinsky understood this to mean collective action that wrested control over financial and decision-making resources from established authorities such as mayors. Those mayors, by contrast, believed *they* should have control over federal projects as elected representatives of their communities, and when it became clear that this wasn't necessarily the case, they became increasingly suspicious, if not hostile, toward such enterprises that threatened their power. Hence, the divisions were sowed within the left that would grow increasingly bitter.[44]

Even avowedly moderate liberal organizations were increasingly radicalized by the mid-1960s. In 1963, Students for a Democratic Society launched an Economics Research and Action Project (ERAP), with the help of a $5,000 grant from the United Auto Workers. The plan was to do SNCC-like community organizing in a series of cities around the country. But the poor people encountered by SDS students were less interested in complex critiques of capitalist society than in getting their trash collected. Disillusioned students who remained in the movement concluded that the problem was that liberal reforms such as the War on Poverty were preventing more systemic critiques of social reform.[45]

A more satisfying experience of student protest took shape in the fall of 1964 at the University of California at Berkeley, the crown jewel in the thriving state system of higher education. When a CORE worker was arrested for setting up a table at a campus location where such activity was prohibited, a student group led by student Mario Savio formed the Free Speech Movement (FSM). Thousands of students gathered to protest the policy restricting personal expression. In the face of such resistance, university officials backed off, and the victory became emblematic of what was rapidly becoming known as "the Counterculture" in its intensifying conflict with what was becoming known as "the Establishment." In the years that followed, the FSM fueled much of the language and logic of protest in the 1960s, including early opposition to the war in Vietnam. The FSM was also an early locus of a crystallizing conservative counterrevolution. "I'd like to harness their youthful energy with a strap," was the assessment of Ronald Reagan, an emerging Republican star running for governor of California, of the FSM.[46]

The FSM spawned a phrase that became popular in the 1960s: "do not fold, spindle, or mutilate," which referred to a statement printed on computer cards that were once commonplace for everyday bureaucratic purposes (such as registering for classes). By the 1960s, computers were becoming increasingly common in major corporations and government offices as well as universities. Though smaller "minicomputers" were becoming more common in some settings, they were still very large, very expensive machines isolated in corporate and government buildings where their power, while real, was also invisible to most people. As such, there was a growing skepticism of technology on the left, which would intensify over the course of the 1960s.

But in the first half of the decade, the locus of challenges to the established order remained the civil rights movement, whose energy was intensifying even as strains were emerging within it. Some of this remained a matter of inter-organizational rivalry; the NAACP, for example, was never entirely happy with the SCLC, which competed with it for attention and donors. Some, too, was a matter of increasingly visible alternatives, such as the stance of the Malcolm X, which was deeply influential in SNCC. But much of the growing tension was a matter of tactics, and how far the movement needed to go in order to change the status quo.

The dramatic possibilities of challenging that status quo in the segregated South came vividly into view at the very center of the nation's political establishment: the Democratic National Convention of 1964, which was held that August in Atlantic City, New Jersey. Lyndon Johnson's re-nomination for president was a foregone conclusion. But in the case of Mississippi, there was some question about *who* would be doing that re-nominating. In the months preceding the conventions, organizers of Freedom Summer had been toiling intensively, as they had in previous years, to work with poor African American children, register African American voters, and in other kinds of political work. The Council of Federated Organizations (COFO), an association linking a series of civil rights groups, went one step further and organized a slate of delegates to represent the Mississippi contingent at the convention. These delegates, representatives calling themselves the Mississippi Freedom Democratic Party (MFDP), challenged the legitimacy of the party regulars, who had denounced the Civil Rights Act. Many of these establishment Democrats were actually expected to support Goldwater, not LBJ, in the general election.

Johnson saw trouble, and acted swiftly to forestall it—the last thing he wanted was a disruption from business as usual. He planted FBI informants to get intelligence on MFDP representatives. When the party regulars threatened to bolt the convention if the MFDP was recognized, taking other state delegations with them, he sent his vice presidential nominee, Hubert Humphrey—a well-established supporter of civil rights—to bargain with the MFDP, offering them two voting seats and allowing the rest of its members to participate on an honorary basis. This wasn't good enough for one of the delegates, Fannie Lou Hamer, the twentieth child of a Mississippi-based African American sharecropper couple, who was driven off her land when she registered to vote in 1962. She was later beaten when she tried to convince other African Americans to register. In a riveting testimony before the party's credentials committee, she said, "We want to register, to become first-class citizens, and if the Freedom Democratic Party is not seated now, I question America." When Johnson heard the stark testimony of "that illiterate woman," he quickly called a press conference in the hope the television networks would cover him rather than Hamer. But the networks covered both. The regular delegation was seated and the MFDP, rejecting the compromise, left the convention. Johnson cruised to re-election; electorally speaking, the whole controversy was merely a blip. But Hamer's angry assertion, "I question America," would linger and intensify.[47]

This became apparent the following year in what, in many ways, was the climatic showdown of the civil rights movement in Selma, Alabama. In January 1965, King, Diane Nash, and her husband James Bevel of the SCLC, along with SNCC leaders John Lewis and James Forman, among others, had targeted Selma as one of the most intractably racist of Southern cities—with a population of 29,000, of whom 15,000 were African American, there were only 244 African Americans registered to vote.[48] Selma was also the home of the Bull Connor-like sheriff Jim Clark, who was likely to overreact to African American protest. In January and February of 1965, Clark jailed thousands of protesters. His state troopers beat people, attacked them with electric cattle prods, and when one protester tried to intervene, he was shot and killed. In response to these outrages, King and his allies organized a march from Selma to the Alabama state capital of Montgomery, 56 miles away, where they planned to petition a hostile Governor Wallace to protect African Americans who wished to register. Upon approaching the Edmund Pettus Bridge, the protesters were met by Clark and his men, mounted on horseback. They attacked, wielding clubs (Lewis ended up with a fractured skull). The event was known as "Bloody Sunday."

The maneuvers that followed were politically complex. As hoped, Clark's violence generated widespread disgust when it was broadcast on national television. White supporters descended on Selma, and calls increased for Congress to do something about voting rights. While public officials called for a cooling-off period, protesters (including a swarm of white clergy who descended on Selma) planned to resume their march in the face of a court order to wait. This put King in the difficult position between angering his allies—disenchantment with King among the rank and file of SNCC had been growing for some time—and a supportive president who wanted him to go slow. King tried to finesse this tension by formulating a secret plan with federal mediators whereby he would lead a march to the Edmund Pettus Bridge but turn around so as not to defy the government or have the marchers get attacked again. Governor Wallace tricked King by unexpectedly having the police stand aside at the bridge, making his decision not to cross it seem all the more puzzling to those who had never been told of his plan. Tragedy also struck after the second march when James Reeb, a white minister, was clubbed in the head by white supremacists, leading to his death, becoming one of 10 casualties in the campaign, which included Jimmie Lee Jackson, who was killed in the early stages of the campaign, and Viola Liuzzo, a white woman from Detroit who was killed by the Ku Klux Klan for her role in transporting demonstrators to and from Selma.[49]

Still, Selma was a win for the movement. After that second attempt to cross the bridge, President Johnson gave a speech on March 15, pressing for the Voting Rights Act, invoking the famous phrase "We Shall Overcome." (King was moved to tears in hearing a white politician use these words.) The following week, the federal government allowed the full march to proceed, and this third try was experienced as a victory lap, with demonstrators flanked by Washington officials and the Alabama National Guard, which Johnson ordered to protect the marchers. When Wallace warned he could not guarantee the safety of the protesters, LBJ summoned him for a full dose of the Johnson Treatment. "If I hadn't left when I did," Wallace mused afterward, "he'd have had me coming out *for* civil rights."[50] On August 6, LBJ signed the Voting Rights Act. Johnson had been hoping so get a voting rights law before Selma, but the movement helped build the support in Congress necessary to get it passed. It was, in many ways, the high-water mark of the Johnson presidency, the civil rights movement, and the 1960s generally.

Five days later, a Los Angeles highway patrolman arrested a young African American man for speeding in the African American Los Angeles neighborhood of Watts. When another officer arrived and clubbed an innocent African American observer, a gigantic riot ensued, one that lasted for 6 days and resulted in the deaths of 34 people and millions of dollars in damage. A despondent King flew to Los Angeles, seeking to persuade African American citizens to stop looting, only to be heckled by young African American men. "We won," one told him. When King asked how this could be true, the man replied, "Because we made the world pay attention to us."[51]

Watts was not the first site of urban rioting in the 1960s. There had been earlier outbreaks in Harlem, Jersey City, and Milwaukee in 1964, for example. But Watts was a crossroads. Surprisingly, it was a relatively comfortable neighborhood, with tree-lined streets and middle-class houses that were considered by some observers as among the best for African Americans in the United States. If riots could happen there, they could happen anywhere. And they did, in dozens of cities, every summer for the rest of the 1960s.

It would be too simple to say that the 1960s split in half. As we've already seen, a series of alternating currents were at work in the first half of the decade, hope and anger colliding at any given moment. And that would continue to be true. But for many of the people who lived through it, and for many of the people who have remembered it, there really was a distinct difference in the balance of mood between the first half and the second half of the decade. The American empire reached its zenith at some point in the mid-1960s. Life would remain good for a great many people, and greatly improve for a great many others in the years and decades that followed. But never again would the nation be quite as powerful and confident in its purpose as it was in the early and mid-1960s.

CULTURE WATCH: "The Times They Are A-Changin'" (1964)

Political protest doesn't really figure all that prominently in the history of pop music. To be sure, there's often an implicit message in what's being said—as well as who's saying it—and there are occasionally songs such as Marvin Gaye's "What's Going On" (1971) and Bruce Springsteen's "Born in the USA" (1984) that explicitly engage social issues (even if audiences overlook or misunderstand their point). But chart-topping performers who have a reputation as political artists are relatively rare.

In this regard as in others, Bob Dylan is exceptional. Though his career has spanned over half a century, he is widely considered the quintessential voice of the 1960s. And though much of his work in fact has little to say about political issues, the songs in his canon that do say anything political loom large in shaping his reputation. No song in this regard has been more

Figure 3.2   CHANGIN' MAN: Bob Dylan, 1965. The voice of the Baby Boom generation, Dylan engaged contemporary liberal politics with a timeless sensibility. That remained true even after he moved from folk music into rock and roll. © Everett Collection Historical / Alamy.

important than "The Times They Are A-Changin'," which captured a rare moment of hope and purpose in American history while resonating across time as a source of inspiration for future generations.

By the time Dylan released the song, and the album of the same name, in 1964, he had already established a reputation among those in the know as a singularly gifted songwriter of the era. His early songs, showcased in his albums *Bob Dylan* (1962) and *The Freewheelin' Bob Dylan* (1963), drew on English, Scottish, and American folk traditions, often writing fresh lyrics to accompany old melodies. The latter album in particular showed an emerging political consciousness, evident in songs such as "Blowin' in the Wind" and "A Hard Rain's Gonna Fall," both of which have a prophetic air that warn of a reckoning if problems go unaddressed.

"The Times They Are A-Changin'," by contrast, has more of a rousing spirit, suggested by the almost biblical cadence of its title. Though marked by some of the same righteous anger as earlier Dylan songs, it asserts a wave of social reform that is both welcome and inevitable: "Your old road is rapidly agin,'" the narrator tells the older generation. "Please get out of the new one if you can't lend your hand."

Though the phrase had not yet come into vogue, Dylan is here describing what would become known as "the generation gap": a perception that young people were able and willing to realize positive social change in a way their elders were not. Such a belief was one of the defining characteristics of the Baby Boom generation that came of age in the 1960s.

"The Times They Are A-Changin'" arrived at a particularly propitious moment in the decade. The album of the same name was released just as the successful struggle to pass the Civil Rights Act climaxed in 1964, which was also the year that the War on Poverty got underway. President Lyndon Johnson would win re-election by one of the most decisive margins in US history, suggesting the triumph of postwar American liberalism. Insofar as there was a debate in mainstream American politics, it seemed to be a matter of just how far left the country should go.

Subsequent events would suggest that the reform spirit that Dylan's song seemed to capture was more fragile than it seemed. The times may indeed have been changin', but within a few years it seemed they were changin' back, as a resurgent American right would stem and reverse the flow of historical change. Dylan himself pursued a more deeply personal— and at times highly cryptic—personal vision. But "The Times They Are A-Changin'" nevertheless stands as a beacon of idealism in American history. And that's unlikely to change.

Suggested Further Reading

The politics of the Nixon–Khrushchev meeting of 1959 can be explored in *The Kitchen Debate and Cold War Consumer Politics: A Brief History with Documents*, edited by Sarah T. Phillips (New York: Bedford, 2014). Richard Nixon's career has been dissected in great detail; two of the more important treatments are Garry Wills, *Nixon Agonistes: The Crisis of the Self-Made Man* (1970; Boston: Houghton Mifflin, 2002) and Rick Perlstein, *Nixonland: The Rise of a President and the Fracturing of America* (New York: Simon & Schuster, 2008). Among the most highly regarded treatments of John F. Kennedy's life and presidency is Robert Dallek's *An Unfinished Life: John F. Kennedy, 1917–1963* (Boston: Little, Brown, 2003). For a short overview, see Alan Brinkley, *John F. Kennedy* (New York: Times Books, 2012), part of the American Presidents Series under the editorship of the late Arthur Schlesinger, Jr., a former aide to JFK.

On the early idealism of the 1960s, see James Miller: *Democracy Is in the Streets: From Port Huron to the Siege of Chicago* (1987; Cambridge, MA: Harvard University Press, 1994). Todd Gitlin provides an insider's perspective in *The Sixties: Years of Hope, Days of Rage* (1987; New York: Bantam, 1993). Morris Dickstein offers a cultural perspective that bridges the 1950s and 1960s in *Gates of Eden: American Culture in the Sixties* (1977; Cambridge, MA: Harvard University Press, 1997).

The preeminent historian of the civil rights movement is Taylor Branch, in the form of *America in the King Years,* his three-volume biography of Martin Luther King, Jr.: *Parting the Waters* (1988), *Pillar of Fire* (2001), and *At Canaan's Edge* (2007), all published by Simon & Schuster. See also *Bearing the Cross: Martin Luther King and the Southern Christian Leadership Council* (1987; New York: Morrow, 2004) and *A Testament of Hope: Essential Writings and Speeches of Martin Luther King, Jr.*, edited by James M. Washington (San Francisco: Harper San Francisco, 1986).

As for Lyndon Johnson, one biographer towers above all others: Robert Caro. See *The Years of Lyndon Johnson,* his (as of this writing) four-volume biography: *The Path to Power* (1982); *Means of Ascent* (1990), *Master of the Senate* (2002), and *The Passage of Power* (2012), all published by Random House. For a good one-volume treatment, see Robert Dallek, *Lyndon Johnson: Portrait of a President* (New York: Oxford University Press, 2007). The most highly regarded history of the Vietnam War is Stanley Karnow, *Vietnam: A History* (New York: Penguin, 1983).

The best modern book on the roots of the new right is Rick Perlstein's *Before the Storm: Barry Goldwater and the Unmaking of American Consensus* (2001; New York: Perseus, 2009). The political trajectory of the Kennedy–Johnson political program—its rise and fall—is dissected with great skill in Allen J. Matusow, *The Unraveling of America: A History of Liberalism in the 1960s* (New York: Harper & Row, 1984).

Notes

1   The official US government transcript of the exchange can be found at http://www.foia.cia.gov/sites/default/files/document_conversions/16/1959-07-24.pdf (April 1 2014).
2   Videos of the two men's exchanges in the television studio are available on YouTube.
3   William Safire, "The Cold War's Hot Kitchen," *The New York Times,* July 24, 2009: http://www.nytimes.com/2009/07/24/opinion/24safire.html?pagewanted=all&_r=0 (April 1, 2014). Safire was writing on the fiftieth anniversary of the Kitchen debate. For coverage on July 25, 1959, see Harrison Salisbury, "Nixon and Khrushchev Argue in Public as US Exhibit Opens; Accuse Each Other of Threats": http://www.nytimes.com/learning/general/onthisday/big/0724.html#article (July 19, 2015).
4   Eisenhower never seemed to like Nixon. Ike really did hope to get rid of him at the time of the Checkers speech, and when asked in 1960 if there was any important decision in which Nixon had played a part during Eisenhower's presidency, Ike replied, "If you give me a week, I might think of one." But the men would be durably linked in any case: Nixon's daughter married Eisenhower's son in 1968. Nixon's "Checkers" speech can be seen on You Tube: https://www.youtube.com/watch?v=0t4SPyeDstk (April 27, 2014).
5   For a good brief analysis weighing the likelihood of fraud in the 1960 presidential race, see David Greenberg, "Was Nixon Robbed? The Legend of the Stolen 1960 Election," *Slate,* October 16, 2000: http://www.slate.com/articles/news_and_politics/history_lesson/2000/10/was_nixon_robbed.html (April 8, 2014).
6   Branch, *Bearing the Cross,* 565–569, 906–914.
7   The Peace Corps was actually Senator (later vice president) Hubert Humphrey's idea; the Special Forces preceded JFK, but he made green berets the badge of their identity.

8   Joshua B. Freeman, *American Empire: The Rise of a Global Power/The Democratic Revolution at Home, 1945–2000* (New York: Penguin, 2012), 191.

9   John Morton Blum, *Years of Discord: American Politics and Society, 1961–1974* (New York: Norton, 1991), 96–97.

10   Freeman, 188; Perlstein, *Before the Storm*, 410.

11   Michael Harrington, *The Other America: Poverty in the United States* (1962; New York: Scribner, 1997), 16.

12   https://lcrm.lib.unc.edu/blog/index.php/2012/10/10/lucy-v-adams-and-the-initial-integration-of-the-university-of-alabama/;http://www.al.com/unseen/stories/index.ssf?cutlines4.html (April 13, 2014).

13   Branch, 536; See Garrow's chapter on the subject (173–230).

14   Katherine Mellen Charron, *Freedom's Teacher: The Life of Septima Clark* (Chapel Hill: The University of North Carolina Press, 2009), 10.

15   King, *Testament of Hope*, 295.

16   James Patterson, *Grand Expectations: The United States, 1945–1974* (New York: Oxford University Press, 1997), 478–479; Freeman, 183.

17   Quoted in Blum, 108.

18   Jonathan Reider, "Songs of the Slaves: The Music of MLK's 'I Have a Dream'," *The New Yorker*, August 23, 2013: http://www.newyorker.com/online/blogs/books/2013/08/songs-of-the-slaves-reflections-on-mlks-i-have-a-dream.html (April 15, 2014).

19   Ronald D. Cohen, *Rainbow Quest: The Folk Music Revival and American Society, 1940–1970* (Amherst: University of Massachusetts Press, 2003).

20   Patterson, 480.

21   James Baldwin, *The Fire Next Time* (1963; New York: Vintage, 1993), 94.

22   Manning Marable, *Malcolm X: A Life of Reinvention* (New York: Viking, 2011), 66.

23   Marable, 127–129.

24   Patterson, 552.

25   Branch, *At Canaan's Edge*, 473.

26   Marable, 201–203.

27   http://xroads.virginia.edu/~public/civilrights/a0146.html (April 16, 2014).

28   SNCC Position Paper, November 1964, *in The United States Since 1945: A Documentary History*, edited by Robert P. Ingalls and David K. Johnson (Malden, MA: Blackwell, 2009), 79.

29   Patterson, 532.

30   The assessment is Perlstein's in *Nixonland*. He, and Johnson, are quoted on p. 5.

31   Matusow, 226–227.

32   Cesar Chavez and *la Causa*, "The Plan of Delano," in Ingalls & Johnson, 120.

33   Blum, 186.

34   Blum, 198–199.

35   Blum, 144; http://www.tradingeconomics.com/united-states/gdp-growth-annual (accessed April 20, 2014); James Patterson, *America's Struggle Against Poverty* (1980; Cambridge, MA: Harvard University Press, 2000), 157–162.

36   Branch, *At Canaan's Edge*, 269–270.

37   http://www.pbs.org/now/politics/foia06.html (April 20, 2014). "Hell, those dumb, stupid sailors were just shooting at flying fish," he is also reported to have said (quoted in Perlstein, *Nixonland*, 170.

38   Freeman, 227.

39   Patterson, 611.

40 http://presidentialrecordings.rotunda.upress.virginia.edu/essays?series=CivilRights #fnref3 (April 20, 2014).

41 Rick Perlstein, *The Invisible Bridge*, 733.

42 Michael Kazin, *The Populist Persuasion: An American History* (New York: Basic, 1995), 233.

43 Dan T. Carter, *The Politics of Rage: George Wallace, the Origins of the New Conservatism, and the Transformation of American Politics* (1995; Baton Rouge: Louisiana State University Press, 2000), 474.

44 Matusow, 243–254.

45 Matusow, 314–316.

46 Perlstein, *The Invisible Bridge*, 83. Perlstein cites his own *Nixonland* as the source (113).

47 Patterson, 553–556.

48 Patterson, 579.

49 For a list of the casualties, see Branch, *At Canaan's Edge*, 192. Branch gives full 200 pages in that volume alone to Selma; it's also covered at the end of *Pillar of Fire*.

50 Patterson, 583.

51 Blum, 255.

4

Fulfillment and Frustration
An Empire in Conflict, 1965–1974

Figure 4.1 ONE GIANT LEAP: Astronaut Edwin "Buzz" Aldrin standing on the moon after planting the American flag, July 20, 1969. The US effort to achieve a lunar landing, executed over the course of the 1960s, represented one of the nation's greatest collective accomplishments. © Chronicle / Alamy.

Democratic Empire: The United States Since 1945, First Edition. Jim Cullen.
© 2017 Jim Cullen. Published 2017 by John Wiley & Sons, Inc.

Over the Moon: Winning the Space Race

ON MAY 6, 1961, President John F. Kennedy hosted a state dinner in honor of Habib Bourguiba, the president of Tunisia. Noticing that the Tunisian leader was speaking to the administration's science adviser, Jerome Wiesner, Kennedy approached the two and said, "You know, we're having a terrible argument in the White House over whether we should send a man to the moon. Jerry here is against it. If I told you you'd get an extra billion dollars a year in foreign aid if I didn't do it, what would be your advice?"

"I wish I could tell you to put it in foreign aid," President Bourguiba answered. "But I cannot."[1]

Kennedy had been never been a fan of the US space program. As a senator, he regarded it as a waste of money. And as president, he at one point favored scrapping the National Aeronautics and Space Administration (NASA) altogether. Kennedy had chosen Wiesner as a science advisor in part because Wiesner believed any space exploration that did take place could be done (relatively inexpensively) with unmanned aircraft. One factor checking Kennedy's instincts were those of Vice President Lyndon Johnson, a strong champion of NASA, in no small measure because it was based in his home state of Texas. Another was the tremendous sense of national prestige associated with space technology; the Soviet Union's launch of the Sputnik satellite in 1957 provoked a good deal of envy, anxiety, and soul-searching in the United States, particularly when the nation's first attempt to launch a satellite into space in December 1957 failed. These feelings were intensified still further in April 1961, when Soviet cosmonaut Yuri Gargarin became the first person to be launched into outer space. In the aftermath of Gargarin's flight, Johnson wrote to the president, noting, "This country should be realistic and recognize that other nations, regardless of their appreciation of our idealistic values, will tend to align themselves with the country which they believe will be the world leader—the winner in the long run." The success of US astronaut Alan Shepard in becoming the first American to make a sub-orbital flight around the earth in 1961, about a month after Soviet cosmonaut Yuri Gagarin, demonstrated that the United States could compete in this increasingly important arena.

Kennedy was getting the message. It was around this time that he sought the opinion of Wernher von Braun, the former Nazi who had worked on rocketry projects for the German government during World War II and was brought to the United States to continue his work after the war. "Can we beat the Russians?" Kennedy asked him. "We have a sporting chance," von Braun replied.[2]

The president revealed his new frame of mind in an address to a joint session of Congress on May 25, 1961. "I believe that this nation should commit itself to achieving the goal, before this decade is out, of landing a man on the moon and returning him safely to earth," he said.[3] It was an audacious aspiration—among the most audacious ever made by a world leader—and one whose implications Kennedy embraced. "We choose to go to the moon," he said in a speech at Rice University in September 1962, an assertion inspiring in its very simplicity.

The nation made such choices, he explained, "not because they are easy, but because they are hard, because that goal will serve to organize and measure the best of our energies and skills, because that challenge is one that we are willing to accept, one we are unwilling to postpone, and one we intend to win."[4]

This was more than mere rhetoric. And it was more than the will of one man—a man who, of course, as with many men and women, did not live to see his dream become a reality. In the aftermath of these speeches, the NASA budget grew tremendously, from an initial estimate of US$7 billion a year to over US$25 billion a decade later—at its peak, NASA received the equivalent of US$26 from every man, woman, and child in the United States annually (which would be much more in twenty-first-century US dollars).[5] The scale of the enterprise was dazzling. The rocket that launched Apollo 8, the mission that resulted in the first trip around the moon, provided a thrust at liftoff that was more than twice the hydroelectric power that would be obtained if all the rivers and streams in North America were channeled through turbines. The engines in that rocket delivered 160 million horsepower, burning a million and a half tons of kerosene and liquid oxygen in two and a half minutes. Hundreds of thousands of people were involved in the project.[6]

It was completed with 5 months to spare. In July 1969, the space mission Apollo 11 headed to the moon. "That's one small step for man, one giant leap for mankind," team leader Neil Armstrong said as he walked on its powdery surface. After his colleague Buzz Aldrin disembarked, the two unfurled an American flag, stiffened with wire so that it would remain erect in an airless world. The astronauts struggled to get it about 6 inches into the ground, just enough so that it could stand upright for a breathless audience of roughly 600 million people, about 20% of the earth's population, watching the event on live television. Mission accomplished.[7]

Landing a man on the moon may prove to be the most impressive thing the United States ever did in terms of its significance in the broader sweep of human civilization—a bookend of sorts to the expeditions of Christopher Columbus almost 500 years earlier—and an accomplishment likely to impress future societies as least as much as anything we've held dear about ourselves. It was a quest conducted against a backdrop geopolitical rivalry with the Soviet Union, and aided by the work of scientists associated with a genocidal Nazi regime (via a secret program code-named Operation Paperclip, launched just after World War II to tap the talents of German scientists). But the sheer scale and speed of the enterprise in the context of its time—and ours—is nothing short of amazing. And for all the competitive, even imperial, dimensions of that enterprise, the United States respected an international agreement that no nation could legally claim to colonize the moon. (A plaque planted on a front leg of lunar module read "We came in peace for all mankind.")[8] President Habib Bourguiba of Tunisia may just have been trying to be polite when he told President Kennedy that he would prefer to see men on the moon than receive a billion dollars in federal aid. But if the belief that the moon landing justified its cost was not unanimous, confidence in the worthiness of the enterprise is not an opinion bound by time, place, or nation. There are human longings that defy logic or self-interest.

The moon landing of July 20, 1969, was, in collective terms, a happy moment in the life of the United States, and one that would be remembered with great feeling as such for those who lived through it (I was 6 years old at the time, and had a t-shirt commemorating the occasion). In that regard, the moon landing was similar to another event from the summer of 1969: the Woodstock Festival, in which hundreds of thousands of young people gathered in upstate New York for 3 days of celebrating what was known in shorthand as "the sixties." Woodstock too had its less attractive sides, from mud to drug overdoses, but it seems churlish at this point to dwell on them.

In retrospect, however, the most remarkable thing about the moon landing is how rapidly it receded from national consciousness. The world was riveted by the almost weeklong saga of Apollo 13 in 1970, in which three astronauts narrowly escaped with their lives (three other astronauts had perished in a fire on the launching pad during Apollo 1 in 1967). By this point, politicians were growing increasingly wary of the astronomical cost of the space program. In the aftermath of Apollo 13, Democratic senator Walter Mondale of Minnesota opposed NASA's proposed space shuttle and space station. "I believe it would be unconscionable to embark on a project of such staggering cost when many of our citizens are malnourished, when our rivers and lakes are polluted, and when our cities and rural areas are dying," he said, posing questions whose answers he considered obvious: "What are our values? What do we think is more important?"[9] In fact, the NASA budget passed that year, and both these projects were realized (the space station is now a joint project with Russia). But in terms of resources and recognition, the US space program receded in public consciousness; the last trip to the moon, Apollo 17, was completed in 1972. The moon landing isn't even mentioned in some of the most prominent US history textbooks.[10]

In the months and years following the moon landing, the attention of the nation was focused on events much closer to home—as well as on events, notably the Vietnam War, taking place on the other side of the planet. On the whole, these developments were not happy ones. The United States entered the 1960s in a state of collective hope, even expectation. By the time the decade was over, however, the dominant mood was one of disappointment and frustration, a mood that dominated the next decade as well.

Imperial Quagmire: The Vietnam Wars

Perhaps the best way to begin explaining why is to look at the situation in Vietnam, where an American empire at the zenith of its power embarked upon a large-scale military intervention with a curious combination of arrogance, anxiety, and half-heartedness. There was no question that the United States had the resources to conduct a long war on the other side of the world. Its Pacific fleet was the largest naval force in the world. And military readiness had been bolstered by a major buildup during the Kennedy administration, part of a long-range strategy to have alternatives available to a nuclear option.

Nor was manpower an issue. The Selective Service System never stopped drafting soldiers after World War II, and the demographic bulge of the Baby Boom provided a supply of young men that exceeded wartime demand. Whereas, in the mid-1950s, 70% of men reaching draft age served in the military, only 40% did so during the Vietnam War, and only 10% actually went there. Exemptions were widespread. They were also heavily influenced by social class; until 1968, being in college or graduate school meant you were excused.[11]

In the early years of the war, support was strong and morale was good. "This war is not going to be won in a day or even a year," a young GI named Jack S. Swender wrote to his aunt and uncle in 1965. "This war and others like it will only be won when the children of that nation [Vietnam] are educated and can grow in freedom to rule themselves." (This soldier died in combat 3 months later.) As late as 1967, a peace resolution introduced at an AFL–CIO convention was defeated 2000 to 6. "I would rather fight the Communists in South Vietnam than fight them down here in Chesapeake Bay," said AFL–CIO president George Meany, expressing a widespread sentiment of the time.[12]

Such confidence and determination notwithstanding, President Johnson always saw the war as a matter of grim necessity undertaken at least as much for the sake of domestic political considerations as geopolitical ones. "I knew if we let communist aggression succeed in taking over South Vietnam there would follow in this country an endless national debate—a mean and destructive debate—that would shatter my presidency, kill my administration, and damage our democracy," he later explained. Johnson was keenly aware that the communist takeover of China had damaged Harry Truman's presidency and aided the rise of Joseph McCarthy. "And I knew all these problems were chickenshit compared with what might happen if we lost Vietnam."[13]

Even as LBJ escalated the war, he also tried to muffle its growing impact. Johnson did not act openly in the aftermath of the Gulf of Tonkin Resolution of 1964, which essentially gave him a blank check to conduct military operations. The coming presidential election and his desire to the get his Great Society underway were higher priorities, both of which would be threatened by sudden military moves. But when enemy forces attacked an American airbase in the town of Pleiku in early 1965, he decided to strike back hard—though not to be open about it, as he would duplicitously downplay the scope of the nation's deepening involvement. The result was Operation Rolling Thunder, a massive series of air strikes that began in March. Meanwhile, the number of soldiers sent to Vietnam ratcheted up steadily: 184,000 by the end of 1965, 450,000 by the end of 1966, and over 500,000 by 1968.[14] This influx of troops was accompanied by a gigantic supply infrastructure that included air-conditioned barracks, movie theaters, bowling alleys, and supply posts that resembled department stores. The Vietnam War helped turn Japan, a crucial way station, into an economic superpower; the imperatives of moving goods quickly revolutionized the use of recently developed container shipping, which transformed world trade—one more example of the way the US government and its military were instrumental in fostering the growth of private enterprise.[15]

It was the American Way of War: using the power of plenty to steamroller opposition. This approach worked in World War II, and at least on the surface, it seemed like it would work in Vietnam as well. Actually, Johnson pushed it to the point of bribery. In a televised speech in April 1965, he promised the communists that if they were willing to lay down their weapons, he was willing to pour resources into the rural Mekong Delta of South Vietnam and transform it in ways comparable to those that FDR used to create the Tennessee Valley Authority that modernized the South in the 1930s. "Old Ho can't turn me down," Johnson said of North Vietnamese leader Ho Chi Minh (though he privately admitted that, were he in Ho's shoes, he would do exactly that).[16] When Ho refused to hold any discussions until the United States suspended bombing missions, Johnson did so. But the North Vietnamese communists simply increased the flow of weapons and supplies to South Vietnamese communists, and the war continued to escalate.

Militarily speaking, the United States faced three core problems in Vietnam. The first is that the Americans were seeking to prop up a South Vietnamese ally that was not only hopelessly corrupt (Johnson described the leadership there as "bottom of the barrel"),[17] but also lacked the will to fight with the same intensity as their opponents, even as a significant proportion of the South Vietnamese population was passively—and in some cases actively—supporting the communists. Second, the North Vietnamese, who had spent the better part of the decade expelling the French and were willing to endure casualties on a scale that dwarfed those of their adversaries, saw themselves as engaged in a nationalist struggle, *not* as pawns in a Cold War chess match. Nor would they be distracted by the charms of American capitalism. Finally, even if Johnson was willing to commit to total war (which, for domestic reasons alone, he decidedly was not), he had to be deeply concerned about antagonizing the Soviets and/or the Chinese to the point where their aid would go beyond supplying their North Vietnamese ally and cross into military intervention.

Under such circumstances, the core strategy of the United States in conducting the war was an attempt to root out communist influence—conducted in highly localized "search and destroy" missions—and an attempt to shut off the supply of weapons to South Vietnamese communists, much of it channeled through the Ho Chi Minh trail, which ran through the neighboring Cambodia and Laos. But this was difficult to do. Because the Vietnam War was in fact a civil war, it was often difficult, if not impossible, to tell the difference between friend and foe, a situation that created frustration for the Americans, who lashed out against both, most notoriously in the My Lai massacre of 1968, in which hundreds of unarmed Vietnamese civilians were murdered by US troops. Twenty-six soldiers were tried for war crimes, but only one, Lieutenant William Calley, was convicted. He served 3 years of house arrest before he was pardoned. American spokesmen reported progress in terms of casualties inflicted on the enemy, yet neither resistance nor supplies seemed to ebb. Johnson had even stronger geopolitical reservations about intervening in Cambodia and Laos as he did invading North Vietnam, and refrained from doing so (something his successor would not).

In a way, it's surprising that the conflict wasn't more disastrous. "Had China been less self-absorbed or the Soviet Union less wary of the Chinese, the war in Vietnam might have proved more embarrassing to American foreign policy than it did," notes historian John Morton Blum. (Indeed, the bad blood between China and the Soviet Union, which reached the point of a brief undeclared border war in 1969, is one of the most important, and widely overlooked, aspects of the Cold War.) "As it was, the American presence in the Mediterranean and the Middle East was marginal, and in Europe the NATO nations grew more and more anxious about the capability of the United States to provide enough support in case of a conventional war."[18]

The war imposed strains on the global economy. Though Vietnam was comparatively cheap compared with previous US wars and occurred during a period of economic expansion, Johnson refused to raise taxes to pay for it until 1967, which created inflationary pressures that would have a serious impact over the course of the next decade. The diminishing power of the dollar, aggravated by a sharp rise in overseas spending, set off a rush to buy gold, destabilizing world markets. This ultimately led to the US decision to relinquish a longstanding policy of linking the value of the dollar to gold, a sign of weakening international pre-eminence.

The greatest damage inflicted by the Vietnam War on the United States, however, was domestic, exactly as Johnson feared. "I knew from the start that I was bound to be crucified either way I moved," he told biographer Doris Kearns Goodwin at the end of his life. "If I left the woman I really loved—the Great Society—in order to get involved with that bitch of a war on the other side of the world, then I would lose everything at home." Johnson was increasingly distracted from his domestic agenda by war concerns, and as the budget for the war got steadily larger, resources for the Great Society steadily ebbed.

But the problem was bigger than one man. The conflicts that came to the surface in the second half of the 1960s reflected not just government policies, but some of the underlying assumptions of American life by those who believed that realizing their strongest desires was within reach—and who became angry to discover that reality proved more complicated than aspiration. The classic example, mentioned in the last chapter, were the Community Action Programs that were part of the Office of Economic Opportunity. The stated goal of CAP was "maximum feasible participation." But the result, in the words of Johnson policy adviser Daniel Patrick Moynihan in the title of a 1969 book, was "maximum feasible misunderstanding." Existing municipal power structures tussled for control with an influx of activists, fraying the unity of the liberal left, as politicians, bureaucrats, and social reformers pointed fingers at each other.

Meanwhile, new federal initiatives proved far more costly than anyone anticipated. Medicaid, a health program for the poor also mentioned in the previous chapter, was tacked on to Medicare, a health program for the elderly, both of which Johnson signed into law in 1965. But, over time, the latter would prove comparably costly—and both would become huge burdens on the federal budget. As with Social Security, Medicare would become an entitlement that millions of Americans would come to depend upon. Reducing, much less ending, such programs became politically impossible, even as those Americans were often painfully aware of their limits no less than their burdensome costs.

Down from the Mountaintop: The Civil Rights Movement

Nowhere, however, did the soaring hopes of the 1960s crash more disappointingly than in the civil rights movement. Paradoxically, the movement was both a victim of its success and a casualty of American racism. Moreover, the movement's victories and defeats revealed fissures within, making it clear that African Americans sometimes disagreed among themselves about what their goals should be and how they should pursue them.

By most reckonings, the apex of what is now known as the "classical" civil rights movement occurred in Selma, Alabama, in 1965, which culminated in federal intervention on the side of protesters and President Johnson signing the Voting Rights Act. That law, along with the Civil Rights Act of the previous year, formed the two pillars marking a turning point in the history of American race relations (see Chapter 3). But these accomplishments, as tremendous as they were, proved to be no magic wand. The civil rights movement would continue in its struggle to consolidate its gains in the South as well as to extend them into the largely untouched territory of the North.

Organizations such as the SCLC, SNCC, and CORE continued their work in the Deep South in the years after Selma, taking on the painstaking work of registering voters and enduring intimidation and violence in places such as Lowndes County, Alabama, near Selma. The unremitting hostility that young SNCC activists faced was especially exhausting. They also found themselves questioning two axioms of the struggle: that Washington was a powerful ally in challenging states' rights, and that non-violence was the only viable tactic for realizing their goals. "As far as I'm concerned, the federal government is the enemy," an exasperated Diane Nash Bevel said at one point during the Selma fight.[19] Nash was at that point married to James Bevel, a key lieutenant of Martin Luther King, Jr. But King himself was a subject of growing impatience, a stratospheric celebrity who tended to pop in and out of strategy sessions; impatient SNCC members mockingly referred to him as "da Lawd." A rising wave of SNCC leaders, who included James Forman, Stokely Carmichael, and H. Rap Brown, were increasingly vocal in expressing their aggravation, even bitterness, toward King's commitment to non-violence, and edged toward explicitly renouncing it.

These tensions, which had simmered over many months, burst into the open in June 1966. James Meredith, the young college student who had led a successful quest to desegregate the University of Mississippi 4 years earlier, now decided to exercise his freedom by walking 220 miles from Memphis to Ole Miss without police or federal protection, an enterprise he described as sponsored by a fictive "World Committee for the Preservation of James Meredith." (Meredith was regarded as an odd duck even by his allies.) He had covered about 25 miles of the trip before he was shot by a racist. Meredith, initially reported dead, survived and was hospitalized. In the aftermath of the shooting, civil rights activists, including Carmichael and King, converged on the scene and vowed to continue the march. When the marchers made brief detours to do things such as desegregate a local movie theater and promote voter registration, tensions with local officials intensified. Carmichael was arrested for failing to provide a permit for marchers to camp outside a local school in Greenwood, Mississippi. (Local officials later reversed this decision.) After making bail, he returned to address a mass meeting of 600. "This is the twenty-seventh time I've been arrested, and I ain't going to jail no more!" he began, before uttering a fateful sentence: "We want black power." It became an incantation: "What do you want?" he asked the crowd repeatedly. "Black power!" came the answer. The movement had taken a decisive turn. Once rooted in Christian non-violence, it was now an increasingly secular and militant force, thrilling some and frightening many.[20]

King was not on hand when Carmichael gave his Black Power address in Greenwood. By that point, he had returned to Chicago, where he had been working for months to open a bold second front in the civil rights movement: taking the struggle from the South to the North, and in particular to the ghettoes of Northern cities (he had settled his family in a run-down apartment on Chicago's West Side). But the Windy City proved a much more elusive target: instead of the *de jure*, or legal, segregation codified by laws that could be challenged and overturned, he faced the unofficial *de facto* segregation of residential patterns and informal customs that were not as easy to crack. Nor were his opponents as easy to confront; Chicago mayor Richard Daley, a Democrat, had African American as well as white allies in seeking to check King from making incursions in the city's ways of doing business. At the same time, the movement faced vicious racism that was all too willing to challenge him openly. On August 5, 1966, King was knocked to the ground by a large rock while protesting housing discrimination, an act that elicited cheers from the crowd. Fellow clergy who accompanied him were subjected to jeering; young residents held up signs that said things such as "the only way to end niggers is exterminate them" and "King Would Look Good with a Knife in His Back." King noted with sadness that members of the crowd called nuns "bitches." "This is a terrible thing," he mused. "I've been in many demonstrations all across the South, but I can say that I have never seen, even in Mississippi and Alabama, mobs as hostile and hate-filled as I have here in Chicago."[21]

King always knew Chicago would be difficult. But he also felt he had no choice but to press on, not only geographically but also in expanding his critique of American society. By the second half of the 1960s, that critique was increasingly economic. King's concern about poverty was not only racial, and he saw it as much in terms of values as he did resources. "We need a rebalancing of our national priorities," he said, noting that the nation spent liberally on the space program but seemed grudging in funding the War on Poverty. King later alluded to another problem as well. "The security we profess to seek in foreign adventures, we will lose in our decaying cities. The bombs in Vietnam explode at home—they destroy the hopes and possibilities for a decent America."[22]

This was edging into dangerous territory. The Vietnam War had been gnawing at King for many years. But he held his tongue, because he needed the support of President Johnson, and because he feared that to comment on the war would be to invite criticism from people who felt he was not qualified to address the subject. He did say in March 1965 that "The war in Vietnam is accomplishing nothing," but the remark did not get much attention.[23] As the 1960s went on, however, King felt it impossible to honorably remain quiet, especially since African Americans were being drafted in disproportionate numbers. His allies in the movement were not as diffident; in the words of one hand-lettered sign at the Meredith March, "No Viet Cong Ever Called Me Nigger."[24] In April 1967, King finally made an address entitled "A Time to Break the Silence" at New York's Riverside Church, where for the first time he directly challenged the Johnson administration for prosecuting the war. "Somehow this madness must cease," he said. "I speak for those whose land is being laid waste, whose homes are being destroyed, whose culture is being subverted. I speak for the poor of America who are paying the double price of smashed hopes at home and death and corruption in Vietnam."[25] King's growing breach with President Johnson, never open, was now fully public. (The two had had their last telephone conversation almost 2 years earlier.)[26]

By this point, the war was like the eye of a growing storm, sucking everything in its path. There had been scattered voices of opposition from the very beginning. Actually, much of that opposition came from within the Johnson administration, which is to say it was from the people who were actually paying most careful attention to what was going on. But LBJ grimly went forward in waging war on what he called "a little piss-ant country," increasingly angry and hostile toward those who questioned his determination, which he cast in fatalistic terms: "American voters will forgive you for anything except being weak."[27]

As the war escalated, critical voices began to emerge with growing intensity outside the halls of government. In October 1965, a young Catholic pacifist named David Miller attracted mass media attention when he burned his draft card outside an army induction center in New York (he was sentenced to 2 years in prison). The move was widely condemned, but made a deep impression. As noted earlier, relatively few men were drafted during the Vietnam War, and relatively few were actually sent there. But the possibility that this *could* happen loomed large over the lives of these people and those who loved them. (It's no accident that President George W. Bush did not reinstate the draft, which ended in 1973, during wars in Iraq and Afghanistan from 2003 to 2014; had he done so, there would likely have been much more domestic opposition.) Those who did go—their average age was 19, much younger than World War II or Korea veterans, and overwhelmingly from working-class backgrounds[28]—encountered an often mystifying conflict with no obvious front and no clear-cut military objectives. "This country is no gain that I can see, Dad," one soldier wrote home. "We're fighting, dying, for people who resent our being over here."[29]

Government spokesmen kept reporting heavy enemy casualties, and yet Johnson felt compelled to keep asking for more men and more money. A new term entered the national vocabulary: "the credibility gap."

Centered on the Vietnam War, the notion of a credibility gap began to envelop the national conversation around other topics as well, as Americans began to question the honesty and effectiveness of their national institutions. Was the government doing what it could and should about civil rights and poverty? Conversely, was it effective in maintaining order as riots broke out in dozens of cities in the summers following the Watts riots of 1965? In multiple—and opposing—camps, hope turned to anger, and anger gave way to violence, notably in the wave of urban riots that convulsed the nation's cities each summer. Democrats suffered serious political setbacks in the midterm elections of 1966, indicating that voter patience with liberalism was ebbing. A despairing King, whose approach to social change was increasingly seen as irrelevant, understood what was happening. "The problem is that the rising expectations for freedom and democracy have not been met," he told a group of ministers in training. "And interestingly enough, in a revolution, when hope diminishes, the hate element is often turned toward those who originally built up the hope."[30]

King wasn't the only one sounding a warning. In February 1968, a task force appointed by President Johnson to investigate racial rioting in the previous year made its official report. Led by Illinois governor Otto Kerner, the so-called Kerner Commission ominously reported that "our nation is moving toward two societies, one black, one white—separate and unequal." By this point, however, Johnson felt he had done all he could do on race relations, and was preoccupied with Vietnam. Little came of the commission's findings.

Turning Point: 1968

The year 1968 was, similar to the outbreak of the Civil War in 1861 or the onset of the Great Depression in 1929, a turning point in American history. A string of setbacks began in January with a military embarrassment when the North Korean Navy seized a US warship, the USS *Pueblo*, off the coast of that country, and took 82 hostages. Because Johnson did not think he could take on the North Koreans and their communist allies while tied down in Vietnam, he was forced into an 11-month negotiation that led to the release of the hostages after an official apology (the North Koreans still hold the *Pueblo*). Later that month came a more unexpected, and devastating, military development: the Tet Offensive, a huge Viet Cong lunge into South Vietnam, one large enough to include the brief capture of the US embassy in the South Vietnamese capital of Saigon. Considered solely in military terms, the Tet Offensive was a defeat for the communists, who failed in their objective of generating a general uprising against the South Vietnamese government. But, in *political* terms, Tet was a disaster for the Johnson administration. How, given regular reports of progress, could this have happened? And, after being told things were under control, how could General William Westmoreland, the US commander in Vietnam, be asking for 200,000 *more* troops? *The Wall Street Journal*, no flaming bastion of radicalism, editorialized that "the whole Vietnam effort may be doomed." Johnson was particularly shaken when CBS news anchor Walter Cronkite— nicknamed "Mr. Credibility"—said on national television that the best that the United States could do was "negotiate, not as victors, but as an honorable people who lived up to their pledge to defend democracy, and did the best they could."[31]

There was also to be a presidential election in 1968, and the widespread assumption when the year started was that Johnson would run for another term. But even before the Tet Offensive, challengers were emerging within the Democratic Party. One, to whom we'll return to shortly, was Alabama governor George Wallace, who had run a surprisingly strong campaign in 1964. Another was Minnesota senator Eugene McCarthy, who declared himself an avowed peace candidate. McCarthy surprised the nation by finishing a stunningly strong second to Johnson (49–42%) in the New Hampshire primary that March. Even more stunning was Johnson's reaction: at the end of the month, he withdrew from the presidential race entirely. One reason for this was an even bigger threat that jumped into the race after McCarthy made it clear that LBJ was vulnerable: former attorney general Robert F. Kennedy, brother of the slain JFK. Johnson and RFK, as he was known, had never gotten along well, and their personal hatred deepened over time.[32] After leaving the White House as attorney general, Kennedy was elected US senator from New York, where he became a leading voice of liberalism. Similar to King, he was increasingly unhappy with the Vietnam War but held off from speaking out. But after it was clear that public opinion was turning sharply, he declared his candidacy and immediately became the front-runner for the Democratic nomination.

Amid all this drama came another stunning event: the assassination of King on April 4, 1968. In the months leading up to the shooting, he was gearing up for his next big undertaking, the Poor People's Campaign, a multiracial March on Washington meant to dramatize economic injustice. Over the course of previous weeks, he had been diverted a number of times to Memphis, where he supported sanitation workers on strike against the city. By that point in his life, King was physically and spiritually exhausted. He was also shadowed by premonitions of his impending death. "Like anybody, I would like to live a long life," he said in "I See the Promised Land," his riveting final speech delivered on the eve of his murder. "Longevity has its place. But I'm not concerned about that now. I just want to do God's will. And he's allowed me to go up to the mountain. And I've looked over. And I've seen the promised land."[33] King was murdered on April 4 by James Earl Ray, a career criminal who shot him while the civil rights leader was standing on a motel balcony.

King's death was devastating. In the days that followed, rioting broke out in a series of cities, among them Washington, Baltimore, Chicago, and Kansas City. It might have been worse; the mayor of New York, liberal

Republican John Lindsay, is widely credited with preventing a riot in New York by bravely venturing to Harlem. Robert Kennedy performed a similar task in Indianapolis, where he paid tribute to King as a man who "dedicated his life to love and to justice for his fellow human beings, and he died in the cause of that effort."[34] The Poor People's Campaign pressed on in his absence, and thousands of participants camped out on the Mall in the nation's capital.

In retrospect, King's death was a blow from which the civil rights movement never recovered. I've been at some pains in this account to make clear that the movement was the product of a great many men and women, some of whom did important work decades before the 1950s and 1960s. And it seems that, in any event, King's greatest moment of influence had already passed by the time of his death. But no one since Abraham Lincoln had been able to so compellingly fuse human aspirations in terms of national ideals the way King did: his dream was truly an American Dream, grounded in Christian faith and in the principles as well as tactics of non-violence. No figure since has matched the breadth and depth of his appeal. Had he lived, he might yet have recovered as a voice of essential moderation.

King's death was followed 2 months later by that of another icon of the era, Robert Kennedy. Long known as a tough-as-nails political infighter, Kennedy had substantially repositioned himself in the years following his brother's death. Actually, there were signs of this even before then; a heated argument with writer James Baldwin and other civil rights leaders at a New York apartment in 1963 seemed to have led to a greater understanding of racial issues, which deepened further when Kennedy visited South Africa in 1966. By the time he entered the presidential race 2 years later, RFK had become a peace candidate, as well as a leading voice against poverty. He had just won the California primary in June—effectively sealing his nomination—when he was assassinated at his victory party. Alarmed by the crowd's reaction to gunfire, he asked if everyone was all right, even as he had been shot in the head.

Kennedy's death threw what was already a tumultuous Democratic presidential race into further turmoil. Eugene McCarthy and George Wallace remained in the race, but the man who finally captured the nomination was another late entrant, Vice President Hubert Humphrey, a liberal lion with strong links to the civil rights movement dating back to the 1940s. Humphrey's biggest problem was his association with Johnson—which is to say his association with the Vietnam War. By the time of the Democratic National Convention in Chicago that July, Humphrey was the leader of a badly fractured party, at a convention that was taking place in a badly fractured city. An umbrella organization of groups under the banner of the National Mobilization Committee to End the War in Vietnam (MOBE) gathered to hold marches and demonstrations, where they clashed with police under the direction of Mayor Richard Daley. Much of the violence was captured live on television, where police beat and bloodied protesters.

Right Rising: The Return of Richard Nixon

But—and it's here we need to finally take note of the other side in the large alternating current that surged through the 1960s—public sentiment was with the police, and not the protesters. Even as the left intensified its radicalism, the right was recovering its footing in the aftermath of the disastrous presidential campaign of 1964, where Barry Goldwater had experienced such decisive defeat.

For if there were lots of people who felt the country had not gone far enough in its efforts to close the gap between ideals and reality, there were others who felt it had gone too far—that the pace and the nature of the changes that had taken place in the 1960s were destroying much that was good and worth preserving. As the decade wore on, there were more and more people who felt this way, many of whom became convinced as they watched the growing radicalism of the civil rights and antiwar movements. To some, the Tom Hayden and SDS of the Port Huron Statement of 1962 had become unrecognizable in their anger and hostility, and some radical groups' hatred forfeited sympathy for their ends, much less their means. "Our whole life," one such group, Weatherman (later the Weather Underground), proclaimed, "is a defiance of Amerika."[35] The term, which evoked the imagery of early-twentieth-century writer Franz Kafka's totalitarian nightmares as well as the late-twentieth-century KKK, suggested just how far the left had gone in abandoning national ideals. Once, the lack of democracy had been distressing. Now the very idea of democracy, at least as most Americans understood the term, had become a joke.

Perhaps the best place to begin tracing the emergence of the new conservative coalition that mobilized in response is by looking at those who were most vocally opposed to social change from the very beginning of the civil rights era. These were the people who flocked to the banner of George Wallace. Ever since the ascent of FDR, the Northern wing of the Democratic Party had become increasingly dominant in national politics, in large measure because this wing of the party was willing to use the government as a means of improving the lives of ordinary people. (Southern Democrats were always nervous about this, because there was always the risk that a strong federal government would interfere in race relations.) The dominance of the Northern wing of the party could be tenuous; Kennedy had picked Lyndon Johnson as his running mate precisely because he needed to strengthen his Southern appeal; many observers believe LBJ provided him with his margin of victory in 1960.

Lyndon Johnson's problem was different. He *had* credibility in the South; LBJ had begun his career associated with segregationists such as his mentor Richard Russell of Georgia. What Johnson needed was the approval of urban Northerners, which is why he introduced a civil rights bill when he was a senator in 1957. Careful to maintain ties with his base, LBJ moved steadily in the direction of Big Government liberalism partly out of conviction—Johnson had a bona fide altruistic streak, as well as a passionate desire to make his mark as a statesman—but primarily because that's where the votes were in 1960 and (especially) 1964. Johnson understood very well that the Great Society, the

Civil Rights Act, and the Voting Rights Act would cost him the support of his old constituency. But he hoped to gain allies, in particular the newly registered African Americans who he correctly believed would eventually transform the Democratic Party into what we know it to be today, which is essentially a party of multiculturalism. But in 1968, this was all in the future.

George Wallace was ready and waiting to harvest these newly disaffected Democrats. It was with their support that he made a surprisingly good showing in 1964. Now, in 1968, he would try again, and do even better. He could no longer do so as a Democrat, however: the party had left his brand of politics behind. So Wallace became the standard-bearer for the newly formed American Independent Party, whose slogan was "law and order."

Of Wallace's racial politics in 1968, there could be no doubt; this was, after all, the man of "segregation now, segregation tomorrow, segregation forever" fame. But it's impossible to really fathom Wallace's appeal without recourse to his class politics as well. As he loved to ask, "Can a former truck driver married to a dime-store clerk and son of a dirt farmer be elected president?" Wallace had nothing but contempt for protesters. "You young people seem to know a lot of four-letter words," he would say. "But I have two four-letter words you don't know: S-O-A-P and W-O-R-K." And yet, Wallace shared the New Left's hostility toward the Kennedyesque "best-and-brightest" types who got the nation into Vietnam. (His approach to ending the war? Nuclear weapons.) Urban elites expressed contempt toward Wallace in ways that did not always reflect well on them; one writer for the *New York Review of Books* wrote of his "plastic-like ill-cut suits, his graying drip-dry shirts, with his sour, dark, unprepossessing look, carrying the scent of hurry and hair oil: if he were not a figure, a star, he would be indistinguishable from the lowest of his crowd."[36] This was exactly the kind of condescension that allowed Wallace to capture five Deep South states in the election, and attract voters from all of the country.

But if Wallace's support was deep and wide, it was also finite. As he well knew, he could never win more than fraction of the overall electorate; his hope was to get enough votes so that no candidate would get a majority and thus throw the election into the House of Representatives. Which brings us to the other major political party about which I have said little in this chapter: the Republicans. Veering to the edge of irrelevance in 1964, they were now in a position to re-emerge in national politics—*if* they could find a way to capture or neutralize the Wallace vote.

Similar to the Democrats, the Republican Party of the 1960s had two major wings. But rather than Northern and Southern, these were, loosely speaking, Eastern and Western. The Eastern wing, led by New York governor Nelson Rockefeller, went even farther than Dwight Eisenhower had in accepting the legacy of the New Deal; in effect, it considered Big Government as the price of Big Business. Leadership of Western wing, which had belonged to Goldwater, passed in the aftermath of his defeat to California governor Ronald Reagan, the former Hollywood actor who had scored a surprising win for that position in 1966 by defeating Democrat Edmund "Pat" Brown (whose son Jerry would later be a four-term governor). Reagan was increasingly a spokesman for an impatient right that was exasperated with student protest at home and abroad. "It's silly talking about how many years we will have to spend in the jungles of Vietnam when we could pave the whole country and put parking stripes on it and still be home for Christmas," he said famously in 1965.[37]

But neither Rockefeller nor Reagan were really in a strong position to land the Republican nomination for president in 1968. Besides ideological questions about the future of the party, Rockefeller was a divorcee at a time when many people believed that difficulties in one's private life signaled unfitness for public office. Reagan was still new to the national political scene, and widely considered too conservative to win general acceptance. The question, then, was who could successfully bridge the poles marked out by Rockefeller and Reagan.

The answer, as it turned out, was Richard Nixon. This is not an outcome that many people would have imagined only a few years earlier. After his narrow defeat in his presidential race against John Kennedy in 1960, Nixon ran for governor of California in 1962 and lost—an especially humiliating defeat that resulted in a churlish performance at a press conference at which he told reporters that "you won't have Nixon to kick around anymore."[38] For the next few years, he effectively went underground, practicing law in New York and doing favors for politicians to rebuild his position. When he re-emerged in 1968, it was reputedly as "the New Nixon," an older, wiser, more seasoned politician. Nixon skillfully positioned himself between the Goldwater/Reagan and Rockefeller wings, and emerged with the nomination.

Writing in 1969, Nixon biographer Garry Wills usefully crystallized Nixon's political vision in terms of "the mystique of the earner." Nixon, Wills said, was a liberal in the classic eighteenth-century sense of the term, a man who believed that the United States was a land of equal opportunity (both economic and civic), that it rewarded hard work (as both ennobling and profitable), and where the private sector functioned as an essential check against government tyranny. This message struck a chord with the increasingly weary "silent majority" to whom Nixon targeted his message. In the words of his acceptance speech, Nixon reached out to "the forgotten Americans, the non-shouters, the non-demonstrators. They're not racists or sick; they're not guilty of the crime that plagues the land; they are black and they are white; they're native born and foreign born; they're young and they're old." As Wills and others noted, there was more than a little mythologizing in this formulation (for one thing, it tended to speak to the white more than the African American, the old more than the young). But even its sharpest critics could not deny its potency.[39]

Nixon was an imperfect vessel for this message. Many doubted the "new" Nixon was all that new; others wondered what he and his Democratic opponent, Humphrey, would actually do about Vietnam. In an off-the-record meeting with newspaper editors, Nixon gestured toward a so-called secret plan to end the war, which involved turning the fighting over to the Vietnamese, a concept that came to be known as "Vietnamization." But his campaign was largely content to let the Democrats self-destruct while following a "Southern

Strategy" developed by campaign aide Kevin Phillips to quietly appeal to Wallace voters with law-and-order language. Given the electorate's mood by late 1968, it's amazing that Nixon almost lost the election. In an apparent effort to aid Humphrey, Johnson halted bombing and called for negotiations in November, while Nixon allegedly worked behind the scenes to subvert them. Humphrey had momentum, but could not prevail in what political scientists call a realignment election that marked the end of liberalism as the dominant ideology in US politics. For the next half-century, voters would view their government's ability to solve problems with skepticism at best.

Women's Work: The Feminist Movement

Calendar notwithstanding, the 1960s hardly ended with the inauguration of Richard Nixon in 1969. The American left may have been losing control of *electoral* politics, but its influence in *cultural* politics, and in a plethora of new social movements, was going strong. This was not so much true of the mainstream civil rights movement, which by the late 1960s had splintered and radicalized. Militant figures such as Bobby Seale, Huey P. Newton, and Eldridge Cleaver led the Black Panthers, an Oakland-based African American self-help group that protested police brutality and got lots of attention. But they were no longer really driving what would prove to be the more durable changes of the era. It was the classical civil rights movement that became the template for all those that followed, drawing on the logic, language, and many of the tactics developed in the 1950s and 1960s.

Nowhere was this more obvious than in one of the most significant developments of the 1960s: the modern feminist movement, also known as second-wave feminism. The first wave, which emerged in the mid-nineteenth century, culminated in the passage of the Nineteenth Amendment to the Constitution, granting women the right to vote, in 1920. In the decades that followed, women continued to agitate for social and political equality in a wide array of issues. But the late 1960s were notable for the way in which these efforts coalesced with a new sense of critical mass. While this feminist movement made its most obvious public impact in the 1970s, it's worth charting its emergence in the 1960s.

Traditional accounts of second-wave feminism cite Betty Friedan's 1963 book *The Feminine Mystique* (see Chapter 2) as an important landmark, even if they also note its white, suburban orientation. They also note that John F. Kennedy appointed former First Lady Eleanor Roosevelt to head the President's Commission on the Status of Women early in his term (she died before the body completed its work). The commission, comprised of men and women, produced a document 2 years later that documented workplace discrimination and recommended better childcare and employment opportunities for women. One thing the report did *not* advocate, despite rather intense discussion, was a constitutional amendment explicitly mandating equal rights for women, instead calling on government leaders to use the Fourteenth Amendment, which defined all native-born Americans as citizens entitled to equal rights at the federal level, to protect women. But the commission did help spur passage of the Equal Pay Act of 1963, which prohibited workplace discrimination on the basis of gender (but only when men and women were doing identical work, which rarely occurred).

In the aftermath of the commission's report, which got significant press attention, Friedan, the Rev. Pauli Murray (the first African American woman Episcopal priest), and 26 other activists formed the National Organization for Women (NOW) in 1966, calling for an Equal Rights Amendment, or ERA. In the statement of purpose that accompanied its founding, NOW called for gender equality in all its forms—economic, educational, legal, *et. al.* In its insistence that modern life had essentially rendered sexual difference irrelevant in terms of how people should be treated in public life, NOW was a proponent of what feminist poet and scholar Katha Pollitt would later call "equality feminism" (which she distinguished from "difference feminism," which roots claims for female power in sex difference—more on this to come). As with so much social activism of the 1960s, this claim for modernity was rooted in technological innovation and economic plenty. "Today's technology has reduced most of the productive chores which women once performed in the home and in the mass-production industries based upon routine unskilled labor," the NOW manifesto asserted. "This same technology has virtually eliminated the quality of muscular strength as a criterion for filling most jobs, while intensifying American industry's need for creative intelligence."[40] In short, women's minds were simply too valuable to waste. For the next decade and a half, the pursuit of the ERA would be a major dimension of the feminist movement.

But not the only one. One of the more striking things about the feminism in the 1960s was the way in which it widened its critique of society. In many cases, this was the result of women's work in the civil rights movement. One of the reasons why Mary King and Casey Hayden's "A Kind of Memo," written in 1965 while they were in SNCC (see Chapter 3), was important was the way in which it explained how discrimination corrupted gender relations in both private and public spheres, a "common-law caste system that operates, sometimes subtly, forcing them to work around or outside hierarchical structures of power which may exclude them."[41]

The growing unrest among women's activists burst into public view during the 1968 Miss America contest, held in Atlantic City. About 150 women from six cities staged a demonstration on the Atlantic City boardwalk, generating a good deal of publicity, as did a series of guerilla protests that included crowning a live sheep Miss America, unfurling a banner reading "WOMEN'S LIBERATION," and throwing shoes, underwear, and other objects into a Freedom Trash Can. (A plan to set the contents on fire—the legendary "bra-burning" associated with the event—was deemed a safety hazard by local police, and never took place.) Pageant organizers got a court injunction that curtailed plans for another protest in 1969, but, by that point, the event had taken on connotations of sexism that have dogged it ever since.[42]

By the end of the decade, a growing number of feminists were describing themselves as avowed radicals, often fusing gender politics with a broader program that included a more radical brand of civil rights as well an embrace of radical class politics as well. A good example was the African American activist Angela Davis, who was a member of the Communist Party as well as the Black Panthers. This was not an easy balance to maintain, not only because it attracted often intense criticism—California governor Ronald Reagan got her fired from her position as a professor at the University of California at Los Angeles (UCLA)—but also because of the inherent tensions involved in identifying as a feminist when many African American leaders (from Martin Luther King, Jr., to Stokely Carmichael) were every bit as sexist as their white peers, who denounced feminists as "women's libbers."

Such complexities, and the ways in which different groups of women grappled with them, resulted in the evolution of at least three distinct streams of feminism by the early 1970s. Liberal feminists tended to focus on the rights and values in the public sphere, defining progress in terms of the ways women gained a sense of parity with men. Socialist (sometimes Marxist) feminism, by contrast, was more attentive to conditions of work, and struck a more collective rather than individualist stance. Radical feminists, for their part, rooted their critique of society in specifically female experiences (especially sexuality) as the proper basis for social reform. These points of departures led toward different priorities. But all were means to the same end of improving the lives of women.[43]

The attempt to come to terms with such complexities and priorities resulted in a new effort for women to gather and discuss the implications of the feminist movement. Among the pioneers in this regard was a radical feminist organization known as the Redstockings, based in New York. The Redstockings helped popularize the practice of "consciousness-raising," where women could meet and discuss without censure topics that many had spent a lifetime suppressing. Central to consciousness-raising was the idea expressed in the slogan "the personal is political"; in the words of one Redstockings writer, engaging the whole gamut of women's lives "would be a way of keeping the movement radical by preventing it from getting sidetracked into single issue reforms and single issue organizing."[44] Yet, this very breadth also carried with it the challenge of bridging considerable differences among and within women across race, class, and other sociological divides.

The late 1960s and early 1970s was also important for the explosion of feminist writing, including many now-classic works such as Australian writer Germaine Greer's *The Female Eunuch* (1970), which achieved widespread circulation in the United States, and *Sisterhood is Powerful*, an anthology of radical feminist writings also published that year. A major theme of these books was the centrality of sexual liberation as a core component of feminism. This ranged from a new emphasis on pleasure to an insistence on women's control of their own bodies.

Medical technology was an important dimension of these developments. Relatively cheap, safe, and painless oral contraceptives became available on a widespread basis in the early 1960s, offering women a powerful new tool for controlling their fertility. By lessening the risk of unwanted pregnancy, "the pill"—in fact, shorthand for a number of different contraceptive medications— also lessened the risk and even stigma attached to women's sexuality, especially premarital sexuality. By 1975, when country singer Loretta Lynn enjoyed a hit song titled "The Pill," it was clear that contraception had reached some of the most conservative precincts of US society.

Similar refinements in the capacity to end pregnancies were also underway. More importantly, women—who had often undergone psychologically and physically dangerous abortions without professional medical care—gained new legal protections. Feminist influence was important in the 1973 Supreme Court decision in *Roe v. Wade*, which for the first time affirmed a woman's right to an abortion if it took place early enough in a pregnancy. *Roe* would be controversial from the moment it was handed down, and much of that opposition came from women, as it does to this day. But few would dispute that it is an important legacy of the movement.

Rainbows: Rights Revolutions

The feminist movement of the 1960s also overlapped—in terms of interests, figures, and opponents—with the gay liberation movement (a term that perhaps had more general gender connotations then than it does now). As indicated in Chapter 2, momentum on this front had been building since the 1940s. All over the country, gays and lesbians had often gathered in same-sex bars. They paid bribes to the police to be free of harassment. But not all police cooperated, or held up their end of the bargain. Such establishments also had difficulties in dealing with local government in terms of getting liquor licenses.

Since at least the late nineteenth century, New York City had been a haven for gender diverse people, whose support helped elect John Lindsay, a liberal Republican, as mayor in 1965. Greenwich Village in particular was the epicenter of queer life, and a favorite haunt for Beat poets in particular. The Stonewall Inn, on Christopher Street, was a gay male bastion (lesbians occasionally visited as well). But in the early morning hours of June 28, 1969, police raided the Stonewall Inn. This time, the patrons fought back. A crowd of hundreds got involved in the melee; thousands congregated in the protests that followed.

From this point on, gay Americans became an increasingly visible presence on the nation's political landscape—which is not to say it was easy, or that all gay Americans were willing to reveal their identities. But the self-assertions that characterized Gay Pride, similar to the increasingly commonly invoked Black Pride, were legacies of the 1960s. "We are refugees from Amerika," the gay activist Carl Wittman wrote in a manifesto soon after he "came out" (to use the then-new language) in San Francisco in 1968. "To be a free territory, we must govern ourselves, set up our own institutions, defend ourselves, and use our won energies to improve our lives." Such language mirrored important separatist strains in the feminist and civil rights movements of the time. Wittman described traditional marriage as "a rotten, oppressive institution," and many gay gender-diverse people of the time, and ever since, would agree. But at least some of them would reappraise this stance by century's end.[45]

The influence of the civil rights movement extended into other racial domains as well. The late 1960s and early 1970s were notable for the emergence of the Yellow Power movement, one catalyzed by "The Emergence of Yellow Power," a 1969 essay by Japanese poet Amy Uyematsu. Noting that Asian Americans had in some respects overcome challenges still afflicting African Americans, Uyematsu noted that Asians were still subjected to various forms of racism. Other key texts of the Yellow Power movement included *America Is in the Heart*, a 1946 novel by Filipino Carlos Bulosan that was reissued in 1973 and quickly became a foundational document for many Asian Americans, and Frank Chin's 1971 play *The Chickencoop Chinaman*, a work that rejected the assimilationist ethos. Chin was a controversial figure, in part for his masculinist sensibility, and entered into a public dispute with another Chinese American writer, Maxine Hong Kingston, whose 1975 memoir *The Woman Warrior* is widely regarded as a classic. Yellow Power advocates noted the racial character of US wars in Southeast Asia.[46]

Native Americans were also among those racial groups with a revitalized sense of militancy. In 1969, one activist group, calling "Indians of All Tribes," captured national attention by seizing the recently abandoned island of Alcatraz off the coast of San Francisco (where the infamous prison had been located), asserting it was Indian land. Protesters occupied the island for 19 months, pro-claiming their intention to turn it into a cultural center. Supporters delivered supplies by boat; the site had no running water or phone service. That standoff ended relatively quietly, though a few protesters were taken off the island in handcuffs. Far more fraught was the 71-day occupation in 1973 of a federal facility at Wounded Knee, South Dakota, site of a massacre of Sioux Indians in 1890, by leaders of the American Indian Movement (AIM). The showdown ended when the government agreed to reconsider the treaty rights of the Oglala, one branch of the Sioux. The US Congress, with Nixon's support, reversed the "termination" policy of the 1940s and 1950s that had sought to end official recognition of Indian tribes in favor of cultural assimilation, now providing for the return of common assets to tribal control.[47]

Latin American inhabitants of the United States were literally and figuratively on the move as well. One of the national minorities in particular that achieved a new sense of prominence and power in the 1960s were Mexican Americans, who increasingly began referring to themselves as Chicanos. In 1962, a young Chicano named Cesar Chavez co-founded the National Farm Workers Association (NFWA), which merged 3 years later with the Filipino-dominated Agricultural Workers Organizing Committee (AWOC) to form the United Farm Workers (UFW). In 1965, Chavez led grape pickers in a strike throughout California's San Joaquin Valley. "We want to be equal with all the working men in the nation," the charismatic Chavez explained in 1966, in language—and non-violent methods—redolent of King. "To those who opposed us, be they ranchers, police, politicians, or speculators, we say that we are going to continue fighting until we die, or we win. We shall overcome!" The strike went on for years; at one point, Chavez went on a 25-day hunger strike to protest against the increasing violence in the union. It has been estimated that 17 million Americans had stopped eating grapes in solidarity with the strike. It finally achieved victory in 1970 when growers recognized the UFW.[48]

Changes in the demographic composition of the United States were not only a matter of what was happening from within, but also from without. In 1965, President Johnson signed a bill into law that ended the system of quotas that had discriminated in the ethnicities of foreigners who could enter the United States, which was heavily tilted in favor of Western Europeans. The law was not really intended to herald major changes. But, thanks to a provision that allowed the migration of close relatives of immigrants without restriction, increasingly large numbers of immigrants arrived on US shores. Also significant was the change in composition in those immigrants, the majority of whom now came from Asia and Latin America. The changes were not especially apparent in the late 1960s and early 1970s; in a nation of approximately 200 million, an additional 400,000 or so legal immigrants was not especially dramatic. (Undocumented immigrants are another story that we will turn to later.) But because the birth rate had stabilized, immigrants became an increasingly significant proportion of the population. By the 1980s, over 700,000 were coming annually. And that number would continue to rise in the decades that followed.[49]

The changes in national consciousness during the 1960s were not only demographic. The decade also marked the beginnings of the modern environmental movement. As with the women's movement, this was not exactly a new development; a concern for conservation of the nation's natural resources dates back at least to the time of Theodore Roosevelt at the turn of the century. Historians often cite the publication of a book as pivotal: what Betty Friedan's *The Feminine Mystique* was to the women's movement, Rachel Carson's *Silent Spring* (1962) was to environmentalism. Carson, a biologist, brought the danger of insecticides on crops to national attention. "The 'control of nature' is a phrase conceived in arrogance, born of the Neanderthal age of biology and philosophy, when it was supposed that nature exists for the convenience of man," she wrote.[50] Carson and others were able to mobilize public opinion in ways that led to a string of new laws: the Clean Air Act of 1963, the Wilderness Act of 1964, the Water Quality Act of 1965, and an Endangered Species Act in 1966. It was during these years that concern began growing about pollution and overpopulation. In 1970, the nation celebrated Earth Day for the first time. This was also the year that Richard Nixon signed legislation creating the Environmental Protection Agency (EPA). Neither Nixon nor Johnson were politicians particularly known for their concern for the environment; they approved these bills usually at the urging of supporters and/or to parry criticism while they focused on issues they regarded as more central to their presidencies.

Indeed, as with many decades, it seemed that there was more than one version of the 1960s. For a feminist in pursuit of consciousness-raising, an environmentalist fretting over the fate of the earth, or a worker on strike for better wages, events in Washington may have seemed far away, if not irrelevant. But even as a variety of centrifugal forces operated on a nation that was fragmented, major national controversies continued to rage on and touched the lives of ordinary Americans, whether they liked it or not.

Grim Peace: Endgame in Vietnam

Above all, there remained the war. Richard Nixon came to office promising to find a way to end it, but the most obvious thing he did in the first years of the his first term was to escalate it. In 1970, he ordered US forces to do something that previous presidents had avoided: invade Cambodia, through which ran the Ho Chi Minh trail that the communists used as a supply line. In 1971, he followed it up with an invasion of the neighboring Laos, through which the trail also ran. These offensives failed to achieve their military objectives, destabilized the nations in question—Cambodia in particular sank into chaos, which resulted in the rise of the genocidal Pol Pot communist regime—and generated angry protests in the United States. One such protest, at Kent State University in Ohio, resulted in the deaths of four students when National Guardsmen fired on the crowd (an event memorialized in the famous Crosby, Stills, Nash & Young song "Ohio"). By the early 1970s, even members of the military were disenchanted with the war, which a great many Americans now saw as unwinnable. In the famous words of decorated combat veteran John Kerry, "How do you ask a man to be the last man to die for a mistake?"[51]

As with so much else about his presidency, Nixon's foreign policy was complex to the point of duplicity. Even as he escalated the war against North Vietnamese communists, he opened lines of communication to the Soviet Union and China. After a series of carefully calibrated diplomatic feelers, Nixon made a surprising announcement in 1972 that we would visit, and recognize, the communist regime of Mao Zedong's China, something the United States had not done since Mao came to power in 1949. What made this so stunning is that Nixon had come to national prominence as a fierce anticommunist. Some political observers noted that a politician without such a record might avoid seeking better relations for fear of being seen as soft on communism, prompting the now-proverbial phrase "Only Nixon could go to China." Seeking to further exploit the long-simmering wedge between China and the Soviet Union, Nixon also negotiated what came to be known as the Strategic Arms Limitation Talks (SALT) treaty of 1972. Lyndon Johnson had taken the first step down this path when he joined with the Soviets and more than 50 other nations in signing the Treaty on Non-Proliferation of Nuclear Weapons in 1968. But SALT represented the first in a string of efforts to control the manufacture and spread of nuclear weapons between superpowers who already possessed them.

Meanwhile, Nixon continued to try to find a way out of the Vietnam quagmire. Negotiations in Paris to end the war had begun in 1968, but proceeded torturously, with arguments about the shape of the table around which participants would talk. These conversations were complicated by the fears of the South Vietnamese government, which was less interested in resolution than the United States was, given the likelihood that its power would be diminished, if not destroyed. When a deal seemed close, but stymied, Nixon reacted with fierce bombing campaigns intended to demonstrate his toughness and dangerous unpredictability. Finally, in January 1973, a treaty was signed in which the United States would gradually disengage from Vietnam. Over the course of the next 2 years, the Americans tried to prop up the South Vietnamese army as it pulled out its own forces, but the effort was fruitless. In 1975, the communists captured Saigon, ending a two-decade long saga. By the end of the decade, Vietnam had gone to war with China in a territorial dispute—disproving the Domino theory that the loss of one nation to communism would result in a chain reaction of collaborative communist domination. Today, Vietnam is a major trading partner of the United States.

Vietnam cast a long and painful shadow over American society for many years. For starters, some 50,000 soldiers lost their lives, leaving behind their families and loved ones. There were also thousands of prisoners of war and men classified as Missing in Action. The Vietnam War was also the first war that the United States ever lost, puncturing its seeming invincibility. For decades to come, the experience would be a measuring stick for future overseas involvements; impatient internationalists would invoke "the Vietnam Syndrome" to explain US reluctance to commit to overseas intervention for geopolitical or humanitarian reasons.

Crooked Justice: The Triumph and Fall of Nixon

But this all took a while to sink in. Meanwhile, Nixon, who cared much more about foreign than domestic policy, adopted similarly secretive and deceptive strategies to keep internal opponents off balance. Assessing Nixon's government record remains difficult to this day because he seemed to adopt conflicting policies. A critic of Great Society liberalism, he explicitly sided with those who criticized protesters—famously donning a hard hat in 1970s to show his solidarity with construction workers in New York after a riot in which they harassed antiwar activists—and used the courts to side with those who resisted racial integration strategies in public schools. On the other hand, Nixon was responsible for some of the most far-reaching government regulation of the late twentieth century, including the creation of the EPA and the Occupational Safety and Health Administration (OSHA).

Sometimes, this was a matter of indifference on his part; in other cases, it represented Machiavellian calculation. Take Affirmation Action. The concept dates back to 1961, when President Kennedy issued an executive order requiring construction companies seeking the federal government's business to hire minorities. Johnson expanded on the idea, but it was Nixon who actually took it farther than either of them in his so-called Philadelphia Plan, which was presumably designed to give employment opportunities to minorities in the construction industry. But this was not because Nixon actually believed in the program on its own merits; instead, he knew it would drive a wedge between minorities looking for jobs and the white ethnics who held them. Both sets of people tended to vote Democratic. Nixon sought to sow discord between them, as indeed the Philadelphia Plan did.[52] In similar fashion, Nixon offered a disarmingly straightforward alternative to Great Society welfare entitlements in his Family Assistance Plan, which sought to get rid of federal bureaucracy and simply guarantee a minimum income to poor people by paying them directly. A Democratic Congress, suspicious of Nixon's intentions (which indeed involved trying to get rid of the considerable bureaucratic welfare infrastructure of the federal government, which again voted Democratic), never approved the plan, and Nixon, whose primary intention was to inoculate himself from suggestions that he didn't care for the poor, never pushed it. But it served his purposes perfectly.[53]

Not all Nixon's machinations were a matter of domestic policy maneuvers— he also resorted to more underhanded tactics that crossed the line into criminal activity. Some of this was a matter of sophomoric pranks, such as the so-called "dirty tricks" played by political operative Donald Segretti, who would send for pizza and liquor to be delivered, along with the bill, to Democrats who never ordered them. But Nixon's desire to crush his enemies could be more serious. He maintained an extensive "enemies" list of people (such as John Lennon of the Beatles, then living in New York) whom he sought to harass by seeking to have them deported, have their taxes audited, or have them followed by private detectives. Furious about leaks of information that he didn't want disclosed in the early months of his presidency, he wiretapped the White House so he could track whether employees were disclosing secrets When, in 1970, the *New York Times* published the Pentagon Papers, detailing the deceptions of the Kennedy and Nixon administrations in Vietnam, Nixon, who wanted such information kept secret so as to allow himself maximum secrecy, arranged to have operatives break into the office of the psychiatrist of leaker Daniel Ellsberg in an effort to discredit him. But nothing of value was found.

Nixon's mania for control ultimately proved self-destructive. He was up for re-election in 1972, and his prospects were excellent. He had scored a major foreign policy coup with his China trip, prospects for peace in Vietnam were improving, and the Democratic Party was deeply divided between its older New Deal constituency and a rising countercultural sensibility (one that had succeeded in implementing reforms in the nominating process after the disastrous 1968 campaign). George Wallace, moreover, had to abandon his third try for the presidency when an assassin's bullet left him paralyzed. But Nixon was unwilling to take these very good odds. He decided that his most serious challenger would be Senator Edmund Muskie of Maine. Nixon's campaign operatives forged a letter claiming that Muskie condoned the use of the slur "Canucks" to refer to French Canadians in Maine; the letter was published in a pro-Nixon newspaper, along with reports that Muskie's wife smoked, drank, and used-off color language.[54] Muskie's denunciation of the latter allegation was so strong—some said he cried; Muskie claimed it only seemed so because he was speaking in a snowstorm—that primary voters wondered if Muskie was too volatile and turned to the more liberal Senator George McGovern of South Dakota, the opponent Nixon much preferred.

A far more serious form of manipulation took place that June. A group of Nixon's operatives known as "the Plumbers" (some of whom participated in the failed Bay of Pigs invasion of Cuba in 1961) were ordered to break into the Democratic National Headquarters in Washington's Watergate Hotel, where they hoped to find embarrassing documents in an Ellsberg-like operation. But the Plumbers were caught and arrested, and to make matters worse, one of them was carrying an address book with White House phone numbers in it. Still, the arrests generated little attention. White House press secretary Ron Ziegler dismissed the break-in as "third-rate burglary," and there was little reason to think otherwise. By that point, Nixon's re-election was virtually assured—he would take 49 states of the electoral college (all but Massachusetts) that November in one of the great presidential victories of all time—and few people believe he would be so foolish as to take such unnecessary risks.

But "Watergate," as this event became known, turned out to be political dynamite with a long fuse. As the Plumbers were tried and convicted, there was growing concern in the White House that they would reveal what they knew in return for lighter prison sentences or extort payment from the administration (which Nixon was willing to pay). Meanwhile, the Watergate story proved to have legs at the *Washington Post*, where two young reporters, Carl Bernstein and Bob Woodward, were the beneficiaries of leaked information by a secret informant who went by the name "Deep Throat" (the name of the lead character in a pornographic movie at the time). Decades later, Deep Throat was revealed as Mark Felt, the deputy director of the FBI who was angered for getting passed over for the top job after the death of J. Edgar Hoover in 1972. Felt fed a steady stream of information to Woodward and Bernstein, who used it to run a series of stories that generated increasing media attention. Two key questions came into focus: what did Nixon know about Watergate? And when did he know it?

In the spring of 1973, Congress, controlled by Democrats, began to hold hearings on Watergate. At the same time, the Nixon administration named a special prosecutor to do an independent investigation. These developments accelerated growing interest in the case still further; the congressional hearings were broadcast on national television. In the process of routine questioning in the summer of 1973, one witness revealed that Nixon routinely taped all his conversations in the Oval Office. The Watergate Committee asked for any tapes that would shed light on his involvement. The Nixon administration refused, and a yearlong legal fight ensued. In the meantime, in a development his lawyer (who testified in exchange for immunity) called "a cancer on the presidency," a string of figures in the Nixon administration were forced to quit as their role in the scandal came to light. A number would be tried, convicted, and sent to jail. In October 1973, Nixon tried to quietly fire the special prosecutor over a weekend; this event, known as "the Saturday Night Massacre," only made matters worse. So did his statement, "I am not a crook," which he made at a press conference. The denial only called attention to an increasingly credible suspicion.

Nixon desperately tried to avoid turning over the tapes, which, Watergate aside, showed him in a bad light (it was during this time that the phrase "expletive deleted" entered common parlance).[55] In grand jury testimony, his longtime secretary claimed to have accidently erased an 18-minute stretch. The Supreme Court ultimately ruled against Nixon and ordered him to turn over the recordings. He then tried to submit written summaries instead, but was refused. Nixon finally complied. In the summer of 1974, the nation discovered what came to be known as "the smoking gun": a recording made 5 days after the Watergate break-in where he agreed to a plan whereby the Central Intelligence Agency would tell the FBI to stop investigating the case because there was a (fictitious) foreign angle, so that, legally speaking, the FBI, over which Nixon felt he had less control, would give up jurisdiction to the CIA. Congress prepared to impeach Nixon for an obstruction of justice, among other crimes, which included tax evasion. Once impeachment—which looked inevitable—happened, Nixon would be tried and likely convicted. He'd lose his job, perhaps even go to jail. In an effort to prevent any of this from happening, Nixon became the first president in American history to resign.

The saga didn't quite end there. Even as Nixon was trying to wriggle free of Watergate in the fall of 1973, Vice President Spiro T. Agnew—widely known as a media hatchet man who went after Nixon's enemies—was forced to quit after his indictment for bribery. (He pleaded no contest and repaid the money he was given.) His replacement, Congressman Gerald Ford, was widely regarded as one of the most honest men in American politics. Upon Nixon's resignation, he became president. A month later, Ford decided—on his own, with little consideration of the political implications—to give Nixon a pardon because he felt it would not be good for the country to remain embroiled in the contentious case. Many observers assumed he did this in exchange for becoming president, but there is no evidence to suggest this. In any case, Ford's reputation was badly damaged, and the pardon probably played a role in his loss in the presidential election of 1976 to Jimmy Carter—another honest man who would have another troubled presidency.

In an important sense, the resignation of Richard Nixon marked the end of an era. For almost 30 years, Nixon had loomed large on the national scene as a congressman, senator, vice president, and president. One of the nation's most successful politicians, he was also among its most disliked. And at no time was he more disliked than his years as president, as his nickname, "Tricky Dick," suggested. The facts as we now know them suggest it was apt.

Considered as a constitutional crisis, Watergate was a national ordeal in which the nation's legitimacy was at stake. And, by some reckonings, at least, the outcome was a vindication of American democracy: the system worked, because a corrupt politician was held accountable. The skepticism of the counterculture was proven correct, and the things Nixon resisted most strongly—the peace movement, civil rights, the most generous promises of American liberalism—were affirmed. In an important sense, Watergate marked the culmination of the 1960s.

But the United States of 1974 was a politically exhausted nation. A war had been lost, a leader had been disgraced, and (as we'll discuss) the economy was in shambles. A new age of reform was not in the offing. Indeed, events would show that the nation would be heading in a very different direction.

In 1976, former astronaut Stu Roosa, who had gone into space 5 years earlier on the successful scientific mission of Apollo 14, visited a granite quarry near Aswan, Egypt. He gazed upon an unfinished 1,100-ton obelisk which, had it been finished, would have stood 137 feet high, the largest of its kind. But sometime before the project was completed, the stone cracked and the workers abandoned it. "I always thought Apollo was like our unfinished obelisk," he reflected. "It's like we started building this beautiful thing and then we quit. History will not be kind to us, because we were *stupid*."[56]

Maybe not stupid, just tired. Sometimes empires just run out of energy. We chose to go to the moon. We also chose—with less unity and perhaps less seriousness—to try and end poverty, centuries of racial discrimination, and social inequality for entire classes of people. These were far more difficult tasks. (Maybe making new things is easier than getting rid of old ones.) Forty years after the final Apollo mission, the American flags planted during the various the moon landings have since turned white, the color of surrender. Eventually, they will disintegrate from the intense temperatures and assaults from micro-meteors.[57] And then all that will remain is that most durable of national creations: our (American) dreams.

CULTURE WATCH: *Easy Rider* (1969)

As its name implies, the counterculture was defined in terms of what it was against, and the main thing it was against was authority. Still, there was more to it than that; the counterculture evinced characteristics that made it distinctive to its time. One such characteristic was a strongly democratic ethos. Another was an embrace of novelty, both as a matter of art (notably popular music) as well as spirit (notably recreational sex and drugs). But there were conservative dimensions to the counterculture as well—not conservative in a political sense, but rather in an environmental one, reflected in its back-to-the-land ethos. There was also a peculiar brand of patriotism grounded in this love of place, one wholly lacking in the militaristic associations that we traditionally associate with the term, but laden with love of the United States as a land of possibility. Such resonances were reflected in one of the landmark films of the era, *Easy Rider*.

Figure 4.2   BORN TO BE WILD: Peter Fonda (front) as Wyatt and Dennis Hopper as Billy at the start of *Easy Rider*. The 1969 movie was a landmark not only of the counterculture but also of the transformation of the Hollywood film industry (1969, directed by Dennis Hopper, produced by Pando Company Inc. [as Pando Company] and Raybert Productions).

In a hidebound Hollywood whose old corporate studio system was lurching to collapse, *Easy Rider* was an unlikely project. Filmmakers Peter Fonda (son of storied Hollywood actor Henry Fonda), Dennis Hopper, and Jack Nicholson had collaborated in various permutations to make movies about drugs and biker culture in the second half of the 1960s that resulted in *Wild Angels* (1966), *The Trip* (1967), and *Head* (1968). For *Easy Rider*, Fonda and Hopper scraped together US$400,000 and put together a soundtrack notable for its lavish use of rock music (acts whose works are featured in the movie include Jimi Hendrix, the Band, and Bob Dylan). Fonda and Hopper's script, co-written with screenwriter Terry Southern, known for his work on the 1964 classic *Dr. Strangelove*, inverted and updated the classic Western by having its buddy heroes, played by Fonda and Hopper, ride motorcycles instead of horses and travel from west to east. Fonda plays Wyatt, nicknamed Captain America, who wears a helmet and leather jacket adorned with the US flag. Hopper plays Billy, whose buckskin jacket evokes a Native American. (Their names also allude to Western outlaw legends Wyatt Earp and Billy the Kid.) Having successfully smuggled drugs from Mexico to Los Angeles, the two take their proceeds from selling their wares to a wealthy man—played by the famous record producer Phil Spector—and embark on a road trip to New Orleans, where they plan to celebrate Mardi Gras. They meet a gallery of characters along the way, among them a young lawyer played by Nicholson, who befriends them when they spend a night in jail together. Wyatt and Billy eventually reach their destination and experience LSD-induced bliss. But they also encounter hostility, violence, and tragedy, and Wyatt's lament late in the film that "we blew it" gives the film a distinctly melancholy air.

The psychedelic ethos of *Easy Rider* is obvious—it's what made the movie stand out at the time, and it's what makes the movie such a rich historical document. But it's equally evident that the film is a love song to America, its gorgeous desert landscapes and baroque urban neighborhoods captured in all their splendor by Hungarian cinematographer László Kovács. There's also affection for its people, among them a Chicano family whose hospitality Wyatt and Billy savor at a western ranch. The filmmakers are less approving of Southern whites, who prove to be the villains of the story, a judgment that seems a little unfair, in that the evils ascribed to them were in many ways national ones. But such were sentiments of the New Left at the time, for better or worse.

Easy Rider was a major hit, grossing 10 times its budget and ushering in a new era in Hollywood. In its wake, a new generation of filmmakers, among them Francis Ford Coppola, Martin Scorsese, and George Lucas, began making deeply personal films with a degree of artistic autonomy that was almost unknown to earlier generations of directors. While a blockbuster mentality would take root by the late 1970s (led by another maverick director, Steven Spielberg), Fonda and Hopper continue to serve as an artistic archetype for young filmmakers pursuing a deeply personal vision. In short, the counterculture has become a tradition.

Suggested Further Reading

The best account of the US space program is Andrew Chaikin's *A Man on the Moon: The Voyages of the Apollo Astronauts* (1994; New York: Penguin, 2007). Tom Wolfe captures the romance of space flight and its broader cultural implications in *The Right Stuff* (1979; New York: Picador, 2008).

Many of the sources cited at the end of Chapter 3 are relevant to discussions of this period, among them those on Lyndon Johnson, the Vietnam War, the civil rights movement, and domestic liberalism, generally. The best account of the period as it appeared from a Republican perspective is *Nixonland: The Rise of a President and the Fracturing of America* (New York: Scribner, 2008). Garry Wills provides an incisive contemporary perspective on Nixon in *Nixon Agonistes: The Ordeal of the Self-Made Man* (1970; Boston: Houghton Mifflin, 2002). The classic account of Watergate is Bob Woodward and Carl Bernstein's *All the President's Men* (New York: Simon & Schuster, 1974), and its sequel, *The Final Days* (New York: Simon & Schuster, 1976).

The literature of feminism is, of course, vast. Perhaps the best place to begin with a one-volume history of the Second Wave is Ruth Rosen, *The World Split Open: How the Modern Women's Movement Changed America* (2000; New York: Penguin, 2006). Rory C. Dicker provides an excellent short overview in *A History of U.S. Feminisms* (New York: Seal, 2008). See also Estelle Freedman, *No Turning Back: The History of Feminism and the Future of Women* (New York: Ballantine, 2002). Seal Press is also the publisher of a similarly concise overview, Susan Stryker's *Transgender History* (2008). See also Martin Duberman, *Stonewall* (1993; New York: Plume, 1994).

A standard multicultural recent history of the United States has yet to be written, in part because an emphasis on racial and ethnic particularity resists master narratives. Though much broader than the purview of this chapter, the best synthesis remains Ron Takaki's *A Different Mirror: A History of Multicultural America* (1993; New York: Penguin, 2008). Takaki is also the author of *Strangers from a Different Shore: A History of Asian-Americans* (1989; New York: Little, Brown, 1998). Vine Deloria, Jr., captures the militant spirit of Native Americans in the 1960s in *Custer Died for Your Sins: An Indian Manifesto* (1969; Norman: University of Oklahoma Press, 1988). Felipe Fernandez-Armesto provides an intriguingly trans-historical approach to US Latinos in *Our America: A Hispanic History of the United States* (New York: Norton, 2014).

Notes

1 Richard Reeves, *President Kennedy: Profile of Power* (New York: Simon & Schuster, 1993), 139.
2 Reeves, 138–139.
3 JFK, Address Before Joint Session of Congress, May 25, 1961, http://www.jfklibrary.org/Asset-Viewer/xzw1gaeeTES6khED14P1Iw.aspx (May 21, 2014).
4 JFK, Speech at Rice University, September 12, 1961, http://www.jfklibrary.org/Asset-Viewer/MkATdOcdU06X5uNHbmqm1Q.aspx (May 21, 2014).
5 http://gizmodo.com/5805457/kennedys-crazy-moon-speech-and-how-we-could-have-landed-on-the-moon-with-the-soviets (May 21, 2014); Chaikin, 2.
6 Chaikin, xiii, 80–81.
7 Chaikin, 212–213; John Noble Wilford, "*Men Walk on the Moon,*" *The New York Times,* July 21, 1969, nytimes.com (May 24, 2014).
8 Chaikin, 212.
9 Chaikin, 336.
10 See, for example, Robert A. Divine et al., *America Past & Present* (New Jersey: Upper Saddle River, multiple editions). Neither James Patterson in *Grand Expectations: The United States, 1945–1974* (New York: Oxford University Press, 1996) nor Joshua Freeman, *American Empire: The Rise of a Global Power/The Democratic Revolution at Home, 1945–2000* (New York: Penguin, 2012) have entries in the index.
11 Freeman, 227, 230.
12 Letter from Jack Swender in *Dear America: Letters Home from Vietnam, edited by Bernard Edelman* (1985; New York: Norton, 2002), 205; Patterson, 608.
13 Patterson, 602.
14 Patterson, 595.
15 Freeman, 231–232.
16 John Morton Blum, *Years of Discord, 1961–1974* (New York: Norton, 1991), 238; Branch, *At Canaan's Edge: America in the King Years* (New York: Simon & Schuster, 2007), 206.
17 Blum, 239.
18 Blum, 247.
19 Branch, 72.
20 Branch, 475–486.
21 Branch, 511. See also the YouTube footage of King's remarks.

22 Martin Luther King, Jr., testimony to the US Senate Committee on Government Operations, December 15, 1966, in *The United States Since 1945: A Documentary Reader*, edited by Robert P. Ingalls and David K. Johnson (Malden, MA: Wiley-Blackwell, 2009), 85.

23 Branch, 23.

24 Branch, 483.

25 Martin Luther King, Jr., *A Testament of Hope: The Essential Writings and Speeches*, edited by James M. Washington (San Francisco: Harper San Francisco), 238.

26 Branch, 305.

27 Patterson, 609; Branch, 16.

28 Patterson, 616.

29 Letter of Philip Woodall in Edelman, *Dear America*, 214.

30 David Garrow, *Bearing the Cross: Martin Luther King and the Southern Christian Leadership Council* (1987; New York: Morrow, 2004), 598. Branch as King saying something similar on pp. 696–697.

31 Blum, 294; Freedman, 245.

32 The best book about the Johnson–RFK relationship is Jeff Shesol's *Mutual Contempt: Lyndon Johnson, Robert Kennedy, and the Feud that Defined a Decade* (New York: Norton, 1997).

33 King, *A Testament of Hope*, 286.

34 http://www.jfklibrary.org/Research/Research-Aids/Ready-Reference/RFK-Speeches/Statement-on-the-Assassination-of-Martin-Luther-King.aspx (May 27, 2014).

35 Patterson, 716.

36 Michael Kazin, *The Populist Persuasion: An American History* (New York: Basic, 1995), 224–225, 240; Wills, *Nixon Agonistes*, 49–50.

37 Sean Wilentz, *The Age of Reagan: An American History* (New York: Harper, 2008), 22.

38 https://www.youtube.com/watch?v=lo9FlPeKKzA (May 27, 2014).

39 Wills, Nixon, *Agonistes*, 583 ff; Richard Nixon, Republican nomination acceptance speech, August 8, 1968, in Ingalls & Johnson, 168.

40 "National Organization, Statement of Purpose," 1966, in Ingalls & Johnson, 141.

41 The King and Hayden memo can be accessed at http://www.uic.edu/orgs/cwluherstory/CWLUArchive/memo.html (November 12, 2014).

42 Jo Freeman, "No More Miss America": http://www.jofreeman.com/photos/MissAm1969.html (November 12, 2014). The piece, from the site of the well-known feminist scholar, includes photographs of the event.

43 This taxonomy is sketched out by feminist scholar Alison Jaggar, quoted Freedman, 72. Freedman uses it throughout *No Turning Back*.

44 Kathie Sarachild, "Consciousness-Raising: A Radical Weapon" (1973), in Ingalls & Johnson, 147.

45 Carl Wittman, "Refugees from Amerika: A Gay Manifesto," 1969, in Ingalls & Johnson, 151.

46 An excerpt of Uyematsu's essay is available at http://www.dartmouth.edu/~hist32/Hist33/Uyematsu.PDF (June 18, 2015); for more on the Yellow Power movement, see Shelley Sang-Hee Lee, *A New History of Asian America* (New York: Routledge, 2014), 298–301.

47 Dennis Banks memoir in Ingalls & Johnson, 124; Nicole Lapin and Jason Hanna, "1969 Takeover Incident Changed the Course of History," CNN.com, November 20, 2009: http://www.cnn.com/2009/CRIME/11/20/alcatraz.indian.occupation (June 1, 2014); Patterson, 722–723.

48   Banks, 123; Patterson, 642–643.

49   Patterson, 577–578.

50   Excerpt from Rachel Carson's 1962 book *Silent Spring* in Ingalls & Johnson, 130.

51   John Kerry, Congressional statement, Vietnam Veterans Against the War, May 4, 1971, in Ingalls & Johnson, 103.

52   Michael Lind, *The Next American Nation: The New Nationalism and the Fourth American Revolution* (New York: Basic, 1995), 188.

53   Schell, *The Time of Illusion: An Historical and Reflective Account of the Nixon Era* (1975; New York: Vintage, 1976), 47–49.

54   Woodward & Bernstein, *All the President's Men*, 127.

55   Rick Perlstein, *The Invisible Bridge: The Fall of Nixon and the Rise of Reagan* (New York: Simon & Schuster, 2014), 236.

56   Chaikin, 577–578.

57   William W., "The Flags We Left on the Moon Have All Turned White," *Space Industry News*, July 20, 2012: http://spaceindustrynews.com/the-american-flags-we-left-on-the-moon-have-all-turned-white/: (June 7, 2014).

5

Experimentation and Exhaustion
Political Culture of the Sixties, 1965–1975

Figure 5.1 STARDUST: (Notably young) adolescents at Woodstock, August 18, 1969. The 3-day festival symbolized the charm—and, for some, the squalor—of the hippie life as the 1960s drew to a close, one that would have a significant influence on subsequent generations. Photo by Rick Manning, used under Creative Commons CC BY 3.0 (http://creativecommons.org/licenses/by/3.0), via Wikimedia Commons.

Democratic Empire: The United States Since 1945, First Edition. Jim Cullen.
© 2017 Jim Cullen. Published 2017 by John Wiley & Sons, Inc.

The Great Divide: Establishment and Counterculture

PURE VENOM.

When Bob Dylan released "Masters of War," a song from his 1963 album *The Freewheelin' Bob Dylan*, he was rapidly emerging as one of the leading figures in folk music, a genre that was at its peak of influence. Of course, for much of US history, folk music *was* American music, but, in the late 1950s and early 1960s, it emerged as a self-conscious counterpoint to what its fans considered the crass commercialism of rock and roll and other forms of popular song. Folk was celebrated for its deceptive simplicity and emotional directness, which Dylan endowed with a new intensity. Sometimes this was a matter of injecting a psychological edge into love songs, as in the surprising passive-aggression of "Don't Think Twice, It's Alright" ("you could have done better, but I don't mind," goes one typical line). Other times, it was a matter of crafting inspiring generational anthems such as "Blowin' in the Wind." In some cases, his social commentary was more direct, as in "Oxford Town," his account of James Meredith's attempt to desegregate the University of Mississippi (though he doesn't mention Meredith or Ole Miss directly); in others, it was oblique, as in his allusive "A Hard Rain's Gonna Fall," which many listeners interpreted as a song about nuclear war. Dylan was always a little cagey in the writing of his songs and the way he talked about them, a strategy that contributed to his mystique—which, for those who were young in the 1960s, was, and remains, enormous.

But in its stark, unbridled anger, "Masters of War" is in a class by itself. Dylan himself understood it this way. As he explained to critic Nat Hentoff in the album's liner notes, "I've never written anything like that before. I don't sing songs which hope people will die, but I couldn't help it with this one."

As with many early Dylan songs, "Masters of War" derives its melody from traditional sources, in this case, the English folk song "Nottamun Town." It's written as a waltz, a rhythm associated with stately dancing. But here that time signature takes on an ironic edge—the dance here is a dance of death—particularly when coupled with the contempt that saturates Dylan's voice. "Come you masters of war," he sneers, listing the guns, planes, bombs, and walls orchestrated by men behind desks. Comparing them directly to Judas and indirectly to vampires, "Masters of War" is a rant of unvarnished hatred. "I'll stand o'er your graves 'til I'm sure that you're dead," he concludes.

As with most of Dylan's political commentary, "Masters of War" does not name a specific target. But observant listeners at the time would have known what he was talking about. "It's speaking against what Eisenhower was calling a military industrial complex as he was making his exit from the presidency," Dylan explained many years later. "That spirit was in the air, and I picked it up."[1]

But one of the things that made Dylan such an exceptional artist was his uncanny way not simply of picking up what was in the air, but in anticipating how the climate was about to change. As he would later sing in his classic 1965 song "Subterranean Homesick Blues," "You don't need to be a weatherman to know which way the wind blows." (An American antiwar terrorist organization of the late 1960s and 1970s, the Weather Underground, took their name from the tune.) The basic critique Dylan was articulating had been widespread in intellectual circles in the late 1950s, notably in the work of sociologist C. Wright Mills. Dylan gave it an arresting sense of currency and literally provided a voice of protest as the Vietnam War became an increasing source of unease and anger in the second half of 1960s.

But "Masters of War" was more resonant still. In suggesting the interlocking set of public and private elites who operated without the knowledge, much less the approval, of the American people, Dylan was describing a concept that would attain extraordinary credibility and currency in the 1960s: "the Establishment."

Though frequently invoked, the Establishment, a term that first entered usage in Great Britain in the late 1950s and migrated to the United States over the course of the next decade,[2] was rarely defined in these years, and indeed no official definition existed. But, in the broadest sense, it referred to traditional institutions in American society—government in its many forms (especially the military); big business (especially global corporations); mainstream churches (and related institutions such as the traditional family)—and the people in charge of them. The rising tide of opposition to the Establishment, much of it consisting of young people, was known collectively as "the counterculture." This, too, could be diffuse, encompassing civil rights activists, war protesters, and less politicized individuals who were labeled, often imprecisely, as "hippies," heirs of the 1950s beatniks recognizable for their long hair, unconventional clothes, and insider language. The conflict between the Establishment and the counterculture, broadly construed, was at the center of the social history of the nation in the decade between the mid-1960s and mid-1970s, a period, usefully, if imprecisely, referred to as "the sixties."

Before going any further in trying to chronicle this social divide, however, it's important to note that a more general collision of two powerful social forces— we'll call them institutionalism and anti-institutionalism—had been the driving engine of US history long before Bob Dylan came along. (In the 1960s, the Establishment represented the latest manifestation of institutionalism, and the counterculture was the latest manifestation of anti-institutionalism.) All societies exhibit tensions between established authority and those who, individually and collectively, resist such authority. But in few societies have challengers to such authority enjoyed as much social sanction, and drawn on as many resources, as those in the United States, in ways that ranged from the Puritans who rebelled against the Church of England (itself a rebellion against the Catholic Church), the Founding Fathers of the American Revolution, or the Confederates who seceded from the Union during the Civil War.

This was never the whole story, however. There have also been *pro*-institutional moments in US history, where Americans actively embraced government power as a solution to social problems, as Federalists did in the early years of the

Republic, abolitionists did during the Civil War, Progressives did in the early twentieth century, and New Dealers did during the Great Depression. Actually, the period between 1930s and the mid-1960s represents the longest stretch of institutional power and confidence in all of American history. Such was its potency that many of the people who lived through it tended to think that this was a fixed norm rather than an unusually high tide.

But, even at the height of twentieth-century institutionalism, alternating currents—those of the left as well as the right—were apparent. Manifestations of them included Beat poetry, rock and roll, and political insurgencies that ranged from the segregationists who rebelled against Harry Truman in the presidential election of 1948 to the racial militancy of Malcolm X in the late 1950s and early 1960s. For the most part, however, the mainstream civil rights movement was decisively institutional, not only in its commitment to religious organizations (as indeed was Malcolm X), but also in its reliance on the federal government to combat the entrenched resistance of states' rights advocates, who often defined their identities in opposition to national power.

So, in some very important ways, the counterculture that began to assume a distinct shape in the mid-1960s was simply the latest chapter in a very old story. In fact, some historians have seen it in essentially religious terms—the most recent of a wave of anti-institutional revivals that challenged prevailing orthodoxies: the First Great Awakening in the mid-eighteenth century; the Second Great Awakening in the early nineteenth century; and the Fundamentalist movement at the turn of the twentieth century.[3] The counterculture was certainly different from earlier ones in its orientation—it looked more to Eastern religions and altered states of consciousness that resembled some Native American practices than to mainstream Christianity—but the notion of spiritual regeneration was central. For its proponents, the 1960s marked the advent of the (astrological) Age of Aquarius—the title of a popular 1969 song—reflected in the newfound prominence of mind-altering drugs, colorful clothes, peace signs, and other symbols of the era. It should be noted, however, that two of the biggest musicals of the era, *Godspell* and *Jesus Christ, Superstar* (both 1971), tapped into conventional religious narratives, albeit in a self-consciously modern way.

The impact of the counterculture was uneven, and it didn't happen all at once. For many Americans, especially in the nation's interior, everyday life in 1964 was not much different from what it had been 10 years earlier. And for a great many, life in 1974 wasn't all that much different, either. Perhaps a personal anecdote would help here. When I was a child on suburban Long Island in the early 1970s, I had a newly married babysitter who lived in a basement apartment down the street. I considered her and her husband almost impossibly glamorous: they were young, good-looking, openhearted people with an infectious sense of confidence. She had been a singer in a rock band; he had played guitar (and had seen the Beatles live in their legendary Shea stadium concerts). By the early 1970s, he was a junior executive at IBM, and the couple's membership privileges at the local country club I often visited gave me many happy childhood memories. Many years later, when I had received an education that allowed me to understand such things, I found myself in their house gazing upon a framed copy of their wedding invitation alongside a photo from the ceremony, which took place in the summer of 1968. This was one of the most agonizing moments in American history, a time of rioting, assassination, and general social upheaval. And yet, here was a pair of upwardly mobile young people about to launch a happy life that would include four children and a general sense of affluence associated with the American Dream. I don't want to sentimentalize these people; they all had their struggles, and my babysitter was killed many years later in an accident on the Long Island Expressway. But their lives suggest the ways in which individual experiences both reflect as well as complicate larger historical narratives.

At the center of this particular narrative is the sense of affluence that dominated US life in the decades following World War II. Even for those who lacked it, a sense of economic plenty was in the air and decisively shaped expectations. The American economy expanded steadily between 1961 and 1969, a stretch of growth that was part of a much larger trajectory of economic expansion since 1945. Industrial production came close to doubling over the course of the decade; the nation's unemployment rate was a mere 3.8% in 1966, and inflation was minimal (the story would be very different a decade later). The growth of the economy was also decisively shaped by the growth of the government *in* the economy. Government expenditure as a percentage of the gross national product had been 12.4% in 1940. It reached 28.1% in 1960, 30% in 1965, and would continue growing for the rest of the century.[4]

Such material realities had important psychological consequences. One is reminded of a passage from Ralph Waldo Emerson's classic 1841 essay "Self Reliance": "The nonchalance of boys who are sure of a dinner, and would disdain as much as a lord to do or say aught to conciliate one, is the healthy attitude of human nature."[5] Many Americans took national affluence for granted, and they took the government's role in fostering that growth for granted as well.

Perhaps paradoxically, this perception of pervasive economic security lay at the foundation of the powerful spiritual longings of the 1960s, from the aching hopes of the Port Huron Statement in 1962 to the Hindu ashrams scattered across the country a decade later. Precisely because they did not fear finding decent-paying jobs, millions of Americans, especially young ones, were determined to avoid the rat race and establish a more authentic basis for their lives, whether in terms of family, sexuality, or other arrangements. The demographic friction between parents, many of whom had experienced the insecurities of the Great Depression, and their children was referred to as "the generation gap," a term that was commonly used to explain the unease surrounding changes of the time.

In 1967, Guy Strait, the publisher of an alternative newspaper in San Francisco—ground zero of the fabled Summer of Love—explained the new hippie ethos. "Many people cannot understand the hippies' rejection of everything that is commonly expected of the individual in regard to employment and life goals: steady lucrative employment, and the accumulation through the years of possessions and money, building (always building) security for the future,"

Strait wrote. "It is precisely this security hypochondria, *this checking of bank books rather than pulses*, this worrying over budgets instead of medicine cabinets, that drives the youth of today away."[6] A 1967 Beatles song titled "She's Leaving Home," which depicts a well-cared-for young woman fleeing her parents, encapsulated this idea: "fun is the one thing that money can't buy." Subsequent generations of young people would be less confident about that.

This uniquely 1960s form of idealism did not only confuse and anger more traditional Americans; it also frustrated older generations of radicals who had grounded their social critiques much closer to orthodox Marxism. Cultural critic Morris Dickstein has noted the "the most striking quality of the cultural life of the sixties, the combination of political militancy and cultural bohemianism."[7] Dickstein noted that such militancy and bohemianism had been present in earlier radical movements, which, similar to the counterculture, had availed itself of the insights of Marx and (especially) Sigmund Freud. But while earlier followers had focused on what might be termed the darker insights of these monumental thinkers—the emphasis on limited resources and the imperatives of repression central to both mass politics and individual psychology—a newer wave of intellectuals, among them Herbert Marcuse and Norman O. Brown, believed that new technologies of mass production meant that such repressive mechanisms could be cast aside if only young people were willing to recognize their freedom and act on it.

One of the most prominent proponents of what this might mean was Harvard University psychologist Timothy Leary. In the early 1960s, Leary began experimenting with lysergic acid diethylamide (LSD), which he argued offered revolutionary possibilities for dealing with seriously mentally ill people such as alcoholics and psychopaths. (History may prove Leary at least partially correct: LSD is now used cautiously to treat some army veterans suffering from posttraumatic stress disorder.) Leary was ultimately fired from Harvard, but became an internationally famous proponent of hallucinogenic drug use, famously urging followers to "turn on, tune in, and drop out." In so doing, he argued, LSD would open the doors of perception, loosen inhibitions, and allow users to create a new relationship to reality for themselves. In the years that followed, millions of Americans would experiment with LSD, along with milder drugs such as marijuana (long in circulation, but now increasingly widespread) and more powerful mind-altering ones such as amphetamines and opioids such as heroin, both of which remained on the fringes of society. These latter two classes of drugs were dangerously addictive, and while ingesting LSD often resulted in experiencing euphoria, there was also always the risk of a "bad trip." So while there has long been what might be termed the dominant narrative of recreational drugs serving a liberating role for young people of the 1960s and ever since, there has also been a counter-narrative of its dangers, which were painfully embodied in the deaths of iconic figures such as rock stars Jimi Hendrix, Janis Joplin, and Jim Morrison (to say nothing of later figures ranging from comedian John Belushi to pop star Whitney Houston).

Another phrase often attributed to Leary was "think for yourself and question authority." Less original, and less quickly associated with him, the phrase nevertheless captures something fundamental about the spirit of the 1960s. It was a time when virtually all forms of authority came into question in the United States. Public institutions such as schools, businesses, and the military experienced challenges to their legitimacy, as did traditional understandings of marriage, childhood, and (hetero)sexuality. While this anti-institutional tide receded in the 1970s and (especially) in the 1980s, the impact of such questioning resulted in dramatic changes in terms of what it meant to be a student, soldier, worker, spouse, parent, or lover. We live with those changes—changes most of us regard as for the better, even if the costs have not been fully tallied—to this day.

It should be emphasized that the wave of anti-institutionalism in national life, while clearly rooted in the rhythms of US history, was part of a larger antiauthoritarian shift in the Western world at the time. Student demonstrations took place in Paris as well as New York in 1968. Nor were such challenges limited to what was often dubbed "the free world." The Prague Spring of 1968 represented a defiant bid for liberalization in Soviet-dominated Czechoslovakia that thrilled freedom-loving people everywhere until Soviet tanks rolled in, as they did 2 years later in Poland. When athletes Tommie Smith and John Carlos raised their fists in a Black Power salute after finishing first and third respectively in the 200-meter race during the 1968 Olympics in Mexico City, the gesture was widely understood as an international statement for human rights and against colonialism globally as well as within the United States. One of the great culture heroes of the 1960s was the Argentine-born doctor-turned-revolutionary Ernesto "Che" Guevara, an architect of the Cuban Revolution who left Cuba to foment Marxist revolution in the Congo and Bolivia. It was there he was captured and killed by the CIA-backed Bolivian army in 1967. Che, as he was known, was lionized long after his death all over the world as well as by radicals in the United States, and his iconic face continues to appear on vintage t-shirts.

(de)Construction Sites: The Rise of Postmodernism

It was in the realm of culture more than politics that anti-institutionalism made its deepest and longest-lasting impact. Beginning in the 1960s, a new term entered the international cultural lexicon: "postmodernism." As its suggests, postmodernism was an outgrowth of modernism, the broad cultural movement that emerged in the early twentieth century. Modernism, too, had represented a bold challenge to established authorities in all the arts, overturning established conventions such as narrative in fiction, melody in music, and the premise of suspended disbelief in theater (shattered by techniques such as breaking through the so-called fourth wall and addressing the audience directly).

Modernism and postmodernism differed in some crucial respects. One was in its stance toward the past. While the characteristic injunction of modernism was, in the words of the expatriate American poet Ezra Pound, to "make it new," postmodernists did not really believe this was possible. Instead, they focused on recombining elements of the past into arresting combinations, using references to other works ("intertextuality") to make commentary designed to reframe our notion of the present.

For our purposes, what matters most about postmodernism is the way in which it democratized our notions of culture, taking apart, or "deconstructing," the often avowedly elitist aspects of modernism. Indeed, postmodernism was concerned—some would say obsessed—first and foremost with relations of power, and the way in which what is presumed to be "normal" is really a way of trying to justify a status quo that serves the interests of a relatively small number of people. Against this, postmodernism promoted a new interest in, and respect for, "low" art forms that ranged from street signage to comic books, in part because postmodernists were always on the lookout for that which would subvert a presumably oppressive status quo.

In highlighting the way in which meaning is constructed through conscious choice and reordering existing arrangements, postmodernism also had a profound impact on individuals' notions of themselves. In the words of one scholar, "postmodern thought, in attacking the idea of a notional center or dominant ideology, facilitated the promotion of a politics of difference. Under postmodern conditions, the ordered class politics preferred by socialists has given way to a far more diffuse and pluralistic identity politics, which often involves the self-conscious assertion of marginalized identity against the dominant discourse."[8]

We've already seen how this dynamic has played itself out in arenas such as the civil rights and women's movements of the 1960s. But its implications for American culture were also more broadly profound. Just as the electoral and social upheavals of the decade affected much of subsequent US history, so did the artistic ferment of the time.

The most vivid illustration of the way in which postmodernism shaped American culture in the late twentieth century can be seen, literally, in modern painting, in particular the subgenre known as "pop art." Andy Warhol became internationally famous for his *Campbell's Soup Cans*, a canvas he completed in 1962. Sometimes seen as a critique of mass-produced capitalism—though Warhol famously professed himself to be apolitical—the painting reveals a fascination with everyday American life and the interpenetration of so-called reality and constructed experience, a fascination that would be further reflected in later Warhol paintings of pop culture icons such as Marilyn Monroe, Elizabeth Taylor, and Elvis Presley. Jasper Johns explored the surprising complexity and depth of the American flag in a series of works in the 1950s and 1960s; Roy Lichtenstein drew inspiration from comic strips for his own far more complex paintings of the 1960s.

System Failure: The Reorganization of Hollywood

Some of the postmodern/anti-institutional turn was a matter of content: songs, movies, shows, books, and other works of popular culture. But some was a matter of structure as well, including the organization of entire culture industries.

One very good example was the US movie business of the 1960s. After peaking in the late 1940s, Hollywood faced a series of cultural and commercial challenges that resulted in a distinct loss of power and influence in the culture at large. A big part of the reason for this lay in legal challenges to the very foundations of the studio system, in which the executives of major Hollywood studios essentially controlled every step of the process, from commissioning scripts to delivering movies to theaters (which they also owned). A series of lawsuits in the 1940s and 1950s weakened this authority, with power increasingly passing to movie stars and the agents who represented them.

While this was going on, the movies also faced a powerful challenge from television. Initially, studios adapted to the new order by offering experiences that couldn't easily be replicated on television, with gimmicks such as 3D movies and big visual extravaganzas such as *Ben-Hur* (1959) and *Lawrence of Arabia* (1962). Sometimes this worked; other times (such as the 1963 flop *Cleopatra*, featuring the superstar Elizabeth Taylor and her husband Richard Burton), it failed, or, in the slang of the time, "bombed." But, over time, the movie business made its peace with the television business as it became clear that television networks were voracious for content and willing to pay for old films, B movies, and shorts such as cartoons along with recent box office successes.

Financial maneuvers were one thing; political maneuvers were another. Hollywood struggled to keep up with political developments such as the civil rights movement, the women's movement, and the Vietnam War. Earnest efforts to grapple with civil rights, such as the interracial drama *Guess Who's Coming to Dinner?* (1967), became cringe-inducing in their conservatism within a few years, replaced by far more confrontational "blaxploitation" films such as *Shaft* (1971) and *Super Fly* (1972), which explored African American life on more avowedly black (though still sexist) terms. With notable exceptions such as Gordon Parks and his son Gordon Parks, Jr., who directed *Shaft* and *Super Fly*, respectively, African Americans and women continued to be underrepresented in power positions in the film industry, something that would only barely begin to change at the end of the century.

That such movies were made at all reflected a Hollywood culture in transition—a crisis of confidence among established filmmakers giving way to those who had new ideas with which to experiment. The studio system had not only collapsed in terms of its structure; it had also lost its way in its ability to tell credible stories to the newer audiences of the late twentieth century, as attested by colossal flops such as *Doctor Doolittle* (1967). In part, that was because American society was changing so rapidly. One important indication of this was the death of the Motion Picture Production Code, which had limited what could been seen and said onscreen, replaced by a ratings system, which has continued in modified form to this day as G, PG, R, and X ratings. Notwithstanding such classifications, American movies now exhibited an unprecedented level of frankness, reflected in the success of *Midnight Cowboy* (1969), the only X-rated film to ever win an Academy Award for Best Picture, and the sexually explicit *Last Tango in Paris* (1972), both of which are relatively tame compared to what came later.

Indeed, it was amid the wreckage of what might be termed Old Hollywood that a New Hollywood began to take shape. It would come to its fullest flower in the 1970s, though the first indications of a renaissance were apparent by the late 1960s. A rising generation of American artists was influenced by foreign cinema, particularly the so-called French New Wave typified by the works of European directors such as Robert Bresson, Jean-Luc Godard, and François Truffaut. These directors, themselves influenced by post–World War II Italian neorealists such as Roberto Rossellini as well as generational successors such as Federico Fellini, broke accepted conventions of cinema by introducing post-modern accents through subjective points of view, informality in expression, and experiments in narrative pacing, lighting, and editing. Such influences were evident in the 1967 film *Bonnie and Clyde*, directed by Arthur Penn, in which Warren Beatty starred with Faye Dunaway. The film, which featured stylized violence new to American cinema, was based on a true-life tale of criminals on the run in the 1930s.

In very different ways, a more directly countercultural sensibility saturated two other generational touchstones of the decade, *The Graduate* (1967) and *Easy Rider* (1969). The former, a quintessential document of the generation gap, starred Dustin Hoffman as a restless young college graduate reluctantly enmeshed in an affair with one of his parent's friends when he's really in love with her daughter. *Easy Rider* starred Peter Fonda and Dennis Hopper as two hippies who successfully wrap up a drug deal and use the money to embark on a long motorcycle ride from the west coast to New Orleans, in time for Mardi Gras. Its unexpected commercial success suggested future possibilities for American cinema in the 1970s (see sidebar in Chapter 4).

Medium Dominant: Television

Television was not as badly shaken by the 1960s as the movie business was. A relatively new medium, it was coming into its own as the dominant form of popular culture in the second half of the twentieth century. Central to its power was the concept of broadcasting: the capacity to reach large numbers of people simultaneously in real time. Radio was a pioneer in this regard, but television took it to a whole new (visual) level. Sometimes this was a matter of television's ability to show Americans the news as it was happening. The McCarthy hearings of 1954 had indicated the potential of television news to compel national attention, and so did the Cuban Missile Crisis in 1962. But the Kennedy assassination in 1963 is widely regarded as the moment when it had become an indispensable element of everyday life. In the years that followed, a number of other events—the Vietnam War, the moon landing, the Watergate hearings—were witnessed and, to a great degree, shaped by the shared experience of watching them live.

Television cast a similar spell in the entertainment realm. Approximately 73 million people—over one-third of the US population at the time—watched the

Beatles appear on *The Ed Sullivan Show* in February 1964. Popular shows at the time, such as the perennial *Gunsmoke* (a Western that ran from 1955 to 1975) or *Mission: Impossible* (an action-adventure series featuring a team of young government secret agents that ran between 1966 and 1973, later becoming the basis of a successful movie franchise) enjoyed audiences many times larger than any television program today. These were prime time shows that were broadcast between 7 and 11 pm; it was during the 1960s that television programming was routinely available, especially in genres such as daytime dramas (also known as soap operas) and game shows, which were generally cheap to make and highly profitable. So were reruns of older shows that introduced subsequent generations to *The Honeymooners* and *I Love Lucy*, which were installed in daily time slots.

For much of the 1960s, television entertainment seemed curiously immune to the cultural changes that ranged around it, even when those changes were depicted as part of news programming. That's because, as a medium that required a lot of money, and therefore a lot of risk, the people who ran networks were reluctant to take chances in offending anyone—especially advertisers, who, if anything, were even more sensitive to backing anything that might damage their reputations. One of the most popular shows of the decade was *The Beverly Hillbillies* (1962–1971), a situation-comedy about a poor backwoods family that strikes it rich in the oil business and brings its cornpone ways to Southern California. Shows with narrative gimmicks—genial Martians, monsters, and talking animals—were popular, as was *Gilligan's Island* (1964–1967), about a motley crew of castaways on a Pacific island, or *I Dream of Jeannie* (1965–1970), in which a well-intentioned and beautiful genie upends a NASA astronaut's life. These shows would continue in reruns for many decades, giving millions of Americans of subsequent generations a somewhat misleading, though indirectly revealing, indication of what the 1960s were about. Other shows, such as *Star Trek* (1966–1969), were short-lived as prime time fare, but enjoyed huge success in reruns and subsequent cultural tie-ins such as books and movies. A parable of liberal tolerance, *Star Trek* featured a diverse crew of professionals undertaking an exploratory mission on the USS *Enterprise*. In one of the show's most famous episodes, its screenwriters sidestepped feared objections over the first interracial kiss to be shown on television by depicting it as the result of forced telekinesis.

Despite such aversion to controversy, there were tentative efforts to acknowledge social changes, for fear that the failure to do so would prove even more risky. African Americans were hardly new to the medium by the late 1960s, but *Julia* (1968–1971), starring Diahann Carroll as a nurse, was the first show to depict black life on anything resembling realistic terms. Sitcoms edged tentatively toward new realities for women in *That Girl* (1966–1971), which starred Marlo Thomas (as a single, though engaged, woman living on her own), and changes in family structure with *The Brady Bunch* (1969–1974), which depicted a blended family, albeit one blended by the marriage of a widow and widower rather than divorce.

And then something surprising happened: television got real—admittedly, a relative term. In particular, three new sitcoms that went on the air in the early 1970s inaugurated what many consider the golden age of the genre. The first of these to debut, *The Mary Tyler Moore Show* (1970–1977) was a milestone for women in television. Mary Tyler Moore was already well-known to television audiences for her role as a suburban housewife on *The Dick Van Dyke Show* (1961–1966), so when she reappeared as a single woman in Minneapolis pursuing a career in television news, she registered social change at face value. A second important sitcom of the era was *M*A*S*H* (1972–1983), a seriocomic saga based on a 1970 movie about paramedics during the Korean War that effectively functioned as an allegory for the Vietnam War. By the time the show was on the air, the latter had become deeply unpopular with the American public, and its mordant wit helped establish a persistent skepticism that affected perceptions of that war long after it ended. Finally, and perhaps most importantly, there was *All in the Family* (1971–1979), starring Carroll O'Connor as bigoted dockworker Archie Bunker, and Jean Stapleton as his dim-witted but lovable wife Edith. *All in the Family* grappled with big issues—racism, abortion, marital tension, and generational conflict—in ways that had never really been broached before in the genre. Developed by the liberal–Jewish Norman Lear and his partner Bud Yorkin, the show was based on a British sitcom called *Till Death Us Do Part* (1965–1975). Characters in *All in the Family* also became the source of a series of Yorkin–Lear spin-offs, among them *Maude* (1972–1978), featuring Edith's salty-tongued cousin (played by Bea Arthur), and *The Jeffersons* (1975–1985), about an upwardly mobile African American family who had been neighbors of the Bunkers.

Fit Print: Publishing

While the movie business and, to a lesser degree, television struggled amid the currents of the 1960s, other media embraced change with greater enthusiasm, even if the results weren't always successful in terms of audience support. The publishing industry was always relatively small compared to other culture industries, though it got larger due to accelerating tendencies toward corporate consolidation. The major format innovation of the time was the introduction of the trade paperback, a kind of midpoint between hardcover titles and the rack-sized paperback. Trade paper books, which were most successfully sold in the rapidly expanding college market, tended to have more intellectual substance than traditional paperbacks, costing more but still a good value compared with the newly published hardcover books. Trade paperbacks were an important vehicle for spreading some of the most influential ideas of the era, especially because titles in that format tended to stay in print for many years.

American novelists of the 1960s broke new ground in two major directions. The first was in terms of content. Ambitious literary artists always challenge their audiences, and this was as true in the 1950s as any other time, when writers such as John Cheever and Philip Roth chafed against the stifling conformity of the early postwar era. But, beginning in the 1960s, American writers waded more decisively into topics that had been largely regarded as taboo, whether in terms of subject matters or who wrote about them. A good example was William Styron's 1967 novel *The Confessions of Nat Turner*, based on the memoirs of the famous slave insurrectionist. Styron was not only controversial for the graphic violence and its positive portrayal of some slave owners in the novel, but also—perhaps more decisively—for writing as a white man who imagined himself into a black man's life, a questionable move as the civil rights movement was taking more of a separatist turn. The legacy of the early women's movement was apparent in Erica Jong's bestselling 1973 novel *Fear of Flying*, which frankly portrayed the sexual desire of women in a positive way (a catchphrase of the novel, "the zipless fuck," entered common parlance).

The more important legacy of the 1960s in American literary history, however, was innovation in the *form* of the novel. For the most part, these experimental writers did not become rich or famous, though they had long careers and achieved durable influence. Once again, the changes they promoted were rooted in the modernist tradition, though again, they avoided, if not punctured, the grand sense of transgression that marked the high modernism of early-twentieth-century writers such as T. S. Eliot. Perhaps the most important of these writers was Thomas Pynchon, who—in a series of novels that included *V.* (1963), *The Crying of Lot 49* (1966), and, especially, *Gravity's Rainbow* (1973)—thrilled and confounded readers with his dense, fragmented approach to storytelling. No one pushed harder against the boundaries of narrative art than short story writer Donald Barthelme, many of whose pieces appeared in *The New Yorker* in the 1960s and 1970s. Barthelme's stories were often quite short—he is considered a founding father of "flash fiction" or short stories that run for a page or two—and confound expectations of a beginning, middle, and end. A similar sense of playfulness and/or irony characterized the work of Robert Coover, whose 1968 novel *The Universal Baseball Association, Inc., J. Henry Waugh, Prop.* depicted a hapless accountant who takes refuge in a virtual world of his own creation, ruled by the roll of three dice. If your identity was little more than what other people convinced you of what it was, why not make up your own?

Though she did much of her path-breaking work in the 1970s and 1980s, African American novelist Toni Morrison was decisively shaped by the 1960s. Her first novel, *The Bluest Eye*, was published in 1970. A tragic tale about a young girl brutalized by incestuous rape, the novel reflected Morrison's characteristic way of rendering the civil rights era through the prism of ordinary African Americans who deal with private struggles against historical landscapes that would prove increasingly panoramic. Morrison drew on techniques associated with modernist master William Faulkner—multiple points of view, deliberate withholding of plot elements, scrambled chronology—and transfigured them to tell stories of people and perspectives that had been long overlooked. Her 1973 novel *Sula* explored the theme of female friendship and the limits of social convention in the first half of the twentieth century. Her reach would only become more audacious in decades to come.

Kingdom of Rebels: The Reign of Rock

In terms of its immediate appeal and long-term influence, no cultural form was more successful in fusing form and content than the popular music of the 1960s. Similar to the publishing business, making and distributing music was a relatively low-cost proposition when compared with film or television, which allowed for more innovation. The most visible site for such innovation was rock and roll, which disseminated through two major channels: radio and records.

Both the radio and record industries underwent key technological changes that had major ramifications for their future direction, even if neither of those technologies was actually new. In the case of radio, this was the rise of frequency modulation (FM) as a competitor for amplitude modulation (AM) radio. In the 1950s and 1960s, as car rides increasingly became the way most Americans listened to radio, AM was the dominant technology, in part because it had the farthest geographic reach. In the mid-1960s, FM, which had originally been developed for television, became a viable radio format, offering higher fidelity than AM. Partly for this reason and partly to carve out its own identity, FM became less of a pop-driven format than AM, featuring longer tracks, less tight playlists, and a general air of experimentation (especially in the world of college radio, which flourished in the decades following the 1960s). By the early 1970s, some major rock acts were bypassing hit radio entirely, building their reputations on FM radio and relentless touring, which helped foster audiences for their records.

Meanwhile, the 33⅓-rpm long-playing (LP) record achieved parity with, and in some musical communities surpassed, 45-rpm records as the format of choice. The LP, which could hold a set of songs on each side of its vinyl disc instead of just one, made it possible to record longer songs as well as suites of songs: to borrow a photographic metaphor, it was possible to present an *album* of musical compositions, the whole of which was greater than the sum of its parts. One of the first artists to seize the possibilities of album-making was Frank Sinatra, a former teen idol of the 1940s who, in the 1950s, reinvented himself as a decidedly adult singer who released albums with a thematic focus, as in *Come Fly with Me* (songs about travel) in 1958 and *Frank Sinatra Sings for Only the Lonely* (songs of loss) later the same year. Albums also created new opportunities to showcase artists visually; poring over album covers and their liner notes became one of the most popular hobbies for adolescents of the 1960s and 1970s.

No one exploited these possibilities more fully and successfully than the Beatles. After scoring a string of hits in the first half of the decade, the Fab Four demonstrated an astonishing capacity for experimentation in musical styles, songwriting acumen, and their ability to exploit recording technology, thanks in no small measure to their producer, George Martin. A growing sense of critical excitement was evident at the release of *Rubber Soul* in 1965, and *Revolver*, with its unmistakable hints of drug use, in 1966. Both albums were notable for the way in which the band stretched thematically, instrumentally, and in manipulating sounds—an accelerated piano here, electronic tape looping there—in songs that remained as catchy as ever. The Beatles 1967 concept album *Sgt. Pepper's Lonely Hearts Club Band* is a landmark in the history of popular music, the record that fully legitimated rock as a form of serious artistic expression. *Sgt. Pepper's Lonely Hearts Club Band* arrived in San Francisco just when the hippie scene—and innovative bands such as the Grateful Dead and Jefferson Airplane, fronted by the charismatic Grace Slick—were coming to their own as an essential musical backdrop for the Summer of Love.

Recognizing which way the winds were blowing, Bob Dylan—who was still managing to stay a step ahead of the curve—took a page from the Beatles' book and adapted it to his own vision. In 1965, he did what many of his most dedicated fans regarded as unthinkable: he abandoned folk music for rock, documented in his rambling, thrillingly bitter hit song "Like a Rolling Stone," released that June, a preview of coming attractions from his landmark album *Highway 61 Revisited*, which came out in August. In July 1965, Dylan made what had become an annual trip to the Newport Folk Festival in Rhode Island, where he shocked fans with his electric-guitar-based performance. The hostile reaction he received has become part of musical lore. In his new rock mode, Dylan went on to follow *Highway 61 Revisited* with a string of subsequent records stretching from *Blonde on Blonde* (1966) to *Blood on the Tracks* (1974), which, while not uniformly celebrated, are nevertheless regarded as a durable part of the rock and roll canon.

In the mid-1960s, both the Beatles and Dylan had serious competition from the California-based Beach Boys, led by the brilliant, if psychologically unsteady, Brian Wilson. Similar to the Beatles, the Beach Boys had a string of light-hearted hits such as "Surfin' Safari" (1962) and "California Girls" (1965) in the first half of the decade. But Wilson was showing growing ambition and assertiveness in the studio, which culminated in his masterpiece *Pet Sounds* (1966). What really distinguished *Pet Sounds*—beyond its gorgeous melodies and the soaring harmonies that characterized the Beach Boys' signature sound—was a sense of melancholy, even depression, that cut against the deceptive innocence of the songs. So, for example, the protagonist in "Wouldn't It Be Nice" daydreams about the day he and his girlfriend might finally be able to spend the night together. He notes that the more they entertain such a scenario, the harder it becomes to live without it. "But let's talk about it," he concludes dreamily, embracing the exquisite ache while the backing vocalists sing in cheery voices that heighten the irony.

One track not included on *Pet Sounds* was also important: Wilson's "Good Vibrations," which became a smash hit when released as a single in 1966. As with many Beatles songs of the time, "Good Vibrations" suggested the influence of psychedelic drugs, which were becoming an increasingly important part of American musical culture. At its best, the spirit of experimentation promoted by drug use bent and stretched popular music in new directions, as when Beatle George Harrison developed an interest in Indian instruments, which became an important vector in the Beatles' sound in 1966–1967. It also fostered a sense of communalism that extended beyond music, captured in the tolerant spirit of the Woodstock Music Festival in 1969 and in some quarters of the antiwar movement.

By the late 1960s, however, it was becoming increasingly apparent that the drug culture of the 1960s had a dark side. Hailed as a form of liberation, it could also result in ruthlessly oppressive addiction. One obvious warning came from the litany of gifted musicians who succumbed to deadly addictions. Jimi Hendrix, a guitar prodigy who virtually reinvented the instrument, died from an overdose of barbiturates in 1970. (Hendrix's almost hideously distorted version of "The Star Spangled Banner," performed at the Woodstock Festival in 1969, has a twisted grandeur that makes it one of the greatest acts of musical interpretation of all time.) The death of Hendrix was followed 2 weeks later by that of Janis Jopin, a brilliant, if self-destructive, blues-based rock singer whose sense of self-assertion inspired generations of women to assert confidence as an act of faith. Jim Morrison, the alternatively spellbinding and overbearing lead singer of the Los Angeles-based band the Doors, also died of an overdose in 1971.

Actually, years before this happened, a kind of counter-narrative to the Flower Power sensibility had been emerging. The Doors positioned themselves as a musical alternative to the cheerier side of 1960s music, with songs such as the minor-chord-heavy "Light My Fire," and the 12-minute Oedipal epic titled "The End" (both 1967). A few months after the release of *Sgt. Pepper's Lonely Hearts Club Band*, the Rolling Stones responded with *Their Satanic Majesties Request*, a psychedelic-influenced album generally not regarded as among the band's finest. (One member of the band, Brian Jones, would also become a casualty to the drug culture of the time in 1969.) Even the Beatles dabbled in more gothic territory, as in their 1968 song "Helter Skelter." New bands, notably Black Sabbath and Led Zeppelin, achieved mass success in the early 1970s with brooding, even threatening, songs that foregrounded loud guitars, caterwauling vocals, and distortion in a rock subgenre known as heavy metal. Led Zeppelin's brooding, thunderous, blues-based sound would prove enormously influential.

These musical currents reflected a distinctly darker quality in the culture at large by the end of the 1960s. The pathologically charismatic cult leader Charles Manson cited "Helter Skelter" as the inspiration for a series of murders he orchestrated with his "family of followers," including that of the rising Hollywood star, Sharon Tate, in 1969. The widely celebrated Woodstock was followed by the Altamont Free Concert in Southern California, at which the Rolling Stones hired a motorcycle gang, Hell's Angels, for security. A series of fistfights resulted, as did the death of one man when he was stabbed after brandishing a pistol (he was high on methamphetamines at the time). Such events, which occurred against a backdrop of race riots in US cities and a raging—and expanding—Vietnam War abroad, contributed to a widespread feeling that the nation as a whole was, figuratively speaking, on a bad trip.

In response to such upheaval, a new mood was taking root in the country in the early 1970s, one that involved the rediscovery of simplicity in art as well as in life. As frustration grew in the country at large about the ability to achieve satisfying collective changes in society, individuals collectively turned inward: if they couldn't change the world, at least they could change themselves. One of the great publishing success stories of the early 1970s was Richard Bach's surprise bestseller *Jonathan Livingston Seagull*, a 1970 fable about a bird that overcomes crippling social conformity and materialism to achieve an authentic individualism rooted in his desire for flight. "The trick was for Jonathan to stop seeing himself as trapped inside a limited body that had a forty-two-inch wingspan that could be plotted on a chart," his mentor, the wise gull Chiang, explains at one point. "The trick was to know that his true nature lived, as perfect as an unwritten number, everywhere at once across space and time."[9] The vague Eastern spiritualism and environmentalist subtext for the story comported well with the age of Earth Day and the back-to-the-land movement that grew out of the hippie counterculture.

This new wrinkle in the counterculture reflected the anti-institutionalism that had been there all along. But it now indicated a splintering effect within the counterculture itself. For a while in an earlier part in the late 1960s, it was easy to believe that the civil rights advocates, antiwar protesters, and feminists were all part of the same bloc fighting the Establishment (which was never quite as unitary as its critics believed, either—the corporate executive and the good old boy didn't exactly see eye to eye, as George Wallace would have been the first to note). Someone aged over 30—the famous counterculture dividing line after which a person should not be trusted—could be forgiven for seeing all members of the counterculture as alike; for one thing, they tended to have long hair. This may sound like a mild joke, but in fact hair—title of a celebrated 1968 Broadway rock musical—was a major political statement at the time (as indeed it was for many African Americans before and since). But there was a big difference between, say, the acid-dropping dropout and the demonstrating political militant, each of whom increasingly viewed the other as unrealistic. "I'm just living my lifestyle," Joe McDonald, bandleader of the Woodstock favorite Country Joe and the Fish, told a reporter who suggested he was a revolutionary. "That's what you should be doing."[10] Sometimes, as already indicated, these tensions played themselves out *within* subcultures (as we've seen, feminism is a good example of this). But the fissures were also obvious *between* factions of the New Left coalition as well.

Once again, pop music offered a clear window into these developments, and, once again, the Beatles were at the vanguard. By 1968, they were less a band than a group of four songwriters who instrumentally backed each other's compositions. The baroque sounds of *Sgt. Pepper's Lonely Hearts Club Band* (and its less well-received follow-up, *Magical Mystery Tour*, in 1967) was followed by the so-called White Album, whose cover consisted of nothing but the band's name in small gray letters against a white background. The album contained Lennon's song "Revolution #1," which expressed skepticism about the political radicalism in which he himself had, and would, dabble. Telling those who would resort to violent tactics to achieve their aims to count him out, the song rhetorically asks, "Don't you know it's going to be all right?" Another version of the song (faster and more well known) was released as the B-side to the Beatles' hugely successful 1968 single "Hey Jude."

A new move toward simplicity showed up in other musical districts as well. The Rolling Stones returned to the blues base that served them so well in a critically acclaimed string of albums: *Let it Bleed* (1969), *Sticky Fingers* (1971), and, especially, *Exile on Main Street* (1972). Dylan, who had suffered a near-fatal motorcycle crash in 1966, returned to public life with *John Wesley Harding* (1967) and the even more rustic *Nashville Skyline* in 1969, an album that veered toward country music (under the apparent theory that it was so retro he could make it hip). In the years before that album, Dylan had been touring with a set of backup musicians, who in an act of simple audacity referred to themselves as The Band. Their first two albums without him, *Music from Big Pink* (1968) and *The Band* (1969), sounded like they could have been made a century earlier; indeed, the cover photo of the second album looked like it was shot during the Civil War. One of the songs from that record, "The Night They Drove Old Dixie Down," became a hit for Joan Baez in 1971. Though nominally a Confederate lament by a defeated rebel, the song was widely heard as an expression of individual resilience in the face of heartless, faceless, organized power, a mood that captured the way many people on the left were feeling at the time.

Actually, the old libertarian strain in Southern culture resurfaced in bands such as the Allman Brothers Band and Lynyrd Skynyrd, who formed a musical bridge between the hippie lifestyle that the Allmans lived by (and, in the case of the legendary guitarist Duane Allman, killed in a 1971 motorcycle accident, died by) and an older conservative mentality that had always viewed government skeptically. Lynyrd Skynyrd's 1974 hit "Sweet Home Alabama" chided liberals for their obsession with Watergate and tossed a barely veiled bouquet—"in Birmingham they love the governor"—to George Wallace, whose national career was built on attacks on big-government liberalism.

The increasingly melancholy vein of the 1970s culture spawned a new musical icon, the singer–songwriter. All these people working in this subgenre, which foregrounded soulful vocals and acoustic instruments, owed a debt to Dylan in one way or another, but as a group they tended toward a more confessional— some would say narcissistic—approach to their work. James Taylor, initially signed to the Beatles' Apple label, made his first records in the late 1960s, and by the early 1970s had become a major success. Joni Mitchell, a Canadian painter and musician, wedded a heartbreakingly pristine voice to searingly beautiful songs. Her 1971 album *Blue* is perhaps the best of the genre. The more mild-mannered Carole King had written a series of hit songs for African American and white artists with husband Gerry Goffin in the 1960s; after her divorce, she made *Tapestry* (1971), a pop perennial as well as feminist statement. Jackson Browne, a Southern California singer–songwriter who collaborated widely with colleagues who were part of "supergroups" such as the Eagles as well as Crosby, Stills, Nash & Young (CSNY), was part of this crowd. All these figures enjoyed multigenerational careers.

There were also signs of change in African American popular music. Some precincts tried to hold fast; Berry Gordy's Motown factory churned out pop hits straight through the decade that retain their freshness a half-century later. And Gordy revealed he still had tricks up his sleeve when he signed the Jackson Five, whose miraculous lead singer, Michael Jackson, cheered the world with singles such as "I Want You Back" (1969) and "ABC" (1970). But, as the 1960s wore on, there was increasing friction within the house of Motown, as major acts such as Marvin Gaye and Stevie Wonder chafed against Gordy's constraints (Wonder would go on to have a hugely successful career after leaving the company). Some of this reflected the politics of the time; Gaye's classic 1971 single and album *What's Going On* commented on the upheaval of the time. But it also reflected a desire to deepen African American engagement with black idioms, an impulse Gaye tapped in his huge hit "I Heard It Through the Grapevine" (1968), and to which Wonder would turn repeatedly in rhapsodic albums such as *Innervisions* (1973) and *Songs in the Key of Life* (1976).

By the late 1960s, the capital of African American music had shifted from Gordy's Motown Records in Detroit to Jim Stewart and Estelle's Axton's Stax Records—a fusion of their names—in Memphis, which became ground zero for the subgenre known as soul music. Soul drew on the energy of gospel music, but bent it in a secular direction, a sensibility that had been tapped to great effect by older artists such as the vastly influential James Brown. It sidestepped the slick catchiness of Motown in favor of an earthier, even ragged sound. Motown was sometimes described as African American music for white people, while soul was African American music for African Americans, a formulation that overlooks the appeal of both for both (and everyone else). But such cultural shorthand does reflect the less decisively integrationist ethos of soul music compared to that which had marked the African American music of the late 1950s and early 1960s, whether in Chuck Berry's lyrics or Smokey Robinson's singing and melodies. Many soul artists recorded for Turkish immigrant Ahmet Ertegun's Atlantic Records, which featured what was arguably the finest roster in pop music history, stretching from CSNY to Led Zeppelin (Atlantic also had a distribution deal with Stax). Among the most important soul artists on the label were Otis Redding, the duo Sam & Dave, and, especially, Aretha Franklin, who tapped her gospel background to record a string of hits, notable among them her feminist anthem "Respect" (1968), originally written by Redding but given a gendered twist with Franklin's reading of the song.

Unfortunately, the very diversity of this music—reflecting the growing diversity of American culture, and American society generally—brought with it a growing sense of fragmentation, segmentation, and, perhaps ironically, segregation. There were a series of reasons for this. The first speaks to the resilience of corporate capitalism, which had been deeply entrenched in American society since World War II. By the early 1970s, a commercial Establishment that had been thrown back on its heels by the challenge of the counterculture had begun to reorganize and exploit the fault lines of that counterculture for commercial advantage. Advertising agencies became ever more sophisticated in positioning products to appeal to specific segments in the marketplace based on race, class, gender, and age, among other factors.[11] This included selling the idea of rebellion itself as a marketing strategy, an approach especially successful for reaching suburban adolescent boys looking for safe ways to challenge authority (hence the success of a string of acts such as Alice Cooper and KISS, who coupled male bravado with a counterintuitive penchant for dressing up in elaborate costumes that would have raised many more questions about sexuality later than were commonly asked at the time). Such specialization became apparent in popular culture as well, as FM radio was gradually tamed and chopped up into specific demographic segments, a process that would only intensify over the course of the coming decades. The record business proceeded in tandem, though it's impossible to disentangle the causality here: did radio airplay drive record sales, or the other way around? Were music business executives simply reflecting audience demand, or shaping it?

In any event, by the mid-1970s, young listeners were often having significantly different musical experiences based on their location, in the broadest sense of that term. Inner-city African Americans, for example, grew up with George Clinton, the O'Jays, and James Brown, while white youth were having formative experiences with acts such as Genesis and Yes, the so called "progressive" rock bands that incorporated ever more elaborate classical music accents into their repertoire. (More avant-garde white kids went for British performance artist David Bowie, who proved lastingly influential.) The two camps were not necessarily exclusive. But the cultural gap was wider than it had been a decade before, when Chicano rock god Carlos Santana, African American folk singer Richie Havens, and white blues singer Joe Cocker crossed racial lines, as did interracial musical ensembles such as Sly and the Family Stone, and Booker T. and the M.G.'s, the Stax house band.

For fans and critics alike, rock and roll dominated the musical discourse of the 1960s and 1970s, but plenty of other pop genres continued to flourish. Country music, which drew less attention but had a broader fan base, is a good example. Some country performers positioned themselves in opposition to the counterculture, which they regarded as effete, if not hypocritical, in its often unwitting elitism. So, for example, Merle Haggard enjoyed a big hit with "Okie from Muskogee" (1969), a song critical of Vietnam protesters. ("We don't burn our draft cards down on Main Street," goes one line.) Johnny Cash, who began his career alongside Elvis Presley on Sam Phillips's Sun label, had a fruitful career amid personal turmoil, recording a landmark album titled *At Folsom Prison* (1968). Women also occupied a prominent place in the country landscape in these years. Alongside Loretta Lynn, who brought a similar working-class perspective into popular culture, Dolly Parton emerged as one of the finest songwriters in the history of country music, along with one of the sweetest of voices (and personalities—Parton long reciprocated the affection of her large gay and lesbian audience at a time when such people were considered deviant). Women also featured prominently in a number of married country music duos, among them George Jones and Tammy Wynette as well as Johnny Cash and June Carter Cash.

Such pockets of vitality notwithstanding, there was a very widespread sense in American life that something had gone wrong in the country in the first half of the 1970s. Explanations as to what, and why, varied, as they always do. But one of the more striking aspects of US culture at the time was a fascination with alternatives to the existing order, a restlessness with traditional institutions of society that were widely perceived to be breaking down.

There were a number of manifestations of this. They included the fascination with alternative fantasy worlds that fueled the popularity of J. R. R. Tolkien novels such as *The Hobbit* (1937), which had achieved cult status by the early 1970s. It also included the violent, and often sexist, themes in heavy metal acts such as Led Zeppelin and Black Sabbath, which rejected the emerging liberal conventional cultural wisdom of the time.

Even Hollywood movies—more specifically, the work of younger film-makers working at the edge of the decaying studio system—captured this sense of restlessness, even despair. Stanley Kubrick's *2001: A Space Odyssey* (1968) depicted a world (or, more accurately, a solar system) in which technology overrode the intentions of the human beings who created it. In different yet comparable ways, Roman Polanski's *Rosemary's Baby* (1968) and William Friedkin's *The Exorcist* (1973), terrifying films with occult themes, challenged the rational, secular pieties that had dominated Establishment thinking. In the latter film, a liberal priest is forced to revise his views when he encounters the demonic possession of a 12-year-old girl whose head spins 360 degrees and who says things such as "Let Jesus fuck you!" while shoving a crucifix between her legs (theater owners began stocking up on kitty litter to absorb the vomit of sickened moviegoers).[12]

Above all, there was a new fascination with explicit violence and the insufficiency of official authority in dealing with it. One early indication of this was *Bonnie and Clyde*, a crime tale of 1930s outlaws with a distinctly late 1960s sensibility. It was followed by *The French Connection*, about a drug cartel, in 1971. Polanski, whose personal life was clouded by the murder of his wife Sharon Tate, and later accusations that he was a pedophile, directed *Chinatown* (1974), a movie that suggested massive government corruption in the Los Angeles of the 1940s (as well as incest, among other violations of genteel convention). There was also a pervasive air of conspiracy in the popular culture of the time, as suggested by films such as *The Parallax View* and *The Conversation* (both 1974). But the king of all crime stories in this era was *The Godfather* saga, the first installment of which was released in 1972. *The Godfather Part II* followed in 1974; both won Academy Awards for Best Picture, the only time a movie and its sequel have ever done so. (A third installment was released in 1990.) Based on the 1970 novel by Mario Puzo and directed by the young maverick film-maker Francis Ford Coppola (who also directed *The Conversation*), the films told a multigenerational saga of the Corleone family, immigrant Sicilians who came to America in the 1940s and founded an organized crime empire of mythic proportions. Policemen and politicians were merely pawns in the Corleones' game; their greatest challenges were internal. Interestingly enough, **the** appeal of these criminals seemed to cross ideological lines: for anyone unhappy with the status quo, the idea of people trying to live by their own code, even a violently illegal one, was deeply appealing.

To a great degree, that's because the United States of the early 1970s was a pitiful giant. As indicated early in this chapter, there were still plenty of people living happy lives: immersed in their childhoods, falling in love, and making a living to whatever greater or lesser degree. But happy or not, the backdrop of those lives had changed dramatically from a generation earlier. Defeat in Vietnam, exhaustion over civil rights, and the protracted controversy of Watergate were only the most obvious examples—and, for some, the less painful ones. It was economic challenges, especially those surrounding the politics of oil, that upended some of the most confident assumptions of the American empire and forced its beneficiaries to reconsider some of the most basic premises of their lives. Liberated, oppressed, or (more likely) somewhere in between, a reckoning appeared to be at hand. How would Americans deal with it? Would their empire survive?

CULTURE WATCH: "Chuckles the Clown Bites the Dust," *The Mary Tyler Moore Show* (1975)

For the first two decades of its existence, the television situation-comedy was centered in the home. The most successful sitcoms of the 1950s and 1960s—*I Love Lucy* (1951–1957), *The Honeymooners* (1955–1956), and many others—revolved around the postwar nuclear family—or, in the case of *My Three Sons* (1960–1972), which dealt with a widower and his family, the struggle to deal with alternatives to it. Even when these shows had alternative settings or dealt with other problems, such as the small-town sitcom *The Andy Griffith Show* (1960–1968), domestic issues still figured prominently. And domestic issues figured particularly prominently for women, who were almost always defined in terms of their roles as wives, mothers, or romantic partners. This reality is what made *The Mary Tyler Moore Show* so striking when it premiered in 1970. Here was a sitcom thoroughly grounded in the workplace—and, more specifically, centered on the career of a single woman who comes to the big city of Minneapolis to make a new life for herself in the aftermath of a broken engagement.

Mary Richards (Moore) works at WJM-TV, a perennial ratings loser in Minneapolis, where she eventually becomes a producer for the local evening newscast. While many episodes in the series are set in or otherwise concern the apartment building she shares with an array of (female) characters, the heart of the show is the newsroom, where Mary interacts with a motley crew of co-workers, among them her gruff-but-caring boss Lou Grant (Ed Asner); the drily comic writer Murray Slaughter (Gavin MacLeod), and the vain, stupid television anchor Ted Baxter (Ted Knight). Many of the episodes focus on Mary's attempts to assert herself in a male-dominated workplace or deal with the incompetence or arrogance of the people around her.

Figure 5.2 TEARFUL LAUGHTER: Mary Richards struggles with conflicting emotions during the hilarious "Chuckles the Clown Bites the Dust" episode of *The Mary Tyler Moore Show* (1975). Moore was a television pioneer who brought a feminist sensibility to the television industry as an actor and head (with husband Grant Tinker) of MTM Productions, a company that produced a string of successful television comedies and dramas (1970–1977, produced by MTM Enterprises, created by James L. Brooks and Allan Burns).

In the classic 1975 episode "Chuckles Bites the Dust," anchor Ted is disappointed when his boss Lou prevents him from participating as a grand marshal at a local circus parade and the honor goes to another local celebrity, Chuckles the Clown. Members of the newsroom are shocked when Chuckles is accidently killed during the parade, where he gets stepped on by an elephant while wearing a peanut outfit. But the sheer absurdity of his demise precipitates a string of bad jokes, which makes Mary increasingly angry at her colleagues' insensitivity. The harder they try to bite their tongues, the harder it seems to keep themselves from laughing. Mary's pique continues when they all attend Chuckles' funeral. But when the minister delivers a eulogy for Chuckles that includes a solemn recital of some of the clown's favorite lines ("a little song, a little dance, a little seltzer down your pants"), Mary finds herself struggling to prevent herself from laughing, her desperation increasingly apparent to the grieving congregation. The minister asks a mortified Mary to stand, consoling her that her laughter is not only understandable but even appropriate: Chuckles lived to make other people happy. It's at this point that Mary—hilariously—breaks into sobbing.

The script for "Chuckles Bites the Dust" was written by David Lloyd, who won an Emmy Award for it, and the episode has been named in a number of best all-time sitcom lists. It captures, as does the show generally, the way the workplace is one of the central sites of friction in a typical American's life, as well as the source of one's friends and daily preoccupations. The show also blazed a trail for a number of other workplace shows, whether comedies such as *Cheers* (1982–1993), set in a Boston bar, or *Murphy Brown* (1988–1998), which was also about a newsroom and featured a female lead too, played by Candice Bergen. One can also trace the influence of *The Mary Tyler Moore Show* to dramas such as *The Good Wife* (2009–) and *Homeland* (2011–), shows where having a career woman as a protagonist is less of a statement than a fact of life—a working life.

Suggested Further Reading

Useful cultural histories of the 1960s include David Farber, *The Age of Great Dreams: America in the 1960s* (New York: Hill & Wang, 1994) and William McNeill, *Dawning of the Counterculture* (1971; Now and Then ebooks, 2011). For a brief overview of postmodern theory, see Christopher Butler, *Postmodernism: A Very Short Introduction* (New York: Oxford University Press, 2002).

The cultural transformation of Hollywood is well captured in Mark Harris, *Pictures at a Revolution: Five Movies and the Birth of the New Hollywood* (New York: Penguin, 2008), which looks at five films from the year 1967 as pivotal in the history of the medium. On what happened in the years that followed, see Peter Biskind, *Easy Riders, Raging Bulls: How the Sex, Drugs, and Rock & Roll Generation Saved Hollywood* (New York: Simon & Schuster, 1998).

The standard history of television is Horace Newcomb's *Tube of Plenty: The Evolution of American Television* (1975; New York: Oxford University Press, 1990). The most incisive study of sitcoms (notably 1970s sitcoms) ever published is David Marc's *Comic Visions: Television Comedy and American Culture* (1989; New York: Wiley, 1997). See also Janet Staiger, *Blockbuster TV: Must-See Sitcoms of the Network Era* (New York: New York University Press, 2000).

For an overview of publishing, see Nicole Howard, *The Book: The Life Story of a Technology* (Baltimore: Johns Hopkins University Press, 2009). Kenneth Davis chronicles a crucial mid-twentieth-century chapter in *Two-Bit Culture: The Paperbacking of America* (Boston: Houghton Mifflin, 1984).

There is surprisingly little in the way of a straight narrative history of rock music. One of the best accounts, now dated but relevant to the period under discussion, is Ed Ward, Geoffrey Stokes, and Ken Tucker, *Rock of Ages: The Rolling Stone Illustrated History of Rock & Roll* (New York: Summit, 1986). A more recent, broader history can be found in *Yeah! Yeah! Yeah! The History of Pop Music from Bill Haley to Beyoncé* (New York: Norton, 2014).

Notes

1   Edna Gunderson, "Dylan Is Positively on Top of His Game," *USA Today*, September 10, 1997: http://usatoday30.usatoday.com/life/music/2001-09-10-bob-dylan.htm#more (June 11, 2014).

2   The *Oxford English Dictionary* records this term coming into common usage in this sense in the 1950s: http://www.oed.com/view/Entry/64536?rskey=YH0lbk& result=2&isAdvanced=false#eid5264352 (July 25, 2015).

3   Morris Dickstein, *Gates of Eden: American Culture in the Sixties* (1977; Cambridge, MA: Harvard University Press, 1977), 19. On religious and social reform waves, see William G. McLoughlin, *Revivals, Awakenings, and Reform* (1978; Chicago: University of Chicago Press, 1980).

4   Alan Wolfe, *America's Impasse: The Rise and Fall of the Politics of Growth* (Boston: South End Press, 1981), 33–34; http://www.forbes.com/sites/ joshbarro/2012/04/16/lessons-from-the-decades-long-upward-march-of- government-spending/ (July 9, 2014).

5   http://www.gutenberg.org/files/16643/16643-h/16643-h.htm#SELF- RELIANCE (June 21, 2014).

6   Guy Strait, "What Is a Hippie?" (1967) in *The United States Since 1945*, edited by Robert P. Ingalls and David K Johnson (Malden, MA: Wiley-Blackwell, 2009), 115–116.

7   Dickstein, 68-ff.

8   Butler, 57.

9   Richard Bach, *Jonathan Livingston Seagull: A Story* (1970; New York: Avon, 1973), 80.

10 Bruce Schulman, *The Seventies: The Great Shift in American Culture, Society, and Politics* (New York: Da Capo, 2001), 15.

11 Elizabeth Cohen, *A Consumer's Republic: the Politics of Mass Consumption in Postwar America* (2003; New York: Vintage, 2004). See especially Chapter 7, "Segmenting the Mass" (pp. 292–344).

12 Rick Perlstein, *The Invisible Bridge: The Fall of Nixon and the Rise of Reagan* (New York: Simon & Schuster, 2014), 205.

Interlude

6

Reassessment and Nostalgia

The American Empire in the Age of Limits,
1973–1980

Figure 6.1 RUNNING ON EMPTY: An iconic image of the 1970s energy crisis. The combined shock of rising prices and constricted supply challenged Americans' self-image as a people of plenty © Classic Stock / Alamy.

Democratic Empire: The United States Since 1945, First Edition. Jim Cullen.
© 2017 Jim Cullen. Published 2017 by John Wiley & Sons, Inc.

1973: Hinge of American History

FOR MANY PEOPLE, in many respects, in many locations, the United States of 1973 was a very attractive place. The nation as a whole was immensely wealthy—rich in natural resources, rich in social capital, and rich in monetary wealth. It had the highest gross domestic product per person—essentially the world's highest standard of living, financially speaking—and had been in this position for some time.[1]

Not only that, but life in the United States of 1973 had improved since the dawn of the 1960s, itself a prosperous time. Over the course of the 1960s, the nation's per capita gross national product had risen by almost one-third; the poverty rate had declined by almost half.[2] But the gains were not merely economic. The passage of the Civil Rights Act of 1964 and the Voting Rights Act of 1965 had demolished the legal foundation of racism in the United States. Women were being educated in greater numbers, and entering careers that had previously been denied them. (It was during 1973 that tennis star Billie Jean King defeated avowed sexist Bobby Riggs, symbolically establishing the parity of female athletes, a parity legally codified with the 1972 amendments to the Civil Rights Act known as Title IX, which required gender equity in education, including physical education.) Laws protecting the rights of workers, the environment, and consumer safety were on the books. By 1973, a wave of new technologies—CAT scans, bar codes, microwave ovens—were on their way to becoming facts of everyday life.

The nation was also increasingly taking advantage of another one of its assets: immense space. Though population was growing (the country grew from 151 million in 1950 to over 226 million by 1980), there was still plenty of room. France had four times as many people per square mile, the United Kingdom nine times, and Japan 12 times. Sure, the Soviet Union and China were larger, as was Canada, but their climates, literal and/or figurative, were less appealing. Nor did the growing US population significantly reduce the amount of forest on the continent; the replanting of trees to replace cut timber, combined with reforestation of abandoned agricultural land—this while the United States remained a major food exporter—meant there were about as many trees as there were during World War II.[3] To be sure, there was colossal waste and destruction in the form of strip mining, oil spills, and other forms of air and water pollution. But awareness of these ills was also beginning to mitigate them.

Though, technically speaking, the nation's frontier had closed in 1890, a collective westward migration continued. A huge swath of territory stretching from Virginia to southern California—known by the new term "Sun Belt"—was growing rapidly. There were a series of reasons for this: an attractive business climate (low taxes and wages); appealing weather (especially when compared with the "Rust Belt" of the Northeast and industrial Midwest); and a relatively new infrastructure (good roads, new construction, and, not to be underestimated, pervasive air-conditioning). A series of cities—more like metropolitan areas, since there was a strongly suburban character to them—were growing rapidly in 1973: Atlanta, Houston, Phoenix, and San Diego, among others. Many of these cities produced or shipped goods for international consumption; all of them benefited from an influx of new immigrant arrivals from around the world who contributed their labor to these communities and spiced them with their folkways. The American empire remained a colossus.

In retrospect, though, 1973 appears to mark the beginning of the end of that empire. The most obvious military manifestation of this was the signing of the Paris Peace Accords in January, which marked the end of a two-decade entanglement in Vietnam and the first military defeat in the nation's history. But it was another war in which the United States was not directly involved that revealed the limits of its power much more suddenly, vividly, and painfully. For it was in 1973 that a war between Israel and Egypt erupted, for which the United States would literally pay a steep price.

The product of a 2,000-year-old dream, the modern state of Israel was born in 1948 in the aftermath of the Holocaust and in a rare moment of agreement between the United States and the Soviet Union, overcoming the resistance, some of it military, of Arab states in the Middle East. The two agreed again in 1956 when they forced Israel, along with Great Britain and France, to give up their occupation of the Suez Canal, which connected the Mediterranean and Red Seas, after Egypt nationalized it. (Submitting to anti-colonial US and Soviet demands to yield control of the canal was particularly humiliating for Britain, and the event is widely regarded as marking the end of Britain as a great imperial power.) But over the course of ensuing decades, Egypt and much of the Arab world generally leaned toward the Soviets, while Israel became an increasingly important US ally. Israel defeated the Egyptians and their allies in the Six Day War of 1967 with American help—an event that bound the Israeli state more tightly to many American Jews.[4] In October 1973, an Arab coalition led by Egypt invaded Israel, but again, with US help, the Israelis prevailed in the so-called Yom Kippur War in the space of a month. The US–Soviet relationship was tested by that contest, but *détente*—the French term for eased tension that had become the unofficial basis of US–Soviet relations in the early 1970s—prevailed.

By this point, however, the Arabs were in a position to retaliate for their military humiliation. The means of doing so was in the politics of energy, more specifically petroleum. Its utility as a cheap, relatively clean fuel was first realized in the mid-nineteenth-century United States, where it quickly replaced (dirtier) coal in any number of enterprises there and around the world, notably naval ones. Until the mid-twentieth century, the United States was an oil exporter, and its ability to supply itself with this crucial fuel—unlike Germany and Japan, which seized, and eventually lost, access to it—was a major dynamic in waging and winning of World War II. It was also during the war that President Roosevelt, on his way back from a trip to meet his Soviet and British counterparts at the 1945 Yalta Conference, met with King Ibn Saud of Saudi Arabia, where huge underground oil reserves had recently been discovered. Despite their different views on the pending establishment of an Israeli state in the Middle East, the meeting established a long and profitable, if often uneasy, relationship between the Saudis and the Americans whereby the United States would buy Saudi oil and the Saudis would buy American products (especially military hardware).

In the quarter-century following World War II, the very cheapness and availability of petroleum led Americans to take it for granted as a fuel to heat their homes and drive their cars. So much so that the nation became a net importer of oil, on which it became increasingly dependent. Meanwhile, Saudi Arabia and a series of the other nations in the Middle East and around the world formed the Organization of the Petroleum Exporting Countries in 1960. By 1973, OPEC was in a position to punish those who supported Israel, imposing an embargo on sales of petroleum to the United States and its major allies that lasted from the fall of 1973 to the spring of 1974. Oil prices took a gigantic leap, and remained high even after the embargo was lifted.

The effect of the "energy crisis," as it became known, proved to be jarring and durable. It was not simply that there was suddenly a shortage of gas for cars—lines at gas stations stretched for miles, rationing became widespread, and energy-inefficient American cars now seemed like dinosaurs compared to nimble rivals such as Germany's Volkswagens and Japan's Hondas. It was also that higher prices for transportation, so central to the world and national economy, translated to higher prices for everything else, triggering a sharp rise in inflation. Though the price of energy in the United States remained lower than much of the rest of the world (in large measure because it was taxed less), Americans were shaken by the sudden change and the realization of their international vulnerability.

Actually, the US economy had not been doing all that well even before the energy crisis. The economy grew at an average rate of 5% annually between 1947 and 1965, but between 1966 and 1975 that figure dropped to 1.9%.[5] President Lyndon Johnson's reluctance to tax Americans to pay for the Vietnam War, coupled with a sharp rise in defense spending, led to price inflation that weakened the US economy and eroded the power of the dollar abroad. Facing severe pressures from other nations seeking to cash in their dollars for gold, President Nixon in 1971 ended a long-standing policy of convertibility, allowing the dollar to float relative to other currencies. While this was surely necessary, it also made clear that the international standing of the United States was weakening. First in the world in gross domestic product per person at the start of the decade, the United States slipped to 11th by 1980.[6]

For most Americans, such statistics were remote abstractions. But the pain was real enough. With an eye toward his looming re-election, President Nixon imposed 90-day wage and price controls in late 1971, designed to tamp down inflation. But when he lifted those controls—which ran contrary to Republican free-market doctrine—the whiplash, which intensified over the course of 1973, was all the more painful, particularly for staples such as food. (The opening credits for the *Mary Tyler Moore Show* at the time showed its main character looking with disgust at the price of meat in a supermarket as she tosses it in her shopping cart.) Inflation, at an average annual rate of 6.2% in 1969, had doubled to 12.4% by 1974. And unemployment, which averaged 4.7% in 1973, reached 7.5% in 1975.[7]

These numbers defied economic logic. High inflation usually meant low unemployment, as people with jobs tended to buy more stuff, driving prices up. Alternatively, high unemployment meant low inflation, since people without jobs bought less stuff, driving prices down. If one was high, the other was supposed to be low. But, by the mid-1970s, the nation was experiencing relatively high unemployment *and* high inflation, leading to the creation of a new economic term: "stagflation." Whatever the reasons for the mystery, it was a source of frustration and anxiety.

But not the only one. In 1973, the nation was in the throes of Watergate, in which the crimes of Richard Nixon vindicated the suspicions of the left and dispirited the hopes of the right. The growing lack of respect for authority, which intensified a longstanding tendency in American society, fed a crime wave that swept over the nation's cities. In the 1960s, urban upheavals had been rooted in political events such as the civil rights movement or the Democratic National Convention of 1968. Now crime was experienced as a less dramatic, but chronic, problem. One could argue, as many people did, that the crime wave of the 1970s was rooted in the unrealized promises of the War on Poverty and the civil rights movement. There was surely some truth to that. But the fact remains that crime levels were higher than they had been during previous or subsequent economic or political instabilities, or would be in later ones, a fact that has never been fully explained, except perhaps that the Baby Boom had produced a bumper crop of young men, who are typically the people who commit most crimes.

Whatever the cause, Americans—at this point, mostly white ones—voted with their feet and fled the nation's largest cities in favor of suburbs or the racially segregated districts of the Sunbelt. (In his cheeky but pointed 1975 song "Chocolate City," bandleader George Clinton of Parliament conferred his blessings on the accomplishments of fellow African Americans concentrated in urban areas even as he cast a benevolent eye on those in "vanilla suburbs.") Northeastern cities such as Philadelphia and Washington DC shrank, while downtown Midwestern ones such as Cleveland and Cincinnati became empty and dangerous husks surrounded by a belt of wealthier suburbs. Between 1950 and 1980, Chicago lost 17% of its population, Detroit 35%, and St. Louis 47%, a process of shrinkage and de-industrialization that was acutely apparent by 1973.[8]

But nowhere were the woes of a municipality more apparent than in the New York of 1973. As with other US cities, its population was also shrinking, taking a significant piece of its tax base with it. And, similar to other cities, New York was losing its industrial base; the closing of the Brooklyn Navy Yard in 1966, an economic hub since it first opened in 1806, was only one example of how thousands of jobs were lost (others disappeared when corporations left New York for the Sun Belt). Similar to other cities, too, New York experienced an influx of poor people, many of them immigrants, who required services it was relatively generous in providing. The city also had a large public sector workforce, whose unions negotiated relatively good contracts. To pay those contracts, the municipal government increasingly relied on short-term loans. Add to this a growing crime problem, corrupt police—as revealed in a sensational 1971 investigation—and difficulty keeping streets and subway cars clean, and you had the nation's largest city teetering on the edge of collapse.[9] Much of New York was actually burning down in 1973, especially in the outer boroughs of Brooklyn and the Bronx, where arson for the sake of collecting insurance money on old buildings was a common practice. (My father, a New York City firefighter, would sometimes respond to 40 calls a night; many were false alarms or ones sounded for other reasons than fire because residents believed police would not respond to calls and so triggered fire boxes instead.) Disaster was only narrowly averted in 1975 when the city's government and unions negotiated a deal that prevented bankruptcy. After President Ford initially refused to help—prompting the infamous New York *Daily News* headline "Ford to City: Drop Dead"—the federal government also agreed to make loans that set the city back on the road to solvency. But that would take years.

The year 1973 was also significant for a reason that would not become clear until decades later: it marked the peak of real median income for men, adjusted for inflation, in US history. To some extent, the retreat from this high point was hidden, not only because it was gradual, and because of the availability of overtime (businesses sought to avoid hiring more people), but also because of the influx of women into the workforce. Women's wages—typically lower for men working the same job—helped relieve the strain that families were feeling.[10] In the years that followed, one of the key sources of that pressure became increasingly obvious: the willingness of workers in other parts of the world to do what Americans did for less, coupled with increasing educational and technological competitiveness.

Nowhere were these trends more obvious than in the auto industry. Labor relations were notoriously tense in the 1930s, when a series of strikes resulted in violence. But, beginning with World War II, and continuing during the postwar decades, the steady demand for American cars made it possible for management to buy labor peace by passing on the cost of salaries and benefits onto the price of the vehicles, a pattern established in the famous "Treaty of Detroit" labor settlement between the United Auto Workers and General Motors in 1950, quickly followed by similar deals with Ford and Chrysler. By the early 1970s, however, this was becoming more difficult in the face of competition from companies such as Toyota, which made high-quality, fuel-efficient cars that were widely perceived to be superior to what Detroit was producing. There were widespread suspicions that American workers had become entitled, and that management had become greedy, neither wishing to strive for improvement. Each side pointed fingers at the other for this state of affairs, and observers at home and abroad pointed fingers at both. Eventually, there would be a reckoning, and the outcome would be smaller companies, lower wages, and fewer benefits—not just in the auto industry, but also in the steel, meatpacking, and other once-high-wage industries.

This downward pressure was intensified by more structural changes in the world economy. Until the mid-twentieth century, advanced economies were rooted in *manufacturing*, which is to say they focused on producing goods. By the late twentieth century, however, the world, led by the United States, was increasingly a *service* economy, in which providing information or performing tasks were more important. Service economy jobs could be lucrative. And they could be plentiful. But unlike classic blue-collar assembly-line jobs, they tended not to be both. Most service industry jobs were concentrated in low-wage sectors such as retailing and hospitality, known as pink-collar work because of its gender connotations.

While it would take decades for the implications of this interlocking series of transformations to become fully apparent, the direction of the country was clear enough. "I don't know a dream that's not been shattered or driven to its knees," Paul Simon mused in his classic 1973 song "American Tune." It's all right, his narrator says: "You can't be forever blessed." Days of rage in the 1960s were giving way to days of sorrow in the 1970s.

So while there were clearly alternating currents to the contrary, the mid-1970s marked an unusual moment in American history in the wave of despair that swept much of the country. Of course, there had been bad times before—the Great Depression was a living memory for millions of Americans. But besides a stratum of intellectuals (and even among them only temporarily), there had never been a sense that the basic premises of American life were in question during the Depression or at earlier moments in US history. Americans—even oppressed Americans—tended to think that they lived in an opportunity-rich society where the future promised to be better than the past. This became harder to believe in the 1970s. That's partly because there had been so many changes, and so many disappointments, in the 1960s. But this sense of uncertainty was also a function of the shifting geopolitical tides. And so millions of people began to wonder: is the American Way of Life—variously defined, but usually grounded in material prosperity in one way or another—truly sustainable? And if not, what could/should Americans be doing differently? For a moment, one that turned out in a number of ways to be temporary, the 1970s were a time when a surprisingly large number of people were willing to peer into a collective abyss.

Apocalypse Now: The New Gloom

One of the first people to take stock of new realities in intellectual circles was sociologist Andrew Hacker. In his 1970 book *The End of the American Era*, Hacker argued that Americans were essentially victims of their success, living in a society that had raised its expectations beyond the nation's capacity to fulfill them. "Their rightful forebears are not the old middle class," he asserted, "but the peasants and proletarians of an earlier time."[11] In a striking passage earlier in the book, he elaborated:

> Ordinary people in this country now have a higher estimate of their endowments and broader conceptions of their entitlements than ever before. Virtually every American possesses a self-esteem hitherto reserved for a privileged or talented few. Black or white, poor or prosperous, society's successes and not a few of its failures are infected with the idea that they are equal to any or all with whom they may choose to compare themselves.[12]

And yet, this rise in collective self-esteem was accompanied by a sense of collective failure. Christopher Lasch opened his surprise 1979 bestseller *The Culture of Narcissism: American Life in an Age of Diminishing Expectations* this way:

> Hardly more than a quarter-century after Henry Luce proclaimed "the American Century," American confidence has fallen to a low ebb. Those who recently dreamed of world power now despair of governing the city of New York. Defeat in Vietnam, economic stagnation, and the impending exhaustion of natural resources have produced a mood of pessimism in higher circles, which spreads through the rest of society as people lose faith in their leaders.[13]

Lasch could be almost laughably grim, and the dour mood he and Hacker evoked was far from universal. Some argued that the problem was not so much that Americans were hopelessly infatuated with themselves but insufficiently assertive in challenging ongoing sources of oppression, whether that of racism, sexism, or corporate tyranny. But the sense that the country was being stretched to the breaking point was hardly limited to grouchy aging white men.

One telling indication of this was a cinematic genre that burst into view in the mid-1970s: the disaster movie. The fad was kicked off in 1970 with *Airport* (followed by three sequels), which tapped into fears about international terrorism. In the more critically acclaimed *The Poseidon Adventure* (1972), a cruise ship is overwhelmed by a huge wave; in *The Towering Inferno* (1974), terror takes the form of a huge fire in a skyscraper. Though it's typically remembered for different reasons, which we'll get to later in this chapter, Steven Spielberg's *Jaws* (1975), about a killer shark, can be classified as a variation on this genre. In all these cases, characters are confronted by malignant forces that defy human intentions or rationality—often, as in the case of the 1978 film *The Swarm*, it's nature run amok. Such problems are compounded by greed and incompetence. Expressions of confidence by people in positions of authority are routinely exposed as fraudulent or foolish: if someone says at the start of the movie that things are under control, you knew they were not.

Such perspectives were also apparent in the work of maverick Hollywood filmmakers of the time. For all their considerable differences, the experience of watching the most widely hailed films in the first half of the 1970s—*Midnight Cowboy* (1969), *The French Connection* (1971), *The Godfather* (1972),

The Godfather Part II (1974), *Chinatown* (1974), *Nashville* (1975), *Dog Day Afternoon* (1975), and *Taxi Driver* (1976), these last two arresting in capturing New York at its grimiest—is to be stunned by the sense of deep cynicism or despair that suffused their creators' attitudes toward the major institutions and traditions of American society. In Sidney Lumet's *Dog Day Afternoon*, the hero is a desperate gay bank robber played by Al Pacino; in Martin Scorsese's gripping *Taxi Driver*, we spend almost 2 hours in the company of the psychopathic Vietnam veteran Travis Bickle, unforgettably played by Robert DeNiro, and the movie climaxes in an explosion of violence that upends the very notion of heroism itself. In large numbers, film audiences of the 1970s literally and figuratively bought this message.

The end of the decade brought with it another kind of disaster movie: films about the Vietnam War. During the war itself, Hollywood only released one movie about the conflict: *The Green Berets* (1968), a strongly anticommunist war film starring the patriotic John Wayne. Post-Vietnam movies, however, were uniformly grim in portraying the fighting and its aftermath, typically far more focused on the home front and the war's impact on individual soldiers than on geopolitical issues. *Coming Home* (1978) traced the travails of a paralyzed Vietnam War vet (Jon Voigt) and the married woman (Jane Fonda, a darling of the liberal left) who meets him while her husband is overseas. *The Deer Hunter* (1978) traced the ravages of the war in a small working-class Pennsylvania town. Francis Ford Coppola of *The Godfather* series fame directed *Apocalypse Now* (1979), a retelling of the classic 1899 Joseph Conrad novel *Heart of Darkness*, which depicted the Vietnam War as a latter-day example of Western imperialism. In all these cases, the war was viewed as a foolish mistake, and the US government as at best irrelevant and at worst deeply malignant.

These movies were made, and resonated, because a very large segment of the US population had lost faith in its leaders. A famous juxtaposition of polls showed that, in 1964, 76% of the public trusted the government; a decade later, that number had dropped to 36%.[14] (Minor fluctuations notwithstanding, that figure has never really recovered, and in recent years has dropped further, especially in more specific judgments, such as that of the US Congress.) In his 1973 book *The Imperial Presidency*, former JFK adviser Arthur Schlesinger, Jr., traced the emergence of a troubling pattern of chief executive arrogance, culminating in Lyndon Johnson and (especially) Richard Nixon, who were increasingly unaccountable to the people in making domestic as well as foreign policy. The key problem, Schlesinger asserted, was the failure of Congress to assert its constitutional authority. In the aftermath of Watergate, however, Congress *did* begin to do this. The 1973 War Powers Act, for instance, stated that the president could only act militarily abroad in cases of "a national emergency created by attack upon the United States, its territories or possessions, or its armed forces." Congress also passed a series of electoral reforms designed to limit the power of money in elections, in the hope of enhancing voter confidence in the political system. In years to come, such reforms would be subject to increasing resistance by special interests, and by the end of the century had eroded to the point of meaninglessness.

Depressingly Decent: Ford and Carter

In the years immediately following Watergate, the most obvious problem with US government leadership could be described as a matter of Americans getting what they wished for. The two presidents who followed Nixon, one a Republican and the other a Democrat, were two of the most decent people to ever hold the office. They were also widely regarded—not entirely fairly—as two of the least successful US presidents, a judgment that may reflect the fecklessness of public opinion much as it does these leaders' shortcomings.

The first of these two, Gerald Ford, could only have become president because the executive branch was viewed as so corrupt that an honest man was desperately needed to salvage its reputation. Born Leslie Lynch King in Omaha, Nebraska, he was renamed Gerald Ford, Jr., in honor of his stepfather, who worked for a paint store in Grand Rapids, Michigan, where he and his mother relocated when he was an infant. A football player at the University of Michigan and coach at Yale, Ford was elected to Congress as a Republican in 1948, where he remained for 25 years, rising to the position of Minority Leader during a long era of Democratic dominance of the House of Representatives. Liked and trusted—President Johnson named him to the commission investigating the death of John F. Kennedy—Richard Nixon chose him to be his vice president after the resignation of Spiro T. Agnew in 1973, who was charged with tax evasion, in large measure because Nixon was confident Ford would have little trouble getting confirmed by the US Senate. Ford was indeed rapidly confirmed, and enjoyed an early measure of goodwill once he became president upon Nixon's resignation (see Chapter 4).

Once in office, Ford didn't do that much. This was partly because both he and Nixon needed him to keep his distance from Watergate. But it also reflected a perception on the part of some that Ford, while honest, was not politically acute. In his typically cutting way, LBJ famously described Ford as playing football once too often without a helmet.[15] (He also once said Ford couldn't fart and chew gum at the same time.)[16] This perception was cemented by comedian Chevy Chase, who depicted Ford as a clumsy bumbler who was constantly tripping over things in the first year of the widely hailed television show *Saturday Night Live* in 1975–1976. In his capacity as a mock news anchor, Chase also mocked his skills as a campaigner: "President Ford kissed a snowball and threw a baby."

Insofar as these jokes were fair, they reflected a sense that Ford was straightforward to the point of being a simpleton. When he said, after making his controversial 1974 decision to pardon Nixon, that he felt it necessary to spare the nation an ordeal that had already gone on too long, he meant it. Some people had difficulty taking this seriously; others who took Ford at his word thought he was an idiot. Yet, there was substance to the argument that the trial of Nixon would have serious complications, beginning with where such a trial could be held and an unbiased jury found. In any case, Ford didn't only anger liberals. His announcement that he would offer amnesty to Vietnam War draft evaders in return for community service, made within weeks of the Nixon pardon, was offensive to those who felt such people should have served their country when called, even as others felt he should be more lenient toward those who opposed an unjust war. (His successor, Jimmy Carter, campaigned on a pledge for complete amnesty, a promise he kept on his first day in office.)

Ford's biggest problem, though, was one largely beyond his control: a weak economy. The inflation, unemployment, and federal deficits of the 1970s were at their worst while he was president, and the actions he took—first raising taxes, then cutting them, and distributing buttons with a the word WIN, an acronym for "Whip Inflation Now"—did little to ease the situation. A similar sense of uncertainty characterized Ford's approach to energy policy, which wavered between price controls and allowing oil companies to raise prices in the hope that it would lead to further energy exploration as well as a decline in consumption by ordinary Americans. By 1976, the nation was actually importing *more* oil than it had been 4 years earlier.[17]

Ford did take some measures to reorganize the White House and reassert American power. He brought a pair of young politicians, Donald Rumsfeld and Dick Cheney, into the executive branch, where they streamlined operations and introduced a new sense of discipline. (The two would reappear in the administration of George W. Bush 25 years later with decidedly more damaging results.) In a final spasm of the Vietnam War, the murderous Khmer Rouge regime that came to power in neighboring Cambodia following the Nixon administration's 1970 invasion seized an American merchant ship, the *Mayaguez*, in May 1975. Ford ordered an air strike on Cambodia and sent a team of marines to rescue the crew, only to learn that they had been moved to the mainland (they were later released). Though more Americans died in the attempt than if the entire crew had been murdered, some Americans saw the incident in terms of restored national pride. "It shows we've still got balls in this country," said former presidential candidate Barry Goldwater, who remained a fixture of the US Senate after his presidential debacle in 1964.

Ford also generated sympathy for being subjected to two assassination attempts in September 1975, both by women, and both in California. The first, Lynette "Squeaky" Fromme, was a Charles Manson follower who was subdued before she could fire her loaded weapon in Sacramento. Ford went ahead with his scheduled meeting. The second, Sara Jane Moore, shot him twice but missed as he was leaving San Francisco.[18]

Notwithstanding the goodwill that Ford enjoyed among many Americans, it was Goldwater's protégé, California governor Ronald Reagan, who by the mid-1970s was emerging as the standard bearer of the Republican Party. Reagan and other conservatives had become increasingly unhappy by what they regarded as the Nixon and Ford administration's policy of *détente*, which they regarded as morally and politically unwise. For the moment, this hardline approach, like a parallel hostility toward domestic spending and the rest of the legacy of the Great Society, remained a minority faction among Republicans. But it was growing stronger.

After initially believing that he would not run for president in 1976, Ford decided that his political credibility in office depended on a belief that he would do more than fill out Nixon's second term. Reagan challenged him for the Republican nomination, and came close to winning it. But for the moment, at least, the Republican center held.

Given the severity of the Republicans' image crisis in the aftermath of Watergate—the midterm election of 1974 brought a bumper crop of new Democrats to Congress—the real question to most political observers was who was going to capture the political opportunity that seemed to be there for the taking on the left. One thing seemed clear: it was time for a fresh face in Washington, someone who offered an alternative to the imperial backstage maneuverings of the Kennedy, Johnson, and Nixon years. The question was who that would be.

The answer was Jimmy Carter. "Who is Jimmy Carter?" is a question a lot of people were asking circa 1975. As indicated, an important part of the answer is who he wasn't: a Washington insider. But Carter had a number of attributes that made him a man of the moment. The first is that he was a Southerner—and a particular *kind* of Southerner. Born in the tiny town of Plains, Georgia, in 1924, Carter was the son of a successful peanut farmer and businessman. He entered the US Navy and became an engineer—an important fact about his skill set and temperament—where he worked on nuclear submarines. After leaving the US Navy, he returned to the family business before entering politics. After running unsuccessfully for governor in 1966, he tried again in 1970, succeeding the old-time segregationist Lester Maddox, in part by taking positions that would not alienate racist voters. Still, it was clear from the start that Carter was the first post–civil rights governor in the region's history: "I say to you quite frankly that the time for racial discrimination is over," he said in his inaugural address.[19] In years to come, Carter's African American supporters—now increasingly numerous, thanks to the Voting Rights Act—would form an important part of his political constituency, even as Southern white voters began migrating to the Republican Party. But this was a process that would take time, and Carter was able to retain some of the old Democratic base.

Another important fact about Carter is that he was an evangelical Christian[20] at a time of religious revival in some districts of American Protestantism. As discussed in Chapter 5, many observers have viewed the upheaval we know as the 1960s as at root a religious revival. As also discussed, much of that new wave of spiritual restlessness sought alternative outlets from traditional forms of US Christianity. By the 1970s, it became apparent that traditional Christianity had *also* experienced a revival. However, that revival was relatively specific. Mainline Protestant denominations such as Episcopalians and Presbyterians were experiencing a decline, while fundamentalists—those who interpreted the Bible literally—were on the rise, as were evangelical congregations not affiliated with a particular denomination.[21] Some of these evangelical congregations were becoming large "megachurches"—defined as those with more than 2,000 members—that provided both religious and non-religious services. A Gallup Poll proclaimed 1976 as "The Year of the Evangelical."[22]

As a devout Baptist and Sunday school teacher, Carter was well positioned to tap this enthusiasm. As one historian has observed, "he discussed his faith in deeply personal, character-based terms, combining the Protestant faith with the therapeutic turn," managing to suggest that "good Christians make good leaders" without threatening secular Americans who didn't share his faith.[23] Carter's sense of personal honesty was key here—"I will never lie to you," he famously asserted—an honesty that led him to say things that could be controversial, as in a famous *Playboy* interview in which he confessed that he experienced lust for other women than his wife. (Much of the controversy focused on the fact that Carter made this disclosure in *Playboy* rather than the statement itself.) In a country still experiencing the polarities of the 1960s, Carter had to walk a fine line in 1976. He did so successfully.

In a way, though, what's remarkable is how narrow that success was. The presidential election of 1976 was one of the closer ones in US history, with Carter taking 50% of the vote for Ford's 48%; he won 297 electoral votes to Ford's 240. Even after Watergate, the Nixon pardon, a bad economy, and Reagan's challenge, Ford almost managed to secure re-election and keep the Republican Party in power. Carter won—thanks largely to his strength in the South—but he didn't exactly win a vote of confidence.

Still, his early steps were positive. Carter made a show of downsizing the imperial presidency by walking during his presidential parade rather than travel by motorcade and wearing a cardigan sweater during a speech on energy conservation. He also announced that he was selling the presidential yacht.[24] Other acts were more than symbolic. Carter sought to link American foreign policy to the human rights behavior of US allies. He also sought to encourage structural, long-term change to US energy policy, seeking both to reduce consumption and encourage the development of alternative sources of energy.

He didn't get very far. Part of the problem was that Carter was attempting to address some very knotty complexities. In the realm of energy policy, for example, he was up against some deeply entrenched attitudes on the part of Americans, who had come to think of cheap energy as a birthright. But even had the collective will been there, the alternatives to petroleum were not entirely satisfactory. While promising, new technologies such as wind or solar energy were still decades away from applicability on a large scale. The most obvious alternative was nuclear power, which made many Americans nervous. The post-counterculture left, in particular, continued to harbor an animus against technological approaches to social problems, typified by the celebrated Musicians United for Safe Energy (MUSE) concerts of 1979 and *The China Syndrome*, a film that was also released that year, depicting the consequences of a meltdown at a nuclear power plant. The fears of such people gained frightening plausibility 2 weeks after the movie arrived in theaters when a malfunction resulted in a nuclear accident that caused a mass evacuation at the Three Mile Island nuclear power plant in eastern Pennsylvania. While there were no clear human casualties, the accident effectively ended the licensing of new nuclear power plants in the United States for decades.

Carter also faced serious difficulties in trying to reorient US foreign policy. It was not easy for the United States to break the longtime Cold War habit of backing deeply repressive regimes that were also staunchly anticommunist. And many Americans objected to any suggestion that they might have to surrender longtime perquisites of power. Particularly contentious was Carter's 1977 decision to sign a treaty returning control of the Panama Control to Panama at the end of the twentieth century, a move that many conservatives considered a craven giveaway, since the United States had built the canal, and since Central America was a troublesome source of political instability. Such fears intensified when Nicaragua fell under communist control in 1979.

But some of Carter's problems were Carter's. He was, to use a later term, a control freak—detail-oriented to the point, as recounted in the famous anecdote, of supervising use of the White House tennis court—and while he had an engineer's sense of precision and design, he lacked the social skills for dealing with Congress, where even Democrats found him to be remote and impractical when considering the human dimensions of policy problems. The behavior of Carter's associates, which included a budget director ultimately cleared of corruption charges and his colorful, beer-swilling brother Billy, didn't help matters.

In some sense, Carter's ultimate problem is that he was a moderate figure in a nation in transition, and while he embodied and responded to shifts taking place in the country, he tended to do so in ways that dispirited allies without satisfying critics. Among the first to be disenchanted were his evangelical supporters, who were disappointed that his personal convictions did not frequently translate to political mobilization—particularly with regard to the increasingly important issue of abortion (more on this below)—and began moving toward the Republicans. In truth, Carter had never commanded more than a minority of their support in any case. By the end of the 1970s, the equation of "evangelical" with "Republican" was nearly complete.[25]

In economic terms, the more conservative accents in Carter's persona became increasingly apparent in the late 1970s. Though we tend to think of government deregulation of the economy as a quintessentially Republican economic objective, it was Carter who made some of the most important early moves in this direction, implementing new rules in the airline and trucking industries that freed them from what were widely regarded as burdensome rules. At the same time, however, Carter also unveiled a complex energy policy in 1977 that included a bewildering array of provisions that included gas rationing as well as a new tax on oil companies, whose huge profits were a source of popular outrage. Given that that plan had something to offend everyone, and that Carter lacked Congressional support, it was effectively dead on arrival.[26] By 1979, Carter faced rumbling on his left that would impede his efforts to run for re-election in 1980.

Carter also presided over a re-intensification of the Cold War when the Soviet Union, anxious about a collapsing satellite regime, invaded Afghanistan in December 1979. Carter cancelled arms talks with the Soviets and announced that the United States would boycott the 1980 Summer Olympics, which were to be held in Moscow. In making these moves, he angered classic liberal supporters as well as *détente*-minded foreign policy analysts without receiving much credit from the increasingly assertive conservative right.

Carter's greatest foreign policy challenge, however, came from Iran. For 25 years following the CIA-engineered coup that put Reza Pahlavi in power as the shah, or king, in 1953 (Chapter 1), Iran had been one of those stalwart and repressive allies that the United States had cultivated during the Cold War. Iran was also a major oil supplier to the United States, and a customer for much of its military wares. As with many leaders of postwar Middle Eastern countries stretching from Egypt to Afghanistan, the shah was an essentially secular figure who viewed modernization as a process that involved the substantial importation of Western values. But, similar to the United States, the Islamic world was experiencing a significant religious revival in the 1970s, in both Sunni Muslim nations such as Saudi Arabia as well as Shiite Muslim nations such as Iran (in calling them Sunni or Shiite, I refer to those who actually ruled these countries; in fact, these two, as with many others, had both Sunni and Shiite populations of varying sizes, along with other Muslims and Sikhs). Religious radicals were instrumental in the overthrow of Afghanistan's pro-Soviet regime in 1979. They were also instrumental, following 2 years of demonstrations, in toppling the shah that year. His place was taken by the recently returned exile, religious leader ("Ayatollah") Ruhollah Khomeini, who founded the first modern Islamic state.

The Iranian Revolution posed multiple problems for the United States. Besides the loss of a reliable ally in a highly volatile region, the upheaval there resulted in a significant loss of petroleum production, which spooked world markets. Once again, prices skyrocketed and shortages appeared, resulting in a return to the nightmarish gas lines of 1973. Non-Arab OPEC members such as Venezuela would ultimately pick up the slack, and oil prices would eventually undergo a sharp decline, though this was not obvious or comforting at the time. A 1979 magazine advertisement depicted a driver with a gas nozzle to his head, as if it were a gun. "Or you can drive a Volkswagen," the caption read, suggesting both the widespread gloom about the energy crisis as well as stoking the now-well-established suspicion that American cars were inferior gas-guzzling dinosaurs when compared with German and Japanese rivals.

But the United States did not simply lose an ally in Iran; it gained an implacable new enemy that made the Soviet Union seem staid by comparison. Anti-Americanism peaked in November of 1979 when a mob of Iranian students, angry that the United States had admitted the ailing shah into an American hospital for medical treatment, broke into the US embassy in the capital city of Tehran and took dozens of hostages. Some were released shortly thereafter, but the remaining 52 remained in captivity for 444 days. Their ordeal riveted the nation's attention and demonstrated—once again—the limits of American power. After an initial wave of support, the length of the ordeal, combined with a failed military mission to free the captives in the spring of 1980, steadily eroded Carter's popularity.

But the turning point in Carter's presidency had probably occurred in July 1979. He had gotten some momentum amid an economic uptick and the successful negotiation of an Egyptian–Israeli peace settlement in 1978, but the renewed energy crisis had sent the national mood spiraling downward again, a problem compounded by a perception that Carter was irresolute. In an attempt to act decisively, he cancelled a scheduled speech and spent a week at the presidential retreat at Camp David to interview Americans from all walks of life (including Christopher Lasch, of *The Culture of Narcissism* fame). When he returned, he went on television to deliver one of the most remarkable addresses in presidential history, which he called the "Crisis of Confidence." While most presidents make speeches to inspire, if not compliment, the American people, Carter questioned some of the fundamental assumptions of national life. "In a nation that was proud of hard work, strong families, close-knit communities, and our faith in God, too many of us now tend to worship self-indulgence and consumption," he told his fellow citizens. "Human identity is no longer defined by what one does, but by what one owns. But we've discovered that owning things and consuming things does not satisfy our longing for meaning. We've learned that piling up material goods cannot fill the emptiness of lives which have no confidence or purpose."

Initial reaction to the speech was positive. Gradually, however, media coverage focused on the idea that a president's job is less to criticize than exhort, and a term that surfaced to describe Carter's critique—"malaise"—was applied to the president himself; "Crisis of Confidence" would henceforth be remembered as the "Malaise Speech." (A 1993 episode of *The Simpsons* depicted an unveiling of a Jimmy Carter statue in the town of Springfield, bearing the words "Malaise Forever.") Carter's approval rating, mired at 25% at the time of the speech, rallied briefly with the onset of the Iranian hostage crisis that fall, but was never restored to the popularity he enjoyed at the start of his presidency.[27]

Solitary Refinement: The Me Decade

Carter's "Crisis of Confidence" speech may not have been wise, and it may not have been entirely fair. But he was on to something, and indeed had been for some time. "We have learned that 'more' is not necessarily 'better,' that even our great nation has its recognized limits," he had said in his inaugural address in 1977. Carter was addressing the broad sense of retreat, even despair, in the wake of the civil rights movement, the War on Poverty, and the War in Vietnam. And he recognized that a sense of individualism and materialism were widespread responses to such disappointments. The problem was that, far from being willing to give them up in the name of the common good, most Americans clung more tightly to them than ever. And this was true on the right no less than the left, though in very different ways.

Before explaining how and why this is so, it's probably worth pausing to emphasize the material realities of American life by the late 1970s, and here there are two, perhaps conflicting, points to keep in mind. The first is that the overall US economy was noticeably less strong in the 1970s than it had been in the 1960s, and so, for millions of Americans, there was a sense of *relative* deprivation, not so much because they had less, but because just about everything (thanks to energy prices) now cost more. Feeling pinched and fearful of losing what you have sometimes has the effect of leading one to focus on creature comforts.

The second point is that the economy never got *that* bad. The nation did not see a return to conditions that resembled the Great Depression, for example—most economists agree that *inflation*, painful as it can be, is not as scary as *deflation*, or falling prices, which has the effect of freezing an economy entirely, and people stop buying things because they're convinced prices will keep going down. Nor did military setbacks ever endanger the US homeland (though terrorism abroad was a growing problem). For the most part, internal turmoil never got to the point where Americans felt they had to collectively fear for their safety, notwithstanding the urban crime problem, real as it was, and troubling as it could be, as when an extended power outage in New York City in the summer of 1977 resulted in widespread looting. In short, Americans could *afford* to indulge their penchant to look inward, which was both a testament to the underlying strength of the American empire even as it was also a factor that would, over time, weaken its cohesion. In the early 1970s, this interiority had been of a more reflective kind, as suggested by the success of singer–songwriters such as Joni Mitchell and popular books such as economist E. F. Schumacher's *Small is Beautiful* (1973), which focused on sustainability. But, by the late 1970s, such individualism had taken on a more materialist—some would say crass—character.

To at least some extent, it was the prevailing economic conditions that put pressure on Americans to spend money. In an inflationary situation, one is acutely aware that putting off buying anything is likely to mean it will cost more later. And rising prices mean that the value of a currency is worth relatively less over time, which means that debt you incur now will be relatively easier to pay back later. Whatever arguments one may be tempted to make about American self-indulgence, this was surely a major factor in a 5,000% (!) increase in credit card debt between 1968 and 1982.[28] Unfortunately, accelerating consumption also put pressure on interest rates—when lots of people want to borrow money, the cost of doing so tends to go up—which by 1980 had reached alarmingly high levels. So while you might want to invest in a new home, for example, because you believed its value would increase, it often became impossible to afford the payments on the loan you would need to buy one.

This economic logic applied no less to businesses than it did individuals, and it was during the 1960s and 1970s that corporate America went on a buying binge of consolidation, giving rise to ungainly conglomerates involved in industries that ranged from parking to moviemaking (to cite the example of the Kinney Corporation). The imperative to search for profit had other implications as well, among them the internationalization of US businesses and growing resistance toward labor, resulting in a growing tendency to move jobs to cheaper parts of the country or abroad, putting the squeeze on labor unions, whose numbers and influence dropped steadily.[29] Until the 1970s, it was widely understood by business executives that corporations were government-chartered organizations that had an obligation to workers, customers, and the public at large. After that, however, the rights of shareholders became increasingly important; by the 1980s, they were regarded as paramount. A business is not the same thing as a person, of course, though in legal terms they could be treated as such. More than ever, businesses were seeking, and getting, such affirmations of their rights.

This sense of fragmentation was discernible in even the most communitarian areas of American life. The civil rights movement, for example, hardly died in the 1970s—activists on a wide variety of fronts pushed, often successfully, to integrate schools, neighborhoods, and workplaces over the course of the decade. Two African American women Democrats in particular are noteworthy: in 1972, Barbara Jordan of Texas became the first Southern African American woman to get elected to Congress, where she played a prominent role in the Watergate investigation; and New York congresswoman Shirley Chisolm became the first African American woman to run for president on a major political party ticket in 1972. Both politicians were important in foregrounding the intersection between race and gender in the 1970s. But there is little question that the civic dimension of the civil rights movement was more diffuse by then; in particular, it lost the core religious cohesion that had done so much to bring it to life in the 1950s. Given the growing indifference—and resistance—to the movement, its advocates increasingly turned to the courts, fostering what some legal observers have called a "rights revolution" focusing on individual entitlement. While this was, in many cases, legitimate, even essential, it represented a basic change in direction from the mass-mobilization approach that characterized the classical phase of the movement.

There were two major fronts in the civil rights battle of the 1970s. The first was the issue of court-ordered busing, a tactic whereby white and African American children were sent to schools outside their residential neighborhoods for the purposes of fostering racial integration. In *Swann v. Charlotte-Mecklenburg Board of Education* (1971), a unanimous Supreme Court ruled that the preservation of neighborhood schools was less important than ending racial segregation. Two years later, the court reaffirmed this principle in *Keyes v. Denver School District #1* (1973), which applied it for the first time outside the South. But, in *Milliken v. Bradley* (1974), a divided court ruled 5–4 against a busing plan involving the largely African American Detroit and its largely white suburbs, establishing limits in extending busing beyond city limits into its metropolitan fringe. Though still largely liberal (Chief Justice Earl Warren, who had promoted the *Brown v. Board* decision in 1954, had retired in 1969), the Supreme Court began a gradual drift rightward under Warren Burger, a Nixon appointee.

Significantly, the most contentious battle over busing in the 1970s occurred in Boston—a non-Southern city with a justifiably liberal reputation. But here, as in many other places, the politics of race were deeply entangled with the politics of class, which in this case pitted white working-class residents of South Boston against white judges and politicians who typically came from more pedigreed backgrounds. Whatever merits of busing its advocates may have claimed, the fact that so many of them (including the state's governor, the judge in charge of the case, and the architect of its urban busing plan) sent their own children to private schools gave rise to complaints of "limousine liberalism"—the notion that social justice was something to be engineered for other people's children.[30] And the fact that we *are* talking about children here is part of what made the whole busing issue so controversial; the notion that a parent's primary obligation—more important than any experimental notion of social justice—rests with the welfare of one's own child suggests the degree to which private life trumped public life.

The other major civil rights flashpoint in the 1970s was Affirmative Action. As indicated in Chapter 4, the attempt to redress racial injustice by adjusting access to educational and professional opportunities began idealistically in the early 1960s and was cynically manipulated by Richard Nixon in the early 1970s. But, whatever the intentions, Affirmative Action was an increasingly obvious fact of national life by the late 1970s, and as such attracted growing hostility from white Americans who were fearful it would hurt their own prospects. In 1973, a 32-year-old engineer named Allan Bakke was denied admission to the medical school in University of California at Davis, even though he had higher test scores than many minority students who were admitted. The medical school had a racial quota allocating 16% of an entering class for such students. Bakke sued the school for reverse discrimination. In the 1978 decision *Regents of the University of California v. Bakke*, the Court narrowly ruled 5–4 in favor of Bakke, rejecting the practice of specific quotas. However, in a key opinion written by Associate Justice Lewis Powell, the court stated that, while schools could not admit or exclude students solely on the basis of race, racial considerations could be a *factor*, along with any number of other academic, geographic, or other qualifications, in the process of assembling a diverse class. Though widely regarded as unsatisfactory—and though many institutions in American life continued to employ de facto "target" quotas for decades to come—Powell's logic represented the prevailing commonsense for the rest of the twentieth century. In any case, Affirmative Action became one more way in which civil rights was promoted and experienced on an individual and procedural level rather than a collective enterprise pursued by activists in demonstrations and/or the ballot box.

Amid the heightening sense of racial self-assertion among African Americans, there was a new emphasis on collective identity among some white Americans in the 1970s, albeit one that was more cultural than political, and one that celebrated personal choice rather than fixed identity. If, as James Brown famously chanted in 1968, "Say it loud/I'm black and I'm proud," perhaps other people—especially those whose ancestors never owned slaves and arrived after the Emancipation Proclamation—could say something similar. In an influential 1971 book *The Rise of the Unmeltable Ethnics*, Catholic intellectual Michael Novak declared the independence of a new generation of Americans—Irish, Polish, Greek, among others—from white Anglo-Saxon Protestant standards of assimilation (and guilt). "Individuals, if they do not wish to, do not have to 'melt'," Novak asserted.[31] One reason why *The Godfather* saga was so widely celebrated in the 1970s was the way it seemed to celebrate Italian identity as powerful and valuable in its own right in American culture. One of the first mini-series in television history, *Roots*, was a multigenerational saga tracing the journey of an African American family from slavery to freedom. It created a sensation in 1977. Less remembered—but not much less widely watched—was another series that aired the following year, *Holocaust*, about a Jewish family's ordeal in the 1930s and 1940s (it starred an emerging young actress named Meryl Streep). As a number of subsequent observers have noted, the New Ethnicity of the 1970s—the era spawned a genealogy craze—exploited the historical reality that not all white people were considered equally white; ethnic minorities such as the Irish Catholics and southern Italians, for instance, *became* white over a number of generations. But such observations, which increasingly became proclamations, often served to obscure contemporary realities of racial privilege by asserting ethnic innocence. Such strategies, as one historian noted, fossilized racism "safely in a past too distant to implicate any but the blood-soaked Nordic American."[32]

Body Politics: Gender and Its Discontents

Nowhere were the alternating currents of solidarity and individualism more apparent than in the realm of feminism. This had been obvious in the very roots of second-wave feminism in the civil rights movement, which dramatized the alternatively complementary and divergent dimensions of race as well as gender for women. But, in the 1970s, it also became impossible to ignore the reality that not even all white women thought alike: issues of class and religion, among others, complicated efforts to advance a feminist agenda. Radical feminists grew impatient with liberal feminists, arguing that issues such as rape, abortion, and sexual expression—an issue particularly important for lesbians—mattered more than equal pay for equal work. African American feminists grew impatient with radical feminists in their focus on matters that seemed to reflect a sense of personal entitlement and myopia about identities other than gender. Liberal and radical feminists grew impatient with cultural feminists, who they regarded as disconnected, if not nostalgic, in their focus on women's art and expression. And so on.

Which is not to say that women as a whole did not make major advances in the 1970s. Feminists successfully reframed problems such as rape, noting, for example, that such crimes were often committed by men who knew—were even married to—the women they assaulted, and helped establish a series of rape crisis centers across the country. In 1975, office worker Carmita Wood coined the term "sexual harassment" to describe the difficulties she was experiencing as an office worker at Cornell University, and the recently established Equal Employment Opportunity Commission led by Eleanor Holmes Norton pursued the problem proactively.[33] Responding to a half-century of activism, Congress in 1972 passed legislation for an Equal Rights Amendment to the US Constitution, which read, "Equality of rights under the law shall not be denied or abridged by the United States, or by any State, on account of sex." At that point, the amendment was sent to the states for ratification, and 35 of the necessary 38, or three-fourths, of the states had approved by 1977. Meanwhile, a wave of same-sex schools went co-ed, Title IX was added to existing civil rights law, and women were admitted to the major military academies for the first time.

Women also occupied increasingly visible roles in politics and the media. In 1971, activist Gloria Steinem founded *Ms.*, a high-profile and agenda-setting feminist magazine. In 1976, journalist Barbara Walters became the first woman to be paid US$1 million as salary when she took a job as co-anchor for the ABC nightly newscast with veteran broadcaster Harry Reasoner (who deeply resented her presence). No fair-minded person would claim that women were anywhere near social or economic equality—it was routinely observed that women made 59 cents to every male US dollar—but even skeptical observers could plausibly feel that such an outcome was on the horizon.

One of the most important victories won by feminists in the 1970s was the constitutional right to an abortion, affirmed in the *Roe v. Wade* Supreme Court decision in yet another momentous development in the consequential year of 1973. Between 1974 and 1977, 3.5 million abortions were performed in the United States, nearly four for every 10 live births. In Washington DC in 1976, the number of abortions was actually equal to the number of live births. Nationally, the number of abortions went up steadily into the 1980s and remained high, averaging 1.5 million a year until 1990, when the rate began to decline.[34] Many feminists viewed abortion as a non-negotiable right, justified as a matter of safety—countless illegal abortions had been performed in conditions hazardous to the mother—as well as privacy and control over one's own body.

Body politics were increasingly important in the 1970s. After millennia of subjugation to the demands of men, many women regarded it as essential that they articulate their desires, sexual and otherwise. A new interest in the female orgasm animated the sexual discourse of the era, along with a new sense of celebration of the female form as expressed in movements such as body art, which emerged in the 1960s and flourished in the 1970s, and in the work of feminist artist Judy Chicago. The 1970 book *Our Bodies, Ourselves* became a bible for generations of women seeking information about women's health and sexuality; similarly embraced was *The Joy of Sex*, first published in 1971 (both books have gone through multiple subsequent editions). Non-marital cohabitation became routine in the 1970s, which was also a period when spouse-swapping was widely discussed and depicted in popular culture.

The new sense of candor was more than sexual. First Lady Betty Ford bravely spoke out about her struggles with alcoholism and breast cancer, effectively taking these issues out of the proverbial closet. The path-breaking sitcom *All in the Family*, which engaged issues such as the counterculture and civil rights in the early 1970s, also included episodes in which the show's actor Jean Stapleton experienced sexual assault and underwent menopause.

Notions of gender presentation were also under revision. The multitalented Barbra Streisand, playing a brassy Marxist Jew, was paired with the conventionally gorgeous Robert Redford in *The Way We Were* (1973), a story set earlier in the century but with unmistakable contemporary accents. Diane Keaton created a (male-inspired) fashion craze with her role in Woody Allen's hit movie *Annie Hall* in 1977. The geeky Allen himself became an unlikely leading man in the 1970s, as did Dustin Hoffman. Sitcom *M*A*S*H* star Alan Alda became the quintessential feminist man for his commitment to liberal causes.

That said, traditional notions of beauty, whether that of beefcake movie star Burt Reynolds or pinup favorite Farrah Fawcett, remained apparent enough. Actually, the new gender/sexual order could be exploited for a less enlightened agenda. As feminist critic Barbara Ehrenreich argued in her important 1983 book *The Hearts of Men*, it was men, not women, who got the most benefit from loosening sexual standards. A new wave of T&A ("tits and ass") television shows, among them the sitcom *Three's Company* (1977–1984) and *Charlie's Angels* (1976–1981), used presumably feminist premises—unmarried cohabitation, women as daring private investigators—to showcase highly sexualized stars such as Suzanne Somers and the iconic Fawcett.

Another crucial factor promoting more liberal values in television was technological: the rise of cable television. Actually, cable had been around since the 1940s; it had first been developed as an alternative for people living in remote rural areas who lacked good reception. In the 1960s, cable was popular for athletic events such as boxing matches. But it took on entirely new dimensions when Home Box Office (HBO), founded in 1972, began showing classic and recent movies, unedited and without interruptions, for a monthly subscription fee. Now levels of nudity and violence previously consigned to dark movie theaters could be seen in the privacy of one's own home. Pornography in particular exploded as a cable (and even more later as a video) genre.

As always, consumer capitalism was ready to tap the indulgent ethos of the era. In the words of a famous commercial for a women's hair dye brand, "This I do for me." ("The commercial would have spoken more directly to the times if it had added 'and this, and this, and this'," one historian snarked.)[35] "Have it your way," went the chorus of a long-running Burger King campaign that began in the 1970s. In the decades to come, the imperative to personally configure one's consumer products, from computers to coffee, became the prevailing basis of American consumerism.

Gender-diverse Americans were at the frontier in affirming the 1970s pleasure principle, fusing sexuality with other forms of personal expression such as fashion. While they were still subject to hostility and discrimination, they were also successful in carving out enclaves for themselves, whether in the Castro district of San Francisco or on the beaches of New York's Fire Island. Their impact on the culture at large was most evident in popular music, where gays were crucial in the emergence of the new subgenre of disco. Disco was a highly urban, technology-driven musical form that exploited repetition and elaborate nightclub settings to achieve a hypnotic effect. Gay audiences were central in making stars of performers such as (the heterosexual) Donna Summer, whose erotically charged "Love to Love You Baby" (1975) became a gigantic hit. Latino music and audiences were also important components of disco and the source of the dance craze known as the Hustle, which was also the name of a huge hit single in 1975. Initially something of an insider's taste—the house music at the notoriously decadent Studio 54 in New York, where celebrities such as Andy Warhol held court—disco exploded in the late 1970s with the release of the 1977 movie *Saturday Night Fever* and its soundtrack album featuring the Australian trio the Bee Gees, a 1960s rock group who reinvented themselves for the disco era.

Yet, even as disco was peaking in popular appeal, racism and homophobia—typified by a disco-burning ceremony held in a Chicago stadium in 1979—drove much of the backlash against the genre.[36] This sense of hostility was more than a matter of bigoted opinions. After activist Harvey Milk became the first openly gay politician to win political office in San Francisco in 1977, he was assassinated the following year by one of his peers on the city's board of supervisors.

Ironically, a number of highly successful rock stars of the 1970s were gay or bisexual, flourishing in what most observers viewed as a bastion of male heterosexuality. Some performers, such as Elton John and Freddie Mercury of Queen, were closeted, though their flamboyant personal style essentially hid their sexuality in plain sight. Others, such as David Bowie, who embodied a postmodern style of shifting identities over the course of his long and influential career, were more open. Perhaps not surprisingly, all three of these performers were British, not American, though, in yet another irony, they all were capable of looking and sounding like raging working-class heterosexuals when they chose to, as in songs such as Elton John's "Saturday Night's Alright for Fighting" (1973) or Queen's "Tie Your Mother Down" (1976).

Rebellion and Revival: Pop Culture of the Late Seventies

Artists such as Bowie and Queen (who collaborated in the memorable 1981 hit "Under Pressure") provoked a backlash in another way, however. Their increasing emphasis on glamour—Bowie was at the forefront of a genre known as glam-rock—and the trappings of classical sophistication in rock music grew tiresome to some critics and audiences. The response was the birth of punk rock, first in New York and then London, which sought to recapture the anarchic energy of early rock and its capacity to shock and offend. In the case of British punk, notably the Sex Pistols and the Clash, this music was tied to economic conditions that were more severe than in the United States. American punk, as played by the New York Dolls or the Ramones, had a more cheerfully brutal quality. Commercially speaking, punk rock made relatively little inroads in the United States. But it did generate an enormous amount of media coverage— especially in the spectacularly surreal Sex Pistols tour of the United States in 1978—and helped revitalize mainstream rock in the form of the New Wave, which emerged in the late 1970s and early 1980s in bands such as Talking Heads and Blondie, fronted by the charismatic Deborah Harry, who enjoyed long-lasting success by infusing other pop genres (including rap music, to be discussed in more detail in Chapter 8) with a punk sensibility.

Punk's attempt to revitalize rock by reconnecting it with its original rude energy was part of a broader alternating current in American culture that looked back even as other facets of that culture looked forward (or simply within). While never really experienced as conservative, the success of Bruce Springsteen as a performer—and especially as a recording artist in his classic 1975 album *Born to Run*—was rooted in Springsteen's rich sense of rock tradition and his dazzling lack of irony in an increasingly self-conscious age. Springsteen alluded to Elvis Presley, Bo Diddley, and a trove of countless one-hit wonders in songs that were decisively his own, especially the title track, a thrilling celebration of the road animated by an air of desperation as well as grandeur.

A similar sense of revitalization could be seen in the movie business. Earlier in this chapter, I classified Steven Spielberg's *Jaws* as a kind of disaster movie, which in some important sense it certainly was. But the movie is widely regarded as a game changer in Hollywood, because its tremendous success as a matter of suspenseful storytelling—and even more as a matter of commerce—gave birth to the phenomenon of the blockbuster movie. Blockbusters transformed the industry by focusing resources on big-budget extravaganzas that would create huge audiences. In many respects, this was a nefarious development that sucked creative oxygen out of other projects, and, to some degree, a dumbing-down of content for mass (and international) consumption. But, at their best—as in the work of Spielberg's friendly rival George Lucas, who directed the first of a series of *Star Wars* movies in 1977—blockbusters enchanted a new generation of moviegoers in ways that recalled the power of movies in the mid-century. Spielberg would perform such magic in his sunny sci-fi movies *Close Encounters of the Third Kind* (1977) and *E. T.* (1982); he and Lucas would collaborate on the classic 1930s action-adventure tale *Raiders of the Lost Ark* (1981). Spielberg and Lucas were successful in large measure because, technical wizardry notwith-standing, both were extraordinarily gifted in their storytelling techniques, which often drew on mythic or otherwise old-fashioned sources (*Star Wars* was essen-tially a sci-fi Western). One could make a similar point about the comedy sketch show *Saturday Night Live*, which was bracing in its sharp, postmodern sensi-bility when it debuted in 1975, but in fact owed a debt to the classic comedy variety shows from the early days of television.

In other cases, this appeal to tradition took the form of more straightforward nostalgia. It was during the 1970s that the 1950s were rediscovered, now celebrated—selectively—as a time of relative innocence in American society. The novelty act Sha Na Na, whose name derives from a line in the 1957 Silhouettes hit "Get a Job," performed golden oldies throughout the decade and hosted a variety show on television from 1977 to 1981. George Lucas had his cinematic breakthrough in 1973 by directing *American Graffiti*, a loving recreation of a memorable night in the Modesto, California, of his youth. ("Where were you in '62?" was the promotional line of the movie, but the 1962 of its setting harkened back to the Eisenhower years much more than the 1960s.) Another celebration of the youthful 1950s, the long-running musical *Grease*, made its debut on Broadway in 1972; it became smash hit film in 1978, with a retro-minded soundtrack that spawned a series of hits, among them ones sung by the two leads, Australian pop singer Olivia Newton-John, and superstar John Travolta, following up on his success in *Saturday Night Fever* the previous year. More cozy sentimentality was offered by *The Waltons* (1971–1981), a television series set in the rural South during the Great Depression and World War II. Other examples of nostalgia for this period were suggested by the success of Herman Wouk's 1971 novel *The Winds of War* (later made into a successful television miniseries) and pop singer Bette Midler's 1972 rendition of the Andrew Sisters' 1940s hit "The Boogie Woogie Bugle Boy."

Right Signal: The Conservative Turn

The sense of longing for a country that was widely perceived as slipping away was more than a pop culture fad. In fact, it was a gathering social and political force that provoked powerful responses. Those responses would be felt most fully in the 1980s, but, by the late 1970s, they were gathering in ways that were experienced by friend and foe alike as a rising tide. The shorthand name given to this tide was the "New Right," or "neoconservatism" (a term coined by the democratic socialist Michael Harrington in 1973),[37] both of which encapsulated a series of components, not all of which were in synch, but which were widely perceived as converging.

Among the more obvious indications of this rising tide was American evangelicalism. The Christian revival that had emerged in the early 1970s did not have a distinct political valence; cultural manifestations such as *Jesus Christ Superstar* and *Godspell* were rooted in the counterculture, and Jimmy Carter had enjoyed at least some evangelical support when he ran for president as a Democrat. By the late 1970s, however, it was obvious that evangelicalism had become a largely conservative phenomenon. A new generation of evangelical leaders, more edgy—and in the minds of many Americans, less reputable—than Billy Graham, was coming to the fore. Jerry Falwell, a Baptist minister from Lynchburg, Virginia, founded the Moral Majority in 1979; its name, redolent of Richard Nixon's Silent Majority, suggested its political orientation, something of a departure, given the general Baptist tendency to avoid partisan politics. "It is time we come together and rise up against the tide of permissiveness and moral decay that is crushing in on our society from every side," Falwell said in a typical pronouncement from 1980. "I am convinced that God is calling millions of Americans in the so-often-called silent majority to join in the moral-majority crusade to turn America around in our lifetime."[38] Another Baptist minister, Pat Robertson, son of a Democratic senator from Virginia, created both *The 700 Club*, a popular religious program, and the Christian Broadcast Network (CBN) in the 1960s, both of which attained national prominence in the 1970s, thanks to the spread of cable television. So did *The Old-Time Gospel Hour* (1956–), a program sponsored by Falwell's church.

The evangelical right was especially focused on issues of gender and sexuality. In 1977, former beauty queen Anita Bryant reacted to Dade County, Florida's decision to pass legislation outlawing discrimination based on sexual orientation by founding Save the Children, an organization that worked successfully to overturn it. When told by an acquaintance that the rule protecting homosexual rights was necessary for the advancement of civil rights, Bryant responded, "What about *my* civil rights? Flaunting homosexual teaching in private and religious schools violates my religious beliefs. I believe I have a constitutional right to protect my children from knowledge of what God calls an abomination."[39] Bryant's strategy of using the language and logic of the civil rights movement against its allies would become increasingly common in the decades to come.

Evangelicals were also instrumental in the defeat of the Equal Rights Amendment. After an initial surge in momentum in the early and mid-1970s, support for ratification receded sharply. The 1982 refusal of Illinois voters to approve the amendment was the final nail in the coffin, but it was clear the ERA was in fatal difficulty years earlier. To be sure, there were plenty of sexist men, evangelical and not, who played a role in its defeat. But, by the late 1970s, it was apparent that feminist proposals to advance the interests of women did not win the assent of all women, some of whom saw genuine advantages in the sense of respect and protection they believed they commanded in a traditional gender paradigm. This was especially true of evangelical women, who were among the most vocal on the issue. Antifeminist leader Phyllis Schlafly, who founded the Eagle Forum in 1972 partly to stop the ERA, was the most prominent figure on the movement. ("I'd like to burn you at the stake!" NOW founder Betty Friedan said to her at a 1973 debate.)[40] Schlafly called on what she called "the Positive Woman" to embrace male–female sexual difference and her responsibilities as a wife and mother. "A Positive Woman cannot defeat a man in a wrestling or boxing match, but she can motivate him, inspire him, encourage him, teach him, restrain him, reward him, and have a power over him that he can never achieve over her with all his muscle," she noted in a 1977 book.[41] Some feminists in the next generation would embrace this notion of sexual difference and take it in an alternative direction, but, in the 1970s, it was widely understood as a conservative position by friend and foe alike.

Conservative women were also important in what was probably the most central issue to evangelicals: the politics of abortion. There's no question that *Roe v. Wade* was a controversial decision when it was handed down in 1973; the first annual March for Life, a ritual that has continued ever since, began in 1974, and did so with significant female support and organizational savvy. But it was not until the late 1970s that the evangelical right marshaled its full energies around the issue. Falwell, for example, did not make a statement in opposition to abortion until 1975. To some extent, Protestants were slow to take up the issue because it was seen as a Catholic preoccupation, and the historic chill between the two was only beginning to thaw in the late 1970s.⁴² But by the end of the decade, it had become arguably its most powerful wedge issue in national life.

Even more than a religious issue (the theological dimensions of it are arguably ambiguous), the abortion controversy was cast in terms of individual rights on both sides, pitting a fertilized embryo—a person from one perspective, a mere mass of tissue from the other—against that of the mother. Actually, as a matter of polling and public perception, there was a tenuous consensus on the issue: as journalist E. J. Dionne noted two decades later, most Americans believed that a woman has a right to an abortion, especially in the case of incest or to protect the life of the mother, and most believe it should not be done lightly or be easy to procure.⁴³ To be sure, there are devils in the details, especially ones involving who should pay for the procedure. But one reason why the *Roe v. Wade* Supreme Court decision hasn't been overturned is that the national balance of opinion has never fundamentally shifted since then. That said, the momentum has been against feminists, beginning as far back as 1976, when the so-called Hyde Amendment (named after Illinois congressman Henry Hyde) banned the use of Medicaid funds to pay for an abortion except in cases of rape, incest, or to protect the life of the mother. The *Roe v. Wade* Supreme Court decision has been chipped away at in subsequent judicial rulings, and the stigma surrounding abortion persists, though, in recent years, feminists have been pushing back against strategies that in any way suggest that abortion is a necessary evil rather than a cherished right. In any case, partisans on both sides of the issue have taken strong positions and attracted ardent defenders, not only in terms of building solidarity—particularly for fundraising and other political activities—but also in viewing abortion as dramatizing a cluster of values (sexual, moral, legal, among others) central to their identities. For all their differences, however, the individual rights dimension of the fight remains central, essentially agreed upon by those on opposite sides of the question.

This notion of rights can help one understand one of the more curious aspects of American politics of the 1970s: the intensifying alliance between the evangelical right and a rejuvenated corporate capitalism. In theory, at least, secular business executives and evangelical Christians would appear not only to have little in common, but be downright hostile to one another. Capitalism rests on notions of competition and the profit motive; Christianity rests on a notion of charity and selflessness. In fact, of course, Christianity and capitalism have managed to co-exist in the United States and elsewhere for centuries. But this has typically been understood more in terms of co-existence and a notion of separate spheres than avowed integration and cooperation. Beginning in the late 1970s, however, the alliance between Christians and capitalists became an increasingly obvious feature the American right.

One longstanding bridge between them was anticommunism, whose relevance intensified as *détente* broke down. "It is sad that it has taken a crisis like the Soviet invasion of Afghanistan to make our leaders realize the terrible threats of communism," Falwell wrote in 1980.[44] Another common trait was a shared language of "personal responsibility," a word that was often invoked by multiple strands of the right. Both evangelicals and capitalists were skeptical, if not hostile, toward post-1960s liberalism, which typically championed welfare programs of various kinds at public expense. Liberals tended to be *socially* libertarian, prizing personal expression but willing to compel workers in unionized work forces to pay dues, whether they wanted to or not, in the name of a collective greater good, to cite one example. But conservatives tended to be *economically* libertarian, seeking to maintain the right to spend their money as they saw fit (presumably some of it for charity), even as they believed in promoting, even prescribing, standards of appropriate behavior in ways the left considered as forms of "legislating morality."

Conservatives developed new institutions—here, they stole a march on the anti-institutional left—to help advance their shared ideological agenda. Activist Paul Weyrich, who had worked on Barry Goldwater's presidential campaign in 1964, helped midwife a number of organizations, including the Heritage Foundation, to articulate the New Right agenda (in fact, Weyrich coined that term, along with "Moral Majority").[45] It was followed by the Cato Institute and the American Enterprise Institute, as well as a series of other so-called think tanks. Such efforts were aided by Richard Wirthlin, a highly regarded conservative pollster who became a strategist for Ronald Reagan.

Absolutely crucial to the all these efforts was the wave of money that sprang up to create and sustain them. The late 1970s saw an explosion of the new political action committees (PACs), which had both grassroots support from small donors as well as hugely decisive corporate backers increasingly willing to throw their weight around. They did so by financing candidates who promoted their interests. Campaign reform laws in the aftermath of Watergate tried to limit the role of money in politics by placing caps on what individuals could donate. But PACs found loopholes around this, chiefly by avoiding direct collusion with candidates but nevertheless paying for advertisements that helped them get elected. This tendency would only become more intense over the course of ensuing decades, aided by the 1976 Supreme Court decision *Buckley v. Valeo*, which struck down some early attempts to limit campaign spending. Subsequent attempts to control it would prove largely fruitless.

Whatever synergies may have been forming between the business community and evangelical Christians, there were plenty of Americans who weren't religious *or* part of the commercial elite who had their own problems with the post-1960s left. Among the most vocal was a new generation of anti-tax activists who sprang up around the country. In 1953, the average American family paid less than 12% of its income in federal, state, and local taxes. By 1977, however, that figure had risen to 22%, much of it driven by inflation, which raised the value of homes and thus property tax bills.[46] Ground zero for the tax revolt of the 1970s was California. Activist Howard Jarvis led the charge for Proposition 13, which capped real estate taxes and limited future increases. Despite opposition from both Democrats and Republicans concerned about its impact on schools and other social services, it passed by a 2–1 margin in 1978. (California schools, which were widely regarded as the best in the country, underwent a steady decline.) A similar proposal, Proposition 2½, passed in Massachusetts 2 years later. Significantly, these were states with strong liberal reputations. To some degree, such referenda had liberal support; in Massachusetts, for example, much support for Proposition 2½ came from local residents angry about sweetheart tax rates for businesses that forced them to carry a heavier burden. There was also a widespread sense of corruption and waste at all levels in the government. But, as with evangelicalism, the conservative character of the anti-tax movement became clear over time.[47]

After surveying the nation's cultural landscape from left to right in the late 1970s, it becomes clear why so many people were dissatisfied with Jimmy Carter's "malaise" mentality by the end of the decade. The left disliked Carter's critique of self-gratification; the right disliked Carter's suggestion that Americans needed to reconsider their sense of entitlement to limitless resources at low cost.[48] The question, as a presidential election year approached in 1980, was who could take his place.

On the left, the answer came from Edward Moore "Ted" Kennedy, who, after some initial reluctance, decided to challenge Carter for the Democratic nomination. Kennedy, who became a US Senator from Massachusetts in 1962 to take the seat vacated by his brother John F. Kennedy when he became president, took over leadership of the Kennedy family after his brother Robert F. Kennedy's assassination in 1968. Unlike his brothers, Ted Kennedy cultivated a reputation as a master legislator in a Senate career that stretched almost half a century, earning a reputation as a stalwart defender of liberal causes (though his critics considered him just another limousine liberal). But the call of the presidency proved impossible for Kennedy to resist. He had serious baggage, however. In 1969, Kennedy had driven a car off a bridge on the Massachusetts island of Chappaquiddick while in the company of a 28-year-old woman named Mary Jo Kopechne. After swimming ashore, Kennedy had gone to bed in a nearby hotel, leaving Kopechne to drown. Kennedy apologized, pleaded guilty to leaving the scene of an accident, and was given a suspended sentence of 2 months in jail. Massachusetts voters forgave Kennedy—he would ultimately be elected to the Senate seven times—but Chappaquiddick, as the event was subsequently known, effectively scotched Kennedy's hopes for running for president in 1972 and 1976. In 1979, however, Kennedy responded to the urging of restless liberals and decided to take on Carter. But Carter, who enjoyed a brief bump in the polls at the onset of the Iran hostage crisis, was able to outlast Kennedy in the primaries and earn re-nomination.

It's a measure of the shifting political landscape that Carter also faced a challenge from the center that came from outside the Democratic *and* Republican parties. John Anderson, a moderate Republican Congressman and evangelical minister from Illinois, decided to enter the race, initially as a Republican. But when he didn't get much traction in a crowded field, Anderson ran as an independent candidate. He was best known for a proposal to levy a 50-cent-per-gallon gas tax coupled with a break on Social Security taxes, a proposal that suggested a curious blend of liberal energy policy and conservative tax policy—qualities that had also characterized Ford's and Carter's approach to the issue. Anderson ended up with 8% of the vote, which seemed to come equally from both parties.[49]

But the most formidable challenge to replace Carter ultimately came from the New Right. At the start of the primary campaign, a lot of the smart money was on George H. W. Bush, a seasoned professional who had worked as a diplomat in China and headed the CIA under Gerald Ford. But much of the passion in the party coalesced around another figure who had become a perennial: Ronald Reagan. Reagan had first come to national political prominence on the basis of a spirited speech he had made in favor of Barry Goldwater in 1964; after getting elected governor of California in 1966, he was regarded as presidential timber by some in 1968, though Nixon got the nomination that year and was re-elected in 1972. In 1976, after having served a second term as governor, Reagan almost edged out Gerald Ford. In 1980, many Republicans believed it was his turn.

In some respects, Reagan was an unlikely standard bearer for the Republicans. A native of Illinois, he followed a stint in radio broadcasting in Iowa by going to California to make a career in Hollywood. Reagan proved to be a quintessential B actor—never really a star, he nevertheless achieved a measure of fame in movies such as *Knute Rockne, All American* (1940) and *Kings Row* (1942) before slowly drifting downward into professional desperation, as suggested by *Bedtime for Bonzo* (1951), in which his co-star was a chimpanzee. A registered Democrat, Reagan spent World War II working for the US Army in Hollywood; after the war, he became a union leader, heading the Screen Actors Guild. But his hostility to communism led him to cooperate in FBI investigations during the Red Scare of the early 1950s, part of a gradual shift to the right that became complete by 1962 when he switched to the Republican Party. Yet, as governor of California, Reagan behaved in ways that did not square with his increasingly conservative reputation: he signed bills raising taxes and making it easier for women to get abortions. Moreover, Reagan, who had never been a regular churchgoer (his mother was Protestant; his father Catholic), was divorced and remarried, a situation that had torpedoed Nelson Rockefeller's presidential ambitions.

And yet, for all this, Reagan became the darling of tax cutters and evangelicals. In large measure, this is because he staked out positions that were clearly in sympathy with such groups, reflecting his steady migration to the right over the course of the 1960s and 1970s. More than that, he was willing to do so boldly, known for lines such as calling for Vietnam to be turned into a parking lot, and "sending welfare bums back to work." But—and this is absolutely crucial to understand—Reagan also projected an often irresistibly sunny personality that drew supporters to him and led even critics to be amused by his charm. Those critics considered Nixon dangerous; they considered Reagan dumb. Nixon, who had reason to be grateful to Reagan for his stalwart, even embarrassing, loyalty all through Watergate, considered him "pretty shallow" and of "limited mental capacity."[50] Added to the fact that, if elected, Reagan would be 69 years old if he assumed the presidency, many Americans concluded that he was hopelessly out of touch.

But Reagan had made a career of being underestimated (many of the same criticisms had been made when he won a stunning upset victory to become governor). After a hard-fought campaign, he won the Republican nomination—during which he considered former president Ford for the vice presidential slot, ultimately choosing his former rival Bush—and went on to challenge Carter, who also had difficulty taking him seriously. But Reagan's simple signature question—"Are you better off than you were 4 years ago?"—was devastatingly effective. During a famous presidential debate with Carter, Reagan replied to Carter positions by saying, "There you go again."

Carter seemed to have a chance, given the concerns about Reagan's age and acuity, which made the race appear close. But economic conditions were poor, and the Iranian hostage crisis in particular was a throbbing symbol of national humiliation. Carter worked tirelessly to resolve the impasse, but the Iranian government proved difficult to conciliate (there have been allegations, never conclusively proven, that the Reagan team persuaded the Iranians not to release the hostages). So, when the polls closed on Election Day, Reagan had defeated Carter decisively, 50.7% to 41%, capturing 489 electoral votes to Carter's 49. Moreover, Reagan appeared to have a significant coattail effect; Republicans gained control of the US Senate for the first time since 1955 and took down a series of liberal lions, among them former presidential candidate George McGovern. It was only on Inauguration Day, 1981, that the hostages were finally released, ending a 444-day ordeal as well as the Carter presidency.

The presidential election of 1980 was a major turning point in American history. In 1968, the American people had signaled that they wanted a change by electing Richard Nixon, though prevailing conditions—and Nixon's notoriously Machiavellian personality—sometimes made it difficult to understand which way the US government was heading. Ronald Reagan promised change far more straightforwardly. The question now was whether he could deliver, and what that would mean. The citizens of an anxious empire were ready to give him considerable leeway.

CULTURE WATCH: *Taxi Driver* (1976)

Every functional society has a series of myths—widely believed ideas whose reality cannot be empirically proven or disproven—that function as a kind of governing common sense. These ideas include notions of the proper relations between men and women, how to explain differences between the rich and poor, and why, despite obvious injustices of one kind or another, ruling authorities still have some legitimacy (if only because imagined alternatives seem worse). Yet, in every functional society, there are also regular challenges to prevailing myths, a questioning process that typically begins among a minority of some kind and may eventually become the basis of new myths. The 1970s were a very active time of questioning in the United States, when authority of many kinds was open to challenge. Yet, doing so could also lead to a personal and political void. A number of Hollywood movies in the 1970s dramatized the moral bankruptcy of established institutions as well as the difficulties in establishing alternatives. And no movie did this as hauntingly as *Taxi Driver*.

Directed by a 33-year-old Martin Scorsese with a script by Paul Schrader, *Taxi Driver* stars a young Robert De Niro as Travis Bickle, a self-contained but troubled Vietnam veteran living in New York City. He takes a job as a cabbie because he has insomnia, and is willing to work long night hours and travel the city's most dangerous neighborhoods. In his spare time, he writes in a journal and attends pornographic movies. Bickle's attempts to break out of his social

Figure 6.2   LONER: An ominous-looking Travis Bickle (Robert De Niro) attends a presidential candidate rally in a scene from *Taxi Driver* (1976). A commercial as well as critical success, the movie captured the profound sense of alienation that became increasingly evident during the mid-1970s, and the ending of the film, in particular, upended cherished national myths (1976, directed by Martin Scorsese, and produced by Columbia Pictures Corporation, Bill/Phillips, and Italo/Judeo Productions).

isolation are unsuccessful. His relations with his colleagues are polite but distant; he befriends a campaign worker named Betsy (Cybill Shephard) for the presidential bid of Senator Charles Palantine (Leonard Harris), but she is put off when he takes her to a Swedish sex film on their first date. Increasingly frustrated, Bickle begins to turn his suppressed rage outward, buying a virtual arsenal of guns and practicing how to use them. The scene in which he speaks before a mirror to an imagined adversary—"You talkin' to me?" he repeatedly asks in variations improvised by De Niro—has become a cinematic classic. It becomes increasingly apparent that Bickle has ominous designs on Senator Palantine, who actually rides in his cab at one point (as does Scorsese himself in a minor role as an enraged cuckolded husband). But a chance encounter with a child prostitute (Jodie Foster in an early signature role) and her pimp, Sport (Harvey Keitel), lead his aggressions in a different direction as Bickle tries desperately to balance altruistic and murderous impulses.

Taxi Driver is a movie set in a milieu of pervasive corruption. Exhibit A in this regard is New York itself, a city teetering on the edge of bankruptcy in the 1970s and depicted here as dirty, dangerous, and depressing. The political process is also a sham; the Palantine campaign slogan—"We are the people"—would be totally inane if it wasn't also all too plausible. Authentic human relations are virtually non-existent; another campaign worker in the Palantine campaign (played by actor/director Albert Brooks) tells Betsy at one point that "I'll play the man in this relationship." The notorious blood-spattered ending of *Taxi Driver* is deeply, even searingly, ironic, upending conventional notions of heroism—and suggesting that heroism itself is a joke.

Perhaps the most disturbing thing about *Taxi Driver* is how successful it was. This is not an artistic judgment; most observers at the time and ever since have regarded the film as a masterpiece (it was also nominated for a bevy of Academy Awards, including Best Picture, with nods to DeNiro and Foster, but didn't win any). But of course, masterpieces are not always big box office successes. That *Taxi Driver* was both is not simply a reflection of its quality, but also indicative a national mood that was swerving dangerously close to collective cynicism and despair. In the coming months, a series of other box office successes—notably *Rocky* (1976) and *Star Wars* (1977)—suggested that the pall was beginning to lift as the nation celebrated its bicentennial. But *Taxi Driver* continues to stand as a rebuke to those who may be too quick to embrace the notion that America is always the beautiful.

Suggested Further Reading

There have been a string of good books about the 1970s. These include Peter Carroll, *It Seemed Like Nothing Happened: America in the 1970s* (1982; New Brunswick: Rutgers University Press, 1990); David Frum, *How We Got Here / The Seventies: The Decade that Brought You Modern Life—For Better or Worse* (New York: Basic, 2000); and, especially, Bruce Schulman, *The Seventies: The Great Shift in American Culture, Society and Politics*

(New York: The Free Press, 2001). For an excellent reading of 1973 in particular, see Andreas Hillen, *1973 Nervous Breakdown: Watergate, Warhol, and the Birth of Post-Sixties America* (New York: Bloomsbury, 2007).

On Gerald Ford, see John Robert Greene, *The Presidency of Gerald R. Ford* (Lawrence: University Press of Kansas, 1994). For a sympathetic reading of his life, see the biography of his former adviser James Cannon, *Time and Chance, Gerald Ford's Appointment with History* (1998; Ann Arbor: University of Michigan Press, 2008). Barry Werth puts the Nixon pardon in the wider context of the Ford presidency in *31 Days: The Crisis that Gave Us the Government We Have Today* (New York: Doubleday, 2006). On Carter, see Burton I. Kauffman and Scott Kaufman, *The Presidency of James Earl Carter, Jr.*, second revised ed. (Lawrence: University Press of Kansas, 2006). Kevin Mattson puts the "Crisis of Confidence" speech in the wider context of the Carter presidency in *What the Heck Are You Up To, Mr. President?: Jimmy Carter, America's "Malaise," and the Speech that Should Have Changed the Country* (New York: Bloomsbury, 2009).

For an excellent politico-cultural history of the 1970s, see Jefferson Cowie, *Stayin' Alive: The 1970s and the Last Days of the Working Class* (New York: The New Press, 2010).

Rick Perlstein covers many of the preceding subjects in his huge panoramic history of the period between 1973 and 1976 in *The Invisible Bridge: The Fall of Nixon and the Rise of Reagan* (New York: Simon and Shuster, 2009).

Notes

1   Joshua B. Freeman, *American Empire: The Rise of a Global Power/The Democratic Revolution at Home* (New York: Penguin, 2012), 297.
2   James Patterson, *Restless Giant: The United States from Watergate to Bush v. Gore* (New York: Oxford University Press), 8–9.
3   Freeman, 302.
4   Melani McAlister, *Epic Encounters: Culture, Media & U.S. Interests in the Middle East Since 1945*, second ed. (2001; Berkeley: University of California Press, 2005), 111.
5   Alan Wolfe, America's *Impasse: The Rise and Fall of the Politics of Growth* (Boston: South End Press, 1981), 38.
6   Freeman, 297.
7   Patterson, 7–8.
8   Freeman, 304–305.
9   Martin Shefter, *Political Crisis/Fiscal Crisis: The Collapse and Revival of New York City* (1985; New York: Columbia University Press, 1992), introduction. Shefter notes that many of the problems that NYC was facing had happened before. See also Hillen, 194–196, 204–207.
10   Freeman, 350–351.
11   Andrew Hacker, *The End of the American Era* (New York: Atheneum, 1970), 37.
12   Hacker, 4.
13   Christopher Lasch, *The Culture of Narcissism: American Life in an Age of Diminishing Expectations* (New York: Norton, 1977), xiii.
14   Freeman, 321.
15   Patterson, *Restless Giant*, 93.

16   Perlstein, 414.

17   Patterson, *Restless Giant*, 96–97; Schulman, 126.

18   Edward Epstein, "Ford Escaped Two Assassination Attempts," *The San Francisco Chronicle*, December 27, 2006: http://www.sfgate.com/news/article/Ford-escaped-2-assassination-attempts-Both-2481771.php (June 8, 2015).

19   http://www.jimmycarterlibrary.gov/documents/inaugural_address.pdf (July 1, 2014).

20   The term "evangelical" is being used here to refer to a believer in a specific sect who seeks to make converts to that sect. In some sense, it's a fairly generic term; Muslims, for example, are evangelicals; Jews are not. In a general sense, all Christians are evangelicals, in that the very faith is predicated on spreading the gospel, or "good news," of Christ's resurrection. But, for our purposes, the term "evangelical Christian" generally refers to those engaged in active efforts to recruit and convert skeptics, as well as those who have been "born again," reaffirming their faith on a new, more ardent basis at some point in their adult lives. These tendencies are less pronounced among members of older Protestant mainline churches as well as most Roman Catholics, though one branch of that faith, Charismatic Catholics, are more energetic in this regard. Catholics and Protestants have long been suspicious, if not hostile, toward each other, but began to converge in the closing decades of the twentieth century as the primary religious divides became less denominational and more cast in terms of believer vs. non-believer.

21   Important to note: not all evangelicals are fundamentalist. Again, "fundamentalist" is a term with a broad meaning, in that there are fundamentalist Muslims just as there are fundamentalist Christians. Christian fundamentalism first emerged in the 1890s as a reaction to Darwinism in particular and modernism generally.

22   Steven P. Miller, *The Age of Evangelicalism: America's Born-Again Years* (New York: Oxford University Press, 2014), 3, 19.

23   Miller, 43.

24   Patterson, *Restless Giant*, 109.

25   Miller, 48–59.

26   Schulman, 127.

27   Mattson, 7, 9, 162–166.

28   Frum, 185.

29   Freeman has numbers on this (350).

30   Frum, 263.

31   Michael Novak, *Rise of Unmeltable Ethnics* (New York: Macmillan, 1972), 270.

32   Matthew Frye Jacobson, *Whiteness of a Different Color: European Immigrants and the Alchemy of Race* (Cambridge: Harvard University Press, 1998), 278.

33   Rory Dicker, *A History of U.S. Feminisms* (New York: Seal Press, 2008), 70–71

34   Patterson, 52; Frum, 107.

35   Frum, 58.

36   Jim Cullen, *A Short History of the Modern Media* (Malden, MA: Wiley Blackwell, 2014), 206.

37   Perlstein, *Invisible Bridge*, 454.

38   Jerry Falwell, excerpt from *Listen, America!* (1980) in *The United States Since 1945: A Documentary Reader*, edited by Robert P. Ingalls and David K. Johnson (Malden, MA: Wiley Blackwell, 2009), 173, 176.

39   Anita Bryant and Bob Green, excerpt from *Raising God's Children* (1977) in Ingalls & Johnson, 164.

40   Perlstein, 459.
41   Phyllis Schlafly, excerpt from *The Power of the Positive Woman* (1977), in Ingalls & Johnson, 161.
42   Miller, 53–54.
43   E. J. Dionne's *Why Americans Hate Politics* (New York: Simon and Schuster, 1991), 341–343.
44   Falwell, 173.
45   Smith, 333.
46   Freeman, 336.
47   Schulman, 206–209.
48   Mattson, 176–177.
49   Patterson, *Restless Giant*, 150.
50   Perlstein, *The Invisible Bridge*, 159.

Part III
Indian Summer

7

Revival and Denial
The American Empire on Borrowed Time, 1981–1991

Figure 7.1 COMMUNICATING: Ronald Reagan in the Oval Office, 1986. Few Americans have ever dominated their time and place to the degree he did. "It can be done," reads the sign on his desk. For better or worse, he did a lot. Credit: Carol M. Highsmith, photographs in the Carol M. Highsmith Archive, Library of Congress, Prints and Photographs Division.

Democratic Empire: The United States Since 1945, First Edition. Jim Cullen.
© 2017 Jim Cullen. Published 2017 by John Wiley & Sons, Inc.

Right Man: The Age of Reagan

IT'S POSSIBLE TO TELL the story of the United States in the 1980s without putting Ronald Reagan at the center of it—there's a good book called *The Other Eighties* that does so[1]—but it isn't easy. (Even the title of that book suggests the marginality of the events it describes.) Reagan was not a new figure to the American political scene at the time of his election in 1980; he had been a Hollywood actor in the 1940s and 1950s, and prominent political figure in the 1960s and 1970s. But, in 1980s, he dominated national life in a way very few politicians in US history have managed to do, and his influence continued long after he left office (and long after his death in 2004). Indeed, it would not be ridiculous to suggest that, even here in the twenty-first century, we continue to live in the Age of Reagan.

To use this phrase is to evoke the reputation of two other presidents of durable impact. The first, Andrew Jackson, was similar to Reagan in that he became a national celebrity—in his case, as a general who defeated the British at the Battle of New Orleans at the end of the War of 1812—long before he ran for office. As with Reagan, he was regarded as insufficiently sophisticated to become president, and as with Reagan too, he was defeated in a bid to do so (Jackson lost the election of 1824 under hotly disputed circumstances; Reagan came up just short of capturing the Republican nomination in 1976). Once they took office, however, both Jackson and Reagan overcame substantial opposition in implementing their legislative agendas. The political vision of both was one of limited government—low taxes, less regulation, power devolving to the states—coupled with fierce patriotism and an assertive foreign policy (leading critics to charge both as dangerously aggressive). And both men redefined the political identities of their parties for a generation after their deaths. In 1945, historian Arthur Schlesinger, Jr.—who would become something of a celebrity himself as an adviser to John F. Kennedy—published a Pulitzer Prize–winning book titled *The Age of Jackson*.[2] Six decades later, another prominent historian, Sean Wilentz, published a book titled *The Age of Reagan* in homage to Schlesinger.

Schlesinger wrote *The Age of Jackson* during the age of another hugely influential president: Franklin Delano Roosevelt, about whom he wrote a three-volume study known collectively as *The Age of Roosevelt*.[3] In many of the respects mentioned earlier—celebrity status, defeat, political success, patriotism, lasting influence—FDR was much similar to Jackson and Reagan, and Reagan as a young man idolized Roosevelt. But there was one crucial difference: unlike the other two, FDR vastly expanded the powers of the federal government and is widely regarded as the founding father of modern liberalism. Reagan, by contrast, is often described as the ideological foil of Roosevelt because his own presidency was, in many respects, an attempt to undo FDR's legacy and make conservatism the governing logic of the nation. Scholars debate the degree to which he succeeded in realizing his goals. But that debate is matter of degree—a matter of how *much*, not *whether*, he succeeded.

In an important respect, however, Reagan's impact, similar to that of his illustrious predecessors, was at least as much a matter of psychology as much as it was a legislative agenda. Lots of presidents have power; Lyndon Johnson and Richard Nixon, to cite two contemporaries of Reagan, exerted their will to great effect while in office. But neither had the famously sunny personality that Reagan did, one that engendered a durable attachment for a generation of supporters. Roosevelt had a sunny personality too, and a surprisingly common touch. But that touch was surprising precisely because FDR came from about as elite a bloodline as it was possible to have in the United States; he had Dutch ancestors dating back to the seventeenth century and a distinguished cousin Theodore—he called him "Uncle Ted"—who also bore the Roosevelt name and had preceded him as president (he also married Theodore Roosevelt's essentially adopted niece, Eleanor, in a White House ceremony). Reagan, by contrast, was the son of an alcoholic shoe salesman; his mother was a devout Sunday school teacher in a Disciples of Christ congregation, described by Reagan historian Rick Perlstein as a "Presbyterian splinter with elements of both liberalism and fundamentalism."[4] Of course, by the time he became president, Reagan was a wealthy man, all the more so because he had spent the previous generation among moneyed men who, in many respects, groomed him for the job of governor of California and chief executive of the United States. But Reagan was known as "the great communicator" not because he was famed for the beauty of his language (such as Lincoln) or his erudite wit (such as JFK). He had that reputation because he seemed so fabulously down-to-earth.

I use the word "fabulously" in two senses. The first is the familiar one of exceptional or extraordinary: friend and foe alike agreed that Reagan was a singularly gifted politician, a man who could light up a room, and even many of his most vehement opponents found it difficult to dislike him. But I also mean "fabulous" in the sense of fable, as in fictional. Fables are stories that are meant to illuminate larger truths that transcend mere fact, and Reagan was especially fond of using anecdotes to this effect. But there were also times Reagan crossed the line and became a bona fide fabul*ist*—someone whose stories veered toward outright lies. It was difficult to call Reagan a liar, not simply because criticism seemed to roll off him—Colorado congresswoman Patricia Schroeder famously dubbed him "the Teflon President," partly because he had a crack political team that carefully stage-managed his appearances—but also because lying means making assertions that you *know* aren't true. And Reagan sometimes seemed like a man who lived in a world of make-believe.

The Reagan story—you might say the Reagan legend—is rich with stories to this effect. Among the most famous is a story he told during the 1980 presidential campaign about the crew of a bomber plane during World War II. The plane was hit and about to crash, so the members of the crew were preparing to bail out to avoid certain death. But a badly wounded member was pinned down and unable to go. The pilot of the plane told the rest of the crew to jump. Then he lay down beside the wounded man and said, "Never mind son, we'll ride down together."[5] The obvious question to the puzzled reporters listening to this story, of course, is how Reagan could know this happened, since neither of the principals survived to explain. So what was Reagan's source? Apparently, it was a Hollywood movie—the 1944 drama *A Wing and a Prayer* (starring Dana Andrews, who would appear 2 years later in *The Best Years of Our Lives*; see Chapter 2). In similar fashion, Reagan repeatedly stated that he had visited Nazi concentration camps during World War II. But, because of defective vision, he had spent the war in Hollywood, working for the army (where he processed color footage of the camps, which clearly made a deep impression on him).[6]

Most of the time, such anecdotes were innocuous. But they were less so when Reagan made imaginary charges against real people, such as about food stamp recipients who supposedly used change from their transactions to buy vodka, or when he distorted real stories—such as the so-called "welfare queen" who bilked the government of at least $150,000—to suggest such cheating was rampant among recipients of government aid.[7] Reagan apparently never doubted the veracity of such claims, and indeed his sincerity is what made him attractive to a great many people.

The great paradox of Reagan, though, is that there was something strangely, even troublingly, mysterious about his transparency: he seemed to be an open book with blank pages. Even those who knew him most intimately sometimes wondered what he was thinking. FDR was notoriously difficult to know; he was a man who withheld information, delegated the same job to multiple people, and could sound more agreeable than he really was. Reagan wasn't devious so much as he was unfathomable. He lacked close friends; his only obvious confidante was his (second) wife, Nancy, and even *she* could find him mysterious. Reagan's biographer, Edmund Morris, enjoyed unique access to Reagan, interviewing him and attending many White House meetings while Reagan was president. But after struggling for years to finish a biography, Morris finally decided that the only way to try to capture the man was to turn himself into a fictional character and reconstruct Reagan's youth that way.[8] When the legendary Simon & Schuster editor Michael Korda worked with Reagan on his memoirs, he was utterly charmed by Reagan's eagerness to make sure visitors got their picture taken with him, and in his sheer pleasure in eating, and sharing, chocolate-chip cookies (jelly beans were another favorite). But he found actually getting Reagan to reflect on his experiences to be an utterly exasperating ordeal.[9]

Perhaps the most chilling such story concerned his oldest son, Michael. On the day Michael graduated from high school, Reagan attended the ceremony and gave a commencement speech. Afterward, he came up to students individually and congratulated them. "Hi, my name's Ronald Reagan. What's yours?" After one such introduction came the reply, "Dad, it's *me*. Your son. Mike."[10] At the end of his life, Reagan would be diagnosed with Alzheimer's disease; there has been much speculation about whether the symptoms were discernible decades earlier, but, given Reagan's famous self-discipline, it seems unlikely that this was the case in any straightforward way.

Making the Cut: Reaganomics

However, at the end of the day, Reagan's personality, however interesting, mattered less than his policies. And for all his self effacing humor—"I worry about problems in government, and it's cost me many a sleepless afternoon," he joked about his well-known tendency to nap[11]—there's no question that Reagan was a genuine conviction politician: a man whose beliefs were his own, and which he consistently sought to implement. However we may feel about Reagan—and he's a man who continues to evoke strong and opposing opinions—we should judge him on his arguments and his actions, not his personality.

In the broadest terms, Reagan espoused two core principles. The first went by the name supply-side economics. The core of this doctrine asserts that the public sector of the economy—which is to say government in its various forms, especially at the national level—was too active and needed restraints in order to unleash the productive capacity of the private sector. As Reagan famously put it in his first inaugural address, which inverted what many had regarded as the conventional wisdom dating back to FDR, "government is not the solution to our problem; government is the problem." Reagan's other core conviction—the sole exception to his belief in limited government—was that the nation's defense capabilities needed to be strengthened in a quest to meet, and finally overcome, the Soviet challenge in the Cold War. We'll consider each of these in turn.

The basic idea of supply-side economics is simple. To posit a supply side, of course, implies the existence of a demand side, and in the context of US economic policy in the postwar era, this consisted, in the broadest sense, of consumers: people who were the recipients of goods and services produced by both public and private sectors. To a great extent, postwar liberalism was a matter of catering to this constituency, which, in the tradition of the great British economist John Maynard Keynes, meant using government spending to stimulate the economy. Doing things such as building roads or schools—or, in the case of a program such as Social Security, simply handing spending money to people once they reach a certain age—creates jobs. When people have jobs, they spend money. And when they spend money (whether on meals, clothes, cars, or any number of other products and services), they create still more jobs. The other thing that happens when people have jobs is that they pay more taxes—the more they make, the more taxes they pay—and this money can be used for more government spending, thus perpetuating a virtuous circle.

Supply-siders have many of the same goals, but they go about pursuing them in a different way. The key is their doubt about government spending: they see it as inefficient, not only because governments have tendencies toward waste and corruption, but also because governments are not necessarily good at knowing what it is that the people in a given society need, or how much, at any given time. Instead, they say, government should *cut* taxes and *reduce* spending. Government should also minimize the amount of regulation it imposes on businesses. If you let businesses and individuals keep more of their money and deploy it as they see fit, they will spend money and create jobs in more effective ways.

Supply-siders were fond of illustrating their counter-intuitive logic by drawing the so-called Laffer curve, named after a prominent economist, who was a widely cited supply-sider, along with his colleague Jude Wanniski. Laffer and his supporters argued that if you cut taxes and allow businesses to prosper, the government would actually end up with *more* money. They'll be taxed at a lower *rate*, but the total tax *revenue* will be higher (a 10% tax on $100 will yield more than a 20% tax on $40). The devil is in the details: in the case of a 0% tax rate or a 100% tax rate—which would destroy the economic incentive to work at all—the government would end up with nothing. Supply-siders argued that the rate should be much lower than had customarily been the case—under Eisenhower, the top bracket was 92%; under Kennedy, it was 77%. By century's end, that rate would be somewhere in the 30s.[12]

It should be pointed out, however, that even if supply-side arguments were correct, its advocates did not actually want the government to keep the added revenue: they believed it should be returned to the people in the form of further tax cuts, which represented a different virtuous circle. They believed that government programs encouraged dependency, even entitlement; cutting or even eliminating them created incentives for individuals to become more independent, less reliant on the state. That's why they weren't especially worried—some were actually pleased—if tax cuts didn't generate enough revenue to sustain current levels of spending as they existed at the time. The real goal was to "starve the beast": to *force* the government to shrink. Though they tended not to emphasize this dimension of supply-side thinking, it was obvious enough to any supporter or opponent attentive to its implications. In the notorious words of conservative activist Grover Norquist, "I don't want to abolish government. I simply want to reduce it to the size where I can drag it into the bathroom and drown it in the bathtub."[13]

In its broadest outlines, this was the theory Reagan offered to the American people in 1980. Amid the lingering economic stagnation of the 1970s, it had genuine appeal: the old demand-side model really did not seem to be working. Given that Reagan actually had a fresh idea, and that he won by an unexpectedly large margin, he got a respectful hearing from Congress, especially since—unlike Jimmy Carter—the Reagan administration made a real effort to cultivate it. Reagan had a notably good working relationship with Democratic Speaker of the House Thomas P. "Tip" O'Neill; they disagreed on much, but got along well with each other, two Irishmen meeting periodically over drinks.

This did not necessarily mean Reagan was going to get his way, however. Democrats were particularly concerned that tax cuts would hurt the poor, since lower tax receipts would likely mean less money for welfare programs, at least in the short run. They derided Reagan's program as "trickle-down" economics: a glib idea that helping the rich would eventually drift down and help the poor.

They also wondered whether businesses would take advantage of lower taxes and lighter regulation and not actually use their gains to hire more people. (Indeed, much subsequent corporate gain piled up in offshore accounts or was used in ways that helped shareholders and executives far more than anyone else.) In the first 2 months of Reagan's presidency, it was far from clear he could prevail. According to polls at the time, he was less popular than his recent predecessors.[14]

And then fate intervened: on March 30, 1981, Reagan was shot by a crazed gunman outside a Washington DC hotel. The wound he sustained was serious—more serious than the White House fully let on. What government officials *did* disclose was the extraordinary grace with which Reagan handled his ordeal. His quips throughout the process—"Honey, I forgot to duck," he told his wife; "I hope you're all Republicans," he told the surgeons in the operating room; "Send me to LA, where I can see the air I'm breathing," he told his Californian nurse—charmed and impressed the American people.[15] Reagan also benefited from the instinctive desire of voters to rally around a president in distress, and his popularity surged in the weeks following his shooting. As a result, his political fortunes revived; Reagan got his tax cuts for the fiscal year 1982. It changed the course of American economic history.

Reagan further bolstered his political position in the summer of 1981 not with his charm but rather in his willingness to take a hard line against those with whom he disagreed. That August, federal employees who were members of the Professional Air Traffic Controllers' Organization (PATCO) went on strike, crippling the nation's airline traffic. Reagan—himself a former union leader in Hollywood who had been endorsed by PATCO when he ran for president—believed the strike was illegal. He demanded that the air traffic controllers return to work within 48 hours. Those who didn't, more than 11,000, were fired.[16] Reagan acted despite concerns that air travel would become less safe, though he brought in military controllers and no serious accidents occurred. The PATCO strike is widely regarded as a milestone in US labor history, a moment when management clearly gained the upper hand on labor. For the rest of the decade, unions found themselves on the defensive, as when, following cuts in wages in the early 1980s, workers at the food company Hormel went on strike in 1985, losing a bruising battle after the Minnesota's governor sent in National Guard troops to protect strikebreakers (also known as scabs) who took union positions at lower pay. In some important respects, the American labor movement never recovered from its setbacks in the 1980s.

By contrast, Reagan legitimated corporate values in ways not seen since the 1920s. As with so much in the 1980s, this was a process that was already underway before he became president. In 1971, 175 corporations had established offices in Washington to lobby the government; by 1981, that number had jumped to 2,445.[17] Reagan's champions would point to economic statistics to bolster the legitimacy of this new corporate environment: over the course of his presidency, the US economy added over 18 million jobs, and the Dow Jones Industrial average more than doubled, from 950.88 in 1981 to 2339 in 1989.[18] This corporate outlook also had a symbolic dimension, as in Reagan's decision to move the presidential portrait of Calvin Coolidge, who had famously proclaimed "the business of America is business," to a more prominent location in the White House. Reagan's lavish, star-studded inauguration stood in marked contrast to Carter's purposefully subdued affair 4 years earlier, and set a tone for the rest of the decade. Critics also argued that the blatant materialism that Reagan embodied—Nancy Reagan's $200,000 White House china generated much outrage—was more than distasteful: it set the nation on a course of growing economic inequality that would only grow worse over time.

While Reagan may have prevailed in some long-term battles over the course of his presidency, his standing remained shaky in 1981–1982. A severe economic recession—the worst, in fact, since the Great Depression—wracked the country, as captured in classic works of popular culture such as Billy Joel's *The Nylon Curtain* and Bruce Springsteen's *Nebraska* (both 1982). By about 1983, however, the economy turned a corner and the country enjoyed the sharpest surge in growth it had in two decades. The way most people today remember the 1980s—an era of prosperity—had begun. Reagan's advertising team exploited the good news for all it was worth, packaging it into the slogan "It's Morning Again in America" for his 1984 re-election campaign.

Should he get the credit for the economic turnaround? In the early twenty-first century, there's no clear consensus among historians (who, it should be said, tend to be left of center). One could argue that much of the economic pain of the late 1970s and early 1980s was a function of high inflation, which was aggressively brought to heel by Paul Volcker, the Chairman of the Federal Reserve appointed by Jimmy Carter, who dealt ruthlessly with the problem by raising interest rates, which hurt in the short term but created long-term placidity. (Volcker was reappointed to a second term by Reagan in 1983.) One could also argue that the mysterious rhythms of the business cycle were most important, and that policymakers—especially presidents—get too much credit/blame for what happens on their watch. Insofar as Reagan does get credit, the praise often falls into the realm of psychological, as it did for FDR: Reagan helped Americans feel better about themselves, and this created a self-fulfilling prophecy. Or perhaps the new climate was a function of exactly what Reagan said it would be: tax cuts and deregulation (which had begun under Carter) unleashing the productive powers of the supply side.

Whatever one believes happened, there's one important outcome about US economy in the 1980s about which there is no ambiguity. Reagan and his Democratic opponents, in effect, compromised: he got his tax cuts, and they kept spending levels high enough not to fundamentally change the basic outlines of the welfare state as it had emerged in FDR's presidency and solidified by the time of LBJ's. Actually, this alone can plausibly explain what happened: the supply side got its stimulus without the demand side having to make any sacrifice in spending.

How could this happen? There's a simple one-word answer: debt. The US government, as with all governments, routinely borrows money, and when there are national emergencies such as wars or depressions, they borrow a lot—sometimes from their own citizens and banks, sometimes from foreign ones. Governments rarely pay back all their debt at any given time; when presidents such as Thomas Jefferson and Andrew Jackson tried to do this in the nineteenth century, they actually damaged the nation's economic health. But as a general rule of thumb, governments seek to bring in as much in tax revenue as they spend on services in any given year (state governments are typically required to do this by law). Lyndon Johnson left a small annual budget surplus when he left office in early 1969. But, in the 1980s, the US government began borrowing to finance good times in a way that had never happened before, routinely spending more than it received every single year. This meant not only a string of annual budget deficits; it also meant the *total* national debt began to grow dramatically. Between fiscal years 1980 and 1989— essentially Reagan's presidency—the national debt tripled from $914 billion to $2.7 trillion, rising to a proportion of GNP that exceeded that of FDR during the Great Depression. In 1985, the United States became the world's largest debtor.[19]

This has essentially been the nation's way of life ever since. Which is fine, as long as people are willing to lend the US government money— and not charge high interest rates to do so. Empires tend to buy time for themselves this way. The question is always about how long they can do so. This is not a question Reagan or his contemporaries had to worry about. (You, by contrast, do.)

Breaking Ice: Reagan and the Cold War

The story of Reagan's foreign policy roughly tracks that of his domestic policy. Some of Reagan's critics derided him as ignorant; others were genuinely scared by what he might do when he came to office. Among the most nervous were Europeans, who believed that the escalating Cold War rhetoric of the late Carter and early Reagan years could land them in the middle of a nuclear war. Deployment of new missile weapon systems resulted in large anti-Reagan demonstrations in Western Europe in the early 1980s. There were also demonstrations in the United States, notably a June 1982 event in New York's Central Park that reportedly drew 750,000 people. Such people were not reassured by his 1983 description of the Soviet Union as "an evil empire" or a 1984 joke in which Reagan, not realizing that microphones were live before a radio address, said, "My fellow Americans, I am pleased to tell you today that I've signed legislation that will outlaw Russia forever. We begin bombing in five minutes."[20] Amid widespread concerns about Reagan's perceived recklessness, proposals for a joint US–Soviet freeze on nuclear weapon development and deployment were widely debated, including in the US Congress.[21]

Another flashpoint of opposition to Reagan administration foreign policy was in Central America. The triumph of the communist Sandinista regime in Nicaragua in 1979 was something that the administration was particularly aggressive in trying to reverse, which involved military aid to the so-called

Contra rebels as well as murderous hard-right regimes in El Salvador and Guatemala. Congress was sufficiently troubled by US human rights violations in the region that it succeeded in passing the Boland Amendments, a series of laws named for Democratic congressman Edward Boland, between 1982 and 1984, making military aid to overthrow the Sandinistas illegal. In 1983, the United States invaded the small Caribbean island of Grenada in response to an exaggerated communist threat. Though the operation was badly executed, it was widely cited as an example of renewed American strength and purpose by the Reagan supporters.

Indeed, while Reagan had vocal and trenchant critics in his approach to foreign policy, he also enjoyed significant support in his hard line toward the Soviets. Some of this had origins in the 1970s, among foreign policy analysts who regarded the policy of *détente* as misguided and who believed that the United States could actually win an arms race. Some of it was rooted in Soviet behavior, notably the Soviet invasion of Afghanistan in 1979—the United States began sending covert aid to the Afghan rebels during the Reagan administration—and in the Soviet downing of a Korean airliner in 1983, killing all of its civilian passengers.

By all accounts, the centerpiece of Reagan's Cold War strategy emerged in 1983 when he unveiled what he called his Strategic Defense Initiative (SDI), popularized by the term "Star Wars" after the hit 1977 sci-fi movie. For decades, the core premise of the US–Soviet nuclear balance was the concept of mutual assured destruction (MAD), in which the launch of a nuclear missile by one nation would presumably lead its opponent to trigger a comparably catastrophic response, leading both to practice restraint. But the key feature of SDI was the promise of intercepting missiles carrying nuclear warheads before they could reach the soil of the United States or its allies, negating MAD doctrine and offering a scenario whereby the United States could actually win such a conflict by launching an attack without fear of a successful counterstrike.

To many, SDI represented a breathtaking prospect for ending a decades-long Cold War stalemate. But the program was deeply controversial. Many experts were skeptical it could ever work; there would be no question that the technical problems would take years, even decades, to be resolved—basic research on the necessary technology continued into the twenty-first century—and it would only take a single missile getting through the US nuclear umbrella to effectively render it useless. But even if one granted the possibility of creating an airtight system, critics said, SDI destabilized the Cold War order and could provoke either or both the United States and the Soviet Union to act irresponsibly, whether out of fear or misplaced confidence.

The Soviets, not surprisingly, publicly denounced SDI. Because communist states were effectively closed societies, it was not widely known how Soviet leaders and their allies were thinking at the time. But subsequent disclosures made clear that they felt threatened by Reagan's administration policies generally and SDI in particular. In 1983, a NATO military exercise known as Operation Able Archer 83 briefly led the Soviets to mobilize their military in the belief that it was a genuine attack.

But Soviet difficulties in the 1980s went deeper than the policies of the Reagan administration. The negative effects of running a centrally planned command economy for 60+ years were becoming impossible to ignore internally or externally. Important Soviet client states—notably Cuba—were a net drain on Soviet coffers, and the quality of manufactured goods coming out of the communist bloc were a joke when compared with that of their Western counterparts, fostering despair and resentment against Soviet puppet governments.

After Nikita Khrushchev was ejected from power in the aftermath of the Cuban Missile Crisis, he was replaced by Leonid Brezhnev, who ran the USSR from 1964 until his death in 1982. As the longest-running general secretary of the Communist Party of the Soviet Union (CPSU) in history, Brezhnev provided a measure of continuity in its empire, and presided over a period when the Soviets reached rough military parity with the United States. But the latter years of the Brezhnev regime were marked by stagnation and decline. Upon Brezhnev's death, the CPSU selected former KGB (the Soviet secret police/intelligence agency) chief Yuri Andropov to succeed him. Andropov was only in office for 15 months before his death in 1984, replaced by long-term insider Konstanin Chernenko, who ran the USSR until his own death less than a year later. Chernenko's successor was Mikhail Gorbachev (more on him shortly). Thus it was that Reagan—a man in his 70s who projected tremendous vitality—dealt with four different Soviet leaders during his own presidency, a symbolically important contrast in the relative health of the two empires.

But the poor state of the Soviet Union was more than symbolic, and extended beyond geopolitics, leaching into the quality of everyday life. Long lines for basic goods, shortages of key supplies, and petty corruption were rampant. The demands of running a police state impeded the circulation of information essential for innovation. At a time when Americans were increasingly acquiring personal computers, Soviets were restricting the use of copying machines. Only 23% of Soviet urban homes at the time and 7% of rural homes had (landline) telephones.[22] Keeping up with the Americans—financially, technologically, and culturally—was becoming impossible, especially since Soviet relations with communist China, a supposed ally that was really a rival, were rocky at best. Such information was available to foreign policy experts in the United States, who tended not to publicize it, whether to discourage complacency or to protect a bustling military–industrial complex that thrived during the Reagan years. For weapons manufacturers, and the people whose jobs depended on them, there's not much money in peace.

Headwinds: Second-Term Blues

Reagan headed into his re-election campaign in 1984 with strong winds at his back, in contrast to the treacherous crosscurrents that he sought to navigate 3 years earlier. The Democrats, for their part, were divided, unsure whether to adopt parts of Reagan's program or challenge him directly. One major candidate,

Gary Hart, was a so-called Atari Democrat who advocated the promotion of high-tech approaches to defense and business, a message that appealed to socially liberal, upwardly mobile young urban professionals—aka "Yuppies"—who represented a new face for the Democrats. Another candidate, Jesse Jackson, picked up the civil rights mantle of Martin Luther King, Jr., for whom he had worked. Jackson's public posture as King's heir was regarded with some skepticism, though there was excitement in the idea of a major-party African American candidate for president. The nomination eventually went to Minnesota senator and former vice president Walter Mondale, who represented the traditional liberal values of his mentor, Senator Hubert Humphrey (who himself had been vice president and lost a close race to Richard Nixon in 1968).

Mondale was a long shot, and he knew it. A principled man, he frankly stated his intention to raise taxes, a position he knew would be unpopular, but which he also felt was essential and responsible for the long-term health of the nation. But he realized that, if he was going to have any hope of winning, it would require him to take a more appealingly bold step, which he did when he asked New York congresswoman Geraldine Ferraro to run as his vice president. As the first woman on a major party ticket, the Ferraro candidacy was widely cited as an emblem of social progress. It also generated some controversy, as when the finances of her husband, real-estate developer John Zaccaro, suggested some improprieties (he later pleaded guilty to a minor crime and was acquitted of other charges), or when Vice President George H. W. Bush said he "tried to kick a little ass" after his debate with her that fall.

But questions about Ferraro's fitness for office, or the sexism that swirled around her, were secondary considerations to the two men at the top of the ticket. Mondale enjoyed a brief moment of momentum when Reagan appeared disengaged, even confused, in the first of their presidential debates, but he recovered in the next one, when he jokingly referred to concerns about senility by saying "I am not going to exploit, for political purposes, my opponent's youth and inexperience." He went on the win one of the most crushing victories in US electoral history, taking 49 states and 525 electoral votes to Mondale's one state (his native Minnesota as well as the District of Columbia) and 13 electoral votes.

As is often the case for re-elected presidents, Reagan's second term was less successful than his first. He enjoyed relatively smooth sailing in 1985 and for most of 1986, but in the latter part of that year he experienced a series of setbacks. The midterm elections of 1986 cost him the majority he enjoyed in the US Senate. Reagan also lost a bruising battle in late 1987, when one of his nominees for the post of associate justice of the Supreme Court, Robert Bork, was rejected by the US Senate because he was considered too extreme in his political positions. His defeat gave rise to a new verb: subsequent nominees for government positions denied after a campaign of systematic vilification were said to be "borked" by their opponents.

Reagan's freewheeling celebration of capitalism also came under increasing public scrutiny. A brief, but deeply frightening, stock market crash in October

1987—the Dow Jones Industrial Average lost almost a quarter of its value in a single day—raised questions about whether his business-friendly approach was economically sound, particularly in light of a series of high-profile cases that led to the successful prosecution of the high-flying financiers Ivan Boesky and Michael Milken in the closing years of the decade. Shortly after he left office, Reagan's lax regulatory approach to savings and loan institutions—once low-profit, community-based alternatives to traditional banks, they increasingly took greater risks in the search for greater returns—triggered a series of bankruptcies that required expensive taxpayer bailouts.

Administration challenges extended to foreign policy as well. Even as he was gaining the upper hand with the Soviets, Reagan found himself facing complexities in international relations that defied traditional Cold War categories. This was true even in his first term. The complicated politics of the Middle East was especially vexing. The United States endured a painful debacle in Lebanon in 1983, when a terrorist drove a truck filled with explosives into a US military base there, killing 241 marines. A particular thorn in the US side was Libya, led by longtime dictator Muammar Qaddafi, a largely secular leader who invoked religious language when it suited his political purposes. United States Navy pilots clashed with the Libyan Air Force off the African coast in 1981 and 1989 over sea lanes that Libya insisted were part of its territory (claims not recognized by international law), and Libyan agents were implicated in the bombing of a Berlin nightclub frequented by US soldiers in 1986. The United States retaliated with an air strike on the Libyan capital of Tripoli, allegedly killing Qaddafi's adopted daughter.

But Reagan's biggest foreign policy headache was probably Iran. Ever since Islamic revolutionaries toppled the US-backed regime of the Shah in 1978, the newly theocratic state regarded the United States with deep enmity. But Iran, a largely Shiite Muslim nation, was also locked in a long and bitter war with the largely Sunni state of Iraq, led since 1979 by a dictator of the Qaddafi stripe, Saddam Hussein. Though US relations with Iraq had been poor since the time of the Six-Day War in 1967, the American government quietly extended aid to the Iraqis over the course of the 8-year stalemate.

It is ironic, then, that the biggest foreign policy disaster of the Reagan administration, the Iran–Contra scandal, was the result of a strange collaboration with an avowed enemy. In late 1986, anti-aircraft gunners for the Nicaraguan government shot down a US cargo plane carrying weapons intended for the Contras seeking to overthrow the Sandinista regime. In the investigation that followed, a survivor of the plane crash provided information that led the American media uncovering an improbable plot: secret White House operatives, working through Israel, asked the Iranian government to intercede on the United States' behalf with Muslim terrorists (with whom the Reagan administration asserted it would never negotiate). In exchange for their help, the Iranians were allowed to buy US military technology. The proceeds from these arms sales were then used to illegally fund American anticommunist operations in Latin America that had been specifically prohibited by Congress. These complex maneuvers were managed by Marine Lieutenant Colonel Oliver North, who adopted a defiant stance when questioned about them during congressional hearings in 1987.

For a time, the Iran–Contra scandal threatened to bring down the Reagan presidency in a way comparable to the way Watergate had. As with Watergate, the question was what Reagan knew and when he knew it. Ironically, Reagan's reputation for disengagement worked in his favor. Unlike Richard Nixon, he could, and did, plausibly claim he had no idea what was taking place (indeed the now-common phrase "plausible deniability" entered common parlance as a way to describe administration strategy). A number of White House officials went to prison, though North escaped jail time when his convictions were overturned because he had been granted limited immunity in return for his testimony. Conservatives hailed North as a hero (he later ran for, but lost, a race for the US Senate from Virginia). Those on the left saw the Iran–Contra as one more illustration of an imperial presidency that had survived Watergate.

For God's Sake: Social Conservatism

In addition to economic and foreign policies, there was a third dimension to the Reagan presidency that requires some examination, and that is Reagan's role as a social conservative on the nation's political scene. The support of evangelicals had been instrumental in Reagan's nomination and election in 1980, and he continued to enjoy that support after he became president. This was the case even though Reagan is the only president in US history to have been divorced. Nor was he an active churchgoer, though many observers have described him as a religious man. But, as with other aspects of Reagan's career, his relationship to social and cultural factions of the New Right was curiously distant in ways that partially protected him as well as frustrated those supporters. Much to the disappointment of abortion opponents, for example, Reagan did little to try and challenge *Roe v. Wade* while he was president. Reagan's only major address to religious conservatives was his 1983 speech to the National Association of Evangelicals convention, where he used the phrase "evil empire" to describe the Soviets—morally charged language that got a lot of attention from supporters and critics alike, but amounted to little beyond his already established foreign policy positions.

Reagan's maintenance of a discreet distance served him well when a series of scandals involving evangelical ministers erupted in the second half of the 1980s. One televangelist, Jim Bakker, admitted to an affair with a volunteer whom he paid hush money (she later went public and posed for *Playboy*). Another, Jimmy Swaggart, confessed to sex with a prostitute. A third, Oral Roberts, threatened his viewers that God would "call him home" unless he received sufficient donations to keep his church afloat. Such shenanigans, which played in the media over a period of months and years, greatly tarnished the reputation of evangelicals in the wider eyes of the American public, a large proportion of whom had always viewed them skeptically in any case. But conservative Christians had long experience with ridicule; to a great degree, they maintained their cohesion and remained a significant force in US politics and culture long after Reagan, whose diffidence included a refusal to condemn them, left office.

Reagan was nobody's idea of a civil rights president; indeed, one of his most notorious acts as a politician was giving a 1980 campaign speech in Philadelphia, Mississippi, site of the murder of three civil rights activists in 1964. "I believe in state's rights," he said there—an unmistakable message to racist Southern whites in the process of switching their traditional party identity to become "Reagan Democrats."[23] Yet, in 1983, Reagan signed off on legislation making Martin Luther King, Jr.'s birthday a national holiday. Similarly, the administration pulled its punches on Affirmative Action. It opposed the policy, but concluded that it would be dangerous to take it on too aggressively.[24] It's also worth noting that, in 1981, Reagan named Sandra Day O'Connor of Arizona as the first woman to serve on the US Supreme Court. Over the course of her 24 years on the bench, O'Connor became a notable figure of moderation in the high court.

Reagan's own moderation was not limited to social conservatism. Even he was concerned about the sharp decline in government revenue that followed his 1981 tax cuts, leading him to sign a tax hike in 1982 to cover the shortfall. Reagan also signed a reform law in 1986 that closed many tax loopholes and ended the long-standing policy of allowing deductions on credit card debt. Compared to later generations of Republicans, who refused to contemplate supporting *any* kind of tax increase (all eight Republican candidates at a presidential debate in 2011 refused to support a dollar in tax hikes even if it was paired with $10 in spending cuts),[25] Reagan's approach to tax policy could seem downright liberal.

A similar sense of moderation characterized Reagan's approach to immigration. The numbers of new arrivals to the United States, especially Mexicans, continued to rise, leading to allegations, never convincingly documented, that they brought with them disease and crime. Charges that they took jobs away from US citizens and/or drove down wages were harder to assess. In 1986, Reagan signed the Simpson–Mazzoli Act, which was sold as a crackdown on the rising tide of illegal immigrants to the United States because it made hiring or recruiting them illegal. But at least as important was a provision in the law allowing any immigrant who arrived prior to 1982 to apply for citizenship—an approach that a later generation of Republicans would deride as "amnesty" and passionately oppose.

Left Ahead: The Legacy of the Sixties in the Eighties

Indeed, beneath the surface of American life—and beyond the reach of some of the most insistent conservative activists—alternating currents were at work. The legacy of liberalism in the 1960s was quietly transforming national life in ways that would continue long after the 1980s were over. Robert Bork's failed nomination for Supreme Court is revealing in this regard. Bork opposed the Civil Rights Act of 1964, Affirmative Action, and *Roe v. Wade*. By the 1980s, the first of these positions had become an embarrassment; opposition to the other two, while considered respectable, never managed to gain enough traction to reverse the gains of the American left, suggesting the seemingly irreversible distance the nation had traversed over the course of the previous generation.

Such changes were more than a matter of public opinion. Even though the 1980s are remembered as a period of Republican ascendancy on the national level, Democrats competed effectively for state and local offices, gradually building on a demographic transformation of American politics. Everybody knew about Jesse Jackson. But the impact of figures such as Chicago mayor Harold Washington, Philadelphia mayor Wilson Goode, and Detroit mayor Coleman Young solidified the gains of African Americans in achieving a measure of integration into the nation's political system. In 1973, there were 48 African American mayors in the United States. By 1990, that number had jumped to 316. Thanks to the Voting Rights Act, the number of registered African American voters doubled over the course of the decade.[26]

Unfortunately, racial tensions also remained high. Harold Washington received a mere 12% of the white vote in his first campaign for mayor.[27] The situation was particularly acute in New York, where the racially motivated murder of a young African American man, Yusef Hawkins, divided the residents of Brooklyn in 1989. Also that year, a group of five African American youths were wrongfully convicted of the rape of a woman in Central Park. Many New Yorkers were also dismayed by the case of Tawana Brawley, a young African American woman from upstate New York who claimed to have been raped, an allegation strenuously supported by African American activist Al Sharpton. A jury later concluded Brawley's charges were untrue, and found Sharpton and two associates liable for making false rape accusations against a Brooklyn assistant district attorney. The air of racial mistrust and hostility in New York and other cities took place against a backdrop of ongoing white flight and widespread African American unemployment, which fostered conditions of crime and hopelessness. To some observers, the 1980s marked a period of bifurcation in African American life where a growing middle class began to thrive even as the "underclass"—a term used by sociologist William Julius Wilson to describe African Americans trapped by low-paying jobs and a lack of education—fell further behind and became geographically as well as socially isolated.

As with African Americans, women of all races were a constituency who also made strides amid the conservative political climate of the 1980s. Geraldine Ferraro's candidacy for the vice presidency generated excitement, but perhaps more important was the proportion of women as elected officials, which rose steadily over the course of the decade. Between 1980 and 1992, the number of women in the House of Representatives more than doubled, from 21 to 48 (even if this was barely 10% of the House), and the number of women in the Senate rose to seven, including the first African American woman, Carol Mosely Braun.[28] Women were particularly prominent in the pivotal state of California, where Senators Diane Feinstein and Barbara Boxer, and Representative Nancy Pelosi, rose to become prominent national figures well into the twenty-first century. In 1985, political activist Ellen Malcolm founded EMILY's List—Emily is an acronym for "Early Money Is Like Yeast"—to seed the candidacies of women running for office. It would become a major source of political fund-raising for decades to come.

That said, the 1980s are often regarded by feminist historians as a relative low point following the surge in activism that marked second-wave feminism in the 1960s and 1970s (and prior to what some regard as third-wave feminism that began to emerge in the 1990s). Membership in the National Organization of Women fell by more than one-third in the mid-1980s.[29] It was also in these years that many young women started explaining their gender politics with the phrase, "I'm not a feminist, but ..." coupling an embrace of equality with a reluctance to embrace the perceived stridency on the part of those who pursued and achieved it. As with so much else in the decade, gender politics acquired a more libertarian dimension that emphasized personal experience more than social solidarity.

Abortion remained a flashpoint. Opponents continued the mobilization that had gotten underway in the late 1970s, and, partly because of their activism, the stigma surrounding abortion continued to grow. By 1987, 85% of the counties in the United States provided no abortion services at all; 5 years later, only 12% of doctors training in obstetrics and gynecology were taught how to perform abortions.[30] Abortion is an issue about which reasonable people disagree, and those who demonstrated outside abortion clinics could plausibly be described as advocating for the civil rights of the unborn. But there were also cases of anti-abortion activists whose life-threatening behavior contradicted their professed pro-life principles: by 1990, there had been eight bombings of abortion clinics, 28 acts of arson, another 28 of attempted arson, and 170 acts of vandalism.[31]

Feminism also continued to experience divisions from within around questions of race, class, and sexuality. As was true in the 1970s, some observers inside as well as outside the movement considered the orientation of mainstream feminism as elitist, more focused on the prerogatives of the privileged than the struggles of ordinary women. There was also a (very old, but continuing) philosophical divide among those who thought about feminism in terms of *protecting* women and those who thought of it in terms of equal *opportunities*. While it's safe to say that most women believed women should live free of sexual harassment *and* have the chance to become a firefighter, for example, their priorities on such matters could differ. For many lesbians in particular, however, the older questions of sexual politics became less important than an entirely new crisis that emerged in the 1980s: a terrifying new disease that went by the name acquired immunodeficiency syndrome (AIDS).

First diagnosed in 1981 and named in the following year, AIDS was initially described as a disease typically, but not solely, transmitted by gay men through sexual contact, blood transfusions, or the use of shared needles by drug users. The key agent in AIDS is the human immunodeficiency virus (HIV), a pathogen that weakens victims by making them vulnerable to any number of other diseases, such as pneumonia. In the early 1980s, an AIDS diagnosis was essentially terminal. By the beginning of 1985, it had killed an estimated 5,600 people; by the end of the decade, there were about 83,000 cases, about half of which would end in death.[32]

Given the uncertainties surrounding its origins and prevalence, AIDS generated widespread panic. Its impact was especially great in gay communities such as San Francisco and New York, where, after great and ongoing adversity, gay people had managed to carve out a place for themselves where they could experience their sexual orientation relatively insulated from the prejudices of those who rejected it. Now, in addition to the decimating impact of a scourge that robbed them of their loved ones, they were forced to confront the hostility of those, especially evangelical Christians, who were inclined to view AIDS as the result—some said punishment—for their deviance from heterosexual norms. In the words of Patrick Buchanan, former aide to Richard Nixon, and President Reagan's director of communications, "They have declared war on nature and now nature is exacting an awful retribution."[33]

What did Reagan himself have to say about the AIDS crisis? Some at the time and since have condemned him for saying nothing, even after his movie star friend Rock Hudson, a closeted gay man (of whom Reagan knew a number), died from AIDS. But Reagan was not in fact silent about the disease. He brought it up 2 weeks after Hudson's death at a press conference where he said, "One of our highest public health priorities is going to be continuing to find a cure for AIDS." He also described it as "public enemy number one." Reagan's Surgeon General, C. Everett Koop, who been opposed by some liberals for his opposition to abortion, was energetic in advocating safe sex education. That said, Reagan at one point tried to reduce AIDS funding research; Congress responded by appropriating more money.

Many observers found the government's approach to the AIDS crisis—much to his own wife's dismay, Reagan was reluctant to advocate the use of condoms—appallingly timid at best. Militant gay activists organized the AIDS Coalition to Unleash Power (ACT-UP), which led demonstrations and demanded more funding for AIDS research. Playwright Larry Kramer, a leader of ACT-UP, asserted that "AIDS is our Holocaust and Reagan is our Hitler." In 1987, the Food and Drug Administration approved the use of azidothymidine, or AZT, which inhibits the spread of the HIV virus. Similar subsequent treatments have made it possible for people with AIDS to live normal lives, though there is no cure for disease, which remains a serious epidemiological problem in Africa for men and women.[34]

It is clear, therefore, that for all of Ronald Reagan's evident impact on American society, a series of social movements remained vibrant in national life during the 1980s, some of them resisting, even overturning, the conservative Republican agenda of the decade. Reagan not only endured embarrassing setbacks such as the stock market crash and the Iran-Contra scandal; there were also tens of millions of Americans who found his view of the world irrelevant—comically when not infuriatingly so. There was little question that many

Americans were attracted to the sense of optimism associated with Reaganism, and yet even many of those who embraced it suspected that it reflected a nostalgia rooted in a selectively remembered past more than genuine confidence in the future. (This cultural disposition is a significant focus of Chapter 8.)

Swan Song: Reagan and the Soviets

But even as his presidency was fading into history, there remained a final act in the drama of the Reagan era. To explain what it was, we need to step back a few years—and shift one's focus outside the United States. One place we need to look is the Vatican, where Pope John Paul II assumed the papacy in 1978. John Paul II was a native of Poland, which had pushed as hard as it could during uprisings against Kremlin domination in 1956 and 1970, just short of provoking a Soviet invasion. The new pope was a vocal critic of "godless communism," and drew large crowds when he visited the United States in 1979. His message to his fellow Poles—"Do not be afraid!"— was widely interpreted as encouragement to challenge Communist Party rule. In the late 1970s, a labor union, Solidarity (which theoretically should have been unnecessary in a communist government presumably controlled by workers), led the latest of a series of protests against the Warsaw regime. Moscow did not send in troops, allowing the Polish government to impose martial law in 1981. Poland's relative success in resisting Soviet domination inspired other subjects of the communist bloc, which encountered growing difficulties in containing such spreading defiance.

The USSR also faced considerable difficulties from within. Defense spending took up two to three times more of its GNP than the United States, leaving less for domestic needs. Ethnic divisions were rife—Russians were only about half of the USSR's population—and the war in Afghanistan was a festering wound comparable to that of the Vietnam War in the United States.[35] The situation was not helped by the fact that the Brezhnev government was followed by the care-taker regimes of Andropov and Chernenko. Informed observers knew that the status quo was untenable. The real question was whether the Soviet Union could be reformed from within.

The ascension of Mikhail Gorbachev to the post of general secretary of the CPSU in 1985 represented an attempt to answer that question affirmatively. Gorbachev was 54 years old when he became general secretary of the CPSU, and brought an unprecedented sense of vigor to reforming the country. One component of this was "perestroika" (restructuring), which involved decentralizing decision-making and fostering private enterprise. Another was "glasnost" (openness), a new emphasis on free expression, including criticism of the government. A third was a crackdown on the social scourge of alcoholism. A fourth was an overhaul of foreign relations, which included renegotiating economic and political arrangements with satellite republics, and, especially, withdrawing from Afghanistan. Gorbachev not only projected tremendous vitality, he also conveyed knowledge of and curiosity about the wider world, which impressed foreign leaders.[36]

Reagan's first meeting with Gorbachev, which took place in Geneva, Switzerland, in 1985, did not go especially well. Though Reagan took the meeting seriously and prepared carefully, their conversations were contentious and relations between the two men's wives appeared frosty, a perception that dominated media coverage of the event. Gorbachev wanted the United States to modify its commitment to the SDI, something Reagan insisted was not on the bargaining table. He did indicate a willingness to share technology, but not to abandon developing it.

The two men met again in 1986 in Reykjavik, Iceland, under surprisingly different circumstances. Though originally billed as a planning session for a more substantial summit, the two leaders began discussing a wide range of proposals to substantially cut their nuclear arsenals. Once again, however, the talks broke down over SDI. But the friction between the two men also reflected a new level of candor. Gorbachev didn't even pretend the Soviets could keep up with the United States technologically. Reagan was even more audacious: late in the negotiations, with their respective planes already on the runways, he proposed that both sides commit on the spot to removing nuclear weapons from Europe within a decade. The Soviets had made similar proposals in the past, but they were never taken seriously because the Soviets always maintained a numerical advantage with conventional military resources, and the assumption was that Soviet troops would overrun the continent if the United States withdrew its nuclear weapons. That Reagan would make such an offer was stunning. Gorbachev cautiously agreed, but again attached the condition that the United States abandon SDI. Reagan angrily walked away. "Goddammit," he said to his chief of staff. "We were *that* close to an agreement."

Actually, this was precisely what made some of Reagan's staffers panicky. One member of the entourage, John Poindexter, asked Reagan to reassure him that he had not offered to actually eliminate nuclear weapons. "I did agree to that," Reagan said. "No, you couldn't have," Poindexter replied. "John, I was there and I did," the president insisted. Some of Reagan's usual supporters were appalled when news of the summit got out. One columnist, George Will, charged that Reagan elevated "wishful thinking to the status of a political philosophy." Another, the normally mild-mannered Kevin Phillips, called Reagan "a useful idiot" for the Soviets.

What was happening? Had Reagan revised his core Cold War convictions? Not exactly. He had always said that he was willing to negotiate with the Soviets if he could do so from a position of strength, which in geopolitical terms he clearly could by the late 1980s. But Reagan was also being influenced by pressures closer to home (some of them literal—Nancy Reagan had been pressing her husband on arms control since the time of his re-election). The Iran–Contra scandal, which was bubbling into national consciousness at the time of the Reykjavik summit, gave him an added incentive to take the initiative in foreign policy—a common refuge for presidents in trouble. Reagan turned to more moderate advisers in the closing years of his presidency, among them National Security Adviser Colin Powell, the first African American to hold that position (he would go on to become the first African American Chairman of the Joint Chiefs of Staff of the US Armed Forces under George H. W. Bush, and the first African American Secretary of State under George W. Bush).

For a while, it seemed diplomatic progress had stalled. Reagan's frustration over the failure of the Reykjavik negotiations was evident the following year, when he journeyed to the Berlin Wall in June 1987 and famously demanded, "Mr. Gorbachev, tear down this wall!" But the effort to accomplish something substantive finally bore fruit later that year, when the two leaders agreed to abolish intermediate-range missiles from Europe. This was a more modest objective than what Reagan had proposed at Reykjavik. But it represented the first time the two superpowers had agreed to actually reduce, as opposed to limit, the number of nuclear weapons. Reagan had gotten this deal without having to abandon SDI, reflecting the strength of his negotiating position. But Gorbachev was able to bask in a public relations coup. He came to Washington in late 1987 to sign the treaty, and charmed Americans with impulsive acts such as stopping his limousine to shake hands with them. The following year, Reagan journeyed to Moscow. When asked if he still regarded the Soviets as "the locus of evil in the modern world," Reagan replied, "They've changed." So had he.

Reagan left office in 1989 with a 68% approval rating,[37] a notably high figure for any president, but especially so given the hit his reputation had taken in the Iran–Contra scandal, among other setbacks. He went back to California with rising esteem from the public, moving many with the understated letter he wrote to the American people in 1994 explaining that he had Alzheimer's disease. The 40th US president died a decade later as one of the most admired presidents in US history.

41: The (First) Bush Years

Who would follow Reagan? One of the strongest indicators of presidential success is not only winning two terms of office, but also being succeeded by another president from the same political party.[38] Andrew Jackson and Franklin Delano Roosevelt did this (as did Washington, Jefferson, Lincoln and Theodore Roosevelt). Would Reagan?

There were some reasons to think not. Reagan himself always tended to be more popular than the policies he promoted, and, notwithstanding his Cold War successes, there was a widespread sense of fatigue with Republican rule by the end of the 1980s. Nor was there an especially compelling heir waiting in the wings. The most obvious front runner was Vice President George H. W. Bush. Bush, a longtime party loyalist who had fought as a US Air Force pilot in World War II, had run against Reagan in 1980, deriding his supply-side policies as "voodoo economics." Once he was named Reagan's running mate, Bush was a quietly dedicated second-in-command who met with Reagan weekly. But

Reagan, deferring to the primary process, did not anoint him as his successor immediately, and Bush faced a few challengers, among them evangelical broadcaster Pat Robertson and Kansas senator Bob Dole (similar to Bush, a World War II vet, and one who had also been seriously wounded in action). Bush eventually prevailed, and got his blessing from Reagan, but overall support for him was notably tepid by the summer of 1988.

Democrats had their own problems. Front-runner Gary Hart fell out of the running in 1987 after a sex scandal, and the remaining major candidates were dubbed "the seven dwarfs." The one who broke out of the pack was Massachusetts governor Michael Dukakis, a technocrat who emphasized his governing credentials. His main rival proved to be Jesse Jackson, who built on his successes in 1984 to win a series of primaries by broadening his appeal beyond African Americans by emphasizing traditional liberal values. The fact that Jackson won a string of Southern states—Louisiana, Alabama, Mississippi, and Georgia—was especially notable; this had been Wallace turf in the 1960s and 1970s.[39] Jackson's success there demonstrated the depth of the transformation of the Democratic Party (though all these states would be reliably Republican in national elections for decades to come, in large measure because white registered voters still outnumbered African American ones). Dukakis was able to rack up enough delegates to win the Democratic nomination, however, and, by the time of the party's national convention in July 1988, famously held a 17-point lead over Bush in a national poll.

And then, just as famously, he lost it. The 1988 campaign was one of those elections where economic issues were not especially important: times were relatively good, something that usually helps incumbent parties. Republican operatives, notably the gifted but ruthless Lee Atwater, burnished Bush's lackluster image by emphasizing social issues. A particularly nasty campaign ad criticized Dukakis's support for an inmate furlough program that allowed one convicted criminal, Willie Horton, to commit armed robbery and rape while on temporary release. Horton was African American, and the racial subtext of the ad was unmistakable; Atwater specialized in using coded appeals—in this case, the message was literally evident at face value—that avoided overt racism but appealed to prejudiced whites. Dukakis was derided as a "card-carrying member of the ACLU" (American Civil Liberties Union), as if membership in a civic organization was a crime or something to be embarrassed about. Dukakis didn't help his own cause in a lackluster campaign that included a bloodless response during the presidential debates as to what he would do if someone raped his wife (he replied by talking about his opposition to the death penalty). Though it was not the electoral drubbing that Mondale had experienced in 1984, Bush won the race handily, becoming the first sitting vice president to be elected president since Martin Van Buren did it 152 years earlier after serving as Jackson's vice president.

Bush had little of Reagan's charisma. Widely regarded as a personally decent man, notwithstanding the hardball tactics practiced in his name (Atwater, who died of cancer in 1991, apologized to Dukakis for his "naked cruelty" in the campaign[40]), Bush claimed little in the way of what he called "the vision thing." A Yale graduate whose professional career included stints as ambassador to China in 1974–1975 and head of the Central Intelligence Agency in 1976–1977, he did not particularly like the give-and-take of national politics, and was not especially imaginative or committed in the realm of domestic policy. His real interests were in foreign affairs. As it turned out, he had many opportunities to pursue them, and on the whole did so with a deft hand.

Bush's first challenge was in China. For most of the Cold War era, the United States regarded China as secondary to the USSR in its dealing with communist adversaries. In the decades following the Korean War, when it had sent troops to fight the United States, China had largely turned inward, focused on two huge internal struggles waged by its leader Mao Zedong, chairman of the Central Committee of the Communist Party of China. The first, known as the Great Leap Forward of the late 1950s and early 1960s, represented a reckless attempt to transform China from an agricultural to an industrial nation, resulting in a famine that killed, by many independent estimates, tens of millions of people (millions more were put to death for resistance). The second, known as the Cultural Revolution, began in the mid-1960s, and was designed to purge the nation of dissent. In encouraging Chinese citizens to denounce each other for deviations from party orthodoxy—including children against their parents—the Cultural Revolution plunged China into further turmoil. It had run its course by the mid-1970s. Mao died in 1976; a subsequent power struggle took up the rest of the decade. Toward the end of it, one of the principal players in that struggle, Deng Xiaoping, a survivor of two party purges in the course of his long career, emerged as the leader of the country. Deng gingerly redirected China in a more capitalist direction, as per his famous assertion "that it doesn't matter whether a cat is black or white, as long as it catches mice." His approach to governing was clear: China was going to move pragmatically toward developing its vast economic potential.

There's little question that Deng's program had a positive impact on the country, which began an accelerating rise to global pre-eminence during the 1980s. There *was* a question, however, about whether China could run a market-oriented *economic* system while still being governed by a communist *political* system. Among those who thought not were a group of student protesters who led massive demonstrations in Beijing's Tiananmen Square in June 1989. After taking an initially conciliatory approach toward the protesters, internal divisions within the Chinese government were resolved in favor of hardliners, who imposed martial law and seized control of the media. Hundreds, perhaps thousands, of protesters were estimated to have been killed.[41] Economic reform in China went on hold, and Deng lay low, his prestige damaged, for years before his death in 1997.

Many Americans, as with other freedom-loving people around the world, supported the Tiananmen protesters and wanted the United States to take a hard line against China. Bush did not. In part, this reflected economic considerations: as a huge—and rapidly growing—market, US corporations were virtually salivating at the chance to reach Chinese consumers, as well as to use Chinese workers to manufacture products at a fraction of the cost to make them in the United States. But there were other factors at work as well. China had (and still has) the largest standing army in the world, and thus could not be provoked without great risk. Nor has it ever been clear if the Chinese people as a whole are committed to the same cultural and political values as those that govern the Western world. Many outside observers believed that a combination of capitalist markets and an undemocratic police state would be unsustainable. While the tensions between the two are unmistakable—often taking the form of corruptions and distortions in both the economic as well as political spheres of the government, where bribery is a simple fact of life—China has challenged some of the deepest assumptions of Western analysts for decades. In any case, in the very old US foreign policy debate about whether the nation should follow its democratic ideals or its pragmatic self-interest, Bush favored the latter.

Bush took a similar—but less morally ambiguous—approach in dealing with the most momentous development of his presidency: the collapse of the Soviet empire and the end of the Cold War. As noted earlier, the real question facing Mikhail Gorbachev when he came to power in 1985 was whether the reforms he tried to implement would prove to be too little, too late. The answer turned out to be yes. In the final years of the decade, Gorbachev shuttled between East European capitals, explaining to satellite governments that the Soviet Union would be offering them new autonomy to run their affairs, but also withdrawing the financial and military support that had propped them up. Without it, however, they began to crumble. In the fall of 1989, the government of communist Hungary dismantled its fence barring entry into Austria, allowing a growing stream of refugees to enter the West. Similar pressures were growing at the Berlin Wall, which for three decades had been the symbolic dividing line between the communist and capitalist worlds. As a result of confusion in the transmission of orders on November 9, the Berlin Wall was thrown open, allowing free passage for a human flood. In the surge of euphoria that followed, anticommunists on either side of the wall began actually tearing it down, chipping away pieces as souvenirs. The speed and impact of these events was stunning.

Bush pointedly avoided triumphalism in the face of these developments, quietly maintaining communication lines with the Soviets. In the months that followed the fall of the Berlin Wall, communist regimes in the Eastern Bloc were overthrown. Especially notable was the reunification of Germany for the first time since World War II; here too, Bush provided reassurance and support as West Germany moved quickly to revitalize a shattered East German economy. Meanwhile, after a cautious start, the Bush administration continued the negotiations that Gorbachev and Reagan had begun to reduce the threat of nuclear war, which resulted in two Strategic Arms Reduction Treaties (START) negotiated during his presidency.

In the months following the fall of the Berlin Wall, the Soviet Union lurched toward its own collapse. The end came in the summer of 1991, when a group of Soviet hardliners, appalled by the disintegration of the Soviet empire, imposed house arrest on Gorbachev, who had become deeply unpopular among disillusioned Soviets whose living standards had seen no real improvement despite glasnost and perestroika. But the move on Gorbachev backfired when a new leader, Boris Yeltsin, emerged to challenge the hardliners, who ultimately capitulated. By year's end, the Soviet Union as a political entity had ceased to exist. The pre-1917 designation of Russia was revived, and a series of formally internal republics such as Ukraine and Belorussia were formally recognized as autonomous entities, some of them under the new umbrella of the Russian Federation.

For someone born after the Cold War ended, it may be hard to appreciate just how amazing an outcome this was. For over 40 years, the logic of the struggle had not just defined American and Soviet life, but shadowed geopolitics generally. Certainly not all global conflicts could be reduced to Cold War terms, as the United States learned to its dismay in Vietnam. But it nevertheless exerted a gravitational pull on virtually every national and international power struggle. For much of that time—especially in the late 1940s and early 1950s, but also as late as the 1980s, when a widely watched 1983 television movie, *The Day After*, dramatized the aftermath of a nuclear holocaust—ordinary citizens widely assumed that the world would eventually end in a radioactive conflagration. That the conflict would end, peacefully, with one side—the American side—an unambiguous victor defied the imagination of all but the most determined Cold Warriors. Reagan certainly gets credit for this outcome. But so do a host of other people, such as Gorbachev. And luck should certainly be considered a factor.

Freely Intervening: United States as Sole Superpower

What would the post–Cold War world look like? How would the United States act, now that it was the sole superpower? In some respects, it didn't take long to find out. For if George Bush acted with restraint in some foreign policy situations, it was also clear he was willing to intervene militarily abroad when he considered it necessary.

One early arena for such action was Panama. Its leader, Manuel Noriega, had been a paid agent of the United States and served as a conduit with the Contras. But he also dabbled in closer relations with Cuba and got involved in drug trafficking, two activities that angered the US government. Tensions increased after Noriega nullified an election that would have removed him from power, and Panamanian soldiers killed a US soldier who had gotten lost and attracted a mob. Bush sent in an invasion force of 27,000 to depose Noriega, who was ultimately convicted on drug charges and sentenced to 40 years in prison. The fighting resulted in 23 American deaths and 394 wounded; Noriega's successor, Guillermo Endara, redirected Panama on to a more democratic path.[42] Meanwhile, the electoral defeat of the Nicaraguan Sandinistas in 1990 was further evidence of the failure of communism in Central America and a victory for US interests. Only Cuba stubbornly held on in the region, but, lacking Soviet support, it was an increasingly isolated and creaky regime.

But the American military intervention that most strongly signaled the arrival of the post–Cold War world was the Persian Gulf War. Its immediate origins lay with the Iraqi dictator Saddam Hussein. Saddam had led Iraq into an exceptionally bloody 8-year war in Iran in 1980, during which he had used chemical weapons against his enemy and murdered thousands of Iraqi citizens. Saddam clearly considered at least some of his people disposable; Iraq as a nation had a cobbled-together quality, with borders that had been drawn by Europeans after the end of World War I. The state consisted of an uneasy coalition of Sunni and Shiite Muslims, as well as the ethnically separate Kurds to the North, whose moves toward independence were quashed ruthlessly by Saddam, who used warfare as a means of political distraction from internal difficulties. Thus, in the aftermath of the Iran–Iraq War, he decided to invade the neighboring Kuwait in August 1990. His official explanation involved post-colonial logic—he claimed that Kuwait had originally been a province of Iraq. His real objectives were economic and military: it was estimated at the time that Iraq controlled 11% of the world's known oil supplies, and Kuwait another 9%. Immediately adjacent Saudi Arabia, which he was now in position to threaten, controlled another 26%.[43] Saddam may have believed that the United States, which had provided him with weapons and financing as a check on Iranian power, would allow him to occupy Kuwait. The US ambassador, April Glaspie, had indicated as much at one point.[44]

Saddam was mistaken, however. Almost immediately, President Bush—who was more militant than many members of his own administration—asserted, "This will not stand." Bush navigated passage of a United Nations Security Council resolution to use force to dislodge the Iraqis, winning a 12–2 vote that included the approval of the tottering Soviet Union. (China abstained; only Cuba and Yemen voted no.) He then assembled a 34-nation international military coalition that included several Muslim nations and won approval for using Saudi Arabia as a staging area for the invasion—a fateful decision that triggered the string of events that would culminate in 9/11 a decade later. Bush perhaps had his most difficulty at home in his efforts to convince a skeptical Democratic Congress to go along with his plans. Many Democrats, mindful of Bush's history as an oil industry executive, looked upon the war as an unnecessary fight to protect large corporate interests. The administration counterargument was that Saddam's aggression created a dangerous precedent and that he was secretly developing nuclear weapons. The Bush administration narrowly prevailed in votes that proceeded along largely partisan lines. In the US Senate, it was the closest tally (52–47) on whether to use military action in the nation's history.[45]

The US-led military operation in Kuwait was massive, as per the advice of the Chairman of the Joint Chiefs of Staff Colin Powell. It proceeded in two phases. The first, which began in mid-January 1991, involved a punishing aerial assault featuring "smart bombs," which were more precise than traditional ones in reaching their targets. Iraqi attempts to retaliate with Soviet-made Scud missiles were partially counteracted with US Patriot missiles, offering a glimpse of SDI-type weaponry at work (as well as the limits of that weaponry, as some Scuds did reach their targets, even if overall damage was minimal). The second phase of the war began in February when US troops invaded Kuwait on February 24, and in the space of 100 hours had driven the confused and demoralized Iraqis out of the country. American casualties were minimal: about 300 dead and another 500 wounded; Iraqi casualties were in the thousands.[46] As per his stated war aims, Bush did not allow US troops to chase after the Iraqis into Iraq proper. He was mindful of the fragility of his coalition, which might come apart if he sought to entirely destroy the Iraqi regime, and he was also concerned about what kind of government might emerge in a power vacuum created by Saddam's removal. While this stance resulted in further atrocities by Saddam against Iraqis who sought to overthrow him, Bush's approach would look much better in retrospect after one of his successors—his own son—took a decidedly different approach a dozen years later.

American victory in the Persian Gulf War proved to be faster and more decisive than even its most fervent advocates expected, and was followed by a huge wave of national self-congratulation, evident in the wave of parades thrown for returning veterans in the months that followed. President Bush proclaimed the arrival of a "New World Order," asserting that "the specter of Vietnam has been buried forever in the desert sands of the Arabian Peninsula."[47] More sober analysts too could not help but be impressed by the emphatic successes of the United States over old adversaries and new in 1989–1991. One such observer, conservative writer Francis Fukuyama, argued that the world had essentially reached "the end of history," the title of a highly influential 1989 article (later a book).[48] Fukuyama's point was that the collapse of communism had demonstrated both the moral as well as pragmatic logic of Western liberal democracies for the entire world. All societies, he believed, would ultimately evolve in this direction. Fukuyama would later back away from such triumphalism; over time, it would become increasingly clear that large numbers of people around the world did not necessarily see the Western way, much less the American way, as a worthy goal.

This sense of triumphalism pervaded popular culture of the time as well. The Gulf War was in effect the first video game war—its methods both benefited from, and fostered, popular electronics. Television studios upgraded their technology, and press coverage was marked by a far more upbeat tone than had characterized the Vietnam War. Vietnam had spawned a series of antiwar songs; the most popular song to come out of the Gulf War, by contrast, was country music artist Lee Greenwood's "God Bless the USA," which was originally released in 1984 but surged in popularity in 1991 (as it would a decade later after the September 11 attacks and during the Iraq War).

And yet, even in this moment of apparent supremacy, there were troubling aspects to the post–Cold War status of the United States. President Bush succeeded in convincing allies to pay for most of the cost of the Persian Gulf War, which made sense, in that many of them—notably Kuwait—were immensely rich and had a territorial stake in the outcome. But this development also reflected the troubled state of the nation's finances: the end of the wave of debt unleashed by Ronald Reagan in 1981 was nowhere in sight, nor was the end of the growing economic inequality, which would only intensify.

There were also signs that, even as the United States was triumphing over its rivals, it was losing ground to its long-term allies. Both Germany and Japan seemed, to many observers, to have more vibrant economies than the United States—and economies that on the whole did a better job than the United States did in providing a social safety net without compromising their evident commercial success. Japan in particular was troubling, even threatening, in its technological vitality and growing financial power, which involved acquiring major American assets, from corporations to real estate. Such concerns could take on xenophobic overtones, as in Michael Crichton's bestselling 1992 novel *Rising Sun*, a conspiratorially minded story of industrial espionage. But a steep and sustained downturn in the Japanese economy that began in the early 1990s lessened such fears.

Actually, the greatest danger the United States faced in the post–Cold War era was the same danger that wildly successful empires always face: complacency. For the next decade, the nation would largely turn inward. The rich, preying on a weaker welfare state, insulated themselves from paying the cost of maintaining it with tax breaks and other devices. The poor would seek solace in a rising wave of new (electronic) toys, which became cheaper even as other kinds of goods (notably education) became ever more expensive. Prosperity, even borrowed prosperity, was simply too powerful to resist.

By and large, however, these would be worries for a later day. New fights, and new pleasures, beckoned.

CULTURE WATCH: *The House on Mango Street* (1984)

"We didn't cross the border," Mexican Americans, also known as Chicanos, sometimes say. "The border crossed us." Unlike other immigrants who traversed oceans to reach US shores, there are millions of people today who inhabit a large slab of US territory stretching from southern Texas to northern California that once belonged to Mexico, with a vast borderland that includes Arizona and New Mexico. In the decades following the Mexican–American War (1846–1848), migration across the boundary between the two nations was relatively small. It began to pick up sharply with the development of the bracero program, an agreement between the United States and Mexico allowing temporary guest workers to enter the United States during World War II. In the postwar decades, Mexican immigration—and Latin American immigration generally—began to accelerate. And, in the closing decades of the century, Chicanos began to spread out from the American Southwest— from meatpacking plants in Iowa to college campuses in Vermont.

The Chicana writer Sandra Cisneros has spent her career exploring the ramifications of this Chicana diaspora. Her first book, *The House on Mango Street*, is a short novel tracing a year in the life of Esperanza, a girl on the cusp of adolescence in a poor Latino neighborhood in Chicago. "Those who don't know any better come into our neighborhood scared," she notes at one point.

Figure 7.2 LATINA, FLOWERING: Sandra Cisneros at the Munich Botanical Garden in the 1990s. Since its original publication in 1984, her novel *The House on Mango Street* has become a perennial, selling millions of copies. © Interfoto / Alamy.

"They think we're dangerous. They think we will attack them with shiny knives. They are stupid people who are lost and who got here by mistake." But as we spend time in Esperanza's company—*The House on Mango Street* consists of 46 chapters ranging from two paragraphs to five pages—we are introduced to a rich gallery of characters who bring her community alive: Elenita, the witch woman who tells Esperanza her fortune (she leaves disappointed); the Earl of Tennessee, a jukebox repair man who gives away records (but not country and Western songs); and Sally, her forlorn friend who lives in the shadow of her abusive father—and who brings about Esperanza's unwelcome introduction into the world of sex. Yet, for all the sorrow she witnesses and experiences, her essential buoyancy—*esperanza* means "hope" in Spanish—sustains her. She takes comfort in the four skinny trees that manage to survive on her street. "When I am too sad and too skinny to keep keeping, when I am a tiny thing against so many bricks, then it is I look at trees," she says. "Four who grew despite concrete. Four who reach and do not forget to reach." By the end of the book, Esperanza's dreams are taking root—dreams of a home and a voice with which she can tell the stories of her people.

The House on Mango Street was first published in 1984 by Arte Público Press, a Latino publishing house based in Houston. The book was revised in 1988, and then issued in 1991 by Vintage Contemporaries, a paperback imprint of Random House. Over time, it has attained the status of a classic, selling over 2 million copies and becoming a staple of middle school, high school, and college courses. Cisneros won a prestigious MacArthur Fellowship (the so-called genius grant where recipients are paid to do whatever they like over a period of years) and has gone on to write a series of books that have been translated into a dozen languages.

Hence, by the twenty-first century, the fictional Mango St. has gone global. And Latinos—US-born and foreign-born, legal and undocumented—have redrawn the map of America. Literally and figuratively, we are all in the process of learning an old language.

Suggested Further Reading

Ronald Reagan's life has been richly and variously chronicled. His most respected biographer is Lou Cannon, who has written extensively about him. See, in particular, *Ronald Reagan: The Role of a Lifetime* (1991; New York: Public Affairs Books, 2000). See also Garry Wills, *Reagan's America: Innocence Abroad* (1987; New York: Penguin, 2000). Because it is semi-fictionalized, Edmund Morris's, *Dutch: A Memoir of Reagan* (New York: Random House, 1999) is complicated to assess but nevertheless useful. For a concise overview of the Reagan presidency, see Edward Schaller, *Reckoning with Reagan: America and Its President in the 1980s* (New York: Oxford University Press, 1994). On the George H. W. Bush presidency, now undergoing a positive reappraisal by some historians, see Timothy Naftali, *George H. W. Bush* (New York: Times Books, 2007), part of the American Presidents series edited by the late Arthur Schlesinger, Jr. See also, Jon Meacham, *Destiny and Power: The Odyssey of George Herbert Walker Bush* (New York: Random House, 2015).

For a good overview of evangelical religion and its role in American politics, see Steven P. Miller, *The Age of Evangelicalism: America's Born-Again Years* (New York: Oxford University Press, 2013). On the persistent perception of racism in modern evangelicalism, see Michael O. Emerson and Christian Smith's ethnographic study, *Divided by Faith: Evangelical Religion and the Problem of Race in America* (New York: Oxford University Press, 2001).

For an overview of the 1980s as a whole, see journalist Haynes Johnson's account, *Sleepwalking Through History: America in the Reagan Years* (1991; New York: Norton, 2003). On social movements that operated outside or against the currents of the Reagan presidency, see Bradford Martin, *The Other Eighties: A Secret History of America in the Age of Reagan* (New York: Hill & Wang, 2011).

Notes

1 See Martin's *The Other Eighties,* cited above.
2 Arthur Schlesinger, Jr., *The Age of Jackson* (Boston: Little, Brown, 1945); Sean Wilentz, *The Age of Reagan: A History, 1974–2008* (New York: Harper, 2008).
3 The three volumes, all published by Houghton Mifflin, are *The Crisis of the Old Order, 1919–1933* (1957), *The Coming of the New Deal, 1933–1935* (1958), and *The Politics of Upheaval, 1935–1936* (1960).
4 Rick Perlstein, *The Invisible Bridge: The Fall of Nixon and the Rise of Reagan* (New York: Simon & Schuster, 2014), 36.

5   James Patterson, *Restless Giant: The United States from Watergate to Bush v. Gore* (New York: Oxford University Press, 2005), 161.

6   Edmund Morris, "Five Presidential Myths about Ronald Reagan," *The Washington Post*, February 4, 2011, http://www.washingtonpost.com/wp-dyn/content/article/2011/02/04/AR2011020403106.html (July 18, 2014).

7   Josh Levin, "The Welfare Queen," *Slate*, December 13, 2013: http://www.slate.com/articles/news_and_politics/history/2013/12/linda_taylor_welfare_queen_ronald_reagan_made_her_a_notorious_american_villain.html (July 18, 2014); Perlstein, 603–604.

8   Morris, see citation number 6.

9   Michael Korda, "Prompting the President," *The New Yorker*, October 6, 1997, 87–95.

10 Morris, 318; Perlstein, 544.

11 Patterson, 160. "I know hard work never killed anybody," he was also wont to say. "But why take that chance?"

12 Hedrick Smith, *Who Stole the American Dream?* (2012; New York: Ballantine, 2013), 41.

13 Smith, 329.

14 Gil Troy, "Ronald Reagan's 100-Day Revolution," in *Living in the Eighties*, edited by Troy and Vincent Cannato (New York: Oxford University Press, 2009), 10–11.

15 Patterson, *Restless Giant*, 156; Del Quentin Wilber, *Rawhide Down: The Near Assassination of Ronald Reagan* (New York: Henry Holt, 2011), 209.

16 Patterson, 158.

17 Smith, 11.

18 Patterson, 171.

19 Patterson, 158; Joshua B. Freeman, *American Empire: The Rise of a Global Power/The Democratic Revolution at Home* (New York: Penguin, 2012), 396; "U.S. Becomes the World's Largest Debtor Country," the *Los Angeles Times*, June 24, 1986; http://articles.latimes.com/1986-06-24/news/mn-21190_1_foreign-investments (July 21, 2014).

20 http://www.nytimes.com/1984/08/13/us/reagan-said-to-joke-of-bombing-russia-before-radio-speech.html (July 19, 2014).

21 Bradford has a chapter on this in *The Early Eighties*.

22 Patterson, *Restless Giant*, 214.

23 Transcript of Reagan's remarks at http://neshobademocrat.com/main.asp?SectionID=2&SubSectionID=297&ArticleID=15599&TM=60417.67 (July 21, 2014).

24 Patterson, 171.

25 Matt Bai, http://thecaucus.blogs.nytimes.com/2011/08/12/debate-showed-why-americans-hate-government/?_php=true&_type=blogs&_r=0 (July 28, 2014).

26 Martin, 123.

27 Martin, 129.

28 Martin, 157.

29 Rory Dicker, *A History of U.S. Feminisms* (New York: Seal Press, 2008), 108.

30 Dicker, 106–107.

31 Dicker, 105.

32 Patterson, *Restless Giant*, 179.

33 Patterson, *Restless Giant*, 180.

34 On Reagan and AIDS, see Patterson, *Restless Giant*, 179; Carl M. Cannon, "Ronald Reagan and AIDS: Correcting the Record," *Real Clear Politics*, June 1, 2014: http://www.realclearpolitics.com/articles/2014/06/01/ronald_reagan_and_

aids_correcting_the_record_122806.html#ixzz38FdREfoE (July 23, 2014). See also chapter on ACT-UP in Martin, *The Other Eighties.*

35 Patterson, *Restless Giant,* 214.

36 Information on previous and ensuing paragraphs from Jim Cullen, *Imperfect Presidents: Misadventure and Triumph* (New York: Palgrave, 2007), 158–160.

37 http://www.gallup.com/poll/11887/ronald-reagan-from-peoples-perspective-gallup-poll-review.aspx (July 24, 14).

38 This is the premise of Robert Merry's *Where They Stand: The American Presidents in the Eyes of Voters and Historians* (New York: Simon & Schuster, 2012). Merry notes that William McKinley meets this criterion, but does not rank him with the other six who did.

39 Freeman, 410.

40 http://www.nytimes.com/1991/01/13/us/gravely-ill-atwater-offers-apology. html (July 24, 2014).

41 Freeman, 414; Patterson, *Restless Giant,* 199.

42 Patterson, *Restless Giant,* 227.

43 Patterson, *Restless Giant,* 233.

44 http://www.globalresearch.ca/gulf-war-documents-meeting-between-saddam-hussein-and-ambassador-to-iraq-april-glaspie/31145 (July 27, 2014).

45 Patterson, *Restless Giant,* 233.

46 Patterson, *Restless Giant,* 235.

47 Freeman, 413.

48 http://ps321.community.uaf.edu/files/2012/10/Fukuyama-End-of-history-article.pdf (July 27, 2014); Francis Fukuyama, *The End of History and the Last Man* (New York: the Free Press, 1989).

8

Innovation and Nostalgia
The Culture of the Eighties, 1981–1989

Figure 8.1 TECHNOLOGICAL FRUIT: First-generation Apple Macintosh, 1984. This early personal computer revolutionized the computer industry much in the way the Model T did the automotive industry at the turn of the twentieth century, by offering consumers a relatively affordable, reliable, and convenient piece of machinery for everyday life. By Maxim75, Used under CC BY-SA 4.0 (http://creativecommons.org/licenses/by-sa/4.0), via Wikimedia Commons.

Democratic Empire: The United States Since 1945, First Edition. Jim Cullen.
© 2017 Jim Cullen. Published 2017 by John Wiley & Sons, Inc.

Small Transformations:
The Rise of the Personal Computer

ONCE UPON A TIME in the history of technology, bigger was better. The Industrial Revolution began in the eighteenth century with the development of the steam engine, a piece of machinery where larger scale—in textile mills, in railroad locomotives, in coal mines—corresponded to greater power. Go to a museum such as Greenfield Village at the Henry Ford museum in Dearborn, Michigan, and you will be dwarfed (and, in all likelihood, awed) by the huge nineteenth- and twentieth-century reapers, tractors, and other vehicles that revolutionized the world of work by making it possible for the person operating them to perform the labor of hundreds of horses, and people, at a time. Which is to say nothing of the massive, multi-football-field-length factories that once hulked around greater Detroit (some still do). Bigger was better in other contexts, too. Putting a man on the moon required the construction of gigantic rockets to power space capsules to travel hundreds of thousands of miles.

The early computer industry was also about bigness. Early electronic computers, first built in the 1930s, were large machines that took up entire rooms and required massive streams of power (as well as air conditioning to keep them from overheating). Even the first minicomputers, pioneered by IBM in the 1960s, were still multi-component machines involving cabinets, large printers, and spools of tape to hold data. They were big in financial terms as well. Only the largest businesses or institutions could afford to actually own them; it was common to rent them for the periods of time necessary to perform the calculations on a scale that, similar to the reaper or locomotive, previously required the labor of multiple people.

And yet, from the beginning, the computer industry was all about getting smaller. The key innovation was the development—and shrinkage—in the core component of computing: the integrated circuit (IC), also known as chip. The IC, which replaced the clunky and fragile vacuum tube technology also used in early radios and televisions, was actually a collection of units of computer technology known as transistors. A transistor is a device containing a tiny piece of material, initially germanium but later silicon—as in Silicon Valley—on which there are a series of electrical connections. Transistors were first developed in the 1920s, but it wasn't until 1959 that the first IC for a computer was patented. Innovation proceeded rapidly in the years that followed, principally in the ability to quickly and cheaply manufacture ever-smaller transistors capable of manipulating and storing ever-larger amounts of information. (Today's chips are microscopic, and, according to Moore's law, which is really an observation rather than a rule, the number of transistors that can be placed on an IC has doubled roughly every 2 years since Caltech PhD Gordon Moore first described the pattern in 1975.) Smaller chips meant smaller computers and, by the mid-1970s, it was possible to imagine machines small enough to be owned, operated—and, to an increasing extent, moved—by an individual person.

The people who actually did that imagining were a distinctive cultural type. They were well versed in the technical dimensions of the computer industry— recognizing, for example, that the exceptionally versatile Intel 8080 micropro- cessor manufactured by Intel Corporation for business clients could be the building block for a do-it-yourself machine. These tech-minded "geeks" or "nerds" also had a countercultural sensibility. Among the best known was Stewart Brand, publisher of the *Whole Earth Catalog*, an ecologically minded resource for buyers and sellers—think of it as an early print version of eBay for hippies. Among Brand's multifaceted interests were early personal computers; in fact, he's considered the first person to put those two words together.[1]

Another important group of people was the Homebrew Computer Club, a group of geeks who met at Stanford, long a center of computer innovation. But geekdom was expanding far beyond Northern California. In July 1974, *Radio- Electronics* magazine ran an article titled "Build the Mark-8: Your Personal Minicomputer." It was followed a few months later by a story in *Popular Electronics* that described another do-it-yourself machine, the Altair 8800, which created a sensation across the country.[2]

By the late 1970s, manufacturers began to produce machines for the consumer market. In 1977, Radio Shack introduced the TRS-80, a computer that was distributed through its large chain of stores. Similarly successful was the Commodore PET, which sold particularly well in Europe. Yet another company, Atari, produced the first generation of computer games, notably Pong, origi- nally an arcade game that was adapted for home television playing. Indeed, it's important to note that early computers did not have screens or keyboards, nor were they used for word processing. As their name suggested, their primary functions were mathematical: they made computations.

The two people who revolutionized what computers could do were a pair of Steves: Steve Wozniak and Steve Jobs, a pair of geeks who in 1976 founded a company they named Apple Computer, Inc., in a Silicon Valley garage. One of their early creations—which *did* have a keyboard and a screen—was the Apple II, which marked the true beginning of personal computing. From this point on, simple word processing programs became standard, initiating a process of transforming the computer from being a specialized apparatus for experts into a tool of everyday life. No one executed this transformation better than Apple, which by the early 1980s controlled one-third of the personal computing business, joining the ranks of *Fortune* magazine's listings of the top 500 com- panies faster than any in history.[3]

In 1981, however, the empire—that is to say IBM, the colossus of the com- puter industry since World War II—struck back. Recognizing both the threat and the opportunity of personal computing, IBM rushed its own model, the PC, into production. Because it wished to tap the entrepreneurial energy of geek culture, IBM allowed the PC's internal design to be replicated and refined by others.

A series of imitators, known as clones, entered the fray, among them Hewlett-Packard and Dell. But the term PC quickly came to connote any non-Apple machine, much in the way "Kleenex" became synonymous with facial tissues.

Apple fought back. In 1984, it unveiled the Macintosh, a personal computer that exploited design features first developed by Xerox before that company got out of the computer business. The Macintosh operating system offered users a series of icons such as folders, trashcans, and a language of windows and desktops, making the machine seem natural and simple for even the least computer-literate person. The Mac also came with a "mouse," a user-friendly means of issuing commands. It became for computers what Henry Ford's Model T had been almost a century earlier: not necessarily the cheapest or most advanced piece of technology, but one that was versatile, beloved, and vastly influential.[4]

Yet, even as IBM and Apple were struggling for supremacy in the new personal computer industry, the nature of that industry was undergoing a transformation. In its haste to get the PC onto the market, IBM licensed a Harvard dropout named Bill Gates to design an operating system for it. The physical objects that comprise a computer, such as the chips, motherboard, and ports, were known as "hardware." The coded instructions that allowed the hardware to function, by contrast, was known as "software." By the late 1980s, software was king. Apple was fiercely protective of its software. Gates's software, Microsoft MS-DOS, was installed in IBM machines, but Gates retained the rights to sell this operating system (short for Microsoft Disk Operating System), to other manufacturers, and in the process became immensely successful. In 1985, Microsoft began selling Windows, an updated operating system that imitated the user-friendliness of Apple computers. By decade's end, Apple was on the defensive, more of a niche than a mass-market company. In large measure, that's because most software, whether business tools or the computer games that soon became a gigantic industry in its own right, were written for PCs.

For Americans of the early 1980s, the rise of the personal computer was an exciting, if sometimes disorienting, event comparable to the birth of cars, radio, or television: everybody wanted one. The new machines seemed to have limitless possibilities and implications, ranging from the paperless office to the effortless transmission of genius. Neither of these came to pass. But there's little question that the mass dispersal of computer technology had a major impact on the daily existence of virtually all Americans, vastly simplifying all kinds of tasks even as it imposed new skills to master. Compared to what came later—mass access to the Internet, social networking, the rise of cellular telephony—the isolated personal computer was dismayingly limited. But, in an important respect, it marked the beginning of what might be termed our time.

The personal computer society happened to emerge in the 1980s. As I've indicated, its roots were earlier—I could have easily included much of this discussion in a chapter on the 1970s (but waited to do so, because on balance I consider this a story of the 1980s more than the 1970s). To some degree, the invention and diffusion of technology operates independently of the culture and politics of a given moment. But however direct or indirect the influences of that moment may have been, it seems fitting that what we call "the digital age"—one in which all kinds of information can be coded, transmitted, and stored into patterns of ones and zeroes—began in the 1980s. The personal computer was a technology well suited to the times.

That's because its essence was libertarian. I mean this in two important ways. In the most literal of sense of the term, personal computers freed people: they allowed them to perform all kinds of tasks much more easily and cheaply than ever before. Take that most tedious of enterprises: writing an essay. This was once something that had to be done in a series of stages, typically involving pen and paper, drafts on a typewriter, rounds of corrections done by hand, and retyping. (If you were lucky enough to have an electric typewriter, you could correct typos relatively easily. If not, you could pay someone else to type for you.) Sometimes you would type on triplicate paper so that you would have more than one version, but this required actually procuring it, along with the other tools of the craft, such as typing ribbons and correction fluid. There was no electronic storage of your work. There was no spellcheck. Features such as bold or italic type were exotic (underlining was relatively easy), and footnoting was a formatting nightmare. About the only advantage of typing papers was the plausibility of a claim that your dog ate your homework as an excuse for not handing it in. Personal computers, by contrast, made writing papers easy. They were also wonderful for things such as running spreadsheets, balancing checkbooks, and other tasks of personal and business life. (One spreadsheet software program that ran on the IBM PC, Lotus 1-2-3, revolutionized commerce in the early 1980s; it was the first "killer app.") Personal computers set people free from their dependence on specialists, and, for the more creatively minded, opened up new possibilities for things such as visual design; Apple computers were especially prized in this regard.

Which brings us to a second facet of computer culture libertarianism: it decentralized authority. This was a significant part of its appeal for the *Whole Earth Catalog* crowd in the 1970s. The Counterculture had tended to view technology with hostility, because it was viewed as an instrument whereby the military–industrial complex maintained dominance and control. Personal computers, by contrast, placed power in the hands of the people.

But this technological populism was more than countercultural. It was also consonant with the spirit of the early Reagan era. Corporate America, which had undergone a period of conglomeration and diversification in the 1960s and 1970s, began to streamline by focusing on core businesses by the early 1980s. Personal computers allowed businesses to complete work in-house that formerly had to be contracted out, which was both cheaper and more efficient. One shouldn't exaggerate the degree to which autonomy channeled downward; the 1980s were in fact a time when the corporate concentration of power, particularly in terms of influence over the government, began to intensify. But the rhetoric of "devolution" was compelling and widespread. A famous 1984 Macintosh advertisement, broadcast during the Super Bowl, previewed the new Apple computer as the antidote for the totalitarian fears first articulated in George

Orwell's famous 1948 dystopian novel, *1984*. In the ad, a beautiful blonde woman in a bright white shirt and red running shorts (the rest of the ad is in muted color) hurls a sledgehammer at a massive screen on which a Big Brother–like character lectures to a numbed audience of workers. "On January 24, Apple Computer will introduce Macintosh," the announcer explains at the end of the ad. "And you'll see why 1984 won't be like *1984*."[5]

Consuming Pleasures: Old Fashions, New Gadgets

This convergence between business culture and popular culture was one of the hallmarks of the 1980s. Both embraced a new sense of materialism. Young people in the 1960s and 1970s were disdainful, sometimes extravagantly so, of the traditional indicators of status in national life, rejecting high fashion and sports cars in favor of tie-dye t-shirts and battered VW Beetles (or vans). But the technological innovations of the late twentieth century, combined with a recovering economy—something that Americans who had suffered through the downturns of the mid-1970s and early 1980s were less likely to take for granted—led many Americans of all ages to revel in newfound buying power. In relative as well as absolute terms, personal computers were more expensive than they are today— routinely thousands of dollars. That made them hard, though not impossible, for many middle-class families to acquire, much in the way cars have been since the era of the Model-T. And, of course, once you bought one, you also bought all kinds of stuff (printers, games, etc.) to go along with it.

But computers weren't the only coveted gadgets of the 1980s. Even more prevalent, at least in the short term, was the rapid proliferation of the videocassette recorder (VCR).

As with many technologies, the capacity to record live television programs for later playback—or to format films, which were quite expensive on reels, in tape form—had been possible long before the 1980s. But they were not commercially viable. Playback devices for consumer use began to gather momentum in the marketplace in the late 1970s. One factor inhibiting their spread was a lack of clarity about which format would become dominant: Sony's Beta or JVC Video Home System, or VHS, tape. (One early sign of ebbing US technological dominance was the withdrawal of a number of American companies from the market, unable to compete in terms of quality or price.) Most connoisseurs considered Beta better in terms of quality, but VHS was cheaper and its cassettes could hold more tape, and so it ultimately prevailed. Once it did, VCR ownership spread rapidly. There were 400,000 in US homes by 1978; 5 years later, that number had reached 4.1 million. In 1985, 20% of all homes had VCRs; by decade's end, more than 75% did. More homes had a VCR than subscribed to cable.[6]

The rise of the VCR had a major impact on television viewing. The ability to record shows or movies for later viewing freed audiences that had been tied to watching a particular show at a particular time. Networks, film studios, and advertisers regarded this development with some concern, especially after the Supreme Court ruled that videotaping shows for time-shifting purposes was legal in the 1984 decision *Sony v. Universal*. But the rise of videotape proved to be a bonanza for such companies, which could now sell vast quantities of content, new and old, to voracious consumers. Films on video, which could cost as much as US$100, could be profitably rented for a few dollars per day, resulting in an explosion in the number of video rental stores across the country. Movies eventually dropped in price to the point where personal film libraries were affordable. For movie fans who could previously only see new films in theaters and old ones in places such as college film societies, this opened up a whole new world, especially for those located outside major metropolitan centers.

A third consumer revolution involved the transformation of a technology that was already long established: recorded music. Actually, sound recording had already gone through a series of previous formats, among them perforated sheets of metal, wax cylinders, and shellac disks. The great innovation of the mid-twentieth century had been the advent of vinyl records, formatted in 7-inch or 10-inch disks to be played on machines spinning at 45 and 33⅓ revolutions-per-minute, respectively. In the 1960s and 1970s, two other tape formats, 8-track and cassettes, could also be used to record music, and became widespread. Here again, record companies were upset about the ability of consumers to make and share tapes, but there's little indication that this hurt sales—indeed, it may well have stimulated them. In the early 1980s, however, the compact disc player, which used laser technology on disks (CDs) that were about 4.75 inches in diameter, entered the marketplace. They too spread rapidly. Consumers liked CDs because they offered generally higher sound quality, were far more durable, and allowed listeners to program songs in any sequence they wished—another element of liberation. Record companies loved them because CDs were sold at higher prices—ridiculously so at first—and, perhaps more importantly, gave them a way of selling old music to consumers all over again in a new format. And, apropos of the point made at the beginning of this chapter, a *smaller* format. Records and music were more portable than ever before, and entire libraries could fit on a snug shelf.

This brings us to a curious paradox about the culture of the 1980s, an alternating current to this breathless sense of excitement about cultural change: many of these new technological bottles were being filled with old cultural wines. For all the sense of excitement and wonder over new gadgets that were transforming everyday life in the realms of work and leisure, Americans spent a good deal of their time looking back. The 1980s are widely regarded as a conservative era not only in terms of partisan politics, or in prevailing economic principles, but also in the realm of art and ideas. It was a time of reawakened attention to tradition—and, after decades of growing skepticism and hostility toward conventional notions of nationalism, a time of reawakened patriotism.

Nowhere was this shift more obvious than in the realm of popular music. Pop musicians have always been known for their acuity to new musical trends, and the 1980s certainly had their fair share, ranging from newfangled synthesizer-based bands such as the Human League, Flock of Seagulls, and Eurhythmics that dominated the charts early in the decade, to the emergence of hip-hop as a major pop music genre in the mid-1980s (more on this in the text that follows). But a self-conscious dedication to older sounds was also a hallmark of the decade. In the 1980s, there had been bands such as Sha Na Na that were understood to be nostalgia acts. But, in the early 1980s, the Stray Cats wrote and performed a string of new songs in a 1950s-based rockabilly style, managing to sound fresh and contemporary at the same time. Billy Joel did something similar in his smash hit album *An Innocent Man* (1983), which was stocked with hit songs written in older pop styles that ranged from 1950s doo-wop to 1960s Motown. This neoclassical trend was even more pronounced in country music, where a new generation of performers—Dwight Yoakam, Steve Earle, Lyle Lovett, and k.d. lang, among others—set themselves apart from middle-of-the-road country by stripping down their sound to the basics and/or accentuating styles from an earlier era. Lang fancied herself as the reincarnated voice of Patsy Cline—she called her band the Reclines—though the sheer power of her vocals, coupled with her quirky (and closeted lesbian) orientation, put her in a class by herself.

This attentiveness to tradition could be as much thematic as it was musical. Over the course of the decade, John Cougar Mellencamp wrote paeans to farm life in albums such as *Scarecrow* (1985), and evolved from a fairly straightforward rock musician to one who incorporated Appalachian instruments into his arrangements for *The Lonesome Jubilee* (1987). Bruce Springsteen showed similar tendencies in his own work of the decade, but became one of the iconic figures of the 1980s by embodying the voice of the receding industrial working class in his hugely successful *Born in the U.S.A.* (1984). The title track of that album was an anguished cry of despair sung from the point of view of an unemployed Vietnam veteran. But not everyone took it that way. In a New Jersey campaign stop while running for re-election in 1984, President Reagan asserted that the nation's future was affirmed "in the message of hope in the songs of a man so many young Americans admire—New Jersey's own Bruce Springsteen." Chrysler CEO Lee Iacocca (whose self-titled hit memoir became a bestselling celebration of the American Dream) offered Springsteen US$2 million to use "Born in the U.S.A." in a car ad. Springsteen fans were appalled by such glib patriotism, as was Springsteen himself, who disassociated himself from Reagan and turned Iacocca down.[7] But when you stand before the flag, as Springsteen did in the iconography surrounding the album, such appropriations may not be all that surprising.

What *was* surprising was the way even the self-avowed alternative artists got in on the act. In 1980, the highly successful rock band Talking Heads released their landmark album *Remain in Light*, which was heavily influenced by indigenous African music and contained some of the most arresting pop music of the rock era—and some of the most bizarre ("Lost my shape/trying to act casual," goes the opening line of the song "Cross-Eyed and Painless"). But, by the mid-1980s, in albums such as *Speaking in Tongues* (1983), *Little Creatures* (1985), and *True Stories* (1986), lead singer/songwriter David Byrne was celebrating the joys of domesticity and roadside Americana in his own inimitable way ("The future is certain/give us time to work it out," he sings with a gospel choir as his backdrop in "Road to Nowhere"). Laurie Anderson, who was much more avant-garde than even the Talking Heads, titled her 1984 album *United States Live*; it included tracks with titles such as "Yankee See" and "Democratic Way." Again, neither the Talking Heads nor Laurie Anderson were patriotic in any conventional sense of the term—indeed, some of their music willfully defied national pieties. But, in their distinctive ways, they rode waves that surged through the body politic.

One could also see this tendency in postmodern architecture. Postmodernism was an intellectual movement that ranged across a variety of fields (it was last discussed in Chapter 5 and will be taken up again in Chapter 9), and it was international. But, in the United States, as elsewhere, it was marked by a new effort to engage the past—often in a style that alluded to more than one period—and move beyond the strictly functionalist character of modernist architecture. Michael Graves's Portland Building (1982) and Philip Johnson's AT&T Building (1984) are marked by a sense of color and play that redefined their moment, one that in many respects lingers to this day.

Other efforts to invoke the past were more transparent—and revisionist. The 1960s in particular underwent a reappraisal in the 1980s. The legacy of the 1960s had a lasting impact on subsequent decades, and did so in the face of some fairly determined opposition. But there were also cultural currents in the 1980s that questioned, even rejected, the oppositional quality of that decade, embracing the sense of cohesion and stability associated with the 1950s, which experienced something of a revival. One of the biggest hit movies of the 1980s, *Back to the Future* (1985, followed by sequels in 1989 and 1990), was a time-traveling re-creation of that decade, portraying it with both a knowing wink and lavish sentiment. The star of *Back to the Future*, Michael J. Fox, was also the star of one of the biggest sitcoms of the 1980s, *Family Ties* (1982–1989), in which he played a young conservative at odds with his post-hippie parents. The creators of the show originally intended the parents to be the stars, but Fox, and the politics of his character, stole the show.

Even television shows that were meant to showcase social progress had deeply traditional accents. *The Cosby Show* (1984–1992) was widely hailed as a landmark sitcom for the quality of its writing and acting. It featured an African American family in a cast headed by the well-established comedian Bill Cosby. This was not a novelty; a number of previous sitcoms had led the way. But the Huxtables of Brooklyn Heights lived an affluent lifestyle that in many ways seemed closer to lily-white suburban Scarsdale than it did, say, the considerably more edgy Brooklyn of Spike Lee's *Do the Right Thing* (1989). The patriarchal families of 1950s sitcoms such as *The Adventures of Ozzie and Harriet* (1952–1966) were far too old-fashioned for the post-women's-movement 1980s. But, with a African American man in the lead, it was once again possible to smuggle in the message that, at least sometimes anyway, father may really know best. Cosby's reputation was severely damaged in the 2010s by allegations (confirmed in a deposition a decade earlier) that he drugged women in order to sexually assault them over a period of many years.

Feminism, too, took on distinctive accents in the 1980s. The hallmark of the movement in the 1960s and 1970s was a drive for equality, especially in terms of issues such as equal pay for equal work. That quest continued, but there was also a more conservative version that tended to define the concept as a matter of succeeding on male terms. One could glimpse it, for example, in the fashion fad of the power suit: trousers, oversized blouse, and a (typically double-breasted) suit jacket with padded shoulders, an ensemble that suggested empowerment through mimicking male couture. Yet this message was also often coupled with more traditional notions of femininity. The two were memorably fused in a perfume ad from the era that featured an attractive woman in a power suit (among other outfits) singing, "I can bring home the bacon/fry it up in the pan/and never let you forget you're a man."[8] Domesticity remained instinctive, even for female breadwinners with assertive sex drives.

Indeed, perhaps the most striking element of gender dynamics in the 1980s was a renewed desire to embrace difference, to assert power by emphasizing that which was distinctive to women even as they laid claim to prerogatives that had always been male. This concept of "difference feminism," as dubbed by feminist poet and essayist Katha Pollitt,[9] typically involved leveraging sexual power in the pursuit of other kinds. It was most obvious in the realm of popular music, where a number of rock bands—and here it's worth emphasizing that they *were* bands, groups of women working collectively, writing, performing, and in some cases producing music—rose to national prominence. The Go-Gos, an ensemble of five attractive young women, became the first all-female group to hit number one on the Billboard charts with their 1981 album *Beauty and the Beat*. The Bangles, another band whose evocative name evoked a widely worn form of women's jewelry, enjoyed a string of hits in the mid-1980s, among them "Walk Like and Egyptian" (1986), "Manic Monday" (1986), and the sexually suggestive "In Your Room" (1988).

Difference feminism was perhaps captured most appealingly by Cyndi Lauper, whose 1983 hit "Girls Just Want to Have Fun" became a generational anthem. "When the working day is done, girls just want to have fun," Lauper sang in distinctive Brooklynese, fusing public and private gender identities in a charmingly wacky visual style that included skirts made out of newspaper and colorfully spiked hair. The significance of the working day was unmistakable. But so was the song's title, bookended by "girls" and "fun," that was decisively gendered even as it was liberating.

No one embraced difference feminism more aggressively—or controversially—than Madonna. In a decade-long string of hits that stretched from "Holiday" (1983) through her 1989 album *Like a Prayer*, the Detroit-born singer/dancer/songwriter embraced and disposed a series of identities in quintessentially postmodern fashion. In the mid-1980s, she became the poster child of Reagan-era materialism with her hit—and hit video—"Material Girl" in 1984. She also engaged a number of hot-button topics such as abortion (the pregnant protagonist of her 1986 song "Papa Don't Preach" expresses her opposition to it) and Catholicism (the earnest tone of "Like a Prayer" conflates religious and sexual ecstasy). Madonna's champions considered her thrillingly fearless; critics, some of them feminist, considered her glib and sexually reactionary. Her controversial 1992 album *Erotica*, and simultaneously released coffee-table book *Sex*, were dismissed as retrograde pornography. But no one doubted her ability to capture, and hold, attention.

Seeing Music: Music Television, or MTV

Figures such as Cyndi Lauper and Madonna were important for another reason: they were pioneers in a mode of expression that became fantastically successful in the 1980s: music video. As with any form of cultural innovation, music video had deep roots, dating back to the days where early cartoons were synchronized to jazz recordings. The fusion of music and images was central to the success of the Beatles, dating back to *A Hard Day's Night* (1964), a film that featured Fab Four performances. But the form really became recognizably modern in Great Britain with the advent of the British TV show *Top of the Pops* (1964–2006), which broadcast clips of musical acts performing lip-synched versions hit songs.[10]

Music video became an international phenomenon with the birth of MTV in 1981. Its immediate precursor was *PopClips*, a 1980 show hosted by comedian Howie Mandel and broadcast on Nickelodeon, one the first cable channels. The late 1970s and early 1980s were a time of experimentation in cable television, when programming executives were just beginning to offer subscribers niche channels dedicated to specific kinds of programming (such as the Weather Channel, launched in 1982). The business model of MTV essentially involved acquiring free programming from record labels, which would supply what amounted to advertising for their acts. Expectations were modest, but MTV took off rapidly, thanks to engaging graphics, hip video disk jockeys (or "veejays"), and, of course, a parade of engaging musical acts. By 1984, Warner Communications, which owned the enterprise, had spun MTV into a separate company that claimed tens of millions of viewers.[11] The influence of the channel went far beyond music video, shaping advertising, fashion, and other television programming—all of which coalesced in the trendsetting show *Miami Vice* (1984–1990).

Because they had experience—and a large inventory of videos—British acts were among the first beneficiaries of MTV, which launched the careers of a series of performers, notably Duran Duran and Culture Club, led by photogenic musicians comfortable in the medium (the androgynous Boy George of Culture Club became an international celebrity on the basis of his colorfully outrageous couture). Established musicians with good budgets were also able to exploit the possibilities of music video, which evolved rapidly as a genre from relatively straightforward performances of hit songs to miniature movies full of plots, dancing, and visual allusions. A number of 1980s albums—Billy Joel's *An Innocent Man*, Bruce Springsteen's *Born in the U.S.A.*, and Cyndi Lauper's *She's So Unusual,* among others—became collections of hit singles, powered by videos timed to the release of singles from those albums.

One conspicuous early absence from MTV was African American artists. Programming executives initially argued that white audiences were not interested in African American performers; media critics derided this policy as racist. When Michael Jackson's 1982 album *Thriller* topped the charts without video support in 1983, his record label, CBS, reportedly threatened to stop providing MTV with videos if the network didn't change its tune. It complied—the first video from the album, for "Billie Jean," went into heavy rotation and became an instant classic. Jackson kicked down the door for a new wave of African American MTV stars, among them Prince, Lionel Richie, and Jackson's younger sister Janet, all of whom became video stars. Prince, a startlingly gifted songwriter and musician—he wrote "Manic Monday" for the Bangles, one of many hits for other artists—starred in a film to accompany his hugely successful 1984 album *Purple Rain,* which in many ways amounted to an extended music video.

However, Michael Jackson was more than a successful musician who thrived on video. He was a bona fide popular phenomenon, a figure that dominated the nation's cultural life like a colossus in the middle years of the 1980s. Part of the reason why he was able to do so was the extent to which he was seen as a vessel of African-American musical history. Though he was only 24 years old at the time *Thriller* was released, Jackson already had a storied career as the child prodigy of the Jackson Five for Motown in the late 1960s and early 1970s. After lowering his profile somewhat in the mid-1970s, he re-emerged in force with the release of his album *Off the Wall* (1979), which featured the disco classic "Don't Stop 'Til You Get Enough." In 1983, he performed on a television special honoring the 25th anniversary of Motown, and the dance he performed—the Moonwalk—earned him comparisons with Fred Astaire (a fan).

But it was *Thriller,* which spawned seven top 10 singles, that turned Jackson into a living legend, and it was part of the reason why he was able to attract unusually-high-quality collaborators, beginning with the album's producer, Quincy Jones, whose résumé stretched from Miles Davis through Frank Sinatra (he had also produced *Off the Wall*). Jackson sang a duet with Paul McCartney in "The Girl is Mine," got guitar virtuoso Eddie Van Halen to perform a heavy metal solo for "Beat It," and landed heavyweight director John Landis to direct the unprecedented 13-minute video for "Thriller," which included dialogue from horror-movie icon Vincent Price. Jackson's ability to evoke the cornucopia of American popular culture and effortlessly blend pop styles, among them rock, gospel, rhythm and blues, and more, made him a uniquely elastic figure, able to appeal to multiple constituencies across multiple generations, a feat he repeated on almost as successful a scale with his 1987 follow-up album *Bad,* which was also an MTV fixture (the video of the title track was directed by Martin Scorsese).

Jackson was also a man of his moment. Like Bill Cosby, he was an African American whom white Americans found unthreatening and appealing. Jackson, for his part, craved approval, and defined success for himself in terms of the size of his audience. This dynamic generated disapproval among African Americans, many of whom were dismayed by Jackson's apparent attempt to downplay his racial identity, which may have included lightening his skin (the explanation for this was publicly ascribed to vitiligo, a condition that causes depigmentation). Jackson's troubled personal life, which derived in part from a grim childhood that involved physical abuse by his father, would eventually erode his appeal and contribute to his tragically shortened life, which ended in a drug overdose in 2009. But at the height of his powers, he was a shimmering embodiment of integration who personified the most appealing aspects of American popular culture in the 1980s.

Yo! African American Culture and the Birth of Hip-Hop

It's important to note that not all major cultural figures of the 1980s tacked to the prevailing winds of the time. Some challenged them by staking out an alternative path, and in so doing became part of the cultural record of the decade. This was especially true in African American America. Lacking power commensurate with their numbers in politics, and disproportionately poor, African Americans turned to cultural expression as a means of getting their message heard, and succeeded to an impressive extent in piercing the nation's mainstream discourse. Indeed, in some cases, African American artists energized or rescued ailing businesses and art forms; MTV was a mere financial curio before the channel started showing Michael Jackson videos, for example, and sitcoms were widely considered to have been in the doldrums until *The Cosby Show* came along.

African American women fiction writers were particularly notable in this regard. The 1980s were a breakout decade for a number of them. Gloria Naylor's debut novel *The Women of Brewster Place* (1982), which explored the lives of a series of seven women in an unnamed urban setting, won the National Book Award and was made into a television miniseries 7 years later. Alice Walker's 1982 novel *The Color Purple*, which traced the life of a poor African American woman in the rural south of the 1930s through a series of letters, also won the National Book Award, as well as the Pulitzer Prize, and was perhaps among the most celebrated novels of the decade. It was made into a 1985 movie directed by Steven Spielberg, and featured newcomer Oprah Winfrey, also known as the star of a talk show. She would go on to become an entertainment impresario responsible for raising the profile of a series of African American women writers (Winfrey's production company brought Naylor's *Women of Brewster Place* to the screen). The towering figure of American fiction generally in the 1980s was Toni Morrison, who had established herself as a major writer on the basis of a series of novels in the 1970s, but whose 1987 novel *Beloved*, a fractured postmodern narrative of slavery set on either side of the Civil War, is widely regarded as one of the greatest books of the twentieth century.

African American actors also made headway in Hollywood in the 1980s. Comedian Eddie Murphy made the transition from *Saturday Night Live*, which had made him a major star (another African American performer rescuing an ailing show), to a series of hit movies, among the biggest of which was *48 Hours* (1982), a buddy–buddy movie with Nick Nolte in which Murphy's racial sensibility was the driving engine of the plot. Denzel Washington was a transracial sex symbol as well as one of the most gifted dramatic actors of his generation, apparent in films like *A Soldier' Story* (1984) and *Glory* (1989), for which he won an Academy Award for his portrayal of an angry slave-turned Civil War soldier. African American women experienced more difficulty gaining traction, though a few, such as comedian Whoopi Goldberg (who starred in *The Color Purple*) and Phylicia Rashad (of *The Cosby Show*), became household names.

African Americans were almost absent from directorial ranks in the 1980s, with the significant exception of Spike Lee, whose 1986 debut *She's Gotta Have It* (1986), about an independent-minded African American woman (Tracy Camilla Johns), marked the arrival of a significant new voice in American cinema. Lee followed it up with *School Daze* (1988), an unusual foray into intra-racial tensions between students at a historically African American college. The 1989 release of *Do the Right Thing*, which traced the lives of residents in a Brooklyn neighborhood on a searingly hot summer day that would culminate in a race riot, is one of the landmark documents in American race relations of the era.

The most significant development in African American cultural life of the 1980s, however, was the rise of hip-hop as the dominant idiom in popular music.[12] Hip-hop, or rap music, as it was once more commonly known at the time, was the latest chapter in an old musical saga that linked Africa and the Americas. (Indeed, the genre was never racially monolithic; one of the earliest manifestations of hip-hop, for example, came from the Ghetto Brothers, led by the Puerto Rican and Jewish gang member Benjy Meléndez.) In previous eras, this musical triangle trade catalyzed the emergence of gospel, blues, jazz, and other musical styles. As explained by historian Jeff Chang, however, there was a crucial difference with hip-hop: while older forms of African American music such as the blues had been rooted in cultures of work (notably the legacy of slavery), hip-hop was, to a great degree, the musical idiom of unemployment.[13] By the 1980s, the soaring hopes of the civil rights movement had been dashed by the persistently poor economic conditions of African Americans in the United States and elsewhere. In particular, New York's South Bronx had been wrecked by interstate highway construction, white flight, the destruction of the city's manufacturing base, and gang violence. These were the sorry conditions out of which, paradoxically, a vibrant culture emerged.

This culture was more than musical. Hip-hop was part of a broader set of practices that began to emerge in the late 1970s, among them urban graffiti (especially in New York's subway system) and a form of dance known as b-boy, or break dancing, which involved stylish poses and the use of hands to support one's body. The genre of music that had accompanied b-boy—also a term used to describe those who embraced this culture—was known as dub, which involved mixing rhythm tracks from different songs, scratching the needle of a turntable backward and forward while playing records, and sampling brief excerpts from pop hits. This musical manipulation was accompanied by improvisational speech by a master of ceremonies (emcee, or MC), who worked alongside the disk jockey (DJ); occasionally, they were the same person. Once such "rapping" migrated from Jamaica to the Bronx, it became a beloved fixture of street fairs and club parties. A number of MCs and DJs became local celebrities whose fame radiated outward, among them the Jamaican-born rapper Kool Herc, Afrika Bambaata, and Melle Mel.

Ironically, the first national hip-hop hit came out of New Jersey. When entrepreneur Sylvia Robinson failed to convince leading Bronx rappers to come to the studio she owned, her son recruited a local outfit, the Sugarhill Gang, to record "Rapper's Delight" (1979), a song that sampled the then-current, now-classic disco song "Good Times" by Chic. It was also around this time that other musicians became aware of hip-hop's appeal. The New York post-punk band Blondie was at the peak of its popular appeal when it released its 1980 album *Autoamerican*. The first single from that album, "The Tide Is High," was a calypso number that topped the charts. Its was followed by "Rapture"—a tribute to Chic that included a silly rap by lead singer Deborah Harry at the close of the song[14]—which also went to #1 on the *Billboard* pop chart and made people far from the Bronx aware that a musical revolution was brewing. That revolution was confirmed, and its political ramifications were amplified, with the release of "The Message" in the following year (see sidebar at the end of this chapter).

It was in the mid-1980s that hip-hop transformed from a local music scene to the center of American popular music. Pivotal in this regard was Run-DMC, a trio hailing from the Bronx-adjacent borough of Queens. The group, consisting of Joseph "Run" Simmons, Darryl "DMC" McDaniels, and Jason "Jam Master Jay" Mizell, was the first rap act to be featured on MTV, and reached a vast new mainstream audience with their cover version of Aerosmith's 1975 hit "Walk this Way." (The video, which featured the rappers breaking down the wall separating them from the rock band, also revived Aerosmith's sagging commercial fortunes.) Run-DMC was also notable for the way it repositioned hip-hop's visual image from the more colorful look and dance-groove sound of early rappers (such as the Grandmaster Flash) to a stripped down ("street") black-and-white style, showcased in songs such as their classic "My Adidas" (1986), which would be adopted by the next generation of hip-hop performers.

Though they tended to be overshadowed in a genre, like many other pop genres, that tended to ignore or dismiss women, hip-hop did have a growing female presence by decade's end. The trio of Salt-n-Pepa formed in the mid-1980s, and enjoyed a string of hits into the 1990s. Rappers MC Lyte and Queen Latifah are regarded as among the founding members of hip-hop with their albums *Lyte as a Rock* (1988) and *All Hail the Queen* (1989). Lyte was notable for the way she rejected traditional femininity in songs such as "Ruffneck" (1993); Latifah, who incorporated the African diaspora into her visual iconography, went on to have a durable career in film and television, and became a feminist icon.

Perhaps the most obvious development in rap music in the late 1980s is the emergence of a more militant style, reflected in politically pointed lyrics and a dense, even aggressive, musical mix. The pre-eminent act in this regard was Public Enemy, led by the serious Chuck D and his comic foil Flavor Flav, who wore a huge clock around his neck. The band's overall profile was severe, with dancers performing in paramilitary gear, and its logo featured the silhouette of an African American man in the crosshairs of a rifle. Public Enemy's widely hailed debut album *Yo! Bum Rush the Show* was released in 1987, followed by *It Takes a Nation of Millions to Hold Us Down* (1988) and *Fear of a Black Planet* (1990), one track of which, "Fight the Power," was prominently featured in *Do the Right Thing*. Public Enemy generated controversy on a variety of fronts, ranging from its dismissive putdown of Elvis Presley in "Fight the Power" ("straight up racist that sucker was") to arguments that the band was anti-Semitic (among the remarks attributed to one member, Professor Griff, was an assertion that Jews "are responsible for the majority of the wickedness that goes on around the globe"; he left the group).[15]

By 1990, hip-hop was widely regarded as the most vibrant site of American popular culture. Its influence stretched in multiple directions; in particular, it was widely imitated by white musicians. This ranged from the seemingly glib and opportunistic, as in Vanilla Ice's 1990 song "Ice Ice Baby," which sampled the 1981 Queen/David Bowie song "Under Pressure" and became the first hip-hop song to reach the number 1 spot on *Billboard* magazine's pop chart, as well as the more critically acclaimed Beastie Boys, whose 1986 album *Licensed to Ill* became the first rap album to top *Billboard's* pop album chart. (*Licensed to Ill* was cheerfully sophomoric, but also genuinely immersed in hip-hop culture, something that would become increasingly clear in subsequent albums.) As these examples suggest, there remained a persistent issue, going back to the rise of jazz a century earlier, as to where the line between racial influence and racist exploitation should be drawn. Many hip-hop fans, white and African American, would surely have been more comfortable, had the most commercially success-ful purveyors of the art form actually emerged from the communities in which they originated, communities that reflected the inequalities that long preceded, and continued beyond, the 1980s. On the other hand, the period was also notable for the rise of African Americans in the ranks of record executives. The Beastie Boys recorded on the Def Jam label, founded by Russell Simmons. A few years later, Dr. Dre and Suge Knight would be among the founders of Death Row Records. Questions of racial identity in hip-hop continued well into the next century, when rappers such as Eminem—his fans as well as his critics—grappled with them. But the success of the genre documented the truly amazing African American capacity for musical reinvention, and the outsized power of a racial minority to shape a national culture.

Bourne in the USA: Dissident Voices

By the end of the 1980s, a growing sense of opposition to Reaganesque conservatism of the kind that typified hip-hop was taking root even in the most traditional precincts of mass media. This was true even in mainstream Hollywood. Though widely regarded as a bastion of liberalism in terms of the vocal opinions of many celebrated actors, the American film industry was actually quite conservative. To a great extent, this caution was the product of corporate consolidation and a blockbuster mentality that actively sought the lowest-common denominator in the so-called high-concept movies, with the result that the decade is often considered a relatively weak one by film critics. The success of Steven Spielberg's *Jaws* in 1975, George Lucas's *Star Wars* in 1977, and the collaboration between the two in *Raiders of the Lost Ark* (1981) led to a relentless focus on sequels and remakes of established properties (such as *Star Trek*, a tepidly received TV show when it ran in 1966–1969, but which subsequently blossomed in syndication) that made lots of money but evinced relatively little in the way of originality or provocation. With cable and home video providing strong competition for trips to movie theaters, the film industry rededicated itself to visual spectacle, and oriented its business model around opening movies in large big-box multiplex theaters that allowed filmgoers to choose among a greater number of screenings than had typically been possible previously. "SEE IT AGAIN (with your eyes open)," went one promotion for *Jaws*, suggesting the economic logic of the blockbuster that became common in the 1980s, which also included cross-promotion in terms of fast-food merchandising, toys, and other kids of commercial exploitation.

Insofar as there were memorable American movies for most of the 1980s, they tended to come from the margins. Martin Scorsese, who enjoyed little of the studio clout of peers Spielberg and Lucas for most of his career, started off the decade memorably with his 1980 black-and-white classic *Raging Bull*, the story of boxer Jake LaMotta (played unforgettably by Robert De Niro) that many regard as the best film of the decade. Scorsese also directed the overlooked *King of Comedy* (1983), a deeply subversive exploration of fame starring De Niro as an insanely driven man who will go to any length to become a stand-up comedian. Another important director, John Sayles, made historically rich films on shoestring budgets, among them *Matewan* (1987), a riveting drama about striking coal miners whose very topic was a pointed statement in the anti-labor climate of the 1980s, and *Eight Men Out* (1988), a depiction of the Black Sox baseball scandal of 1919 that has similar class overtones. A third maverick director, Jonathan Demme, made a joyfully hip documentary about the Talking Heads, *Stop Making Sense* (1984), and provocatively scrambled genres in his romantic comedy/dark thriller *Something Wild* (1986).

There were a few commercially successful major studio Hollywood movies with real bite that surfaced toward decade's end. One of the most memorable was director Oliver Stone's *Wall Street* (1987), released in the weeks following the stock market collapse that October. As with a number of Stone movies, this one gives us a young protagonist, Bud Fox (Charlie Sheen), trying to choose between two fathers—his airline worker dad (real-life dad Martin Sheen), who's the president of the machinist's union, and his dark, charismatic foil, corporate raider Gordon Gekko (Michael Douglas in a signature role, for which he won an Academy Award for Best Actor). At one point, Gekko delivers a speech to stockholders modeled on a speech given by predatory capitalist Ivan Boesky, who once asserted that "greed is healthy." Gekko's version: "Greed, for lack of a better word, is good. Greed is right. Greed works." We learn, as we so often do, that crime doesn't pay, but a big part of the film's appeal is the silky appeal of its villain.

Stone was also an important Hollywood figure in the 1980s because he made a pair of notable movies that challenged US foreign policy. His 1986 drama *Salvador* used the story of a cynical journalist (James Woods) to depict Reagan administration's atrocities in Latin America. Stone, who was an infantryman during the Vietnam War, also directed *Platoon* (1986), which won the Oscar for Best Picture that year. Whereas Michael Cimino's *The Deer Hunter* (1978) and Francis Ford Coppola's *Apocalypse Now* (1979) were, in their different ways, epic films with panoramic settings, *Platoon* typified a pattern that showed up in a number of 1980s films on the war—among them Barry Levinson's *Good Morning, Vietnam* (1987) and Stone's subsequent *Born on the Fourth of July* (1989)—that sought to downplay geopolitical questions by focusing on the experience of individual American soldiers. *Platoon* starred Charlie Sheen, again caught between mentors (Tom Berenger and Willem Dafoe) who pull him in opposite directions. This tight-focus ideological strategy had the effect of engendering sympathy for Vietnam vets, who had often been ignored or scorned in the 1970s. But it came at a price of ethnocentrism and an unwillingness to really consider the costs of American imperialism.[16] At times, such as in the Sylvester Stallone star vehicle *First Blood* (1982) and its sequels, such evasion resulted in a weird combination of whininess and imperial hubris. "Do we get to win this time?" asks Stallone's protagonist in *First Blood Part II* (1985), who is sent back to recover possible prisoners of war, in the second of four films in the series. (A fifth was in development at the time this book was written.) But whatever their explicit and implicit politics, none of these movies posits the Vietnam War as anything other than a mistake.

American victory in the Cold War and its triumph in the Persian Gulf War had the effect of dissipating some of the instinctive antipathy toward US military interventions abroad. Indeed, the turn of the decade was a moment of unusual good feeling when the patriotism of the Reagan era enjoyed a final flowering as Reagan himself rode into the sunset. But, even here, oppositional voices never entirely disappeared. It seems fitting to close this discussion with a musical icon who delivered a final shot as the decade ended.

By 1989, Canadian native Neil Young had already been a major figure in American popular music for 25 years, dating back to his days with Buffalo Springfield in the 1960s and as a member of Crosby, Stills, Nash & Young in the 1970s, when his 1970 song "Ohio," a protest against the death of four college students at Kent State, became a generational anthem. Young continued producing memorable music throughout that decade, notably *Rust Never Sleeps* (1979), widely regarded as one of the great rock albums of all time (one side of the vinyl disk consists of meditative acoustic songs; the other consists of fiercely distorted electric-guitar-based ones where he's backed by sometime-collaborators Crazy Horse). In the eyes of some observers, Young lost his way in the 1980s, not only because he released a string of commercially unsuccessful albums, but also because he expressed support for some Reagan administration policies.[17] In November 1989, just as the Berlin Wall was coming down, he released *Freedom*, a deeply caustic attack on American complacency. In the signature song from the album, "Rockin' in the Free World," recorded in acoustic and electric versions, Young juxtaposes images of flag-waving patriots with homeless people—one, a drug addict, has just murdered her own child. He takes on President George Bush directly, mockingly citing Bush campaign celebrations of "a thousand points of light" (civic volunteers who, Bush seemed to imply, make government intervention unnecessary) and Bush's attempt to parry the perceived heartlessness of Reaganism by calling for a "kinder, gentler nation." "We got a thousand points of light for the homeless man," Young sneers, "a kinder, gentler machine-gun hand." The title of the song, repeated in the chorus, is a thrillingly vicious repudiation of American self-regard, and as such a bracing warning that imperial victories abroad have hardly improved the lives of all too many US citizens at home.

Though he was certainly heard, in a song that still resounds decades later, Young was in some respects a lonely voice as the 1980s ended. Imperial victory and domestic prosperity—both paid for with borrowed funds—would lead Americans to turn inward in the coming decade. The ability to do so would, to a great degree, be fueled by the intensifying possibilities of computers, which let Americans of the 1990s into ever-deepening virtual worlds. Public discourse, which by some reckonings was being whittled away, would be marked by often petty squabbles as well as deep-seated cultural divides. But relative to our vantage point of the early twenty-first century, it would be an era of relative insulation, both enviable and disappointing.

CULTURE WATCH: "The Message" (1982)

By the early 1980s, the genre of popular music we now know as hip-hop was ready to explode into national—and global—prominence. Up until this point, rap music, as it was typically called then, was generally regarded as music of good times, a release from the often challenging conditions its most passionate fans encountered in their day-to-day lives. One early rap song, however, opened the way for more overt social commentary in the genre, expanding its frontiers for artists and audiences alike.

Figure 8.2   MESSENGERS: Cover of the Grandmaster Flash and the Furious Five's 1982 album *The Mess*age. The title track from the album has become a hip-hop classic for its path-breaking social commentary, establishing a new dimension for the emerging genre of rap music. © CBW / Alamy.

While its musical roots—and the geographical roots of many of its most gifted practitioners—were in the Caribbean, rap had taken on specific cultural contours in the New York City borough of the Bronx in the mid-1970s. The musical scene there involved large neighborhood parties presided over by a disk jockey who mixed, scratched, and otherwise manipulated records, while an MC provided commentary, often in the form of rhyming couplets performed with a high degree of showmanship and interaction with DJs.

Rap music had first achieved a national profile with "Rapper's Delight," a playful song by the Sugar Hill Gang, a New Jersey–based outfit recorded by entrepreneur Sylvia Robinson. Robinson had failed to convince Bronx rappers to record "Rapper's Delight," but when a member of the Sugar Hill Gang, percussionist Duke Bootee, wrote another song, "The Message," she tried again to convince a leading rap group, Grandmaster Flash and the Furious Five, to record it, hoping their name would lend the song prestige. But most its members declined. Robinson and Bootee did convince Melle Mel, a member of the ensemble, to participate (Grandmaster Flash and other members participated in a subsequent unsuccessful recording session). "The Message" was released in the summer of 1982, credited to Grandmaster Flash and the Furious Five.

"The Message" is a gritty urban chronicle of barely suppressed urban rage, notable for its frank social commentary. "It's like a jungle sometimes," Melle Mel says in its opening line. "It makes me wonder sometimes how I keep from going under." He elaborates in the first verse:

Broken glass everywhere
People pissing on the stairs, you know they just don't care
I can't take the smell, I can't take the noise no more
Got no money to move out, I guess I got no choice
Rats in the front room, cockroaches in the back
Junkies in the alley with a baseball bat
I tried to get away, but I couldn't get far
'Cause a man with a tow truck repossessed my car

The chorus of the song is literally its message, a collective one to those who would challenge or condemn the coping strategies of those dwelling in the urban underclass: "Don't push me, 'cause I'm close to the edge / I'm tryin' not to lose my head." Each time the chorus is sung, Mel adds a seemingly incongruous, syncopated laugh that stands in ironic counterpoint to the lyrics of the song. So does the catchy synthesizer and percussion lines, which mark "The Message" as a piece of early 1980s pop at the seams of rock, disco, and the increasingly distinct genre of rap music.

The music video for "The Message," released in the heyday of the MTV era, featured street scenes of New York alternating with Mel and other rappers (including Bootee) on a city stoop. At the end of the song, the actual members of the Grandmaster Flash and the Furious Five appear at a street corner and greet each other warmly—only to be interrupted by the arrival of a police car carrying two white officers, who hustle them into the vehicle and drive them away. In the 1980s, they're saying, you could be arrested for walking while black.

In a number of ways, "The Message" was an atypical hip-hop song. And yet, almost from the beginning, it was regarded as a classic. It also laid the foundation for a wave of subsequent music acts, among them Geto Boys, Niggaz wit Attitudes (NWA), and Public Enemy, all of whom embraced hip-hop as a vehicle for political commentary. Clearly, "The Message" was heard—and continues to be heard—even if it also continues to be ignored.

Suggested Further Reading

Much of the material in this chapter draw on a series of books I've written on the history of popular culture, and are mentioned in the following text.

On transistors and the birth of Silicon Valley, see David A. Kaplan, *The Silicon Boys: And Their Valley of Dreams* (New York: HarperCollins, 2000). Katie Hafner and Matthew Lyons capture hacker culture in their now-classic *Where Wizards Stay Up Late: The Origins of the Internet* (New York: Touchstone, 1998). Walter Isaacs renders the definitive version of Steve Jobs' life in his biography of the same name (Simon & Schuster, 2011).

On the rise of music video, see Rob Tenenbaum and Craig Marks, *I Want My MTV: The Uncensored History of the Music Video Revolution* (New York: Dutton, 2011). The best narrative history of rap music and culture is Jeff Chang's *Can't Stop, Won't Stop: A History of the Hip-Hop Generation* (New York: Picador, 2005). See also Tricia Rose has written a pair of important books: *Black Noise: Rap Music and Black Culture in Contemporary America* (Middletown: Wesleyan University Press, 1994) and *The Hip-Hop Wars: What We Talk about When We Talk About Hip-Hop—and Why It Matters* (New York: Basic Books, 2008). See also Jeffrey O. G. Ogbar, *Hip-Hop Revolution: The Culture and Politics of Rap* (Lawrence: University Press of Kansas, 2007). African American studies scholar Michael Eric Dyson has also written extensively about hip-hop; see, in particular, *You Know What I Mean? Reflections on Hip-Hop* (New York: Basic, 2010).

Notes

1   Carole Cadwalldr, "Stewart Brand's 'Whole Earth Catalog,' the Book that Changed the World," The Guardian, May 4, 2013: http://www.theguardian.com/books/2013/may/05/stewart-brand-whole-earth-catalog (August 1, 2014).

2   Much of the ensuing description of early personal computers is taken from my treatment of the subject in *The Art of Democracy: A Concise History of Popular Culture in the United States*, second ed. (New York: Monthly Review Press, 2002), 297–299.

3   Jim Cullen, *A Short History of the Modern Media* (Malden, MA: Wiley-Blackwell, 2014), 248; Fortune 500 cited in *The Art of Democracy*, 299.

4   Previous and next paragraphs draw on Cullen, *A Short History*, 248–249.

5   The ad can be viewed on YouTube: http://www.youtube.com/watch?v=VtvjbmoDx-I.

6   Cullen, *The Art of Democracy*, 243.

7   Jim Cullen, *Born in the U.S.A.: Bruce Springsteen and the American Tradition* (1997; Middletown, CT: Wesleyan University Press, 2005), 76–77.

8   The ad, for the fragrance Enjoli, can be viewed on YouTube: http://www.youtube.com/watch?v=jA4DR4vEgrs (August 5, 2014).

9   Katha Pollitt, "Feminism at the Crossroads," in Robert Atwan and Jon Roberts, editors, *Left, Right & Center: Voices from Across the Political Spectrum* (New York: Bedford, 1996), 239–244.

10   This and subsequent description of MTV comes from Cullen, *The Art of Democracy*, 277–281.

11   For more on the Jackson controversy, see the Tenenbaum and Marks chapter on this subject in *I Want My MTV*, 143–158.

12   Much of the following draws on Cullen, *The Art of Democracy*, 283–284 and *A Short History of the Modern Media*, 206–209.

13   On the Ghetto Brothers, see Chang, 48, 50–52, and Ed Morales, "The Story of How a Puerto Rican Jew Jump-Started Hip-Hop," ABC News, December 18, 2012: http://abcnews.go.com/ABC_Univision/Entertainment/ghetto-brothers-nuyorican-roots-hip-hop/story?id=17974037 (June 19, 2015). The quote about work comes from Chang, 13.

14   http://www.nilerodgers.com/about/projects/chic (August 5, 2014).

15 Robert Christgau, "The Shit Storm," http://www.robertchristgau.com/xg/ music/pe-law.php (August 5, 2014).

16 Pat Aufderheide advances this line of argument in "Vietnam: Good Soldiers," in *Seeing Through Movies*, edited by Mark Crispin Miller (New York: Pantheon, 1990), 81–111.

17 Peter Glenn, "10 Political Notes from Neil Young," *Calgary Herald*, January 18, 2010: http://blogs.calgaryherald.com/2014/01/18/10-political-notes-from-neil-young/ (August 5, 2014).

9

Prosperity and Distraction
The Post-Cold War Era, 1991–2001

Figure 9.1 TESTIFYING: Anita Hill appears before the Senate Judiciary Committee hearings on the candidacy of Clarence Thomas for the Supreme Court, October 11, 1991. Hill's accusations of sexual harassment galvanized the nation and highlighted the complex intersection of race and gender in US national life. © Rob Crandall / Alamy.

Democratic Empire: The United States Since 1945, First Edition. Jim Cullen.
© 2017 Jim Cullen. Published 2017 by John Wiley & Sons, Inc.

Opposing Justice: The Hill–Thomas Imbroglio

PUBIC HAIR.

Not a pair of words you expect to see in a history textbook. Nor a pair of words you would expect to hear at a US Senate confirmation hearing for a prospective justice to the Supreme Court. But because these words were discussed during (and long after) that hearing, and because they reveal a lot about the state of the nation then, they bear discussion now.

The person who uttered them—a highly dignified individual who surely felt awkward—was a 35-year-old woman named Anita Hill. On October 11, 1991, when she sat before the Senate Judiciary Committee to testify on the candidacy of Supreme Court nominee Clarence Thomas, Hill was a professor of law at the University of Oklahoma. But, a decade earlier, Hill had served as the attorney–adviser to Thomas, who was then serving as assistant secretary of the US Department of Education's Office for Civil Rights. In 1982, Thomas was named by President Ronald Reagan to be Chairman of the Equal Employment Opportunity Commission (EEOC), and Hill followed to serve as his assistant in the new post. Both Hill and Thomas were African–American; the fact that Thomas was a conservative black Republican made him a valuable resource for the Reagan administration, whose policies were opposed by most African Americans.

Hill liked these jobs. She did not like her boss. The principal reason, she explained to the panel of senators, was that Thomas kept hitting on her. When he wasn't asking her out or commenting on her clothing, he talked incessantly about sex (including his penis size), and, in particular, about pornography. And then there was what Hill called "one of the oddest episodes I remember." This was a day when Thomas was drinking a can of soda in his office. "He got up from the table at which we were working, went over to his desk to get the Coke, looked at the can, and said, 'Who has put pubic hair on my Coke?'"[1]

Hill's testimony was shocking, and it put Thomas's nomination to the Supreme Court in doubt. Actually, Thomas had never been a particularly easy sell. He was nominated for the position by President George H. W. Bush to take over the position of the retiring Justice Thurgood Marshall, the legendary African American jurist who had argued the *Brown v. Board* case in 1954 and had been a leading liberal lion on the court since named to the position by President Lyndon Johnson in 1967. Bush had claimed that the 43-year-old Thomas was "the best qualified" person for the job when he announced his choice in July 1991, but this was a difficult assertion for many to accept. Thomas had spent less than 2 years as a judge, and it had been more than a decade since he had actually practiced law (and then at entry-level positions). Bush also claimed that "the fact that he is a minority had nothing to do with this," which was even more difficult for most Americans to believe. Thomas's backers were clearly counting on the difficulty that white liberal supporters of Affirmative Action would have in challenging an African American man on the legitimacy of his qualifications, since white liberals were among the more insistent in trying to create professional opportunities for minorities. Thomas' supporters were also betting on his compelling personal story, which included a broken home and childhood poverty in rural Georgia, would make him seem like a poster child for the American Dream (even if there was less privation in his background than was commonly claimed).² These strategies, combined with a highly sophisticated lobbying effort that involved the mobilization of a series of conservative organizations, helped overcome the reservations surrounding Thomas to the point where it looked as though he had achieved clear sailing by October 1991. But then Anita Hill came along and accused him of sexual harassment, which threatened to undo everything.

At least initially, Hill was a reluctant witness. Though she firmly rejected his advances, she never accused Thomas of harassment while working for him and continued to maintain contact with him after she left the EEOC to take a teaching position at Oral Roberts University Law School in 1983 (by most reckonings, this was a step down professionally, but one that allowed her to get away from Thomas's direct supervision). These facts—that Hill stayed with Thomas when he changed jobs, and remained in touch, even meeting with Thomas when he made periodic trips to Oklahoma—raised questions about Hill's credibility. Hill responded to them by emphasizing how important Thomas was to her career ambitions; confronting or antagonizing one of the most powerful African Americans in the federal government could be highly damaging to her future. Only after Thomas was named as a candidate to one of the highest offices of the country, and Hill was urged by confidantes who had heard her complain about him at the time and offered to corroborate her testimony, did she decide she had a duty to speak out, lest others suffer the harassment she did.

Thomas was surprised and hurt by Hill's accusations. He also categorically denied them. His supporters mounted a furious counterattack on her credibility, suggesting, among other accusations, that Hill was acting as a spurned partner who had psychological problems—in the memorable description of conservative journalist David Brock, she was "a little bit nutty and a little bit slutty." In his rebuttal to Hill's testimony, Thomas portrayed himself as a victim of racism on the part of those who were using her testimony to oppose his nomination: "This is something that not only supports but plays into the worst stereotypes about black men in this society," he asserted, characterizing the hearings as a "high-tech lynching for uppity blacks."³

To a fascinated American public, the Hill–Thomas hearings appeared to be a classic he-said/she-said situation. A series of figures came forward to support both, but none conclusively. There were witnesses who could have independently confirmed Thomas's penchant for pornographic movies and magazines (which, it should be said, was not a crime, and he was protected by the First Amendment), as well as other examples of sexual harassment.⁴ However, they were not called to testify.

Why not? In part because Hill and her attorneys declined an opportunity to provide further testimony, believing they would only result in further attacks. But, to a great extent, this was because the Senate Judiciary Committee—all of whose members were white and male—were eager to end a discussion that they would have preferred not to have in the first place. The committee was chaired by future vice president Joe Biden, who, in his determination to be seen as fairminded, was regarded by some as too accommodating to Republican demands.[5] One figure who, under different circumstances, might have spoken out more forcefully against Thomas was Massachusetts senator Ted Kennedy. But Kennedy's own checkered sexual history made this difficult, especially since he had recently gone out drinking with his nephew, William Kennedy Smith, the night before Smith was charged with rape (he was later acquitted).

When the Senate Judiciary committee voted on the Thomas nomination, it was deadlocked, 7–7. The subsequent vote in the Senate as a whole, largely on partisan lines, went narrowly in Thomas's favor, 52–48. One of two Republicans to vote against Thomas, Bob Packwood of Oregon, later resigned from the Senate amid allegations that he himself was guilty of sexual harassment. The other Republican, Jim Jeffords of Vermont, later left the Republican Party, disenchanted with its rightward tilt.

Thomas took his seat on the court, and for the next quarter-century became one of the most consistently conservative—and conspicuously silent—of justices. Hill went on with her own career, eventually settling down as a professor of law at Brandeis University. But the reverberations of the Hill–Thomas controversy proved profound for a series of reasons. They're worth unpacking, because we live with them to this day.

The first, and perhaps most important, is that the Hill–Thomas conflict made the issue of sexual harassment—one that had sometimes been regarded as the obsession of militant feminists—one of open and spirited discussion in American homes and workplaces. Millions of American women from all walks of life sympathized with Hill's experience, as well why she remained silent about it. They didn't simply sympathize: they also voted. The congressional elections of 1992 were hailed as "The Year of the Woman," which brought a series of durable new faces to the Senate: Patty Murray of Washington; Diane Feinstein and Barbara Boxer of California; Barbara Mikulski of Maryland (re-elected) and, the first African American woman to win a seat in Senate, Carol Moseley Braun of Illinois (she lost it 6 years later amid charges of corruption). And while public opinion polls initially supported Thomas, the general drift of sentiment over time seems to have moved in Hill's favor. David Brock, who had used the "nutty/slutty" phrase, wrote a critical 1993 book, *The Real Anita Hill*, but later recanted his attacks on her in his 2002 book *Blinded by the Right*.[6]

A second reason why the hearings were important is that they also foregrounded the discussion of another issue that, similar to sexual harassment, had been bubbling up over the course of the previous two decades: Affirmative Action. Initially implemented as the result of executive orders by Presidents John Kennedy and Lyndon Johnson in the 1960s, it had become a subject of increasing resentment among whites during the 1970s. The 1978 Supreme Court *Bakke* decision made race a legitimate consideration as a basis of hiring or school admission but outlawed explicit quotas. In the years since, the issue continued to roil, but Thomas brought a fresh wrinkle to the subject as a prominent African American who was critical of it, in large measure because he believed it stigmatized beneficiaries whose attainments were perceived as primarily the result of their race. (In 2013, he compared Affirmative Action to slavery.[7]) Many of Thomas's critics claimed he was a hypocrite because he himself was a beneficiary of the policy, perhaps most obviously in his admission to Yale Law School. Thomas replied by saying Yale's having done so did not make it right.[8]

More subtly, the Hill–Thomas imbroglio made something unmistakably clear to those Americans who might not have been paying attention: whatever its limits or defects, Affirmative Action had made a discernible impact on national life by the early 1990s. Whichever side they may have come down on regarding Hill or Thomas, there was now a generation of "Affirmative Action Babies" (to use the phrase of jurist Stephen L. Carter, who counted himself among them) who were attaining some of the highest reaches in American society. Americans were used to seeing African American athletes and movie stars, but this was something a little different: a critical mass of professionals clustered in rows at government hearings that had previously been the province of middle-aged white men. Those white men remained dominant. But it was now possible to more easily imagine a time when they wouldn't be.

Not Black and White: The Changing Colors of Race

The country was changing. Even the terms of national debates were changing: it was increasingly difficult, for example, to talk about race as a matter of black and white, the way so many Americans had always assumed. The number of people, a great many of them racial minorities, flocking to the United States as a result the Immigration and Nationality Act of 1965 surged in the 1990s. By the year 2000, the number of foreign-born residents of the United States was about twice as high as the previous record (14.2 million people) in 1930. The number of people who had one foreign-born parent (56 million) reached 20%. While much of this rise was concentrated in populous coastal states such as California, Texas, Florida, and New York, immigrants were also beginning to fan out across the country. By 2000, 10% of the population of Green Bay, Wisconsin, for example, was African American, Hispanic, or Asian. By that point, more than half the states in the country had at least 5% immigrant populations. The two largest states, California and Texas, joined Hawaii and New Mexico as states that were less than half white.[9]

It's also important to note that there were often shifts *within* racial groups in the closing decades of the twentieth century. The axis of migration among Asian immigrants, for example, shifted south and east as refugees from the fallout of the Vietnam War—not just the Vietnamese, but also emigrants from Laos and Cambodia—found their way to the United States, where they were sometimes regarded with disdain or hostility by other ethnic groups or more established arrivals from the same native country. Mexican immigrants remained a strong presence in the United States all through the twentieth century, but their relative prominence receded a bit as Mexico itself became more economically stable and migrants from further south in Central America made their way to El Norte.

Actually, the very term "race" was increasingly problematic. At the turn of the twentieth century, it had been applied widely and freely by Americans, who would speak of "the Italian race" as easily as they would "the Negro race," for example. In mid-century, in the wake of World War II, in which rabid racial politics had resulted in the Holocaust, the term had narrowed to apply to three sets of people: whites (or Caucasians, an imprecise reference to people whose DNA originated on the Russian steppes of Eurasia); African Americans (sometimes "colored" or "negro" when not slandered as "niggers"); and Asians (sometimes called "Mongoloid," "yellow," or "Oriental," terms which, similar to "negro" and "Chinks," became dated, even offensive). But, by the end of the twentieth century, that tri-partite approach itself began to seem too limiting. People from Latin America—sometimes euphemistically referred to by whites as "Spanish" and increasingly as "Hispanic"—now preferred the racially tinged "Latino" (though there may have been a bit of a class tilt to this; in the words of one Latin American comedian, "a Latino is a Hispanic with a job"). Alternatively, however, such inclusive terms were also a source of increasing skepticism and even hostility: lumping the experiences of, say, a Dominican, Mexican, and Columbian could obscure far more than they revealed. Similarly, using the term "Asian" to refer to, say, a Korean or Chinese immigrant overlooked the distinctness of their cultural traditions—and the historic tensions between them. Perhaps the most appalling illustration of this was the brutal 1982 murder of Vincent Chin, a Chinese American who was mistaken for being Japanese and was killed by two Detroit-area whites who were resentful over Japanese economic prowess, which they felt had cost them their jobs. Yet, amid such confusion, Americans who were members of minority groups also became increasingly conscious and assertive about their identities. The number of people who identified themselves as Native American tripled between 1970 and 2000, less because of a rising population than a desire to reclaim a heritage that, in most cases, was highly blended among multiple Indian tribes and other races.

This sense of ethnographic awareness—supporters called it multiculturalism; opponents dismissed it as identity politics—became sharper in the 1990s, and has been with us ever since. As had been the case earlier, racial identity intersected with other kinds, notably gender (indeed, words such as "homosexual" and even "gay" were increasingly regarded as imprecise and even unacceptable to describe a multitude of identities). Such complexity was familiar to feminists, who had been dealing with it for decades, but which, again, became more foregrounded in everyday discourse. It was also one that could be partially sidestepped or ignored. This was something that Anita Hill experienced to her regret. "I had a gender and he had a race," she observed in a 2014 documentary about the Thomas hearings. She later explained what this meant: "There were people who tried to ignore the fact that I was an African American woman, and very importantly, there were senators and the people in the country who ignored the fact that, in Washington, DC, particularly in 1991, there was a great deal of entitlement that went along with being a male. ... They didn't take that into account and instead they portrayed him as an African American who could use the lynching metaphor to his advantage."[10]

The complexities of race were evident in some other major events of the early 1990s. Among the most troubling were the Los Angeles riots of 1992. The origins of the riots date back to March 1991, when an African American motorist, Rodney King, was chased down by Los Angeles police for speeding; after he stopped his car, he resisted arrest. A local resident videotaped what happened next: a beating by baton-wielding white officers as King lay on the ground. Four policemen were charged with assault, but the trial was moved to nearby Simi Valley, an area that was known to be more white and conservative than much of metropolitan LA. In April 1992, three of the officers were acquitted and the jury deadlocked on a fourth, an outcome that triggered demonstrations, looting, and burning in much of the city. The 4-day conflagration resulted in 53 deaths and injuries to an estimated 2,300 people, in addition to causing the destruction of 800 buildings and an estimated US$1 billion in property damage.[11]

Significantly, the LA riots were a multiracial event. Half the people arrested in the violence were Latino; many rioters targeted Korean and other Asian businesses, which had become a source of resentment for their relative success in poor neighborhoods. When a white truck driver, Reginald Denny, was attacked at a traffic light, two African Americans, Titus Murphy and Bobby Green, came to his aid. Green, who was also a truck driver, drove Denny's vehicle to the hospital and saved his life. It was also an African American, the Reverend Bennie Williams, who saved the Guatemalan construction worker Fidel Lopez from a similar attack that took place minutes later.[12]

Some whites in the United States reacted to the changing complexion of US society with resentment and fear. One of the most obvious manifestations of this was California voters' passage of Proposition 187, which banned public services for undocumented immigrants, a law that was overturned by state courts. There were also intensifying battles over bilingualism in school districts with large Latino populations, and the vocal voices of broadcasters such as Fox TV's Bill O'Reilly and CNN's Lou Dobbs as well as politicians such as Pat Buchanan who decried what they considered the pernicious impact of Latino immigration, which they claimed raised crime rates, reduced wages, or took away jobs from native-born workers. Such voices received a lot of attention in the 1990s, and had real electoral potency. And yet, even as they achieved prominence, many of their most ardent supporters too recognized they were fighting a rear-guard action against demographic and economic changes that were impossible to resist.

Thug Life: Gangsta Rap

In an important sense, of course, the LA riots were at least as much about class as they were about race, the result of persistent and glaring economic inequality that banished some residents of that city, among others, into a state of hopelessness and frustration. This intersection of class and race was apparent in an important musical phenomenon: the rise of gangsta rap.

Emerging from gang culture such as that of the rival Crips and Bloods of Los Angeles, gangsta was a militant, sensory-challenging subgenre of hip-hop that reflected a more separatist approach to race relations. To some extent, it was clearly a product of its time; Malcolm X enjoyed a cultural revival in the early 1990s, as reflected in the brilliant 1992 biopic directed by Spike Lee and starring Denzel Washington as the title character, and the confrontational Public Enemy was at its peak of influence. But, in another sense, gangsta rap represented a departure by focusing more on local conditions and personal situations than explicitly articulated cultural critiques. In 1988, the early gangsta group N.W.A. (Niggaz Wit Attitude) released *Straight Outta Compton*, an album about the gritty city just south of LA; it became a generational anthem for the hip-hop set. One song from that album, "Fuck tha Police," became a lightning rod for criticism, but its view of police brutality was later regarded as prophetic, especially in the wake of the Rodney King case. A number of members in N.W.A., among them Ice-T and Dr. Dre, would go on to have significant solo careers as performers and producers.

Another important figure associated, though not solely, with gangsta rap was Tupac Shakur. Born in East Harlem, Shakur was the son of Black Panthers and named after Tupac Amaru, the last Inca monarch to resist Spanish conquest in the sixteenth century. His family moved to California when he was a teenager, his home at the time of the release of his highly influential debut album *2Pacalypse Now* in 1991. Over the course of the next 5 years, Shakur built one of the most celebrated bodies of work in hip-hop music, notably his 1994 group effort *Thug Life: Volume 1*. His classic song "Dear Mama," a tribute to his mother from his 1995 album *Me Against the World*, was later added to the Music Registry at the Library of Congress. Shakur, who also worked as an actor, was a controversial figure; he was convicted of sexual assault in 1993 and served a short prison term. In 1996, he was shot to death in his car in Las Vegas. His posthumous hit "Changes" (1998) is regarded as one of the greatest of his career.

Shakur's murder has never been solved. Suspicions surrounded Christopher George Latore Wallace, also known as the Notorious B.I.G. or Biggie Smalls, a leading practitioner, along with figures such as Puff Daddy, of so-called East Coast rap, which tended to have a more lyrically dense quality than typically funkier West Coast rap. Biggie Smalls was murdered in 1997 in another killing that remains unresolved but which has long been rumored to be a reprisal for Shakur's death. Puff Daddy (who has since gone by a number of other identities, including his birth name of Sean Combs) teamed up with Smalls' widow Faith Evans, an accomplished rapper in her own right, and released "I'll Be Missing You," a song that samples the 1983 Police hit "Every Breath You Take" and has since become one of the classic songs in modern popular music.

By the mid-1990s, hip-hop had become the most prominent genre in popular music, and gangsta in particular had a high profile, reaching beyond its African American base to include acts such as the Cuban/Chicano/Italian outfit Cypress

Hill, who enjoyed a string of commercially successful albums in the 1990s. However, in its most common manifestations, gangsta rap created something of a class and race paradox: poor African American men describing thug life for an eager audience of white suburban boys who knew little of this life but were eager to emulate it (in, for example, the baggy jeans that were issued, one-size-fits-all, to prison inmates). Gangsta rap in particular had a particular obsession with authenticity—or, in the lingo of the time, "keeping it real," which has been defined by hip-hop scholar Jeffrey Ogbar as implying "an intimate familiarity with the urban, working-class landscapes that gave rise to hip-hop in the 1970s." What made this situation even more complicated is that many of these rappers alternatively celebrated and lamented that life. Some rappers could seem trapped by authenticity: not really considered legitimate to their audience, their peers, or themselves unless immersed in gangsta life, yet chafing at its demands and costs (there was a wry observation among some hip-hop fans that you never heard Motown's Four Tops threatening to kill label-mates the Temptations, or shootouts between soul divas Gladys Knight and Aretha Franklin). This dynamic was especially pronounced in the work of Eminem, a Detroit-based white rapper whose struggles with success *and* failure, sometimes dramatized through his alter ego Slim Shady, earned him a large audience in the first decade of the twenty-first century. Characters in Eminem songs—including himself—projected frustration in questionable ways, among them a vein of misogyny that laced a good deal of hip-hop generally in the 1990s, a tendency that drew criticism from across the race and political spectrum.[13]

One might speak of a parallel trend to gangsta rap in some female hip-hop of the 1990s. Just as male acts embraced the bad-boy image rooted in African American culture dating back to the mythic figure of the bad-boy Stagolee, some female performers—among them Lil' Kim, Foxy Brown, and (slightly later) Nicki Minaj—invoked images (some would say stereotypes) of assertive female sexuality as a form of personal empowerment. Such a stance was controversial among many feminists, part of an active *intra*-racial as well as *inter*-racial dialogue in an age when intellectual discourse was increasingly defined in terms of personal identity.

Running Saga: The O. J. Simpson Case

The porous, yet polarized, relationship between race, class, and gender was also a significant factor in one of the most notorious events of the decade: the LA murder trial of former National Football League star O. J. Simpson. In June 1994, Simpson's estranged wife Nicole was brutally stabbed to death along with her friend Ron Goldman outside her home. Los Angeles police issued a warrant for Simpson's arrest; he promised to turn himself in. Instead, he fled, leading to one of the most indelible images of the television era: Simpson driving his white Ford Bronco with former Buffalo Bills teammate A. C. Cowlings and trailed, seemingly in slow motion, by police cars on an Artesia Freeway closed to all other traffic. Simpson ended up back at his home and put a gun to his head before finally surrendering.

The saga was only beginning. Simpson's trial, which took place over most of 1995, was a gigantic media circus and a non-stop cable news story, creating a prototype for subsequent coverage of news stories and leading to a series of television careers for photogenic attorneys. Afforded the best defense money could buy, Simpson assembled a team that exploited a series of weaknesses in the prosecution's case, among them the presence of a racist police detective, Mark Fuhrman, and the fact that a glove Simpson allegedly wore during the murders did not fit his hands (in the memorable words of his lead attorney, Johnnie Cochran, "if it doesn't fit, you must acquit," though many observers cited shrinkage of the blood-stained glove as the reason it was too small). Simpson was ultimately acquitted of the murders, but was later found criminally liable and ordered to compensate the Goldman family (most of the penalty went unpaid). In 2008, he was sentenced to 33 years in prison for armed robbery in an attempt to recover sports memorabilia from dealers.

The Simpson trial was often covered as a soap opera celebrity story, reflecting what critics considered a trivialization of American public life (Simpson's friend Kato Kaelin leveraged having been Simpson's houseguest at the time of the murders into instant celebrity and new opportunities for his tottering television career). But the implications were serious, among them the way it revealed a chasm in racial perception. During the trial, 61% of whites considered Simpson guilty. Only 32% of African Americans did—and, of that number, only 8% were confident that he committed both murders, the remainder expressing uncertainty.[14] And yet, Simpson, similar to Michael Jackson, somewhat distanced himself from his racial identity during the height of his fame; he was often quoted as saying, "I'm not black, I'm O. J."[15] Still, when the chips were down, Simpson, again similar to Jackson—and, in a very different context, Barack Obama—was embraced by African Americans, which is perhaps fitting given that, for most of American history, a mere proverbial drop of African American blood made someone non-white. Perhaps less fittingly, Simpson was widely regarded as the perverse beneficiary of racial payback: after centuries of injustice in which many African Americans were convicted of crimes they did not commit, here was a African American man acquitted a crime he did.

Family Matters: Demography and the Assault on Patriarchy

The ambiguities of racial identity were only one facet of a larger demographic transformation of American society that was becoming increasingly clear in the 1990s. Nowhere was this emergent fluidity more obvious than in the realm of the family—and, in particular, changes in the structure of white families. In the 1950s, an archetypal image of the modern American home as a white heterosexual domestic arrangement, consisting of a married man and wife with their biological children, solidified as a standard by which future generations would be measured. By the 1990s, that standard was less relevant. Part of the reason, as already indicated, was the increasing racial diversity of the country. But, in some respects, white families were becoming more similar to African American ones; in particular, the percentage of white women having children out of wedlock was now rising steadily, and the vast majority of all teen mothers were unmarried. The national abortion rate was also high: by the late 1990s, the number of abortions was about one-third of the total of live births. By 1995, only 60% of US children lived in the same residence with two biological parents, and, by the turn of the millennium, less than a quarter of US households consisted of nuclear families.[16]

Such developments were met with anxiety, even alarm, in some quarters of American life. Anti-abortion activists, for example, found the abortion rate shocking in what they regarded with widespread indifference to a human catastrophe. (By the turn of the millennium, they began using the language of antislavery, comparing the human being constituted by a fertilized egg as having rights comparable to those of slaves whose rights were denied in the *Dred Scott* Supreme Court decision of 1857.) But for a great many Americans, the demographic changes of the late twentieth century were experienced as liberation, not genocide.

One obvious way to glimpse at the new order was the same way the old one had solidified: on television. The wise patriarchal dads of 1990s sitcoms were replaced by the cartoon character Homer Simpson: befuddled and foolish, if usually harmless. In 1997, another sitcom star Ellen DeGeneres of *Ellen* (1994–1998) came out of the closet as a lesbian—"Yep, I'm Gay," read the cover of *Time* magazine's April 14 issue—and, in 1998, a new sitcom, *Will & Grace*, featured a gay lead character. This is not to say such alternative sexual orientations experienced smooth sailing: DeGeneres, whose show was canceled in 1998, the year after her character came out, was mocked as "Ellen Degenerate," while some activists were disappointed by the prevalence of stereotypes in *Will & Grace*. But those struggling with adversity could nevertheless take comfort in a widespread belief that time was one their side.

One way to think about what was happening—and one way to connect it to other things that were happening in the final decade of the twentieth century—is to remember the rising tide of anti-institutionalism that had been driving American society since the end of the 1960s. If those on the American *right* most successfully pressed their anti-institutionalism primarily in *economic* terms, those on the American *left* most successfully pressed their anti-institutionalism in *cultural* terms. The principal villain for those on the right was government; for those on the left, it was patriarchy—a concept that had a notion of family at its root, but one that was elaborated as a series of concentric circles that rippled outward from private to public life.

The principal place where that elaboration took place was in the academy—especially in elite liberal arts institutions, where new fields such as Afro-American, women's, and ethnic studies began to gain a secure footing in the closing decades of the century. Perhaps paradoxically, such institutional establishment became a basis for institutional subversion, as scholars in these fields taught students to question some of the governing assumptions of intellectual life for much of the twentieth century.

Nowhere were such scholarly currents more potent, if often puzzlingly obscure, than in the field of literary criticism. In the 1970s, a series of postmodern European writers, notably Jacques Derrida of France and the Belgian-born Paul de Man, who taught at Yale, pioneered a mode of analysis known as deconstruction. At the heart of deconstruction was a practice of reading against the grain of a given text, to the point where its meaning could sometimes be construed as the very opposite of what it appeared to be saying. So, for example, if I were to say, "I can't stand him! He's so full of himself! Did you see that belt he was wearing?" one might think I was expressing my dislike of someone. But a deconstruction of those sentences would focus on the unusual intensity of engagement in my expression, the very passion of my denunciation suggesting a deep degree of engagement, and my attention to a piece of clothing such as a belt might suggest the pull of attraction, my very attempt to repel it—perhaps a sign of panic over erotic tendencies I'm furiously trying to deny?—a signifier of its power.

Indeed, the concept of power was central to the project of deconstruction. Practitioners were highly attuned to the way in which forms of writing were actually means of making a set of arrangements that benefited a particular group of people seem natural or inevitable, preventing readers from challenging them. So if I were to say, "People who follow instructions are much less likely to encounter difficulties," a deconstructionist would be more interested in my covert attempt to impose domination over those whom I'm addressing than the particular instructions or difficulties to which I'm referring.

By the early 1990s, deconstruction and the wider constellation of what was known as critical theory had become a powerful force in American academic life. It affected—critics would say infected—a series of traditional disciplines, among them the writing of history and legal scholarship, where "the crits," as they were known, attacked some of the most basic assumptions of Anglo-American jurisprudence. Because the language of critical theory was often highly technical, and because these scholars typically operated outside the arenas of the mass media or national politics, they attracted relatively little attention beyond the academy in the late 1990s and early 1990s. But their influence—most crucially, the notion that our notion of reality is really nothing more than a social construct reflecting prevailing political arrangements—was powerful. And potentially dangerous. If, for example, concepts such as truth or justice are simply labels that powerful people apply to their pet notions of reality, who's to say we shouldn't replace them with our own—or discard them altogether? Deconstruction and related theories could easily give way to cynicism, anarchy, or even justify fascism. Such a scenario became less than theoretical when media reports after de Man's death in 1986 revealed that he had written pro-Nazi articles as a young man during World War II. Of course, any philosophy can become destructive if pursued to its logical conclusion, and the discrediting of one scholar doesn't mean that critical theory—or even some of de Man's ideas—were worthless or purely fascist. But they do indicate how a sense of limits, even humility, is an important element in the maintenance of a stable social order. (Go ahead and deconstruct that.)

Culture War: The Fall of George Bush

The direction of intellectual life on the American left was an indication of a larger polarization of national life generally. One striking indication of this was the fate of President Bush, who experienced political whiplash during his one-term presidency.

Bush was never really a comfortable fit in the Republican Party of the 1980s. The son of liberal Republican senator Prescott Bush of Connecticut, he had come of age in the 1970s as a moderate and positioned himself as such in running against Ronald Reagan in 1980, dismissing Reagan's fiscal platform as "voodoo economics." The two put their differences aside once Reagan chose Bush to be his vice president, and enjoyed a relatively close working relationship during the 1980s, allowing Bush to position himself as Reagan's logical heir. But, in order to do that, Bush had to move farther to the right, famously telling GOP voters in 1988 to "read my lips: no new taxes." Such promises, along with the hardball tactics of political adviser Lee Atwater, allowed Bush to win the presidency. But, in effect, he did so as Reagan-lite.

As far as some Republicans were concerned, Bush was a little *too* light. He enraged the right wing of the party in 1990 when he signed off on tax increases that violated his campaign pledge. His choice that year of David Souter to replace the retiring William Brennan on the Supreme Court upset some supporters, because Souter was perceived as a liberal—which his subsequent record would indeed show. (Bush promised at the time that his next court pick would be a stalwart right-winger, which is why Clarence Thomas got the nomination the following year.[17]) Bush also signed one of the few significant pieces of welfare legislation in the last quarter of the twentieth century: the Americans with Disabilities Act (ADA), a law similar to the Civil Rights Act of 1964 in protecting those with physical or mental impairments and requiring the provision of handicapped access in new or renovated public facilities.

For a while, it seemed as though Bush might have been able to get away with such moves, especially in the aftermath of the Persian Gulf War in early 1991, when his approval rating crested at an astonishing 89%.[18] From there, however, it was all downhill. A big part of the reason for his slide was the US economy, which plunged into a relatively short, but also relatively deep, recession. Bush had always been more interested in foreign policy than domestic policy, and the prevailing Republican ideology was such that he was not inclined to intervene to bolster the economy in any case. Such passivity angered many voters, and generated particular dissension among young people. The post-punk subgenre of grunge music, popularized by Seattle-based bands such as Nirvana and Pearl

Jam, made a huge impact in the early 1990s, in part out of a growing sense of cynicism about the promises of the American Dream. Nirvana's "Smells Like Teen Spirit," a caustic critique of consumer and media culture, became one of the most important works of popular culture in the decade.

But Bush's immediate problem continued to be on his right. He was running for re-election in 1992, and found himself challenged by Pat Buchanan, a former Nixon and Reagan adviser who had moved on to a prominent career as a conservative commentator and columnist. Buchanan was never an especially serious threat to take the Republican nomination away from Bush, but his high-profile presence both pushed Bush toward more uncompromising positions and gave committed conservatives a more appetizing alternative to the incumbent. Bush's problems were further magnified at the Republican National Convention of 1992, where Buchanan gave a rousing speech that excited convention-goers but repelled some television viewers. "There is a religious war going on in our country for the soul of America," Buchanan said. "It is a cultural war, as critical to the kind of nation we will one day be as was the Cold War itself." In attacking "abortion on demand" and "radical feminism," Buchanan's "Culture War" speech contributed to the perception that the Republican Party was too extreme.[19] Others found it merely out of touch, as when Vice President Dan Quayle criticized the main character on the television sitcom *Murphy Brown* (1988–1998), a television anchor played by Candice Bergen, for having a child out of wedlock. "It doesn't help matters when prime-time television has Murphy Brown, a character who supposedly epitomizes today's intelligent, highly paid professional woman, mocking the importance of fathers by bearing a child alone and calling it just another lifestyle choice," Quayle said. While Quayle was clearly identifying an emerging pattern, and one where many felt he had a point, his remark was greeted with a fair amount of ridicule, even contempt.[20]

Dissatisfaction with Republicans did not necessarily mean voters flocked to the Democrats, however. A powerful third-party alternative emerged in the candidacy of Ross Perot, a Texas billionaire who had become wealthy in the business of data processing (one of his major clients was the US government, which paid for his services in managing Medicare, to cite one example). Perot's major issue was the growing federal deficit—the toxic combination of federal tax cuts and borrowing to which politicians had first become addicted in the Reagan years and which showed no sign of tapering. Perot memorably likened the deficit to "a crazy aunt we keep down in the basement. All the neighbors know she's there but nobody wants to talk about her."[21] Perot was also concerned about the export of American jobs, especially to Mexico, where American companies were inclined to hire workers for less money and be subject to less regulation. Though the self-financed Perot, who ran his campaign chiefly through television commercials, was regarded by some as a crackpot, his message stuck a powerful chord: he got 19% of the vote in the 1992 election, the highest percentage for a third-party candidate since Theodore Roosevelt's insurgent campaign in 1912.

The great political question of 1991–1992 was whom the Democrats were going to nominate for president. At first, Bush's phenomenal popularity scared off a number of candidates. But by the spring of 1992 a sizable field came forward. In the early going, the leading candidate appeared to be Massachusetts senator Paul Tsongas, a moderate who, similar to Perot, expressed concerns about fiscal issues. But 1992 ultimately belonged to Bill Clinton.

Comeback Kid: The Rises and Falls of Bill Clinton

If anyone was ever born to be president, it was Clinton. This is not because he was, as with the two Roosevelts or John F. Kennedy, a child of privilege; in fact, the modest circumstances of his birth in 1946—in the mythically named town of Hope, Arkansas—made him seem like the quintessential American Dream story come true. (Part of Clinton's personal mythology is that he actually met JFK while on a school trip in 1963.) His father, William Blythe, died in a car accident before he was born. His mother, who turned the child over to her parents for a few years while she pursued a career in nursing, gave him the last name of her second husband, with whom she had a second child. Though they remained close until his death from cancer in 1967, Clinton's stepfather was a violent alcoholic against whom he intervened to protect his mother and half-brother on multiple occasions. Despite such family strife, Clinton was an excellent student renowned for his superb social skills. He won a scholarship to attend Georgetown, as well as a Rhodes Scholarship (he studied at Oxford University in England), and then went on to Yale Law School, where he met Hillary Rodham, whom he married in 1975.

After receiving his law degree, Clinton returned to Arkansas and began a life in politics. He lost his first race for Congress in 1974, got elected as the state's attorney general in 1976, and won the governorship in 1978. He was 32 years old, and dubbed "the boy governor." After losing his re-election campaign in 1980 over tax hikes on car registration fees, Clinton publicly repented to voters, who subsequently elected him to four more 2-year terms. In late 1991, he announced that he was running for president.

To many of those who knew him as a young man, Bill Clinton was a rocket who was clearly going places. But there was another side to him—a reckless, opportunistic side—that dogged him throughout his political career. One issue in particular that came back to haunt Clinton was his lack of military service in the Vietnam War. He received draft deferments while in England and made plans to join the Reserve Officers Training Corps (ROTC) when he came back, but then withdrew from the program after he decided to go to Yale Law School. This exposed Clinton to the draft, though he drew a high number in its lottery system that made his compulsory service unlikely. There were later accusations that he used political connections to ensure he never went to war. Clinton's conduct, and the somewhat evasive way he talked about it, helped spawn the nickname "Slick Willie." (A similar issue was the way he talked about his experience with marijuana while running for president: he said he smoked a joint but didn't inhale, an explanation that elicited widespread derision.) In fact, a great many middle-class men avoided the draft during the Vietnam era, including some prominent Republican politicians. Among them were vice presidents Dan Quayle and Dick Cheney, who of course was the major architect of wars in Iraq and Afghanistan (critics called him "a chicken hawk"). Their explanations could be comically self-serving, as when Cheney replied to queries as to why he didn't serve by saying "I had other priorities," or when right-wing Texas congressman Tom DeLay said that "so many minority youths had volunteered for well-paying military positions to escape poverty that there as literally no room for patriotic folks" such as himself.[22]

Clinton's other major problem was that he was a compulsive womanizer. His extramarital fidelity was something he was generally able to keep out of the spotlight until he was running for president, at which point a series of so-called "bimbo eruptions" damaged his image and distracted his campaign. Yet, in an odd way, Clinton was also able to use the media hoopla surrounding his indiscretions to his advantage. In the aftermath of Gary Hart's dashed presidential campaign of 1988 over similar infidelities, there was a growing, if not universal, sense that a politician's personal life should be private. Clinton was also able to frame his dogged persistence amid such difficulties to craft a narrative of resilience, dubbing himself the "Comeback Kid" after finishing a strong second to Paul Tsongas in the New Hampshire primary. From that point on, he became the Democratic frontrunner, ultimately sealing the nomination and bolstering his position by naming Tennessee senator Al Gore—who despite doing relatively well in 1988 was one of those people reluctant to run again in 1992—as his running mate, creating a perception of vibrant young leadership.

By that fall, it was clear that Bush was wounded and that Perot was damaging his own prospects. Clinton did indeed win the election, but did so with only 43% of the vote—less than a solid majority, and an indication of the increasing polarization of American politics that his opponents were determined to maintain, even widen. Though he began his presidency in a spirit of optimism, it was also clear he had his work cut out for him.

Clinton had two major items on his political agenda when he came into office. The first was realizing the long-time Democratic dream of reforming the American health care system, which had become an increasingly expensive patchwork run largely through employers, not all of whom provided it to their workers. The second was an overhaul of the nation's welfare system, which had become an increasingly visible target for conservative criticism since the Reagan years for its cost (though low when compared with middle-class entitlements and the defense budget) and reputation for promoting dysfunctional behavior (such as citizens becoming addicted to handouts rather than seeking jobs).

Instead, however, Clinton began by addressing problems he would have rather deferred. The first was the budget deficit, and a perception of fiscal responsibility for the sake of Wall Street, whose goodwill he would require in order to advance his legislative agenda. "You mean to tell me," he famously shouted during a meeting before his inauguration, "that the success of the program and my reelection hinges on the Federal Reserve and a bunch of fucking bond traders?" The answer he got was a "yes," and Clinton complied: he dropped plans for targeted middle-class tax cuts and a stimulus plan, and pushed through a tax hike to improve the government's ledger. These moves were widely credited with helping to stabilize the still-shaky US economy, which began the longest stretch of expansion in the postwar era on Clinton's watch. Less difficult, though still tricky, for Clinton was his emphatic support for a North American Free Trade Agreement (NAFTA) with Canada and Mexico, which generated widespread opposition from unions and other liberal constituencies before its passage in 1993. Securing NAFTA was another indication of Clinton's relatively conservative approach to economics: he championed free trade, acknowledging but minimizing his concern about the risk of job losses, environmental damage, and other issues raised by the deal.[23] Was NAFTA a good idea? The trade agreement remains controversial, but a 2015 report from the non-partisan Congressional Research Service suggests that NAFTA was neither as good as supporters asserted nor as bad as its critics feared.[24]

The other unwelcome development of Clinton's early presidency was the policy that came to be known as "Don't Ask, Don't Tell." For generations, gay Americans who served in the military or other government offices were subject to expulsion because their sexuality was deemed deviant and/or exposed them to extortion (they would presumably do anything, even give up government secrets, rather than reveal their orientation). While sympathetic to gays, who were among his most stalwart supporters, the issue was highly controversial, and fed into right-wing criticism that Clinton was determined to impose alien post-1960s values on Middle America. He tried to finesse it with DADT, as it was known, which amounted to a compromise: while homosexuality was still a basis for expulsion from the military, the government would make no active effort to determine the sexuality of recruits. Opponents of the policy on the right complained that the policy would hurt morale; those on the left saw it as a civil rights question comparable to that of the racial integration of the military under President Truman. In the first decade that DADT was in force, 10,000 servicemen and women who revealed their homosexuality were discharged.[25] However, the uneasy truce the policy represented remained in place for almost 20 years, finally repealed in 2011, when gay enlistees were free to serve without concerns about their sexuality affecting their military status.

Clinton didn't have much better luck in fighting the battles he sought, either. After weighing his options, he decided to prioritize health care over welfare reform, deputizing his wife, Hillary, as the leader of the initiative (which was soon popularly dubbed "Hillarycare"). Her task force, which initially operated in some secrecy to protect it from criticism, developed a complex plan that avoided single-payer government systems such as those in Canada or much of Europe in favor of something closer to the traditional American model, but relying on large regional purchasing plans that would give consumers buying power in dealing with commercial health care providers. The Clinton proposal also called for managed competition among insurance companies, in the hope that it would result in lower monthly premiums.

At first, it looked as though the Clinton plan might get through Congress. But then conservative advocacy groups and medical lobbies mobilized against it, as indeed they had when President Truman had tried this back in the 1940s. Particularly devastating were a series of commercials sponsored by an insurance industry group featuring the fictional "Harry and Louise," ordinary Americans who talked about the Clinton plan at their kitchen table and discussed any number of reasons why it would be terrible. In the end, the plan never even made it to the floor of Congress for a vote.

In addition to policy setbacks, Clinton also found himself enmeshed in a series of scandals and investigations. Staffers of the White House travel office were fired for what turned out to be political reasons (most were eventually rehired). The suicide of Clinton friend and advisor Vince Foster led to lurid speculation about the reasons, which were personal. There was also considerable speculation and investigation into Clinton family finances. It was revealed during Clinton's presidency that Hillary Clinton managed to make suspiciously successful investments speculating in the cattle markets in the 1970s, but no proof of insider trading, bribery, or other illegality ever emerged. However, tremendous scrutiny was focused on the couple's failed investments during the late 1970s and early 1980s in the Whitewater Development Corporation, a real-estate company, without turning up evidence of financial wrongdoing. The president's most vociferous critics likened Whitewater to Watergate, though, if Clinton was actually guilty of everything he was accused of, it would not rise to the level of wrongdoing committed by Nixon (or, for that matter, Reagan or Johnson).

Still, there's little question that Clinton's stature had taken some serious hits by the time of the midterm elections of 1994. A large conservative apparatus consisting of think tanks, media outlets, and aggressively conservative politicians were effective in articulating their opposition to Clinton and promoting a version of free market ideology that went beyond that of the Reagan years. A key player in leading the charge was Newt Gingrich, a Georgia congressman who formulated a "Contract with America" consisting of a series of conservative proposals, such as term limits and requiring a three-fifths congressional majority for any tax increases. The ensuing midterm elections were a GOP triumph, giving the party a majority in the House for the first time in 40 years and control of the Senate as well. Gingrich, elected the new Speaker of the House, was widely perceived as the most powerful man in the US government.

Clinton, by contrast, was forced to assert that he had not become irrelevant. Most of his energy was devoted to fending off Gingrich and his supporters, which included vetoing provisions of the Contract with America (he called it the Contract *on* America). Indeed, one might say that the signal achievement of Clinton's presidency was less a matter of what he accomplished in terms of his own agenda than his ability to parry the most aggressive moves of the right, such as proposals to privatize Social Security.

To a great extent, he was able to do this because Gingrich and company overplayed their hand. In negotiations for the 1996 budget, they decided to take a hard line, threatening to cut off funding for day-to-day government operations if they didn't get what they wanted. Clinton decided to call their bluff, resulting in two government shutdowns in late 1995 and early 1996. Polls revealed that voters—who, as it turned out, found many things to like about post offices, national parks, and any number of other government functions—tended to blame republicans for the shutdown. Gingrich was lampooned in a famous New York *Daily News* cover that depicted him as a crybaby for allegedly imposing the shutdown because he was annoyed that Clinton kept him waiting at the back of Air Force One when the two traveled together to a state funeral.

Clinton pressed his advantage by tacking to his right, famously declaring during his presidential State of the Union Address of 1996 that "the era of big government is over." By this point, he was deeply engaged in welfare reform, focusing on policies that Republicans were likely to find palatable without giving in to their more draconian proposals. The result was the Personal Responsibility and Work Opportunity Reconciliation Act of 1996. As its name suggests, the law was designed to encourage welfare recipients to move away from government support. It abolished Aid to Families with Dependent Children (AFDC), a program that had been in place since the Great Depression, and replaced it with Temporary Assistance for Needy Families (TANF), a program that had time limits, after which recipients would be cut off. By the turn of the twenty-first century, the number of Americans receiving cash assistance had dropped significantly, as proponents hoped it would. Whether this was the result of a healthy economy or people simply going hungry was difficult to say; what is clear is that Clinton deeply disappointed his liberal supporters, who cited it as another example of his opportunism. One important step that Clinton did take for poor people, however, was his expansion of the Nixon-era Earned Income Tax Credit (EITC), which made cash payments to taxpayers who made less than a specified annual wage. The EITC had originally been offered as part of Nixon's attempt to dismantle the federal bureaucracy by eliminating it in favor of direct payments, but Clinton made it an effective antipoverty measure.

By the time he was seeking re-election in 1996, then, Clinton had substantially enhanced his fortunes. (Part of the reason was a political adviser he'd employed over the course of his career, Republican Dick Morris, whom Clinton brought on in 1995 to reposition him with the electorate.) The Republicans nominated Senate Majority Leader Bob Dole of Kansas, a decorated World War II veteran who had run unsuccessfully for vice president with Gerald Ford in 1976. Dole was a relatively safe choice for a party seeking to soften its hardest edges, but he was no political match for Clinton, who cruised to victory, even if he didn't quite get 50% of the vote (Ross Perot, who ran again, took 8% this time). Clinton was well-positioned to clear sailing in a successful second term.

But he blew it. The reason, once again, was his sexual behavior. In late 1995, Clinton had secretly begun a sexual relationship with a 22-year-old White House intern named Monica Lewinsky. Suspicious staffers had Lewinsky transferred to the Pentagon in 1996, where she would work for the Defense Department instead. But the affair continued until the spring of 1997. While at the Pentagon, Lewinsky befriended a woman named Linda Tripp, who taped conversations about Lewinsky's relationship to Clinton and leaked them to the press. The Lewinsky scandal became a national news story in January 1998, exposing Clinton to anger and ridicule from friend and foe alike.

Bad publicity was hardly his only problem, however. As part of his investigation into the failed Whitewater deal, an independent prosecutor named Kenneth Starr pursued reports that Clinton had sexually propositioned an Arkansas state employee named Paula Jones in 1991. Jones sued Clinton for sexual harassment, for which he ultimately paid an US$850,000 settlement. Starr believed that establishing a pattern of lying and dishonest behavior could connect Whitewater and the Jones cases—and, in turn, he believed the Lewinsky affair could be part of this larger pattern. After the story broke, Clinton gave a presidential address in which he angrily declared, "I did not have sex with that woman." When called to testify by Starr's investigators, however, Clinton was more equivocal. Asked by a grand jury whether he was lying when he had said "there's nothing going on between us," Clinton famously declared "it depends on what the meaning of 'is' is." While he may have been technically correct in making such distinctions—between past and present tense, and in regarding vaginal intercourse as the standard by which to determine whether one has had sex—he came across as both highly opportunistic (as in "I didn't inhale") and arguably committing perjury. Starr, for his part, introduced a dress that had Clinton's semen stains into evidence, documenting that oral as well as phone sex took place. Amazingly, Clinton and Lewinsky's trysts took place in an alcove just outside the Oval Office, where the door was always partially ajar.[26] As one might imagine, such reports became topics of endless conversation and media coverage. Right-wing media feasted on the Lewinsky scandal; in particular, the Fox News Channel, launched in 1996, was a major beneficiary. So was conservative radio, notably the show of host Rush Limbaugh, who used his perch to become one of the most powerful voices of US conservatism for the next two decades.

When Starr submitted his report in September 1998, Republicans in Congress believed that Clinton's evasions amounted to the "high crimes and misdemeanors" specified in the US Constitution as a basis of impeachment. The process of making this case stretched into early 1999. During that time, polls revealed growing support for Clinton and growing distaste for Republican tactics. In the midterm elections of 1998, Democrats actually gained seats in Congress, which was highly unusual, given that the party holding the White House almost always loses ground. An embarrassed Gingrich, who had led the attack on Clinton, resigned as Speaker of the House, further humiliated by the exposure of an extramarital affair on *his* part. The man chosen to replace Gingrich, Rep. Bob Livingston of Louisiana, also had to resign when it was revealed he *also* had such an affair. The pornography publisher Larry Flynt offered US$1 million to anyone who came forward with documentary evidence of affairs by members of Congress or high government officials, and Livingston got caught in that net.[27] Such are the wages of hypocrisy. (Then, again, his replacement as US Senator, "Family Values" conservative David Vitter, was involved in a prostitution ring circa 2007. He was re-elected in 2010.)

Meanwhile, the impeachment process moved forward. As expected, the House, in highly partisan proceedings, voted to impeach Clinton, but the Senate voted to acquit him of the charges, in effect repeating the outcome of the only other president to be impeached, Andrew Johnson in 1868. Clinton's remaining 2 years in office were relatively placid politically, but he sustained one more self-inflicted injury to his reputation on his way out in 2001 with a series of high-profile presidential pardons for some dubious characters, among them a financier who fled the country to escape charges of tax evasion. Still, he left office with even higher approval ratings than Ronald Reagan.[28]

Why? One could say that Clinton was lucky in his enemies, even if they caused him much difficulty (and even if his greatest enemy was himself). One should also credit Clinton's tremendous skills as a politician, which included an unusually sure grasp of policy as well as tremendous political instincts. But the most important element in Clinton's popularity was the wider climate in which he operated, a period of unusual prosperity and relative placidity in the United States.

La Vida Loca: The Roaring Nineties

There were three major trends in the Clinton years that contributed to a subsequent impression of them as an innocent age—if one can speak of an age where pubic hair and semen-stained dresses were topics of public conversation as innocent—compared to what followed.

The first was the surprising strength of the US economy. The 1970s and early 1980s had been a period of stagnation, marked by a combination of high inflation, high interest rates, and high unemployment. The economy recovered in the Reagan years, struggled during the Bush years, but then went on a sustained period of expansion under Clinton. Despite concerns about the flight of American jobs abroad, the unemployment rate dipped to 4% in 2000, the lowest it had been in decades (though the jobs available weren't necessarily good ones). Poverty declined sharply, down to 11.3% of the population by the end of the century, roughly half of what it had been in 1959. Per capita income, which rose slowly in the early 1990s, picked up in the second half of the decade; median household incomes rose from US$38,362 in 1995 to US$42,141 in 2000, a jump of almost 10% in 5 years. Even minorities fared relatively well; the financial position of Native Americans, who only enjoyed about half of white per capita national income on average, improved by roughly one-third during the decade. In 2001, the United States produced 22% of the world's output— far lower than after World War II, but still far higher than Great Britain at its imperial zenith in 1913.[29]

The second trend might be termed the supersizing of America. In the 1990s, it seemed, bigger was better. A good example was the auto industry. The hot vehicle of the decade was the sport utility vehicle (SUV). Lobbyists succeeded in having them classified as trucks, which exempted them from Environmental

Protection Agency standards on gas emissions. Houses also became larger; while the original Levittown homes of the 1950s typically occupied 750 square feet, the single-family house averaged 2,200 square feet by the year 2000. A third of American homes had four or more bedrooms. So many were mass-produced that they were dubbed "McMansions."[30]

Finally, much popular culture in the 1990s had a sunnier character than that of the dour mood of the grunge era circa 1990. The 1990s marked the final flowering of the major network sitcom, epitomized by *Friends* (1994–2004), which traced the lives of a set of attractive twenty-somethings living in New York's Greenwich Village who enjoyed a notably upscale lifestyle. Similar in setting, though more caustic in tone, was *Seinfeld* (1989–1998), which starred comedian Jerry Seinfeld and an ensemble of often hilariously venal compatriots in a show that was famously "about nothing." The decade was also a golden age for often anarchic animated series that were often far more knowing, even graphic, than any live action show, among them *The Simpsons* (1989–); *South Park* (1997–); and *Family Guy* (1999–2001; 2005–), a show that found greater success after it was initially cancelled. Though not upbeat in any conventional sense, they were gleeful in their subversion of conventional wisdom in a time when it seemed safe to do so.

Sunniness was also widespread in American popular music, dominated by the likes of Mariah Carey, Celine Dion, and Whitney Houston. Perhaps the most gifted pop singer of her generation, Houston's rendition of "I Will Always Love You," which transformed a country tune by Dolly Parton into a torchy *tour de force*, was included in the hugely successful soundtrack of the otherwise forgettable movie *The Bodyguard* (1992), in which Houston starred. Country music also continued to enjoy significant mainstream appeal in the work of Garth Brooks and Shania Twain, whose *Come on Over* (1997) became the best-selling country album of all time. (Country music assumed a more prominent place on the commercial landscape around this time, as the *Billboard* charts switched from a survey-based approach for record sales to one based on computerized records of actual copies sold.) The songs of such performers, while not always upbeat, generally sidestepped political issues or social themes in favor of romance and good times. Pop musicians of all times have done the same, of course, but the 1990s are not typically remembered for the great social anthems such as those of the 1960s, for example. On the other hand, the decade was important in the emergence of some of the hip-hop artists discussed earlier, some of whom went mainstream. It was also a decade when Latino artists increasingly seized national attention, among them Cuban–American Gloria Estefan, Puerto Rican Ricky Martin, and the Mexican–American Selena Quintanilla-Perez (known simply as Selena), the Chicana phenomenon whose career was cut tragically short when she was shot to death by a fan in 1995.

That's not to say, of course, that work of social significance was not produced in the 1990s. Musicians such as R. E. M. and Lauryn Hill; filmmakers such as Martin Scorsese and Jonathan Demme; and novelists such as Toni Morrison and Philip Roth continued to do their finest work, much of which was deeply challenging of accepted national pieties. But they often did so against a broader backdrop of triviality and sensationalism that was not limited to the O. J. Simpson trial. The 1990s were the decade when the nation was transfixed by the story of John Bobbitt, whose penis was severed by his angry wife Lorena in 1993 (he was acquitted of rape, she was acquitted of castrating him by reason of insanity, and he went on to star in a 1994 pornographic movie with the title *John Wayne Bobbitt Uncut*). More tragic was the 1996 death of 6-year-old JonBenet Ramsey, which turned into a lurid media marathon that focused on her family's affluence, her parents entering her into beauty pageants that sexualized her, and the fact that the crime was never resolved. Again, such stories were hardly limited to the 1990s, but a densely elaborated media infrastructure (notably the need of the new cable news channels to fill programming time), combined with a lack of obvious economic or political problems—or maybe just the desire and ability to ignore them—made the decade distinctive in this regard.

Tech Sec: Toward the Internet

There were nevertheless important developments in the 1990s that had a significant impact on everyday life then and long afterward. Perhaps the most obvious was the technological sector of the economy. Americans living in that decade were very aware that they were living on the cusp of the millennium—Bill Clinton's campaign slogan in 1996 was "Building a Bridge to the 21st century"—and the near future would be one where science fiction would become reality. The most obvious manifestation of this truth: cell phones. Once upon a time, they had been the realm of fantasy, notably the sci-fi television series *Star Trek* (1966–1969), where characters communicated across space with hand-held devices. As with many technologies, cellular telephony existed decades before it actually became commercially available—in this case, in the early 1980s. By the early 1990s, mobile phones became a must-have gadget for the elite; by decade's end, they had become a fact of global life, the way cars, radios, and televisions had in earlier decades of the century.

One scientific frontier of particular importance was biology. It was during the 1990s that a series of public and private enterprises mobilized to map the human genome, a gigantic undertaking to identify, map, and publish the entire genetic code of human beings (initially believed to be about 2 million genes, it's now estimated to be closer to 20,000). Genetic research also made it possible to clone animals—beginning with a sheep named Dolly in 1996—and create genetically modified organisms (GMOs), notably food. Such practices were deeply controversial, and to some degree remain so (the US government has given more latitude toward farmers using genetically modified crops than is the case in Europe, for example). The possibilities of such research, which include preventing famines and curing diseases, jostle with nightmarish scenarios that include epidemics and marauding armies of clones.

But no technological development of the decade was more obvious, and more transformative, than the rise of the Internet.[31] Here too, there was a long history that preceded what was experienced as a revolution. As discussed at the beginning of this book (see Chapter 1), modern computing was, to a great degree, the product of US government investment and talent, enlisted to win World War II and then to fight the Cold War. In the early 1960s, a government researcher named Paul Baran focused on how computers might coordinate activities with each other amid the likely communications breakdown that would accompany a nuclear war. Working with other researchers, Baran developed a method that came to be known as "packet switching," in which messages sent between two destinations in a connected series of computers would be broken up into small pieces upon their departure and sent through different routes before being reassembled at their destination. This networked approach reduced the risk that the destruction of any one channel of communication would sever military planners' access to information.

Though there were many intermediate steps in the process, the concept of packet switching between inter-networked computers—abbreviated as the "Internet"—became central to the development of one of the most important innovations of the computing era: electronic mail, or e-mail. In 1982, ARPA developed the Simple Mail Transfer Protocol (SMTP) to simplify the process, which included the use of the "at symbol"—@—to route messages. Baran's work with other technologists, among them another network theorist named J. C. R. Licklider, are often cited as pivotal in the development of modern electronic communications, in which the government's role continued to be central.

Indeed, the private sector was, in some ways, an obstacle to the coming of the Internet. Until the late 1970s, its scope was relatively narrow, not only because of technical difficulties, but also because Bell Telephone, which held a monopoly, made it difficult, if not impossible, to connect computers via phone lines, the most obvious means to expand the domain of data transmission. A series of antitrust decisions, however, broke Bell's power, decentralizing the phone business in the 1980s. In the early 1990s, the government eased restrictions on commercial Internet activity. A new mass medium was emerging.

The fact that such a medium existed, however, didn't mean people could easily access it. A key link in bridging individuals to the Internet involved the dissemination of devices known as modems, which connected computers with phone lines, allowing data to travel. Modems had been around a long time before they became household devices; once they did, connectivity to the Internet exploded.

If the modem was the car, and the individual computer a steering wheel, there was still the question of the roads by which to reach an information desti-nation. E-mail was one; File Transfer Protocol (FTP), a system by which bodies of data could be moved between machines, was another. But such roads worked best for those who had good travel directions and knew exactly where they were going. Discovering what you didn't know remained difficult. One source of help were Internet service providers (ISPs). Among the best-known among them was Prodigy, a joint venture between IBM, Sears, and CBS (CBS dropped out of the deal before its formal launch); and America Online (AOL), which, similar to Prodigy, facilitated users by offering a portal with lots of signage through which they could find information such as news, weather, and shopping options.

The best means for accessing the Internet came from British computer scientist Tim Berners-Lee, based at the Geneva-based European Organization for Nuclear Research (CERN). Berners-Lee developed a system of instructions, written in HyperText Markup Language (HTML), to link an individual computer and a source of information. Berners-Lee referred to the vast domain of data, for which he provided labeling, as "the World Wide Web." It was now possible for a relative novice to locate information on the Internet with a relatively simple address and domain.

Being able to find what you were looking for is one thing—a big thing—but still only one thing. One tool that made this easier was a type of computer program we have come to know as the search engine. Among the first were those made possible by a protocol developed by the University of Minnesota, known as "Gopher," named in honor of the school's mascot (it was also widely regarded as a form of shorthand for "go for"). Gopher enabled the creation of search engines such as Archie at McGill and Veronica at the University of Nevada (both named in honor of characters from a popular comic strip.) These were widely used by hackers in the early 1990s, but were quickly outpaced by competitors such as Lycos and Yahoo! The reigning champion of search engines is Google, founded in 1998 by a pair of Stanford PhD students, Sergey Brin and Larry Page.

The other great innovation in web surfing was the development of the browser. The breakthrough here was provided by Marc Lowell Andreessen, a 21-year-old undergraduate student at the University of Illinois, who in 1992 led the effort to develop a program called Mosaic that allowed users to browse through lists of data on a particular subject. Andreessen commercialized his invention the following year as Netscape, which for a while was the most popular browser on the Internet. Netscape's supremacy was contested by Microsoft, the software powerhouse that, having missed the Internet boat, tried to recover its dominance by installing its own browser, the Internet Explorer, as part of every operating system it sold, using strong-arm tactics with computer manufacturers and retailers that were later declared illegal. By the early twenty-first century, however, browsers such as Firefox (an open-source browser developed by the Mozilla Foundation and its subsidiary, the Mozilla Corporation), Safari (an Apple product), and Chrome (Google's entry into the sweepstakes) had become about as widespread.

The last major piece in the emergence of a recognizably modern Internet experience was the replacement of traditional telephone lines as the primary source of computer connections. Though relatively cheap, phone lines were slow and highly limited in terms of the volume and type of information they could carry. Phone service was increasingly replaced by Integrated Service

Digital Network (ISDN) lines, typically offered by phone companies; digital subscriber lines (DSL), typically offered by cable companies; and wireless communication networks, typically offered by both. Until this point, most Internet traffic took the form of text and graphics, which were almost too cheap to meter. Now, however, music, photographs, and video, all of which took up more volume in traveling across space, could be moved efficiently, if more expensively.

At first, the Internet seemed most potent in the way it provided new ways to do familiar things. An obvious example is shopping. One of the most important exemplars of e-commerce is Amazon.com, founded in 1994 as an online bookstore. It has since become the greatest retailer in American history since the rise of Sears & Roebuck in the nineteenth century. While online shopping appeared to have some initial advantages over traditional retailing, particularly in sparing merchants the tremendous overhead costs of operating an actual brick-and-mortar building, it took a while for consumers to get acculturated to practices such as giving their credit card numbers online, accepting the delayed gratification (and costs) involved in shipping, and other considerations. Such factors continue to give traditional merchants important advantages that keep them in business. But wider selection, lower prices, improved shipping options, and 24-hour convenience have established e-commerce as a major factor in the US economy.

The Internet also provided a new means of delivering journalism. It provided a forum for self-styled guerilla journalists such as Matt Drudge, whose website became the first to break the Clinton–Lewinsky scandal. For the most part, though, the emphasis here needs to be on *delivering*; similar to early radio, the online world was not so much a *source* of news reporting as it was an *outlet* for it. From a fairly early stage, the nation's newspapers established an online presence, typically free, whereby readers could access news stories. So did major television news organizations such as the Cable News Network (CNN) and MSNBC, a joint enterprise started by Microsoft and the National Broadcasting Company (NBC) that launched in 1996 (it became solely owned and operated by NBC in 2012).

These are the ways in which the Internet is reshaping that which we consider familiar. But it was also apparent from the start that the Internet would look different from anything that came before it. The most obvious manifestation is that distinctively Internet-centric phenomenon we know as the website. At the most basic level, a website is little more than a database— a discrete body of information. The question has always been a matter of how to organize that information. In effect, websites make information three-dimensional, in that "behind" selected pieces of data such as text or a photo, one can click on a particular link that branches out toward additional data in multiple directions. In this regard, a website is a more horizontal experience than print, which is typically read from top to bottom. But the print analogy nevertheless holds firm: one speaks of a particular desktop presentation in a website as a "page."

Insulated Intervention: US Foreign Policy

Technological innovations such as cellphones, cable TV, and the Internet provided plenty of distractions in everyday American life. And the roaring economy provided an added element of cushioning. Meanwhile, however, much of the wider world continued to seethe. Most Americans weren't paying attention: this is one of the great luxuries of empire for its ordinary citizens. However, notwithstanding Vietnam-era fears about intervening in other nations' civil wars, the US government certainly was periodically asserting itself in foreign affairs for the sake of maintaining *Pax Americana*.

Actually, some US military intervention abroad in the 1990s had a genuinely humanitarian basis. In the early 1990s, the east African nation of Somalia was wracked by civil war. United Nations efforts to provide food and other aid were hampered as rival warlords prevented the delivery—or stole—supplies. As a result, the UN's Security Council voted to allow the use of force, and asked the US government to lead the effort. President Bush sent 25,000 American troops, joined by about half as many from other countries. Apparently a success, the newly elected Bill Clinton began a withdrawal, which again seemed to trigger violence. The most notorious incident occurred in October 1993 when warlord Mohamed Farrah Aidid ambushed two highly advanced US Black Hawk helicopters and waged a daylong battle against the Americans in the capital of Mogadishu, the Somali capital, with civilians caught in the crossfire. Pictures of Somalis dragging the body of a dead US solider through the street appalled and outraged the international public. (The incident was chronicled in the highly regarded 2001 movie *Black Hawk Down*.) In the aftermath of the Soviet Union's collapse and the successful Persian Gulf War, the US mishap in Somalia did not seem to wound collective American self-esteem, but it did tap a latent sense of isolationism that had always been the default setting in American foreign policy before World War II and the Cold War. Clinton withdrew US troops.

In 1994, amid much criticism (most of it from Republicans), Clinton intervened abroad again, this time in Haiti, another nation plagued by chronic discord. When the military of that country overthrew the government of President Jean-Bertrand Aristide, Clinton was initially wary of sending American troops, despite humanitarian calls to do so. When the coup created a refugee crisis, however, Clinton felt he had no choice, and dispatched US forces to prevent chaos in accord with a UN Security Council resolution. They landed without incident, and ultimately facilitated Aristide's return to power.

But humanitarian aid, like more self-interested kinds, was always conditioned by geopolitics—or, perhaps more accurately, a lack thereof. The United States did not get involved in the raging civil war in the African nation of Rwanda, which, unlike Somalia, was located in the less strategically important central Africa. This proved tragic when the nation's ethnic Hutu majority launched a genocidal campaign against the minority Tutsi, resulting in the death of approximately a million people in the spring and summer of 1994. American reluctance to act was not a matter of pure heartlessness; the debacle in Somalia, combined with a rational concern that intervention could make things worse if it led to further escalation or geographic expansion, checked any instinct to intervene in the conflict. But US inaction contributed to a perception that an often moralistic US government could be selective in its application of humanitarian principles.

One place where the US government felt it could not afford to stand aside was in the Balkan region of southeastern Europe, an area where religious and ethnic strife had triggered World War I, and which had served as a crucial buffer zone between the still-fragile states of the former Soviet Union and prosperous Western Europe for most of the twentieth century. During the communist era, a series of ethnic enclaves had been forged into the single unit of Yugoslavia by Josip Broz Tito, an independent-minded military strongman who shunned the West and managed to get away with snubbing Stalin for much of the Cold War. After Tito's death in 1980, however, centrifugal forces pulled Yugoslavia into multiple pieces that included Catholic-dominated Croatia, Orthodox Christian–dominated Serbia, and Muslim-dominated Bosnia (with significant minorities of all three in each other). By the early 1990s, the region was in serious disarray, with an aggressive Serbia under the leadership of the genocidal Slobodan Milosevic seeking to expand its borders. The US refused to get involved until the massacre of over 7,000 unarmed Muslim men in the Bosnian city of Srebenica provoked the Clinton administration to act in concert with NATO. The 78-day intervention in the form of air strikes with state-of-the-art weaponry stopped Serbia without a single loss of American life. The resulting Dayton Accords of 1995, which were followed by stationing a US peace force in Bosnia, ranks among the more successful military operations in American history. However, the US intervened again—much more aggressively—in 1999 when Serbia invaded the neighboring nation of Kosovo. This time, the Serbs only stopped when the US began bombing the Serbian capital of Belgrade. (Milosevic was ultimately captured and convicted as a war criminal by a UN tribunal. He died in a prison cell in 2006.) Though civilian casualties were significant in this conflict, once again there was no loss of American lives, an outcome that perhaps contributed to a belief that the United States could project its power painlessly at will. In this regard, success would prove to be a dangerous thing.[32]

Indeed, by the end of the twentieth century, US military supremacy seemed complete, with hundreds of bases around the globe—many of them secret—and military personnel stationed in about 150 countries.[33] Though there was a decline in defense spending in the years following the Cold War, the government still sought to maintain global supremacy, informally defined in terms of an ability to wage a war across two oceans at the same time. By 2001, the United States accounted for 37% of the world's military expenditures.[34] To at least some extent, such spending reflected domestic and economic imperatives: weapons systems create jobs, profits for arms merchants who sell them to the government, and a market for foreign governments.

But the weak always find ways to challenge the strong. Even at its most seemingly invincible, the nation was still vulnerable to threats on native soil. The breakdown of the Cold War order—never total in any case—was conducive to a wide variety of splinter movements within nations as well as the growing phenomenon of transnational radical movements, sometimes tacitly or secretly supported by their host states. This was especially true in the Middle East, where the fundamentalist era that began with the Iranian revolution of 1979 had now spread across the region. In February 1993, one such radical splinter group succeeded in detonating a bomb beneath New York's World Trade Center, a symbol of American capitalist pre-eminence. The explosion killed six people and injured about 1,000, causing significant damage to one of its two buildings. Four Muslim men were captured and convicted in the bombing, which was led by Ramzi Yousef (believed to be an alias) of Kuwait.

But the most challenging threat to emerge in the 1990s was Al Qaeda, an extremist group led by the charismatic Osama bin Laden. Bin Laden, a Saudi, was the son of an extremely wealthy building contractor who had started his career working for the Arabian–American Oil Company (Aramco), a joint-national enterprise that had helped transform Saudi Arabia from an impoverished desert to one of the wealthiest nations on earth. The elder bin Laden practiced polygamy; he had 22 wives and Osama was one of 54 children. Though he didn't see much of his father, bin Laden was raised in comfort and inherited a substantial fortune. Unlike many of his siblings, however, he did not travel widely and was not educated in the West, instead becoming deeply religious and politically radical. He spent much of the 1980s in Afghanistan, personally funding the creation of a force of foreign fighters to assist the Afghanis in resisting the Soviet invasion. Though his contributions didn't amount to much—at one point, the fighters began to refer to themselves as "the Brigade of the Ridiculous"[35]—he developed a reputation as one of the leading Muslim radicals in the world.

After Soviet defeat in that war, bin Laden turned his attention to the United States as a cause of Muslim oppression. He felt that the US use of Saudi Arabia as a staging ground for the invasion of Kuwait during the Persian Gulf War was a desecration of Islam, and masterminded simultaneous truck bombings of US embassies in Kenya and Tanzania in 1998 that killed 224 people. President Clinton retaliated for these attacks by ordering missile strikes at sites in Sudan and Afghanistan, where Al Qaeda was believed to be operating. Neither worked; the site in Sudan that the US government suspected was a weapons manufacturing plant was actually a pharmaceutical factory—one person was killed and the country was deprived of a medically important asset. Clinton's ability to act credibly and decisively was also hampered by the Lewinsky scandal, and there were widespread rumors that he ordered the attacks as a distraction from his political woes (a scenario that happened to coincide with the premise of a hit 1998 movie, *Wag the Dog*). Al Qaeda was also responsible for the explosion on an American warship, the USS *Cole*, in the Yemini port of Aden in 2000. It killed 17 sailors.

It's worth noting that, while terrorism in the 1990s was often undertaken by foreign operatives in the United States, the single most destructive attack in US history at the time was the work of a native-born American citizen. In 1995, a Gulf War veteran with right-wing political affiliations named Timothy McVeigh detonated a bomb in a parked rental truck outside a federal government building in Oklahoma City, killing 168 people and injuring many others. McVeigh was convicted on all counts in 1997 and executed in 2001. The torture and killing of gay high schooler Matthew Shepard in Wyoming in 1998 and the murderous spree of two other white youth, Eric Harris and Dylan Klebold, at Colorado's Columbine High School in 1999 are other reminders of rage that seethed below the surface of American life among ordinary (often read as white) young people in the turn-of-the-century United States.

Terrorism was a troubling reminder to Americans that they were never entirely secure, and incidents such as these received intensive media coverage. But the relative rarity of such events is precisely what made them so haunting. In a way, they obscured equally troubling, but less spectacular, problems, much in the way deaths in a single plane crash attract far more attention that the much greater aggregate number of car fatalities. And yet, at the same time, the fact that the USS Cole *didn't* sink, and that the World Trade Center remained standing, could contribute to a feeling of complacency. Either way, the overwhelming collective desire remained in a here and now where the dominant impression was one of peace and prosperity, even if both were far from universal.

Recount: The 2000 Election

Actually, one of the major political questions going into the presidential election of 2000 was how the United States should best capitalize on its prosperity. After a generation of red ink, the nation's finances were significantly improving. The closing years of the Clinton presidency were marked by the first US government surpluses in 30 years: thanks to the tax increases of 1993 and overall prosperity, the government collected more than it spent in fiscal years 1999 and 2000, which is to say it came in under budget in those years. It's important to note that there's a big difference between that and the *overall* national debt, which had accumulated sharply during the Reagan era as the result of year after year of the government spending more than it took in. But that overall debt too was shrinking, and, as Clinton was finishing his presidency, US finances were in the best shape they had been in a half-century.

This is exactly why some Republicans said this revenue should be returned to the people. Returning surplus revenue as tax cuts (as opposed to paying down the national debt or spending money on new programs) had been the GOP approach to just about every financial issue since 1980, and it was still gospel in 2000. The question was who would best spread this good news. The answer proved to be another George Bush—George W. Bush, as opposed to his father George H. W. Bush (the younger was sometimes referred to as "W," or, in his home state of Texas, "Dubya"). Bush's principal rival for the nomination was Arizona senator John McCain, a decorated US Navy pilot during the Vietnam War who was captured and imprisoned from 1967 to 1973. McCain was an avowed conservative, but he was also known as a "maverick" willing to take principled stands as well as cut deals with Democrats. McCain surprised many observers by winning the New Hampshire primary in February 2000, but the party establishment threw its weight behind Bush, who received the nomination with a solid base of support. Bush created a search committee for a vice presidential candidate headed by Republican stalwart Dick Cheney, who had been a congressman from Wyoming and worked in the Ford administration. But Bush ended up choosing Cheney himself.

The Democrats nominated Vice President Gore, who was a logical choice for a number of reasons. Similar to Bush, he had a political pedigree—his father, Albert Gore, Sr., had also been a US senator from Tennessee (as had Gore himself) and an opponent of the Vietnam War. Gore had also been a candidate for president in 1988 and was long familiar to voters, particularly in areas such as technology (he dubbed the Internet, which he fostered as a legislator, as "the information superhighway") and was a highly regarded environmentalist. But perhaps most importantly, Gore was a visible lieutenant for a two-term president who was finishing his political career on a relatively strong note. After surviving a challenge from Senator Bill Bradley of New Jersey, Gore secured the nomination. He attempted to bolster his prospects by choosing Senator Joe Lieberman of Connecticut as his running mate; Lieberman was notable because he was the first Jewish major-party candidate on a presidential ticket. He was also a vocal opponent of Clinton in the Lewinsky scandal, though he voted against impeachment.

The presidential campaign of 2000 was a relatively uninspiring one. Though Bush impressed voters with his geniality, there were questions about the depth of his knowledge of the issues. Gore tended to have the opposite problem; no one doubted his qualifications, but he could seem stiff and pretentious. In some important respects, the basic logic of American politics had remained unchanged since 1980: an alliance of Wall Street and white evangelicals taking on a pro-government coalition of white liberals and racial minorities clustered on the east and west coasts, with women increasingly seen as a core Democratic constituency.

Ironically, at the very moment the candidates were wrangling over the best way to exploit the strong US economy, it was unraveling in the latest of a series of recessions that were sharper than those prior to the 1970s. The expansion of American stock markets in the 1990s had been unusually dramatic, so much so that even Alan Greenspan, the strongly pro-market chairman of the Federal Reserve, warned against "irrational exuberance" in 1996. A principal source of that exuberance was the Internet. In an important sense, however, it the *idea* of the Internet—according the US census, only 19% of US homes were online in 2000[36]—rather than the prevailing reality. The heart of that idea, as far as Wall Street was concerned, was e-commerce as the future of the American economy. This could lead to some ridiculous financial speculation—the most famous example is that of Pets.com, a pet supply store that found plenty of buyers when its stock became available in 2000. However, in less than a year, its stock price nosedived from US$14 to US$1 a share, and the company burned through US$147 million before crashing into bankruptcy. Even relatively blue-chip Internet companies saw their share prices undergo severe declines; Amazon. com's share price was over US$100 per share in 1999; but, within a couple years, it came down to less than US$10 (though within another decade it would be US$400).[37] Tech stock prices in general fell 78% between March 2000 and October 2002 amid a growing concern that these and other companies weren't actually making anything and that banks were engaged more in financial manipulation rather than providing the capital necessary to build thriving enterprises.[38] As is often the case, however, the larger economic impact of this turbulence would not be felt right away. Wall Street was getting hit in early 2000; Main Street would not feel the full impact of the downturn until 2001.

Meanwhile, the presidential campaign climaxed in a country that was notably divided. Gore won the popular vote by over half a million votes nationally—four times the margin that secured John F. Kennedy's victory in 1960 (another close and fiercely contested election).[39] But of course, presidential elections are not decided by the popular vote; under the US Constitution, they're decided by the Electoral College, an antiquated mechanism by which the Founding Fathers had hoped to slow democratic passions. At the end of Election Day in 2000, Gore appeared to have a lead in the Electoral College, 267 to 246, but was three votes short of the necessary majority. Moreover, a number of states were still too close to call, notably Florida, whose trove of 25 electoral votes would effectively decide the winner. The question was when—and how.

The situation in Florida was complicated by a series of irregularities. One was a confusing ballot, in which thousands of voters, many of them elderly Jews, voted for Pat Buchanan, who ran as a conservative alternative to Bush, when they really intended to vote for Gore. Another was partially punched ballots—known as chads—that were alternately "hanging," "dimpled," or "pregnant," creating questions about whether they should be counted or not. There were approximately 175,000 votes that fell into this category. Then there was the fact that election officials in Florida had incorrectly invalidated the registrations of thousands of African American and Latino voters and tossed out ballots in African American neighborhoods. Unlike many states, under Florida law, convicted felons could not vote. But thousands of legitimate voters were incorrectly included in this category. Finally, there were reports of voter intimidation in some counties of northern Florida. The fact is that there is often inaccuracies and outright fraud in US elections (Kennedy's election in 1960, for example, was marked by some dubious practices in Illinois). But the situation in Florida was notable for its multifaceted, and specifically racial, dimensions.[40]

In the immediate aftermath of Election Day, Bush held a narrow lead in Florida, with ballots from overseas and legally mandated recounts yet to be tallied. Once they were, Gore cut into Bush's lead in that state. At issue now was how to proceed next: recount all of Florida's votes? Just those in contested counties? Armies of lawyers descended on the Sunshine State to wrangle over such questions. On November 21, 2000, 2 weeks after the election, the Florida Supreme Court approved recounts in four Florida counties that would likely hand Gore a victory. Republicans, complaining that the Florida court was dominated by Democrats and that recounts were likely to be inaccurate, took their case to the United States Supreme Court. Democrats noted that, in so doing, Republicans were contradicting their professed preference for states' rights rather than turning to the federal government to resolve such questions.

The Supreme Court, which had a conservative majority, agreed to hear the case on December 1. Three days later, an apparently divided body referred the case back to the Florida Supreme Court, asking it to explain whether it had followed the relevant portions of Constitutional law. When the Florida court responded by directing the recount to continue, Republicans once again asked the US Supreme Court to intervene, this time by issuing an order to delay it. The five justices appointed by Reagan and Bush agreed to do so on December 9, setting aside December 11 to hear arguments in the case. By a 5–4 vote the next day, the court ruled in favor of Bush, arguing that the attempt to straighten out irregularities was potentially unfair to those voters whose votes had actually been properly counted. It was a highly controversial decision and one made all the more so by the court's assertion that its legal logic was unique to this case. In a way, this reasoning mattered little, since the recount had been stopped and, under Florida law, a winner had to be declared by December 12. Since Bush still held the lead, he was declared the winner, and in so doing became president of the United States.

Was Gore cheated? Many would say so. Others argued that Gore ran a lackluster campaign, failing to win his home state of Tennessee, a basic threshold for successful presidential campaigns. The third-party candidacy of consumer advocate Ralph Nader, a liberal darling who captured 2% of the vote in Florida, was another complicating factor. Still, it's hard to avoid a conclusion that the will of the voters had been thwarted, especially since Gore had won the popular vote, even if the election went to Bush on technical grounds.

Perhaps the most remarkable aspect of the election is that its outcome was accepted. Gore conceded defeat the day after the Supreme Court ruling, and subsequently referred to himself, only half-jokingly, as "a recovering politician." Even though a lot of people were unhappy, and the credibility of the legal system was widely in question, the American people did not take to the streets. The core stability of the republic was sound.

And so, George W. Bush took office in January 2001: life went on. The economy was not as good as it had been in recent years, but in many respects it was still the 1990s. Bush, acting on campaign pledges, successfully pushed for massive tax cuts that included small rebate checks to all voters and massive benefits for the wealthy, effectively erasing the government surplus. The big story that summer was the disappearance of a young woman named Chandra Levy, and whether or not the married congressman she worked for, Gary Condit, with whom she had an affair, was responsible. (The answer was no; Levy was murdered in Washington DC's Rock Creek Park by an illegal immigrant from El

Salvador.) Cable TV shows speculated breathlessly on the latest twists in the case, as did Internet websites. Business as usual, you might say.

And then came September 11.

CULTURE WATCH: *Exile in Guyville* (1993)

We often think of American culture as national, even global, but most great works of art are products of far more specific subcultures. Consider, for example, the post–World War II working-class culture of Liverpool, England, that so decisively shaped the Beatles. One can say the same of American rock and roll music—Elvis Presley saturated in the Memphis of the early 1950s; Bruce Springsteen was a product of the Jersey shore bar scene of the late 1960s; and Liz Phair, not nearly as well known as any of these figures, emerged from the Chicago neighborhood of Wicker Park in the closing decade of the twentieth century. Her 1993 album *Exile in Guyville* is the product of a specific time and place, yet it resonates with an appeal that continues to ripple outward.

Phair, who was adopted, was born in 1967 and moved around early in life before settling in the affluent Chicago suburb of Winnetka, where she attended the highly regarded New Trier High School before going on to Oberlin College. She returned to Chicagoland, settling in Wicker Park in the early 1990s, which, as with a lot of urban American neighborhoods at

Figure 9.2   ROCKING: Liz Phair performing in Chicago, 2011. Her 1993 album *Exile in Guyville*, a response to the Rolling Stones' 1972 album *Exile on Main Street*, became a feminist manifesto. © Zuma Press, Inc. / Alamy.

the time, was just beginning to reemerge from postwar decline. The location was good, rents were cheap, and roommates were plentiful for twenty-somethings trying to find their way. Wicker Park and Chicago generally—as with other cities of the time, notably Seattle—could boast of a vibrant alternative rock scene for independent bands and their fans trying to pursue their passions outside the corporate mainstream. It was a time before musical downloads and the Internet, when most fans acquired music on compact discs. The primary form of information about new bands came from the alternative newspapers that sprouted up around the country.

Phair was deeply immersed in this subculture, but there was one respect in which she stood out: her gender. The notion of rock and roll feminism was not exactly new: Janis Joplin, Chrissie Hynde, and Joan Jett had shown the way in the 1960s through the 1980s, and there were women such as Kim Gordon and P. J. Harvey who were prominent in the alt-rock scene before Phair. But her 1993 album *Exile in Guyville* was nevertheless a bold statement that got a lot of attention—not all of it positive.

Exile in Guyville was notable for its audacity. It was conceived as a generational response to the classic 1972 Rolling Stones album *Exile on Main Street*. Similar to the Rolling Stones' record, *Guyville* was a double album with 18 songs, with the same number of tracks per side (something no longer obvious in this post-vinyl age). And, again similar to the Stones, Phair's album has an improvisatory, almost sloppy, sonic quality that compels attention. But Phair is distinctive in the way she responds to the male bravado of Mick Jagger & Co. with her own brand of assertive sexuality. "Every time I see your face / I get all wet between my legs," begins her song "Flower," which only gets more specific from there. Yet, *Guyville* is no exercise in pornography. "I want a boyfriend," she laments in "Fuck and Run," a song of romantic disappointment. "I want all that stupid old shit / Like letters and sodas." Crucially, however, she doesn't express guilt over her sexuality. *Guyville*'s songs include laments about housework, roommates, and, in the case of "Divorce Song," a startlingly believable lover's quarrel conducted while driving. Phair had captured a moment—a third-wave feminist, alt-rock moment—that would become part of recorded history.

Suggested Further Reading

The 1990s is a decade that awaits a full-scale academic treatment. The best extant journalistic account, which includes coverage of many of the topics covered in this chapter, is Haynes Johnson's *The Best of Times: America in the Clinton Years* (New York: Harcourt, 2001).

The fullest rendering of the Hill–Thomas affair is that of reporters Jane Mayer and Jill Abramson: *Strange Justice: The Selling of Clarence Thomas* (New York: Houghton-Mifflin, 1994). On the O. J. Simpson affair, see Jeffrey Toobin, *The Run of His Life: The People vs. O. J. Simpson* (New York: Random House, 1996) and Lawrence Schiller,

American Tragedy: The Uncensored Story of the Simpson Defense (New York: Random House, 1996).

On gangsta rap, see Eithne Quinn, *Nuthin' but a "G" Thang: The Commerce and Culture of Gangsta Rap* (New York: Columbia University Press, 2004). See also suggestions for further reading at the end of Chapter 8.

On the birth of the Internet, see Stephen Segaller, *Nerds 2.0.1: A Brief History of the Internet* (New York: TV Books, 1998). Tim Berners-Lee recounts his pivotal work in *Weaving the Web: The Original Design and Ultimate Destiny of the World Wide Web* (New York: HarperBusiness, 2000).

Important books on Bill Clinton include David Maraniss, *First in His Class: A Biography of Bill Clinton* (New York: Simon & Schuster, 1995); John F. Harris, *The Survivor: Bill Clinton in the White House* (New York: Random House, 2006); and Joe Klein, The *Natural: The Misunderstood Presidency of Bill Clinton* (New York: Random House, 2002). Klein is also the author of the anonymous fictional account of the 1992 Democratic presidential primary process, *Primary Colors* (New York: Random House, 1996).

On the 2000 election, see Jeffrey Toobin, *Too Close to Call: The Thirty-Six-Day Battle to Decide the 2000 Election* (New York: Random House, 2001); Howard Gillman, *The Votes that Counted: How the Supreme Court Decided the 2000 Presidential Election* (Chicago: University of Chicago Press, 2001); and Richard Posner, *Breaking the Deadlock: The 2000 Election, the Constitution, and the Courts* (Princeton: Princeton University Press, 2001).

On terrorism and the rise of Osama bin Laden, see Lawrence Wright, *The Looming Tower: Al Qaeda and the Road to 9/11* (2006; New York: Vintage, 2007).

Notes

1 Hill's testimony is available on the University of Maryland's Institute for the Humanities database: http://mith.umd.edu/WomensStudies/GenderIssues/Sexual Harassment/hill-thomas-testimony (August 22, 2014).
2 Bush quoted in Mayer and Abramson, 20–21. Without challenging significant adversity in his early life, they also assert that, once taken in by his grandparents, Thomas lived a relatively affluent life. See in particular pages 40–41.
3 Mayer and Abramson, 299.
4 Mayer and Abramson discuss these throughout *Strange Justice*. They devote a chapter, "The Other Women," reviewing the evidence (321–350).
5 Kate Phillips, "Biden and Anita Hill, Revisited," *The New York Times*, August 23, 2008: http://thecaucus.blogs.nytimes.com/2008/08/23/biden-and-anita-hill-revisited/?_php=true&_type=blogs&_r=0 (August 22, 2014).
6 A key excerpt of Brock's retraction in *Blinded by the Right* can be read online: http://www.randomhouse.com/boldtype/0203/brock/excerpt.html (August 22, 2014).
7 "Slaveholders argued that slavery was a 'positive good' that civilized blacks and elevated them in every dimension of life," Thomas wrote in his opinion *Fisher v. University of Texas at Austin*. "A century later, segregationists similarly asserted that segregation was not only benign, but good for black students." http://www.huffingtonpost.com/2013/06/24/clarence-thomas-affirmative-action_n_3491433.html (August 22, 2014).
8 John Blake, "Three Questions for Clarence Thomas," CNN, June 25, 2013: http://www.cnn.com/2013/06/09/us/clarence-thomas-three-questions/ (August 22, 2013).

9   Patterson, *Restless Giant: The United States from Watergate to Bush v. Gore* (New York: Oxford University Press, 2005), 294–295; Joshua B. Freeman, *American Empire: The Rise of a Global Power/The Democratic Revolution at Home* (New York: Penguin, 2012), 448; Juan Gonzales, *Harvest of Empire:* A *History of Latinos in America*, revised ed. (2000; New York: Penguin, 2011), 197.

10 Dahlia Lithwick, "All These Issues Are Still with Us: Talking with Anita Hill," *Slate*, March 21, 2014: http://www.slate.com/articles/double_x/doublex/2014/03/talking_to_anita_hill_at_57_the_woman_who_stood_up_to_clarence_thomas_is.html.

11 James Patterson, *Restless Giant*, 245; see also *Time*, "The L.A. Riots: 15 Years After Rodney King" http://content.time.com/time/specials/2007/la_riot/article/0,28804,1614117_1614084_1614831,00.html (September 1, 2014).

12 Penelope McMillan, "Victim of Mob Assault Meets Man Who Saved His Life," *The Baltimore Sun*, May 9, 1992: http://articles.baltimoresun.com/1992-05-09/news/1992130030_1_lopez-newton-love-church (August 22, 2014); Mary Harris, "Good Samaritan Remembers the LA Riots 20 Years Later: 'I Had to Do Something,'" NBC4, Television News, Southern California, April 28, 2012: http://www.nbclosangeles.com/news/local/A-Good-Samaritan-Remembers–148613585.html (November 20, 2015).

13 Jeffrey Ogbar, *Hip-Hop Revolution: The Culture and Politics of Rap* (Lawrence: University Press of Kansas), 1, 39; for a critique of authenticity, see Tricia Rose's chapter on "keeping it real" in *The Hip Hop Wars: What We Talk about When We Talk About Hip Hop—and Why It Matters* (New York: Basic Books, 2008), 133–148. For a survey of hip-hop's critics, see Ogbar, 118–128.

14 Johnson, 140. Johnson devotes a section of his book to the Simpson case.

15 Johnson, 120.

16 Freeman, 446; Patterson, 271; Johnson, 459, 462.

17 Mayer and Abrahamson devote the first chapter of *Strange Justice* to the politics of the Thomas nomination for Bush; see in particular pages 16–18.

18 http://www.gallup.com/poll/116677/presidential-approval-ratings-gallup-historical-statistics-trends.aspx (August 24, 2014).

19 Pat Buchanan, "1992 Republican National Convention Speech," August 17, 1992: http://buchanan.org/blog/1992-republican-national-convention-speech-148 (August 24, 2014); Patterson, *Restless Giant*, 252.

20 Isabel Sawhill, "20 years later, it turns out Dan Quayle was right about Murphy Brown and unmarried moms," *The Washington Post*, May 25, 2012: http://www.washingtonpost.com/opinions/20-years-later-it-turns-out-dan-quayle-was-right-about-murphy-brown-and-unmarried-moms/2012/05/25/gJQAsNCJqU_story.html (August 24, 2012).

21 Patterson, 251.

22 Katharine Q. Seelye, "Cheney's Five Draft Deferments During the Vietnam Era Emerge as a Campaign Issue," *The New York Times*, May 1, 2004: http://www.nytimes.com/2004/05/01/politics/campaign/01CHEN.html (August 25, 2014); Johnson, 402.

23 Freeman, 420.

24 The Congressional Research Service report on NAFTA is available at https://fas.org/sgp/crs/row/R42965.pdf (June 21, 2015).

25 Patterson, *Restless Giant*, 328.

26 Timothy Noah, "Bill Clinton and the Meaning of 'Is,'" *Slate*, September 13, 1998: http://www.slate.com/articles/news_and_politics/chatterbox/1998/09/bill_

clinton_and_the_meaning_of_is.html (August 26, 2014); Johnson, 333. Johnson devotes a section of *The Best of Times* to the Lewinsky case.

27 Johnson, 408.

28 http://uspolitics.about.com/od/polls/l/bl_historical_approval.htm; http://www.gallup.com/poll/116584/presidential-approval-ratings-bill-clinton.aspx (August 26, 2014).

29 Patterson, 357–358; https://www.census.gov/hhes/www/poverty/data/census/1960/ (September 1, 2014).

30 Freeman, 455–456.

31 Much of the following discussion is a condensed version of the rise of the Internet in my book *A Short History of the Modern Media* (Malden, MA: Wiley-Blackwell, 2014), 246–257.

32 Freeman, 437–438; Johnson, 3.

33 http://www.cnn.com/interactive/2012/04/us/table.military.troops/ (August 30, 14).

34 Freeman, 434.

35 Wright, 127.

36 http://www.census.gov/prod/2001pubs/p23-207.pdf (August 31, 2014).

37 "Ten big dot.com busts," http://money.cnn.com/galleries/2010/technology/1003/gallery.dot_com_busts/ (November 20, 2015); Jean Folger, "5 Successful Companies that Survived the Dotcom Bubble," *Investopedia*, July 11, 2011: http://www.investopedia.com/financial-edge/0711/5-successful-companies-that-survived-the-dotcom-bubble.aspx (November 20, 2015).

38 Joseph Stiglitz, *Freefall: America, Free Markets, and the Sinking of the World Economy* (New York: Norton, 2010), 4.

39 Patterson, *Restless Giant*, 419.

40 Patterson, *Restless Giant*, 413.

Part IV
Present Tense

10

Comfort and Dread
The American Empire in Decline, 2001–present

Figure 10.1   FLAGGING: Wreckage in the aftermath of September 11, 2001. The most crippling single blow the United States sustained after Pearl Harbor, the attack was followed by a wave of national solidarity—and polarizing conflicts at home and abroad. US Navy photo by Journalist 1st Class Preston Keres [Public domain], via Wikimedia Commons.

Democratic Empire: The United States Since 1945, First Edition. Jim Cullen.
© 2017 Jim Cullen. Published 2017 by John Wiley & Sons, Inc.

Towering Collapse: 9/11

SEPTEMBER 11, 2001, was a spectacularly beautiful day in New York City. The weather turned a corner in sloughing off the hazy, limp humidity of summer—the sky was crystalline, and the air, while warm, lacked the edge that generates sweat.

I was getting ready for my second day in a new job as a high school history teacher at a school with one campus on the upper west side of Manhattan, and the other in the northern tip of the Bronx, where I was now heading. As was my wont, I had the *Today* show on television as background as I got dressed, circa 8:45 am, a little later than would become my custom because I didn't have early classes that day. A local reporter was explaining that a small plane had apparently flown into one of the two towers of the World Trade Center (WTC). This didn't distract me from getting into my pants and socks. However, by the time I had finished getting dressed, it was clear that the plane was not a small one and that the disaster it had caused was a very big one. While I was watching, I thought I saw another blip across the television screen. Whether or not I had actually seen it live on television, the fact was a second plane had flown into the second tower of the WTC.

By now, it was clear that I was watching a catastrophe unfold. I was located in southern Westchester County, about 20 miles away from the site of the explosions, and it was also clear that the disaster's impact was rippling in my direction: roads, bridges, and schools were closing. Should I go to work? Would I be able to get there? If I did, how—and when—would I get back? I wasn't sure who to call, and wasn't sure who I could reach (the answer, soon enough, would be no one). My wife and children had already scattered to their respective locations at work, school, and day care. After mulling it over while continuing to watch coverage of the event, I decided that I had to go to work: people might need me there. Less high-mindedly, I worried about the status of my job—what would people think, what would happen, if I failed to show up? The drive to work was eerily easy: there were few cars going southbound into the city, and no cars coming from there.

I was waiting at a red light when I heard on the radio that the South Tower of the WTC had collapsed. When I got to work, there were reports of hijacked planes—three? four? five?—heading in different directions. One crashed into the Pentagon, the symbol of US military supremacy, killing approximately 200 people. Another, apparently headed for the White House or the US Capitol, crashed in Pennsylvania after passengers mobilized to resist the hijackers. All perished, probably saving the lives of many more people.

I arrived at school in a state of anxiety. Parents of elementary school students descended on the adjacent building to pick up their kids. High school students made arrangements to get home; faculty, myself included, volunteered to provide lodgings to anyone who needed a place to go or stay. (I didn't get any takers, in part because I was still an unfamiliar face.) All our students eventually made their way home. But not all their parents did.

As September 11 stories go, mine isn't much of one. As with most Americans, I was not directly affected by the attacks. However, in an important sense—and this is really the point—the event was a watershed event in all our lives: a day, similar to the day President Kennedy was shot, that anyone who lived through it would never forget. But 9/11, as the event came to be known, was also a turning point in US history. It jarred the nation out of the relative sense of complacency that had characterized it since the end of the Cold War, and fostered a sense of security-consciousness that increasingly pervaded everyday life. This was particularly apparent in the role of government. To cite only the most obvious example, air travel became a much more complicated proposition with the creation of an entirely new bureaucracy, the Transportation Security Administration (TSA). There was also a much less obvious, but more insidious, intensification of surveillance in terms of the government's monitoring of phone traffic and Internet activity, largely resulting from passage of the USA Patriot Act in 2001, which gave the federal government vast new powers to monitor the activities of citizens as well as foreigners.

And yet, even as this was happening, there were also other developments— potentially quite dangerous ones—that were taking shape. If not exactly unnoticed, they were also not adequately addressed, either. These included a shift in the balance in geopolitical power in Asia; another sharp rise in national debt, more serious than that of the Reagan years; and a lack of regulation in financial markets that would cause an explosion of another kind by decade's end.

We continue to live in the shadow of 9/11: it in effect marks the beginning of the current historical moment—our time, as it were—in the way a pervasive notion of national decline began to take root in American life. Yes, there are alternating currents in this period in American history, and we'll get to them. But the feeling that the nation was just not what it used to be, that it was taking a wrong turn, was broad and deep.

As with all turning points in history, 9/11 was an event whose origins date back to long before 2001. These origins were the product of just over a century of American intervention in the affairs of other nations beyond the shores of the continental United States, beginning with the nation's colonization of the Philippines in the aftermath of the Spanish–American War of 1898. This is what empires do: they project their power as far as they can for as long as they can, bending other people to their will.

But—and this is crucial to keep in mind—expanding empires never enter a political vacuum. Even when they are unquestionably the most powerful actor in an international situation, there is always a prevailing set of conditions—as often as not, a prevailing set of conflicts—that require attention for mastery to be attained. Local rulers must be removed or appeased; rivals to those rulers require assessment and response. Sometimes a new power will even broker an agreement between warring factions in the name of peace (another name for imperial stability). But this isn't always possible. Sometimes pre-existing hatreds or new alliances complicate the picture; sometimes imperial powers misunderstand— or just plain fail to see—prevailing realities. Stability proves temporary; crises require attention; decisions prove to have surprising and unwelcome consequences. Personality and coincidence keep history from simply becoming an impersonal process of inevitable outcomes.

In no region of the world have US interactions been more complex than in the Middle East. A region that stretches from Turkey to Iran, embedded within the continents of Europe, Asia, and Africa, it is about as remote—culturally no less than geographically—as any part of the world from the United States. And yet, since the time of World War II, no region has consistently absorbed as much US government attention as the Middle East has.

There are three core reasons for this. The first, in a word, is oil. As noted in Chapter 6, the United States began the twentieth century as a major oil exporter, but it was discovered in the 1930s that Saudi Arabia had the world's largest oil reserves. The United States played a crucial (self-interested) role in helping that nation to develop its most valuable strategic resource—and, given its voracious energy needs, maintaining access to a stable oil supply became one of the most important considerations of US foreign policy.

The second major reason for US engagement in the Middle East was the birth, and subsequent survival, of the state of Israel. American support was crucial in the creation of a Jewish national state, and subsequent economic and military aid were vital, given the hostility of Israel's neighbors, who resented it for a number of reasons, principal among them the displacement of the native Palestinian population. In the decades following Israel's establishment, the nation became an increasingly important strategic ally of the United States, a relationship that has been intensified by longstanding ancestral ties between Israelis and a politically important minority of Americans. There has always been a significant element of domestic politics involved in US support for Israel.

This in turn leads to a third important reason why the Middle East has loomed large in the American imagination, one that was well established before the other two: the region's role as a religious crucible for the Abrahamic faiths of Judaism, Christianity, and Islam. This is not simply a matter, significant in its own right, that all three religions have long been represented in American life. It's also that they've been *used* in the service of a series of sometimes overlapping and competing mythologies. Since the 1970s, for example, evangelical Christians have had an enormous psychological investment in the state of Israel for their own prophetic (often apocalyptic) reasons. African Americans have long drawn parallels between Israelite captivity and exodus and their own—and, especially in the last half-century, others have identified with persecuted Muslims (sometimes at Israeli hands), a tendency obvious in Black Nationalist movements such as the Nation of Islam. Egypt is an Arab country and a Muslim country, but also an African country with significant sub-Saharan cultural dimensions, a point of pride for many African Americans. All these facts have elements not only in the way Americans have viewed the Middle East, but also in how they've viewed themselves.[1]

Within the region, the key dynamic has also been religious. The Middle East has been the cradle of a series of world religions, but, in the last 1,400 years, the pivotal one has been Islam. The Muslim faith was born in the Middle East (specifically Arabia), and the region has been the seat of a series of great Islamic empires, most recently that of the Ottomans. The slow decline of the Ottoman Empire, which included significant segments of Europe and North Africa, subjected the region to increasing colonial European influence in the first half the twentieth century, influence that passed to the United States in the second half of the century. Coming to terms with such outside non-Muslim forces—whether as a matter of accommodation or resistance to them—has been the central question in Middle Eastern politics for the last century.

This project of coming to terms has been complicated by the great diversity of the region, one that not only involves what is now a series of autonomous nations, but an ethnic division between Arab states such as Egypt and Jordan was well as non-Arab ones, notably Iran. There are also non-Arab Muslim states beyond the Middle East, among them Pakistan and Indonesia (which has the largest Muslim population in the world). Moreover, there are a series of varieties within Islam, not just the main branches of Sunni and Shiite (Shiites looked to Islamic founder Mohammed's son-in-law as his successor; Sunnis elected theirs), but also fundamentalist and mystical variations, comparable to those found in Christianity and Judaism. For much of the postwar period, control of Middle Eastern governments was largely in the hands of secular leaders who would alternately cut deals with religious figures as well as persecute them. With the Iranian Revolution of 1979, however, militant Islamists became a more powerful factor in regional politics, sometimes gaining control of governments, and a forceful presence to be reckoned with even when they didn't.

This was the context from which Osama bin Laden emerged. Bin Laden's vision of a rejuvenated Islam, one shared by many other radical Islamists—and appealing to some non-radical ones—initially focused on expelling the Soviets from Afghanistan in the 1980s. Once that objective was achieved, bin Laden turned his attention to the United States. Certainly, there had been people in the Middle East who hated Americans long before bin Laden came along, and were willing to resort to terrorism to make their point. But bin Laden was unique for the scope of his ambitions, his wealth of resources, and the logistical skill he brought to the task—which is not to say that he always succeeded. Early bin Laden–supervised terrorist efforts were amateurish; many were unsuccessful. But, by the late 1990s, he had established a name for himself on the basis of simultaneous bombings in Kenya and Tanzania and on the American warship USS *Cole* (see Chapter 9).

Bin Laden's objection to the United States in the 1990s was its military presence in Saudi Arabia during and after the Persian Gulf War, which he regarded as obscene. He also believed that, while Americans were imperialists, they were also a weak-minded people who would crumple once they were forced to fight a committed enemy, a proposition he supported with reference to the American withdrawal from Vietnam and from Lebanon after a 1983 bombing there. His goal, typical of terrorists everywhere, was to provoke a militarily more powerful enemy, expose its inability to protect its own citizens, goad it into action—hopefully *over*reaction—and mobilize opposition from within and without that would lead to its destruction.

To a significant degree, bin Laden succeeded. The September 11 attacks, which involved 19 suicide bombers working for months to plan, train, and execute the operation, was the most devastating attack on US soil since Pearl Harbor (and on the nation's capital since the War of 1812). The death toll of almost 3,000 people made it the bloodiest day in American history since the Civil War. Once the initial shock passed, the overwhelming American response was anger, and there was little question that the United States was going to retaliate. The question was how. The answer proved to be deeply problematic.

There were suspicions from the outset that bin Laden was responsible for September 11, in part because a number of investigators from the FBI and CIA were closing in on the planned attacks but were tragically suspicious of each other and unwilling to share information and/or authority. There was also testimony of bin Laden himself in a series of videos he released at the time. But once there was reasonable confidence that 9/11 was an al Qaeda operation, the US government was faced with the difficulty of responding to an adversary that was not a traditional nation-state. Some wondered if the better way to frame the challenge was in terms of a police action rather than a war footing. The policing framework was rejected by President George W. Bush, who declared a "War on Terror," though FBI posters at the time declared that bin Laden was wanted "Dead or Alive," giving the quest to capture him the flavor an old Western. What was also odd about the Bush administration's approach to the War on Terror was that the president also emphasized that Americans should go about their business, and engage in activities such as shopping rather than try to mobilize a sense of collective purpose. His political program, meanwhile, continued as if nothing had happened. "How urgent can this be," asked Democratic senator Joe Biden of Delaware, "if I tell you that this is a great crisis and, at the very time we're marching to war, I give you the single largest tax cut in the history of the United States of America?"[2]

It was widely believed that bin Laden's operations were based in Afghanistan near the Pakistan border, a favored locale since the time of his operations against the Soviets in the 1980s. For a number of years, he had been the guest of the Taliban, the fundamentalist faction that ruled most of Afghanistan since the time of the Soviet withdrawal. When, in the weeks following the attacks, the Taliban refused to turn over bin Laden, Congress voted to give Bush the authorization to go to war with Afghanistan. By November 2001, a coalition of the United States, its allies, and opponents to the Afghan regime succeeded in toppling the Taliban. Bin Laden, however, escaped into the remote mountains of Pakistan, whose government would prove to be an unreliable ally in the years that followed.

Though defeating the Taliban was relatively easy, capturing bin Laden and imposing a stable order in Afghanistan were significant challenges for the American military. Similar to the Mongols, British, and Soviets before them, Americans found that the nation—if such a term can be applied to a highly tribal society—proved very difficult to govern. The United States officially ended combat operations in Afghanistan in 2014 (though US troops still remain there), making it the longest armed conflict in US history. Achieving a stable order in that country might have been manageable, and more quickly accomplished, had not another agenda ended up dominating US foreign policy: a second war with Iraq.

Unknown Unknowns: The Iraq War

Though the United States had won the Persian Gulf War against Iraq with surprising speed in 1991, there were a number of influential Americans unhappy with the outcome. President George H. W. Bush, mindful of the multinational coalition he assembled with the understanding that war aims were limited to expelling Iraqi forces from Kuwait, decided to leave Saddam Hussein in power after that objective had been achieved. But this decision left Saddam free to brutally put down challenges to his rule, which proved particularly murderous in the case of Kurds in the northern part of that country. Others worried about Saddam's ability to cause ongoing mischief outside his borders, which included a foiled plot to assassinate Bush. The imposition of a US Air Force–monitored no-fly zone, which effectively made much of the country off-limits to Saddam's military, helped keep him in check. Nevertheless, senior Republican policymakers during the 1990s argued that the United States needed to go in to finish the job, and, in 1998, a Republican Congress succeeded in pressuring a politically weakened Bill Clinton, mired in the Lewinsky scandal, to sign the Iraq Liberation Act, which called for regime change in that country.[3]

Once George W. Bush took office, Iraq hawks—among them Vice President Dick Cheney, Defense Secretary Donald Rumsfeld, and Rumsfeld's assistant Paul Wolfowitz—were in a much better position to press their case. Officials in the administration floated the idea of taking on Saddam the first month Bush was in office, and within minutes of the September 11 attacks Wolfowitz told his aides that he suspected Iraq was involved. According to notes taken that day, Rumsfeld said he wanted "best info fast. Judge whether good enough hit S. H. [Saddam Hussein] @ same time. Not only UBL [Usama—meaning Osama—bin Laden]."[4]

Was Saddam Hussein involved in the 9/11 attacks? There's no question of his enmity toward the United States: he would have been if he could have. Saddam had already demonstrated his willingness to go to any length to attack his enemies; he had used poison gas not only against Iran in the long and bitter war with that country in the 1980s, but also against the Kurds, who were citizens of Iraq (though not Muslim). There were also longstanding suspicions that he was developing biological, chemical, or nuclear weapons of mass destruction (WMDs). On the other hand, Saddam was pretty boxed in by 2001. Moreover, he was not a natural ally for Osama bin Laden: though both were Arab Sunni Muslims, Saddam was a largely secular leader whose governing style resembled that of an older generation of Middle East military strongmen, such as Egypt's Gamal Abdel Nasser or Libya's Muammar Qaddafi. Such people looked upon Muslim fundamentalists with suspicion if not hostility. It was hardly unthinkable that bin Laden and Saddam would collaborate. But the evidence that they'd actually done so was murky at best.

For key members of the Bush administration, however, establishing such a tie was not especially important. As far as they were concerned, Saddam simply had to go, and the administration and its supporters would make any plausible claims to make their case, which many journalism outlets accepted. Administration officials asserted that there was a meeting between a representative of the Iraqi regime and one of the September 11 hijackers in the Czech city of Prague, for which there was no clear evidence; they continued to say that Saddam had tried to acquire materials to build nuclear weapons in the African nation of Niger, even though the evidence they cited was demonstrably untrue. In the end, though, the burden of proof was not on the Bush administration. Instead, it was on members of Congress who were afraid of claiming that Saddam was not a threat and subsequently having to answer for another September 11. Over the course of 2002, the administration led a steady drumbeat against what the president called an "Axis of Evil" consisting of Iran, North Korea, and Iraq, only the last of which could attacked in relative safety (North Korea had the backing of China; Iran was a much larger and more dangerous adversary).

When faced with a resolution to support the Bush administration in a pre-emptive war of choice to overthrow the Iraqi regime in October 2002, some of the nation's most prominent politicians, among them New York senator and future presidential aspirant Hillary Clinton, decided that the safe vote was one for war. Both houses of Congress approved the war resolution. In February 2003, Secretary of State Colin Powell, who had strong reservations about attacking Iraq, nevertheless made a presentation to the United Nations, claiming that Saddam had WMDs. The UN at that point had been conducting years of inspections in Iraq, and had found no substantial evidence. But the administration was no longer willing to wait. In March 2003, the invasion of Iraq got underway.

Once again, the US armed forces achieved rapid and decisive success. Within a matter of weeks, the Iraqi army was defeated, Saddam was overthrown, and the United States was in control of the country. Secretary of Defense Rumsfeld was determined to win the war on a shoestring; a lean fast army prevailed in a way that made him look like a genius. (After a long manhunt, Saddam himself was captured in December. He was turned over to the Iraqis, who tried, convicted, and hanged him.) On May 2, 2003, a triumphant President Bush landed on a returning aircraft carrier off the Pacific coast of California, and gave a speech marking the end of major combat operations. A huge banner behind him bore the words "Mission Accomplished."

And then Iraq began to fall apart. The nation's infrastructure, which was fraying under Saddam, began to break down—electrical outages became widespread, sewage systems failed, civic institutions ceased to function. Even worse, looting became widespread. The skeletal force that the United States sent into

Iraq could conquer, but it was simply too small to maintain order, much less rebuild the country, and the Iraqi exiles that the United States brought in lacked credibility among the nation's inhabitants. The administration had been adamant all along that Iraq could be rebuilt quickly and cheaply—to say otherwise would have weakened support for the war. The administration budged US$50–US$60 billion for the effort. When a Bush economic adviser suggested that the war would cost US$100–US$200 billion—a 2013 estimate by the news agency Reuters put it at over US$2 trillion—he was fired. Similarly, when Army Chief of Staff Eric Shinseki told the Senate Armed Services committee before the war that he believed the United States would need twice as many troops as Rumsfeld was advocating, Bush and Rumsfeld pointedly declined to attend his retirement ceremony.[5]

The American postwar plan for Iraq was focused on the Coalition Provisional Authority (CPA), a civilian agency headed by Lieutenant General Jay Garner, who had run a humanitarian operation that saved the lives of many Kurds after the Persian Gulf War. But the growing disorder in Iraq led to his replacement by Paul Bremer, a Rumsfeld protégé. Both Garner and Bremer worked feverishly to restore normalcy to everyday Iraqi life, but while substantial resources were often allocated to this work, contracts often went to less-than-qualified people and/or those with close ties to the Bush administration, giving rise to suspicions of cronyism. Such problems were made worse by the fact that the CPA operated in a highly fortified area of Baghdad known as the Green Zone, effectively isolated from the Iraqi people. The Green Zone had air conditioning, a swimming pool, sports bars, and a fleet of SUVs. But there were almost no Americans who could speak Arabic.[6]

The United States' failure to maintain order in Iraq was not only embarrassing—it was also dangerous. Pre-war planning had turned on the question of WMDs. But Saddam, who had dismantled his WMD program several years back, played a cat-and-mouse game with the United States, the UN, and even some of his own advisers. What he really focused his energy on was developing the means to conduct an insurgency.[7] Saddam was never able to control the country after the invasion, but many of the people he trained were able to continue the fight in a combat style known as "asymmetrical warfare": avoiding direct conflict with a militarily stronger enemy, but using methods—in the case of the Iraqis and the foreign allies who flocked to their banner, this included improvised explosive devices (IEDs)—that kept an occupier off balance. The CPA played into this strategy by disbanding the Iraqi army and firing all government workers who had achieved anything over minimal standing in Saddam's Baath Party, a move that cleansed the country of past misdeeds but also deprived it of considerable know-how and provided US enemies with fresh recruits.

Meanwhile, civil unrest fostered the growth of radical militias who alternately competed for the allegiance of Iraqis and terrorized them. Ironically, while there's no evidence of al Qaeda collaboration with Saddam Hussein *before* the war—he routinely harassed radical Islamists—there is evidence that al Qaeda fighters did flock into the country *after* the war.[8] Whatever the source of subversion, overstretched US forces were under increasing threat in trying to conduct the business of rebuilding the country. They were also increasingly exhausted; manpower shortages in Iraq as well as Afghanistan led the government to force US soldiers to endure multiple tours of duty, fraying bodies as well as minds.

The reputation of the United States was also severely damaged by the way it handled captured enemies. There was widespread disgust at home and abroad in 2004 when media reports revealed the brutal treatment of Iraqi prisoners at Abu Ghraib prison in the capital city of Bagdad. Though the government denied it, most observers agreed that the tactics practiced there—and at the US military base at Guantanamo Bay, Cuba, where suspected terrorists and enemy combatants from the Middle East and Afghanistan were brought and could be handled outside the confines of US law—met the definition of torture. This sense of disgust was intensified by the series of memos written by Attorney General Alberto Gonzales and his deputy John Yoo, which argued that the United States was not obligated to honor the Geneva Conventions, a series of rules adopted by many nations and strongly supported by the United States, to ensure humane treatment of prisoners of war. (The Bush administration's position was that enemy non-combatants were not covered by the Geneva Conventions, and that techniques such as waterboarding, a method of simulated drowning that dates back to the United States' handling of the Filipino insurrection of 1899, did not amount to torture.[9]) Over time, Guantanamo Bay became a huge headache for the American government, because many prisoners who were not deemed a threat could not go home safely, be taken in by other countries, or accepted into the United States (local and state governments were afraid of the security risk). Americans were received rapturously as liberators in Europe after World War II. This had been the hope for the wars in Iraq and even Afghanistan. Instead, people there and elsewhere found themselves wondering how much different Americans were from the tyrants that preceded them.

Ironically, the most obvious beneficiary of the Iraq War was Iran, an avowed US enemy. Similar to Iran, the majority of the Iraqi population is Shiite, but, for many centuries, Iraq had been ruled by Sunnis (Baghdad is an important Sunni cultural and religious center dating back to the time of the breach within Islam in the seventh century). The overthrow of the Saddam regime created a political vacuum in which Shiites—and, in particular, fundamentalist and militant Shiites—moved rapidly to fill with Iranian help. Actually, the United States also favored the Shiites, who had been shut out of power by Saddam's Ba'ath Party. This is why much of the armed opposition in Iraq came from Sunnis. That said, one of the most prominent sources of opposition to the US occupation came from the so-called Mahdi army, led by the Shiite political leader Moqtada al-Sadr, son of a highly respected cleric who was especially successful in rallying opposition to the United States.

By 2006, Iraq had fully descended into military and political chaos. Secretary of Defense Rumsfeld, who continued to insist that his approach to the war and its aftermath was legitimate—"stuff happens" was his famous response to the outbreak of looting in Iraq—became a subject of worldwide derision and resigned. Vice President Cheney kept his job, but his influence in the Bush administration waned. Bush now paid more attention to moderate voices, such as Condoleezza Rice, who succeeded Colin Powell as Secretary of State, moving up from her position as National Security Adviser (where she had failed to act on warnings of an imminent attack using airplanes in the weeks before September 11).

Some influential voices, among them Arizona senator John McCain, and General David Petraeus, who commanded multi-national forces in Iraq, argued that the United States needed to intervene more, not less, aggressively. They called for a "surge" of US troops and resources. The proposal was controversial, but the Bush administration acted on this advice in 2007, and it did help stabilize the country. Violence diminished, state functions resumed, and a new government was organized. But oil production remained below what it had been under Saddam. And the war, the bloodiest in US history since Vietnam, had resulted in an estimated 4,500 US and over 100,000 Iraqi deaths.[10] American forces finally withdrew from Iraq in 2011, leaving behind a shaky country wracked by internal violence and external threats, notably that of the Islamic State of Iraq and Syria (ISIS), an extremist transnational Muslim regime that invaded the country in 2014 and became a significant geopolitical force in the region.

The September 11 bombings and failures in Iraq and Afghanistan effectively erased the sense of triumphalism that pervaded American society in the dozen years following the fall of the Berlin Wall. This sense of despair and frustration did not extend to the military, which, most observers agreed, had generally performed with impressive proficiency. Its shortcomings—even terrible ones such as the treatment of prisoners at Abu Ghraib—were substantially ones of leadership: of underestimating costs, literal and figurative; of demanding too much of soldiers, who endured multiple tours of duty under often harrowing physical and psychological conditions; and of deceit and willful ignorance in the way the Bush administration and its most hawkish ideologues waged war and peace.

That said, not all the blame for the fiasco (the title of an important account of the war)[11] can be laid at the feet of the Bush administration. The American journalism establishment, which prided itself on the independence and skepticism of its reporters and editors, largely failed to challenge the administration's version of events. Meanwhile, war critics and supporters alike tended to speak in abstractions and take undue pleasure in the other side being proven wrong; any given fact that emerged about the war was often used to justify a pre-existing position.[12]

The fact that there was no military draft in the Iraq War, and that the government made no effort to reinstate it, was crucial. Had more young Americans been compelled to go abroad and fight against their will, the war would surely have engendered resistance of the kind the nation saw during Vietnam. Instead, volunteers were saddled with an unfair burden. The Bush administration's unwillingness to admit the real costs of the war, whether among themselves or to anyone else, was in a sense realistic: if the nation fully faced the cost of nation-building in Iraq in financial terms, not to mention human ones, support for it would surely have been significantly weaker.

Spending Resources: The Debt Society

For all the tumult in the first decade of the twenty-first century, most citizens of the United States experienced the war in isolation, which, while hardly blissful, was nevertheless substantial. On the surface at least, the domestic economy was relatively tranquil once the nation emerged from the sharp downturn of 2000–2001. In particular, the real-estate market began to grow rapidly by mid-decade. The rise in price valuations made Americans who owned their homes richer. Many used the rising value of this asset as collateral to borrow money—often at surprisingly low interest rates—against the value of their property, which was spent in ways that ranged from making home repairs to taking family vacations. This could be a smart strategy when it enhanced the value of a property or helped pay down other kinds of debt. But such home equity loans could be potentially dangerous if property values declined, in which case it was possible a homeowner could end up owing more than a house was worth. Yet, to many, that seemed unlikely, even impossible.

The American government took a comparably debt-driven approach in its own finances, taking advantage of low interest rates to pay for annual budget deficits that resumed after the Bush administration passed tax cuts. The galloping national debt—greatly intensified by the wars in Iraq and Afghanistan, paid with borrowed money—was increasingly financed by foreign nations. China was an especially important source of capital, in large measure because its heavily state-run economy was growing so rapidly that it needed a place to park its growing surplus of cash. The Chinese also manipulated their currency to keep the price of its products low, encouraging foreign buyers while maintaining cultural and economic barriers for foreign companies seeking to do business in China. Between 2001 and 2010, Americans bought almost US$2 trillion more in Chinese goods than the Chinese did American goods. By that point, China was also the largest holder of US debt, with financial reserves in excess of US$3 trillion. By cutting off loans or dumping reserves, China was in a position to wreck the US economy, though only at great harm to itself, suggesting the uneasy embrace that characterized relations between the two nations.[13]

Though he was a conservative Republican who professed to dislike government bureaucracy, Bush implemented a few major programs during his presidency. His legislative agenda was helped by Republican control of the House, coupled with a narrowly split Senate where he only needed a stray vote or two to go his way.

One of Bush's signature programs was No Child Left Behind (NCLB), an ambitious educational reform package passed in 2001 that focused on teacher accountability through standardized testing. The law was controversial, and especially unpopular with the education establishment, but enjoyed some support among liberals (among them Ted Kennedy, in the final years of his long Senate career), who believed that a focus on educational outcomes, if coupled with greater resources for students and teachers, made sense. In recent years, the NCLB approach has gradually lost ground, especially amid concern that educators simply "teach to the test" at the exclusion of many other important topics and approaches. Much attention in the 2010s has focused on the Common Core, a set of shared curricular standards. Initially bipartisan, the Common Core has become increasingly controversial (neither left nor right tends to like prescriptive standards). Contentiousness over educational reform in the United States is seemingly inevitable in a country where schooling remains a matter of local financing and control, a situation unique in the Western world, and one that permits a vast disparity in educational resources and outcomes in rich and poor communities.

Another major law passed by Bush during his presidency was an expansion of Medicare in 2003 that, for the first time, allowed significant coverage for prescription medication. This was hailed as an important expansion of the welfare state. But the law was complicated. One example of this was the "doughnut hole" provision, whereby, after a certain point, coverage stopped until an individual had reached a maximum out-of-pocket limit, after which it resumed. The Medicare expansion also reflected a broader Bush administration strategy of giving a relatively modest benefit to a lot of people, and then giving a *huge* benefit to small economic elites. In this case, the elite group in question was the pharmaceutical industry, which now in effect had a major new customer in the form of the federal government. Of course, such economic windfalls for private companies—particularly among those with close ties to the administration in power—are typical consequences of all forms of welfare. But the new law was notable for preventing competitive bids on drugs, which would have made prices lower and given Americans more options. Powerful drug companies also sought to prevent the expiration patents on older medications by paying off manufacturers of generic drugs not to make them when they were legally entitled to do so. This kept even older drugs more expensive than they otherwise would be.

The Bush strategy of small benefits for the many and big handouts for the few was most obvious in tax policy. A second wave of tax cuts in 2003 meant most Americans got a bump in their refunds in their tax returns, or less withheld from their paychecks. But the real bonanza went to the wealthiest Americans, who garnered a greater share of national wealth—52.5% of the Bush tax cuts went to the richest 5% of households.[14] Such reductions in tax revenue meant less income for the federal government, which continued to spend money on wars abroad—for the first time in wartime, an administration did not raise taxes—and go deeper into debt with domestic programs. This is exactly what some conservatives wanted: a starve-the-beast situation in which the government would eventually become incapable of sustaining such spending and start to dismantle the welfare state.

Bushed: Second-Term Blues

Bush's domestic policies in his first years in office were reasonably popular, and sustained the base of political support that rallied around him after September 11, when his popularity soared. This was important because, by

2004, it was clear that the Iraq War was not going well. Going into his re-election bid, Bush was vulnerable, but a highly divided electorate might still break his way.

To challenge him in that election, the Democrats turned to John Kerry of Massachusetts, who prevailed in the primary campaign after a surprisingly strong early showing by Governor Howard Dean of Vermont, who mobilized the party's left wing (another challenger, John Edwards of North Carolina, was chosen for the vice presidential ticket). A decorated Vietnam War veteran who later became a prominent critic of the conflict, Kerry was seen as an effective challenger because his military experience stood in sharp contrast to "chicken hawks" such as Bush and Cheney who had avoided serving in that war. Bush supporters mounted a direct assault on Kerry's military service that proved surprisingly effective, however. Shadowy private funding—"527" groups (named for their place in the tax code) who were officially separate from the presidential campaigns but in fact did dirty work for both sides—paid for a series of ads by the "Swift Boat Veterans for Truth," which made a series of factually inaccurate claims questioning Kerry's role in the mission on a swift boat naval vessel for which was he awarded a Silver Star for bravery in combat.[15] The ads were nevertheless effective in sowing doubt about Kerry, who voted in favor of war with Iraq, though he claimed Bush mishandled it.

Patrician in manner and extremely wealthy due to a fortuitous marriage, Kerry was less than an entirely charismatic politician. He also had a reputation for irresolution. In a 2003 Senate vote, Kerry supported a US$87 billion bill to fund operations in Iraq before voting against the version that passed, leading him to defend himself against critics by saying "I actually did vote for US$87 billion before I voted against it," a line critics used to paint him as a ip-flopper on the issues.[16] The most riveting moment of the 2004 Democratic National Convention came when a relative unknown, Barack Obama of Illinois, gave a speech on his behalf.

The 2004 election results showed a closely divided electorate that resembled the electorate of 2000: Democrats strong on the coast, the upper Midwest, and generally in cities; Republicans strong in the South and the rural heartland. Bush won 50.7% of the popular vote, his Electoral College majority hinging on the state of Ohio. He was thus able to lay claim to the electoral majority that eluded him in 2000.

Even Bush partisans would concede that his second term, as with so many presidential second terms, did not go well. A 2005 bid to privatize Social Security, replacing the New Deal–era insurance program with personal savings accounts, ran into implacable resistance. Bush also suffered a political setback with the Supreme Court. When Justice Sandra Day O'Connor announced her retirement in 2005, Bush nominated John Roberts, a conservative judge who had served in the Reagan administration. Roberts was a generally well-received choice and was quickly confirmed. When Chief Justice William Rehnquist died of cancer a few weeks later, Bush sought to promote Roberts to the top slot—again not a problem—but nominated White House counsel Harriet Miers, a woman widely regarded as lacking sufficient qualifications for the job, to fill the seat Roberts vacated to take that of Rehnquist. After a poor showing in meetings with senators, she withdrew her candidacy (the job eventually went to Samuel Alito, who has been a stalwart conservative voice on the court). Miers was also involved with Attorney General Gonzales in a highly controversial mass firing of Justice Department attorneys for what appeared to be political reasons.

Bush's biggest domestic failure, however, was his handling of Hurricane Katrina and its aftermath in the late summer of 2005. The storm, which killed over 1,800 people and caused economic damage in excess of US$100 billion, devastated the Mississippi, Alabama, and Louisiana coasts. But New Orleans bore the brunt of the storm, which plunged much of the city underwater. And yet, what may have been worse was the aftermath, which revealed local and national government mismanagement on a colossal scale. While the Federal Emergency Management Agency (FEMA) was created in 1979 to assist local authorities in the aftermath of natural disasters, the Bush administration sought to privatize its functions and named two political associates, Joe Allbaugh and his deputy Michael Brown, to run the agency, even though they had little experience in disaster management. (Allbaugh left before Katrina.) Bush was slow to react to the crisis in New Orleans, and slow to recognize that the government's response was appallingly deficient. "Brownie, you're doing a heckuva job," he famously praised Brown, who would resign in disgrace 2 weeks later. There were widespread suspicions that the inadequacy of the government's response had something to do with the fact that a large proportion of the city's population was African American. Countless people died waiting for help, and the facilities set up to help them, among them the New Orleans Superdome, were dangerous and harrowing. "People died in the camp," one woman later related of her experience. "We saw bodies lying there." She described officials at the scene as "all about detention, as if it were Iraq, like we were foreigners and they were fighting a war. They implemented war-like conditions. They treated us worse than prisoners of war."[17] Democratic New Orleans mayor Ray Nagin, who also came in for severe criticism, ultimately went to jail for bribery committed before and after Katrina. Louisiana governor Kathleen Blanco, also a Democrat, and also politically damaged by the storm, did not run for re-election.

No one was more politically damaged than Bush, however, who in domestic terms had become a lame duck by the end of 2005. In 2006, a scandal involving Florida Representative Mark Foley's sending of sexually suggestive messages to congressional interns, and Republican efforts to cover it up despite their stance of being the party of so-called family values, weakened the Republican brand generally and allowed Democrats to retake both the Senate as well as the House, where California Rep. Nancy Pelosi became the first woman ever to be elected Speaker of the House. It was at this point that a sense of political gridlock set in; neither party was able to gain a decisive upper hand—a situation that remained largely true for the next decade.

Downloading: Twenty-first Century Pop Culture

For all the turmoil roiling the nation in the first decade of the twenty-first century, there were also alternating currents of excitement and possibility. As has often been the case, much of this excitement was in the realm of technology. In particular, new media were reshaping the most fundamental experiences of what it meant to read a book or listen to a record—and, for that matter, the very definition of words such as "book" or "record."

The first, and perhaps most pervasive, transformation occurred in the world of music, where a sound recording had always taken the form of some kind of physical object. At the turn of the twenty-first century, the accelerating pace of computer technology made it possible to replace the once-cutting-edge compact disc with computer files that could be recorded, stored—and, thanks to the Internet, transmitted—instantly from one computer to another (or one computer to a great many others).

The problem for record companies and musicians was that you didn't have to buy anything to do this. The music industry was never happy about the way magnetic tape made it possible to copy recordings. But the ability to move entire record collections via downloads through music-sharing programs such as Napster, which flourished on college campuses at the millennium, posed a mortal threat to the industry's entire economic model. Legal action against Napster led to its shutdown in 2001. Eventually, commercial operators in the music business harnessed Napster's ability to move files online to a market model, most notably Apple, whose iTunes Store began selling individual songs for 99 cents, cheap enough that buying seemed easier and safer than illegal methods. Apple's breakthrough listening device was the iPod, first introduced in 2001. With the development of the iPhone in 2007, listening to music completed a transition that began with Sony's Walkman a quarter-century earlier, becoming a fully portable experience integrated into a device that performed any number of everyday tasks, be it taking a picture, playing a game, or shopping for shoes. This made popular music both more pervasive and perhaps more ancillary to American life. Certainly, the music industry suffered; record sales dipped sharply early in the century and have never recovered. In the second decade of the century, the digital music business began to shift away from downloading to streaming, a subscription-based model where you didn't even buy music anymore but simply accessed a seemingly limitless database, a model successfully developed by services such as Pandora and Spotify (eventually Apple would get into this game, too).

The financial basis of the industry had changed. Once musical acts toured as a means to promote the sales of records (or royalties from radio broadcasting); now, records are a means to support tours, and, if there's money to be made on a song, it's more likely to come from its use in a commercial or a movie than a hit on radio (which has also migrated online to a significant degree). The diffusion of technology has made it easier than ever to make a record. But it's also harder than ever to become a star.[18]

There still were a few, however. Most of the big ones had established themselves during the heart of the rock era, such as Bruce Springsteen and U2, who could still fill stadiums effortlessly. But a handful of new ones also emerged in the 2000s, notably Taylor Swift, a Pennsylvania native who moved to Nashville at the turn of the century and established herself as a country star. Similar to earlier generations of female country singers such as Shania Twain, Swift edged her way into pop music. Her breakthrough album in this regard, *Fearless* (2008), showcased her ability to capture a female adolescent experience with a freshness that made familiar emotions seem compelling. By the time of *Red* (2012) and *1989* (2014), her tribute to 1980s pop, Swift had demonstrated her ability to work in a series of pop genres, as well as her staying power with an emerging generation of young women. Another important female pop singer, Beyoncé Knowles, began her career as a member of the successful R&B group Destiny's Child before striking out on her own in a career that suggested the unprecedented degree to which women now dominated the music business. Her 2008 album *I Am … Sasha Fierce* made Beyoncé—famous enough to be referred to by her first name—the most dominant figure in pop music since Madonna a generation earlier. The video for a hit single from that album, "Single Ladies (Put a Ring on It)," was patterned on an African ring shout that dated back to the age of slavery, simultaneously conveying Beyoncé's gifts as a dancer and her ability to embody a sense of up-to-the-minute cool, though many of the moves for that video were borrowed from choreographer Bob Fosse's famous "Mexican Breakfast" performed by Gwen Vernon.

By the first decade of the twenty-first century, hip-hop had been the most influential genre in American music for 30 years. This gave it a sense of depth and self-awareness that its most gifted practitioners were able to exploit to great effect. The rapper without peer in this regard was Kanye West, whose 2004 debut album *The College Dropout* was a treasure trove of musical allusions documenting the complexity of the African American experience in the new century. Another rapper, Jay-Z, attained a comparable level of prestige and staying power with *The Black Album* (2003), a record often cited as landmark in the history of hip-hop. His 2009 collaboration with pop star Alicia Keys, "Empire State of Mind," a tribute to New York City, evokes grandeur comparable to Frank Sinatra's 1977 hit "New York, New York." Jay-Z's 2008 marriage to Beyoncé' made them the reigning couple of American popular music (amid chronic rumors of breakups).

Dramatic as it was, the transformation of recorded music in the twenty-first century pales in comparison to what happened to book publishing in that decade, which experienced its biggest shakeup since the codex, or bound book, replaced scrolls as the dominant format for reading in Roman times. The revolutionary development in question was the arrival of the e-book as a viable reading technology. Its arrival was long foreseen; the spread of the Internet, which permitted the creation, storage, and transmission of large written records in portable document format (PDF), meant that electronic books were at least informally in existence since at least the 1990s. But Amazon.com's 2007 introduction of the

Kindle, an electronic device dedicated to reading, made e-books practical, attractive, and economically viable. By 2012, e-books accounted for 22% of the publishing market, and seem poised to go steadily higher as technological refinements (among them the ability to download books instantly, search and highlight text, synchronize reading across devices, and other features) gradually chipped away at the most attractive features of bound books.[19] Paper seems unlikely to disappear entirely however; the portability of printed volumes, which do not require batteries or Internet access, still offer advantages, and their sensory appeal, from sight to smell, remains considerable. The bound book, one of the most successful technologies ever invented, will not disappear overnight.

The same might be said for reading as a pastime. Though print publishing is the oldest, and from a market standpoint, smallest, of the mass media, it continues to have a disproportionate impact on popular culture. In part, that's because it remains a potent source of content for other media, ranging from radio talk shows to latest Hollywood films. But amid what seems like perpetual laments about the benighted state of reading in the United States, important books and articles continue to be written and read.

One of the more notable developments in publishing in the early twenty-first century is the emergence of young-adult fiction as an engine of the industry as well as an important source of artistry that compelled attention from adolescents and adults alike. The international star without peer in this regard was the British writer J. K. Rowling, whose *Harry Potter* books (1997–2007) were wildly popular globally and were made into blockbuster movies. So were the novels by the US writer Suzanne Collins, whose *Hunger Games* trilogy (2008–2010) also went Hollywood, as did the *Twilight* vampire novels of Stephenie Meyer (2005–2008). Vampire stories were especially popular early in the century across a variety of media, ranging from video games such as *Castlevania* to the hit television series *True Blood* (2008–2014), based on the Sookie Stackhouse novels (2001–2013) of Charlaine Harris, interpreted by some as an allegory of gay rights.

In literary fiction, the first decade of the twentieth century was marked by the prominence of big social novels and a new emphasis on the importance of plot. Some writers (notably non-fiction-writer-turned-novelist Tom Wolfe) had been calling for this since the 1980s, but, by the twenty-first century, even products of graduate writing programs, which typically focused on other literary elements such as character and language, were now paying new attention to the role of narrative. So it was, for example, that novelist Jonathan Franzen wrote a pair of family sagas, *The Corrections* (2001) and *Freedom* (2010), which incorporated significant elements of social history. Philip Roth enjoyed a late-career burst of creativity that included *The Human Stain* (2000), a fierce critique of political correctness, and *The Plot Against America* (2004), a counter-history that imagines the defeat of Franklin Delano Roosevelt in the presidential election of 1940 and his replacement with the isolationist, anti-Semitic Charles Lindbergh. However, postmodern fiction continued to maintain, even consolidate, its place in contemporary US fiction. Toni Morrison extended her run as a major—in many eyes, *the* major—American novelist with work such as *A Mercy* (2008), which projected her fractured, multivalent exploration of African American life to the earliest days of slavery. David Foster Wallace became the premier voice of the successors to the Baby Boom, Generation X, with celebrated novels such as *Infinite Jest* (1996), as well as postmodern non-fiction such as his 2005 collection of essays, *Consider the Lobster*. Wallace's writings were notable for their Internet sensibility—they were laced with footnotes and sidebars that changed a reader's spatial relationship to reading. His career was cut tragically short by his suicide in 2008.

The popularity of such writers suggested the degree to which new technological changes did not necessarily or immediately change cultural discourse. While the arts always operate in a larger social, political, and technological context, the source of creativity is never solely defined by such considerations: good storytelling has a mind, and a heart, of its own.

The complex interplay between the changing structures of media industries and old-fashioned storytelling was especially obvious in the case of television. By the early twenty-first century, traditional network television had already been experiencing decline for a generation, as alternative forms of broadcasting such as cable ate into their market share and competing media provided new ways for Americans to spend their free time. But the changing rules of the game also created opportunities for the industry—and for the artists who flocked to cable channels for the opportunities and creative freedom no longer widely available in a Hollywood obsessed with blockbusters, sequels, and comic book franchises. The advent of high-definition television, which had to overcome a series of technical hurdles and commercial disagreements, finally became widespread early in the century, prompting a new wave of television-buying and a better viewing experience for movies and sports. Cable networks in particular were able to thrive in the twenty-first-century environment. Flush with cash from subscription fees, networks such as HBO and Showtime began developing their own shows. Freed from the conventions and censorship regulations of traditional broadcasting, they inaugurated what could fairly be called a television renaissance. The HBO series *Sex and the City* (1998–2004) was considered pathbreaking in its treatment of female sexuality and independence, while its gangster drama, *The Sopranos* (1999–2007), was hailed as among the best-written and acted television shows of all time. By the second decade of the twenty-first century, even second-tier basic cable networks such as American Movie Classics (AMC) were broadcasting water-cooler fare such as *Mad Men* (2007–2015), which had a national impact on fashion and other dimensions of pop culture. Eventually, non-cable companies such as retailer Amazon, and Netflix, which began in the movie rental business, began developing shows that could be streamed on a computer or a television (the line between the two gradually effacing over the course of the decade). Television shows, once considered generally inferior to movies in quality and prestige, now attracted the best talent. And movies, whose economic and cultural powers were once rooted in theatrical exhibition in multiplexes, were increasingly conceived in terms of mass distribution via streaming. Here too, the very concept of "film," a term that connoted a literal description of reality, had become entirely virtual, even at movie theaters that now relied on digital projection. Once a mass pursuit, going to the movies was increasingly seen as an old fashioned, and relatively expensive, pastime.[20]

The biggest growth industry in the twenty-first century was video games, where revenues routinely exceeded those in the movie, television, or music business. Since the turn of the century, much of this had migrated online and had become increasingly specialized in terms of the kinds of games played and the consoles used to play them. There was also a growing audience for viewers to watch other people play games online. Gaming is now achieving the same degree of prestige and intellectual attention as other media that had once similarly been viewed as "mere" entertainment, as evidenced by the proliferation of academic programs, museum exhibitions, and other indications of cultural influence.

Posting: Web 2.0

Even as other media were catching up to it, the Internet continued to evolve.[21] The major innovation of the early twenty-first century was the rapid emergence of social networking. Its roots date back to the earliest days of the Internet in the form of "bulletin boards," in which individuals could share two-way information. These were small-scale and informal enterprises, but the advent of web browsing took them to an all new level, exploited with particular success by San Francisco entrepreneur Craig Newmark, who launched craigslist in 1995 as a means for individuals to easily advertise goods for sale. Other forms of early social networking included a type of site known as a multiple-user domain (MUD), some of which took the form of games. At many of these sites, users invented anonymous or fictive identities, which could get quite elaborate. By 2000, they had become widespread, as had chat rooms and dating sites such as Match.com. The next step was the emergence of sites such as Friendster and MySpace.com, which relied on a high degree of personalized content in the form of individual web pages and the ability to build a personal network of contacts. Sometimes these sites were personal; others, such as LinkedIn, founded in 2003, were intended primarily for career development.

The quintessential social networking site of the early twenty-first century, however, was Facebook. As you probably know—indeed, much of the story has become a form of modern folklore, mythologized in the 2010 hit movie *The Social Network*—Facebook began as a social networking site for Harvard University undergraduates. A number of Ivy League students were pressing administrators to publish such directories online (an early version went up at Stanford), but the concept really took off once student Mark Zuckerberg built one in 2004 at Harvard that he called thefacebook. It was notable for its simplicity and the voluntary basis of membership, and it caught on quickly. Within months, Zuckerberg had relocated to Palo Alto, where he and his collaborators refined and expanded their reach to an ever-growing number of colleges and universities. In 2006, the refashioned and now officially commercial site, now simply called Facebook, became available to anyone over the age of 13. In 2012, the site added its one billionth user.

For all its global power, Facebook remains only one prominent feature of the contemporary social media landscape. Twitter, a so-called micro-blogging site launched in 2006, also generated considerable excitement, particularly after one of its users sold the company on the concept of the hashtag, which made it easy to group and find tweets on the same topic. Twitter's requirement that all postings take up no more than 140 characters was well-suited to the demands of mobile computing of the kind found on smartphones. Other sites such as Instagram (2010) and Snapchat (2011) had a more photographic orientation.

Social networking of a more expansive kind emerged in 2005 with the arrival of YouTube, a site that allowed users to upload videos—and for viewers of those videos to post comments. Not all the content that has ended up on YouTube is user-created; indeed, the site has become a de facto repository for popular culture of the last century, dating back to silent movies. As with Napster, YouTube, which was acquired by Google for US$1.65 billion in 2006, became a locus of scrutiny for copyright violations, which has partially restricted the availability of content. But it appears to have a promising future as a source of programming that can compete with (and possibly displace) traditional television.

In the 2010s, social networking became a genuinely democratic locus of popular culture in the United States, offering individuals the opportunity to interact on a basis of relative equality unequaled in American history. And yet, that sense of democracy was fragile, limited—if not besieged—by larger forces that sought to check if not destroy it. Though they were often created in a hacker ethos of experimentation and openness, social media have resulted in a level of personal surveillance, which, if revealed, would probably shock many of those who readily disclosed details of their lives wittingly and unwittingly over a period of years. Advertising, which initially had little traction in the online world, has become increasingly intrusive at inserting itself between user and content. As in so many other arenas of American life—and unlike Europe, which restricts the collection and distribution of private information—the imperatives of private enterprise tend to trump broader civic considerations. The only exception is the security state in the wake of 9/11: now the government *and* corporations can monitor every movement of your fingers on a keyboard. In fact, your data in some cases has become more important than anything you buy, because it's now a product in its own right that's bought and sold without your knowledge, consent, or profit.

Freely Unequal: The Tottering US Economy

By the second decade of the twenty-first century, laments about a growing sense of economic inequality in American life—the concentration of financial power in the hands of the few, the ebbing tide of earning power for the many—had become widespread in national political discourse. New gadgetry such as laptops, tablets, and smartphones notwithstanding, the big-ticket items in everyday life—homes, educations, health care—were becoming difficult, even impossible, to afford. (Health care was difficult even *with* insurance, and health difficulties, along with job loss, were the most common reasons for bankruptcy.) Big box retailers such as Wal-Mart, and virtual ones such as Amazon.com, made lots of products affordable, but that's in large measure because they paid low wages to workers and low prices to suppliers. Another low-wage employer, McDonalds, counseled their workers to go on welfare, in effect forcing taxpayers to shoulder an economic burden that had been once understood to be that of employers, while compensating their executives hundreds of times more than the compensations of their lowest-paid workers (and doing so whether or not the companies they led were profitable).[22]

Inequality of *condition* had never really been considered a serious problem in American life, because of a strong collective belief in equality of *opportunity*, a notion that anyone could achieve financial success (or simply a decent standard of living). If anyone *could*, then it was not a problem that not everybody *did*; success could be attributed to at least a kernel of merit beyond good luck, and failure a matter of insufficient effort. However, by the end of the second Bush era, confidence in this version of common sense was rapidly disappearing amid a barrage of statistics indicating that social mobility in national life was declining and was actually below that of nations against which the United States had always measured its success. Affirmations of the American Dream were common, particularly among candidates on the campaign trail. But faith in the American Dream was weakening in the face of realities that were becoming impossible to ignore.

The roots of contemporary economic inequality—slowly but surely giving way to other kinds—have origins that date back far beyond the onset of the Bush presidency, or, for that matter, the Reagan presidency. It was Jimmy Carter, a Democrat, who signed the first important pieces of financial deregulation in the airline and trucking industries in the 1970s. It was a Democrat who followed Reagan, Bill Clinton, who signed the 1999 law repealing the New Deal–era Glass–Steagall Act, which had created a "firewall" between retail and commercial banks designed to prevent dangerous financial speculation. Clinton's Secretary of the Treasury, Robert Rubin, was a Wall Street financier.

These developments reflected an understanding that government regulation could be onerous, and that promoting economic growth at the top of the society was a goal that would benefit a wide range of constituencies in US society. But it also reflected the rising power of special interests to bend government to their will. In 1971, there were 175 companies with offices in Washington DC, ready to lobby the government. A decade later, there were 2,445, and the number has only grown since. Corporate interests became ever-more sophisticated in their ability to influence policymaking, and the role of money has become ever more important, despite attempts to limit it—such as the McCain–Feingold Act of 2002. Of course, lobbying is a legitimate activity undertaken by any number of groups, including labor unions. However, by the time of the 2010 elections, business was outspending labor by a ratio of 16–1.[23]

By the early twenty-first century, the degree to which the nation's economic and political deck was stacked was becoming difficult even for those on the right to ignore. The richest 1% of Americans reaped two-thirds of the nation's economic gains between 2002 and 2007; in the year 2010, it reaped 93%. Though the Bush administration touted tax cuts as a means to stimulate the economy, and successfully implemented them in 2001, 2002, and 2003, annual average economic growth in 2001–2007 was the slowest since World War II. The reasons for such slow growth are complex. But they did raise the question about whether the reigning supply-side paradigm really made as much sense in 2005 as it had in 1980. As wealth got concentrated—and moved offshore—there were also questions raised about whether the rich were even capable of spending and circulating money in ways that really would stimulate the economy.[24]

The decades on either side of the millennium were ones of growing economic stress for families trying to maintain their standard of living. In 1960, only 15% of women with children under the age of 6 years worked outside the home for wages. Fifty years later, that figure was 64%, the highest in the world.[25] Even taking into account the role of feminism and the desire of many women to pursue professional careers, the fact remains that many mothers of young children, and some fathers, would prefer to stay at home in the first years of a child's life, or to have access to free or low-cost daycare of the kind routinely available in other Western nations. In 1993, President Clinton had signed the Family and Medical Leave Act, which required employers to give workers time off to care for a child or tend to a sick relative. But such leaves were unpaid.

Meanwhile, the workplace itself became increasingly insecure. In 2005, about one-third of the US workforce was classified as contingent, meaning part-time or of limited duration, and thus ineligible for benefits such as health care. Not coincidentally, the percentage of unionized workers in the private sector shrank from 27% to 7% between 1979 and 2012. This is despite the fact that US worker productivity had risen 80% between 1973 and 2001, meaning that employers were getting more value from their workers even as they were paying them less. One problem, of course, is that American workers were increasingly subject to competition from low-wage workers abroad, which put downward pressure on their earnings. The practice of US companies "offshoring" their operations, continuing to benefit from the access to US markets but avoiding US taxes and regulations, became a chronic issue, but one in which business lobbyists held the upper hand. So was the growing reliance on increasingly sophisticated robot technology that threatened to make even relatively sophisticated jobs obsolete.[26]

To a great extent, Americans dealt with the squeeze by going into debt, encouraged by the proliferation of credit cards and home loans that often offered low teaser rates but which could quickly prove ruinous, especially when faced with job loss or medical problems. (Late fees and other charges were also an important source of banking profits.) Yet, here too, the government was more inclined to answer to business interests rather than consumers. A 2005 law, the Bankruptcy Abuse Prevention and Consumer Protection Act, made it harder for individuals to declare bankruptcy, and increased the power of businesses to garnish the wages of workers. By 2010, 2 million Americans were going bankrupt each year.[27]

For the approximately 70% of Americans who owned their own homes circa 2000, all this might have been tolerable while real-estate prices were going up, since it meant that, in theory, at least, they held a valuable financial asset. But this wealth foundation rested on sandy ground. In 1985, Americans collectively owned 69.2% of the value of their homes (lenders had the other 30.8). But, by 2011, that amount had plunged by almost half, to 38.4%, a decline that reflected the degree to which they had borrowed money against the value of their homes.[28]

Meanwhile, the major players in the real-estate industry—banks, insurance companies, and regulators—were behaving with increasing recklessness. In the aftermath of the tech bubble of 2000, investors disenchanted with that sector of the economy looked to real estate as an attractive vehicle for financial speculation. Banks and other lenders stoked the appeal of the housing sector through a variety of tactics. One was the proliferation of newfangled loan products. Traditionally, taking out a home loan meant taking on a 30-year mortgage, which allowed a homeowner to slowly but steadily pay back the loan and gain a valuable economic asset. Increasingly, however, banks pushed, and consumers signed on for, complicated variable rate mortgages, which could cost very little in the early years and then require sharply higher payments. The idea was that before such payments kicked in, homeowners would get new mortgages, which would allow them to pay off the old one and start over again. This was possible as long as the value of homes was rising. And they did: nationally, home prices rose 51% between 2000 and 2005.[29]

Banks now showed less interest in actually *holding* the mortgages they issued. Instead, they bundled pools of mortgages, divided them into segments, or "tranches," of creditworthiness, and sold them off as highly complex financial instruments to investors. Whereas once a bank or credit union was rooted in a particular community, and lenders evaluated their customers personally, the large corporation that actually held the debt a given house could be based thousands of miles away. Lenders were more interested in *issuing* mortgages, because they generated fees that were highly lucrative and could be tallied as profits quickly instead of waiting for years for a consumer to pay back a loan. And since lenders didn't plan to actually keep the mortgages they issued, they had less incentive to *care* whether the people they lent money to could actually pay it back. They increasingly resorted to so-called liar loans, where consumers were not required to document their income, and persuading real-estate appraisers to overestimate the value of a home to make buying one at the actual price to seem like more of a bargain. To deal with the potential problem of widespread defaults, the financial industry created a series of complicated financial products designed to insure a lender in case a given set of loans went bad. Such financial insurance policies were not only complicated, but increasingly corrupt: it's one thing to insure *your* house, another to insure *somebody else's* house, and—as increasingly became the case—something else again to bet on someone's house going into default, which you now had an incentive to make happen. By decade's end, investors were aggressively, and in some cases frantically, trying to dump shaky holdings on each other, betting on each other's failures, and trying to hide their own shaky positions. Once content simply to lend money, they were now deeply enmeshed in speculation themselves, sometimes trying to pass off junk investments to their own customers. Actually, the complexities were that such many bankers didn't really *know* the value of many of their assets.

The first tremors of an economic earthquake began attracting public attention in 2007. Increasingly panicky about the state of their portfolios, banks began raising the interest rates they charged each other: knowing *they* were in trouble, they weren't sure they couldn't trust anyone *else*. As this feedback loop began cascading through global financial markets, government officials tried to maintain optimism. "I feel good about the state of the economy," President Bush said amid rumblings in the stock market in October 2007. The following month, he affirmed that "the underpinnings of the economy are strong." By December, he was trying to stake out a safer position: "There's definitely some storm clouds and concerns, but the underpinning is good."[30]

It was not. In March 2008, the storied trading firm of Bear Stearns collapsed under the weight of its bad investments. The federal government stepped in and brokered a deal whereby the company would be sold to bank JP Morgan Chase for US$2 a share—this for a company whose shares were valued at US$170 a year earlier. But when another investment firm, Lehman Brothers, got in similar trouble in September, the government decided it would not repeat its questionable precedent of trying to save a corporation from its own poor choices. But, with Lehman's collapse, it was now unambiguously clear that the US economy— the engine of the global economy generally—faced its worst crisis since the Great Depression. Amid a sinking stock market, a plunging real-estate market, and a the loss of almost 2 million jobs in the first 9 months of 2008 alone, the question was once again how to save American capitalism from itself.[31]

Audacious Hopes: The Rise of Barack Obama

The US economic collapse was particularly pressing and dramatic because it was occurring as a presidential election was coming to a climax and candidates were suddenly faced with the issue of what to do about it. For Democrats in particular, the key issue at the start of the 2008 campaign had been the Iraq War: given how badly it turned out, new attention was focused on whether key political figures had voted to authorize it or not. Most Democrats had, including the presumed frontrunner, Hillary Rodham Clinton. Since spending 8 years in the White House as Bill Clinton's First Lady, she had spent another 8 years representing New York in the US Senate. There, she had acquired a reputation as a hard-working and effective legislator. However, her vote for war was now haunting her in her quest to become the first woman president of the United States.

That's because she faced a rising star who publicly denounced the war authorization in 2003. It had been a risky decision—he would have looked bad if the war had been a big success—but it was a decision rooted in conviction. This challenger had more going for him than a high profile and increasingly popular opinion, however. He was also a deeply charismatic politician and an unusually intelligent and compelling speaker who had authored a compelling 2004 autobiography, *Dreams from My Father*. And, similar to Clinton, he had the potential to make history by dint of his demographic identity—in this case, as the first African American to be elected president.

Barack Obama was in some ways an unlikely political superstar, but his rise, once it began, was steep. Born in Hawaii to an American mother and a Kenyan father in 1961, Obama's parents divorced when he was very young (he only saw his father once subsequently before the elder Obama's death in a 1982 car accident). After her remarriage in 1964, his mother took him with her when she relocated to Indonesia for a few years in the late 1960s. Obama returned to Hawaii in 1971 and lived with his grandparents for a few years while his mother did graduate work in anthropology. He attended a prep school in Honolulu before going on to Occidental College in Los Angeles and finishing his bachelor's degree at Columbia. He worked for as few years in the 1980s as a community organizer in his adopted home of Chicago before going on to earn a law degree from Harvard in 1991. He then returned to Chicago and taught constitutional law at the University of Chicago Law School.

Obama entered politics in 1996 when he won election to the Illinois state senate, where he served for 7 years. In the middle of this stretch, he made a bid for a seat in the US House of Representatives, but failed to unseat his Democratic opponent in the primary race for the nomination. His big break came in 2004, when he entered an exceptionally crowded field for an open US Senate race after the incumbent Republican decided to retire. Obama managed to win the Democratic nomination on a base of African Americans and white liberals, and then found himself in a favorable position when the Republican nominee was forced to withdraw because of a sex scandal. His replacement, the conservative African American commentator and former presidential candidate Alan Keyes, was handicapped by his recent move to Illinois from Maryland, and by political positions that were regarded as outside the state's mainstream. Tapped as a rising star at the Democratic National Convention in 2004, Obama's speech for John Kerry catapulted him to the forefront of American politics with its tantalizing vision of national unity. "There are those who are preparing to divide us, the spin masters and negative ad peddlers who embrace the politics of anything goes," Obama said before launching into a famous series of assertions that established his claim to fame. "Well, I say to them tonight, there's not a liberal America and a conservative America; there's the United States of America. There's not a black America and white America and Latino America and Asian America; there's the United States of America. We are one people, all of us pledging allegiance to the stars and stripes, all of us defending the United States of America."[32] Obama won the Senate race handily that fall.

Even as he was taking his seat in Washington, the presidential buzz had already begun. After 2 years on the job, Obama decided to make his move and announced his candidacy for the Democratic nomination in early 2007. It was clear from the start that the race would come down to Obama and Clinton, which inevitably made it one of historical proportions, because both candidates represented a first—an African American man or a white woman—getting a major party nomination. Given the likelihood that either would prevail over the eventual Republican nominee, the race was among the most exciting in US history.

Obama had a series of factors in his favor. One is that he represented a fresh face at a time when much of the electorate was tired of a country that had been dominated by Bushes or Clintons for a generation. Another is that Obama launched a sophisticated grassroots operation notable for its technological savvy. A third is that his campaign shrewdly planned for the long haul, successfully harvesting delegates from caucuses and primaries that were not expected to be important. However, Clinton was no pushover; after losing the first contest in Iowa in January 2008, she bounced back to win in New Hampshire a few days later. But Obama staked out a substantial lead in the weeks that followed, and was able to maintain it in a grinding stretch of campaign that went on for months. By June, he finally secured enough delegates for the nomination.

While not as dramatic, the Republican race for the nomination was also compelling, given that Bush was not eligible for re-election and the race was up for grabs. Key contenders included Arkansas governor Mike Huckabee, who was a favorite with evangelical voters, and businessman Mitt Romney, who appealed to the GOP's traditional business constituency. Senator John McCain, who had made a spirited but unsuccessful challenge against George W. Bush in 2000, also entered the race, but his campaign experienced early disarray in personnel and was widely considered over by the time of the Iowa caucus, which went to Huckabee. Yet, McCain bounced back to win the New Hampshire primary and steadily gained momentum thereafter, eventually winning the nomination.

McCain had a daunting challenge in 2008, however. Though it was clear that he was hardly a Bush minion, he nevertheless was a strong supporter of an unpopular war and the standard-bearer of the party that had started it. He also lacked the inherent excitement that Obama offered to younger voters, particularly since he was 72 years old in 2008. Republicans essentially resorted to two strategies against Obama. The first was to paint him as a dangerous radical. There was fuel for this fire in Obama's relationship with the Reverend Jeremiah Wright, the fiery pastor of Obama's church, who was captured on video saying "God damn America" in response to the nation's repeated racial inequities. Obama distanced himself from Wright's remarks, though the association lingered. Some Republican partisans also called attention to Obama's middle name—Hussein—to suggest that he was an alien figure; others asserted, inaccurately, that he was Muslim, believing that this would render him unfit for the presidency. There were also accusations that Obama was closely associated with Bill Ayers, the founder of the radical leftist organization the Weather Underground, whose botched terrorist bombing in 1970 resulted in the deaths of two members, though Obama and Ayers were more acquaintances than friends.

McCain sidestepped the most aggressive attacks on Obama, and corrected those who tried to smear him as Muslim. This led to the second GOP strategy, which involved giving his campaign some excitement of its own. McCain did this by selecting Alaska governor Sarah Palin as his running mate. Palin electrified the Republican right with her nomination speech at the GOP national convention in St. Paul in which she described herself as a hockey mom. (The only difference between a hockey mom and a pit bull? "Lipstick.") But there were soon questions about whether Palin, who had not been vetted closely, was sufficiently knowledgeable about national and world affairs to become president of the United States in the event something happened to McCain. The ridicule surrounding Palin shaded into elite condescension—comedian Tina Fey's uncanny but cutting imitation on *Saturday Night Live* thrilled liberals—which only mobilized her supporters all the more. On balance, Palin proved to be more of a distraction to McCain than the energizing jolt he had hoped she would be.

By fall 2008, however, it ceased to matter. The collapse of Lehman Brothers on September 15 effectively sealed McCain's fate, because the sharp downturn in the economy that followed was widely blamed on Republican policies. In November, Obama, riding the tide of a high turnout that included an increasingly important bloc of non-white voters, won the race with almost 53% of the vote to McCain's 45%, and 365 electoral votes to McCain's 170. A new era appeared to be at hand.

But change was not as rapid or decisive as Obama partisans had hoped. Though he enjoyed majorities in the House as well as the Senate, Congressional gridlock, which had been gradually intensifying since the 1990s, had become overpowering. In the 1960s, only 8% of significant legislation was subject to delaying tactics such as the filibuster. A half-century later, that figure had risen to 70%, with special—and often secret—interests able to block passage of just about any bill with cash contributions or other special favors for cooperative legislators.[33] Though Obama became famous for his desire to unite the American people, he was largely unable to realize this goal.

He did, however, achieve three major objectives. The first was stabilizing the national economy. Even before he became president, Obama (as well as McCain) expressed politically important support for the Troubled Asset Relief Program (TARP), which was signed into law by President Bush in October 2008—though not before Congress initially balked at the huge amount of money involved, precipitating a nosedive in the stock market that was only reversed after Congress changed course and voted to approve the bill. The TARP gambit was one of a series of steps to rescue the banks by having the government purchase many of the assets on their books—even though those assets may well have been worthless had they been put up for sale on the open market. The Federal Reserve also made huge cash reserves available to banks at little or no interest to ensure their liquidity, money they were then encouraged to lend to borrowers at a profit. In some cases, the government bailed out tottering firms by buying their stock to prevent their dissolution; the fear was that some, such as Citibank, were "too big to fail," that is, that their collapse would trigger serious damage to the economy as a whole. On September 15, the American International Group (AIG), a corporation that insured a great many mortgages, said it needed US$20 billion to emerge from insolvency. Then next day, this figure was US$89 billion. A little later, when fewer people were paying attention, it was US$150 billion, and then US$180 billion. The government ultimately found itself owning 80% of the company.[34] (It was later able to sell most of it off at a profit.) In the transition between Bush and Obama, the government also approved the use of TARP funds to save major US automakers (Ford, Chrysler, and General Motors), who, while not grossly mismanaged the way the banks were, suffered a sharp drop in demand as the economic crisis deepened, threatening to destroy an important component of the nation's manufacturing base.

Once he came into office, Obama tapped Democratic majorities in Congress to push the American Recovery and Reinvestment Act of 2009 into law. This was an over US$800 billion package of government spending on projects to improve the quality of the nation's roads, bridges, and other elements of its infrastructure. The idea here was not only to build and repair resources that would promote economic development, but to create government-funded jobs that would put people to work, which would prompt them to spend money, and thus get the country as a whole moving again.

These measures were quite controversial in 2008–2009. Some conservatives were appalled by the enormous scale of government spending, which drove the federal budget deeper into debt and put the government in control of large segments of the national economy, a state of affairs that approached that of socialist nations. Some liberals, for their part, were furious about the way government bailouts to banks were not accompanied by anything resembling a comparable scale of assistance to homeowners—indeed, even as they were receiving free money from the government, banks refused to renegotiate loans to consumers by lowering interest rates or reducing the amount owed. Still other liberals, notably the Nobel Prize–winning *New York Times* columnist Paul Krugman, were concerned that the size of the stimulus was much too small, running the risk that economy recovery would be dangerously slow or even reverse. While anything such as a durable consensus on the Obama economic program is probably years away, it is clear that it stanched the flow of damage in the immediate aftermath of the crisis. By the middle of the 2010s, the stock market appeared to have largely recovered from the crisis. That said, household income had not reached 2007 levels. Moreover, attempts to reform banking practices were largely beaten back (notably the so-called Volcker Rule, which sought to restrict banking investments that did not help customers); there were no widespread prosecutions of those who got the nation into a serious mess (only one top executive went to jail)[35]; and corporate financial power got even more concentrated. Casual and informed observers alike continue to believe that the largest banks remain too big to fail, and that it's only a matter of time before another disaster hits.

Obama's second major policy achievement—one that reflected a campaign promise rather than a response to a crisis—was the passage of the Affordable Care Act (ACA), also known as Obamacare, in 2010. This was another hard-won victory, and it too tried to steer a middle course in dealing with the serious national problem of rising medical costs and the growing number of Americans without health insurance. Conservatives were bitterly opposed to any further involvement of the government in health care; many liberals thought the country should move to a single-payer model where the government paid for all health care, the way it's done in many Western nations. The ACA was a complex law with many provisions, among them the elimination of pre-existing condition clauses that prevented sick people from getting coverage, and others that allowed parents to keep adult children on family policies until up to age 30 years. But its key feature was the creation of a series of so-called insurance exchanges where Americans could select from a wide variety of private plans and ensure a basic floor in coverage while stopping well short of socialized medicine.

Obama's third major accomplishment was in the realm of foreign policy. After a decade-long manhunt, a US Navy SEAL team finally managed to find Osama bin Laden in Pakistan, where he was killed in a firefight in May 2011. His death brought a measure of closure to the 9/11 attacks, and reinforced the degree to which al Qaeda had become a shell of its former self in the years following 2001. Obama also withdrew all US forces from Iraq at the end of 2011, and made plans for completing withdrawal of American troops from Afghanistan later in the decade. Here, again, there was controversy—some wanted a US exit sooner, others questioned its wisdom at all, especially after the outbreak of a civil war in Syria created regional instability and the emergence of ISIS as a major military force in 2014, once again overturning the fragile equilibrium that had prevailed in Iraq.

Substantial as they may have been, however, Obama's successes in office seemed, for friend and foe alike, to be limited. Though many hoped and feared he would lead a transformation in American politics—his winning of the Nobel Peace Prize in 2009 seemed more prospective than retrospective—this did not happen. From the moment he took office, widespread opposition to him, personal and political, emerged in many quarters. Among the more organized efforts in this regard was the rise of the Tea Party, whose name was an acronym standing for "taxed enough already" and whose members invoked the American Revolution as a tax revolt. There was vigorous debate about whether the Tea Party was an indigenous grassroots movement or a creature of wealthy conservative activists such as billionaires Charles and David Koch. But there was little question of the Tea Party's success in getting their preferred Republican candidates elected to local and state offices, and generally pulling the national party to the right. The Tea Party was widely cited as a major reason for Republican success in the midterm elections of 2010, which returned the GOP to the majority in the House and narrowed the Democratic margin in the Senate, once again restoring gridlock.

There was nevertheless a widespread perception in American politics that the Tea Party and Republicans generally were fighting a rear-guard action in the face of demographic change. For all its success, the Tea Party also hurt the GOP when it succeeded in getting candidates such as Todd Akin on the Republican ballot for the US Senate race in Missouri in 2012. Akin, a strong foe of abortion, caused an uproar when he asserted that "legitimate rape" rarely causes pregnancy. Such comments reinforced the growing gender gap dating back to the 1980s whereby women, especially single women, abandoned the Republican Party. The party also faced challenges, given the growing number of African American, Latino, and Asian voters, all of whom were voting Democratic in larger numbers in the 2010s. At times, it appeared that the GOP's primary strategy in dealing with the problem was to make it harder to vote at all. Republican governors and legislators around the country passed anti-fraud laws requiring photo identification, though there was little evidence of voter fraud in US elections. The fact that such identification could be difficult and expensive for poorer citizens to acquire seemed, to some people, to be the real reason why such laws were passed.

A sense that Republicans had little to offer beyond instinctive opposition to anything and everything that Obama was for hurt them in the eyes of that sliver of the electorate that was undecided in the presidential election of 2012. Obama's opponent was Mitt Romney, who emerged as the Republican candidate after a long primary campaign where he tacked right to play to the Tea Party constituency. (At one memorable presidential debate, all eight candidates raised their hands to indicate their opposition to a proposal to raise taxes at a rate of US$1 for US$10 in spending cuts: the very *idea* of *any* tax increase *whatsoever*, even if its overall effect was to shrink the size of government, was now standard Republican dogma.)[36] Romney also damaged his standing when he was caught on camera saying that 47% of Americans pay no taxes and consider themselves "victims, who believe the government has a responsibility to care for them, who believe that they are entitled to health care, to food, to housing, to you-name-it."[37] Factually inaccurate and disparaging of Americans whose contributions to society involved serving in the military or raising good citizens, the remark reinforced perceptions that Republicans were the party of the rich. Obama won the election with just over 50% of the vote and 332 electoral votes to Romney's 206. The voting tracked recent presidential elections—Democrats on the coasts and cities, Republicans in the interior—but showed a continued weakening GOP hold on the South, even if Obama lost North Carolina, which he had won in 2008. Republicans gained back significant lost ground in the midterm elections of 2014, amid hopes that key voting blocs (among them the young) might be tacking back in their direction. Demographics still seemed to be going against them in the long term, but observers said many of the same things in the 1970s on the eve of Ronald Reagan's election in 1980.

However *politically* divided the nation remained in the second half of the second decade of the twenty-first century, it seemed clear that, in *social* and *cultural* terms, the nation was moving to the left. Perhaps the most obvious manifestation of this was the surprising triumph of gay marriage, both as a matter of legal reality and social custom, in the nation at large. In the 2004 presidential campaign, George Bush used it as a so-called "wedge" issue to alienate moderate Democrats from the more progressive wing of their party; a decade later, it was Republicans opposed to gay marriage who found the issue nettlesome. Other indications of the leftward tilt of the country were more about anger than acceptance, notably the outcry that erupted after a series of high-profile police brutality cases in Ferguson (Missouri) and Staten Island (New York) in 2014. The white police shooting of another unarmed African American man in April 2015, and the murder of nine members of an African American church by a white supremacist in June 2015—both happening in Charleston—resulted in a change that had been resisted for 150 years: the removal of the Confederate flag from Southern statehouses, and from its position as a socially acceptable symbol of heritage in American life. It also sparked the birth of the Black Lives Matter movement, which fostered antiracist protests in cities and college campuses around the country. And while the political will to do something about climate change was still lacking as the Obama years drew to a close, consensus was growing as to its bona fide reality, even if there remained uncertainty about how to respond. It was not entirely clear which way the nation's alternating currents were tending, but the underlying energy was unmistakable.

Future History: The Present as Past

We are now largely out the realm of history and in a zone of living memory where it's difficult to tell whether any given experience reflects receding trends or intensifying ones. Future observers will certainly reinterpret the recent past, and may be more likely to revise it than more remote history. By way of a provisional conclusion, however, I will suggest that Obama's presidency in retrospect may well be more about what he *didn't* do than what he did. As with Bill Clinton, he spent much of his term in office resisting the force of his opponents, who were willing to shut down the government by refusing to pass an annual budget—as they almost did in 2010 and actually did for almost 3 weeks in 2013—rather than allow spending that they didn't like. (As was true under Clinton, Republicans ultimately backed down in the face of public anger that placed most of the blame on them.) Resorting to tactics such as executive orders that did not require legislative sanction, Obama took any number of steps in areas such as civil rights, immigration, and financial regulation that checked Republican initiatives.

In any case, it's probably more useful at this point to think less about what this leader or that party did right or wrong and think about the United States in the wider context of its imperial history. By 2016, it was 75 years since Henry Luce had proclaimed "the American Century," and citizens from all walks of life could hear that clock ticking. The nation had achieved global preeminence on the basis of its government's capacity to marshal vast powers to defeat external opponents. As with all empires, it maintained its cohesion by distributing finite wealth, rights, and privilege, less on the basis of equity than as to compel loyalty and forestall subversion among key (if shifting) constituencies. And, as with all empires, there remained many people, especially racial minorities, who stayed ignored or oppressed.

Still, even the most shrewdly managed empire eventually finds that the centrifugal distribution of power, whether to economic elites or to agitating minorities, results in growing paralysis. It remains unclear how or when this paralysis will be broken in the United States, and whether the resulting national reorganization will take the form of a faction from within gaining the upper hand, a challenge from without breaking the established order, or some combination of the two. The question now, as you finish this book, is how you're going to react when that happens. To some degree, your response will be a function of how you feel you arrived at that point, something this book is meant to help you figure out.

CULTURE WATCH: "Made in America," *The Sopranos* (2007)

For well over a century, the (rural) cowboy and (urban) gangster have been crucial male archetypes in American culture, essential sources of escapism for those seeking a psychic alternative to the often deadening routines of modern industrial

Figure 10.2 (MOB) FAMILY VALUES: Scene from "Made in America," the final episode of *The Sopranos* (1999–2007). As the family gathers in a New Jersey diner, the man in a Members Only jacket in the upper-right-hand corner may or may not be responsible for what happens next (1999–2007, created by David Chase, and produced by Home Box Office [HBO], Brillstein Entertainment Partners, and The Park Entertainment).

society. By the early twenty-first century, however, it was increasingly difficult for men, especially white men, to sustain such fantasies. Often cited as the locus of societal ills, they faced a series of challenges—notably those of the feminist movement—that questioned male prerogatives in the realm of imagination no less than real life. In the 1970s, it was still possible in *The Godfather* saga for a patriarch to credibly preside over the fates of families, literal as well as criminal. But by the time of the television show *The Sopranos* (1999–2007), the Mafioso as embodied by Tony Soprano (James Gandolfini) was a man besieged, enmeshed amid a domineering mother (Nancy Marchand), a strong-minded wife (Edie Falco), and unruly children (Jamie-Lynne Sigler and Robert Iler)—and uneasily seeking the services of a psychotherapist (Lorraine Bracco)—while presiding over a motley crew of criminals in the suburbs of New Jersey.

The Sopranos was the brainchild of David Chase, a television scriptwriter, director, and producer who tried to sell his idea for a drama series to a number of networks before bringing it to Home Box Office (HBO). The cable network, which had begun making its mark as a source of distinguished programming with shows such as *The Larry Sanders Show* (1992–1998), *Sex and the City* (1998–2004), and *Oz* (1997–2003), financed a pilot in 1997, but the show didn't actually begin its run until 1999. It became an instant hit, generating roughly 10 million viewers a week—not huge by traditional network television standards, but making it clear that cable television was now competitive with anything on broadcast television.

But *The Sopranos* was nothing like broadcast television. It was not simply a matter of the sex and violence that had always been the province of cable. It was also that the show broke some of the basic conventions of the medium in ways that could be shocking. In the classic Season 1 episode "College," for example, Tony takes his daughter Meadow on a college visiting trip in Maine. While there, he sees an ex-mobster-turned-government-informant who had enrolled in the federal witness protection program. Tony makes a detour while Meadow is otherwise occupied and, in a brutal 1-minute and 16-seconds-long scene, strangles his former associate's throat with electric wire. While we often find ourselves rooting for Tony—sympathizing with his woes, believing he may be turning a new leaf—his viciousness is never far from the surface of his character.

By the time of the series finale of the show, "Made in America" in 2007—the title alludes to gangsters being officially adopted, or "made," into a crime family, among other connotations—the walls are closing in on Tony and his crew. With key members of his entourage dead or wounded, and his family sequestered in a safe house, he finds himself in the uncomfortable position of cooperating with federal authorities. Seeking a respite from their troubles, the Soprano family decides to meet at a local diner for dinner. Tony arrives first, carefully scanning the restaurant for threats. The rest of the family arrives as a mysterious man wearing a Members Only jacket (a brand popular in the 1980s) heads into the men's room. Tony puts the 1981 Journey song "Don't Stop Believin'"—a cheesy tune somewhat out of character for the setting—on the jukebox sitting on his table. The family, now together, is engaging in small talk when—

The ending of *The Sopranos* is widely regarded as one of the most controversial—though, on balance, most highly praised—climaxes in the history of television. Viewers at the time thought there was something wrong with their televisions or cable providers, and argued among themselves about how to interpret what had happened. If you're puzzled, consider this an invitation: go check out the show—from the beginning.

All good things, and bad things too, come to an end. But for now, at least, *The Sopranos*, and the culture that spawned it, live on.

Suggested Further Reading

As mentioned in the Suggested Reading section in Chapter 9, the best book by far on the coming of 9/11 is Robert Wright's *The Looming Tower: Al Qaeda and the Road to 9/11* (2006; New York: Vintage, 2007). Jim Dwyer and Kevin Flynn offer a narrative account in *102 Minutes: The Unforgettable Story of the Fight to Survive Inside the Twin Towers* (2004; New York: Times Books, 2011).

On the Iraq War, George Packer provides a deeply informed and highly readable account in *The Assassin's Gate: America in Iraq* (2005; New York: Farrar, Straus, and Giroux, 2006). For the military side, see Thomas E. Ricks, *Fiasco: The American Military Adventure in Iraq* (New York: Penguin, 2006).

On the corrosion of American society and democracy, see Hedrick Smith, *Who Stole the American Dream?* (New York: Random House, 2012). David Cay Johnston provides details on how the American government is rigged in *Perfectly Legal: The Covert Campaign to Rig Our Tax System to Benefit the Super Rich—and Cheat Everybody Else* (New York: Portfolio, 2003) and *Free Lunch: How the Wealthiest Americans Enrich Themselves at Government Expense (and Stick You with the Bill)* (New York: Portfolio, 2007). Among the best writers on inequality and its implications for the United States is Kevin Phillips, who has written a series of books on the subject. Recent books include *American Theocracy: The Peril and Politics of Radical Religion, Oil, and Borrowed Money in the 21st Century* (New York: Viking, 2006) and *Bad Money: Reckless Finance, Failed Politics, and the Global Crisis of American Capitalism* (New York: Viking, 2008). See also Charles Morris, *The Trillion Dollar Meltdown: Easy Money, High Rollers, and the Great Credit Crash* (New York: Public Affairs, 2008). Andrew Ross Sorkin has written what many consider to be the definitive account of the financial crash of 2007–2008 in *Too Big to Fail: The Inside Story of How Wall Street and Washington Sought to Save the Financial System—and Themselves* (New York: Viking, 2009). See also Joseph Stiglitz, *Freefall: America, Free Markets, and the Sinking of the World Economy* (New York: Norton, 2010).

Much of the cultural material in this chapter draws on Jim Cullen, *A Short History of the Modern Media* (Malden, MA: Wiley-Blackwell, 2014) Important books on the emergence of Web 2.0 include Ken Auletta, *Googled: The End of the World as We Know It* (New York: Penguin, 2010); David Kirkpatrick, *The Facebook Effect: The Inside Story of the Company that Is Connecting the World* (New York: Simon & Schuster, 2011); and Andrew Lih, *The Wikipedia Revolution: How a Bunch of Nobodies Created the World's Greatest Encyclopedia* (New York: Hyperion, 2009).

The best horse-race chronicle of the election of 2008 is John Heilemann and Mark Halperin's *Game Change: Obama and the Clintons, McCain and Palin, and the Race of a Lifetime* (New York: Harper, 2010). They are also the authors of *Double-Down: Game Change 2012* (New York: Penguin, 2013). *New Yorker* editor David Remnick has written a highly regarded biography of Obama in *The Bridge: The Life and Rise of Barack Obama* (New York: Knopf, 2010). Chuck Todd offers a balanced chronicle of the Obama presidency in *The Stranger: Barack Obama in the White House* (New York: Little, Brown, 2014).

Notes

1   On the role of the Middle East in the American imagination, see Melani McAlister, *Epic Encounters: Culture, Media & U.S. Interests in the Middle East Since 1945*, second ed. (2001; Berkeley: University of California Press, 2005).

2   Packer, 386.

3   Packer, 23–24. The first chapter of *The Assassin's Gate* traces opinion in leading Republican circles in the decade following the end of the Persian Gulf War.

4   Packer, 39–40.

5   Smith, 358; http://www.reuters.com/article/2013/03/14/us-iraq-war-anniversary-idUSBRE92D0PG20130314 (September 25, 2014); Nicolaus Mills, "Punished for Telling the Truth about the War," CNN, March 20, 2013: http://www.cnn.com/2013/03/20/opinion/mills-truth-teller-iraq/ (September 12, 2014).

6   Joshua B. Freeman, *American Empire: The Rise of a Global Power/The Democratic Revolution at Home* (New York: Penguin, 2012), 471.

7   Packer, 298–299.

8   Packer, 310.

9   Freeman, 472.

10   Freeman, 471.

11   Thomas Ricks, *Fiasco: The American Military Adventure in Iraq* (New York: Penguin, 2006).

12   Packer makes this point on p. 384.

13   Smith, 260.

14   Smith, 131.

15   Kate Zernicke and Jim Rutenberg, "Friendly Fire: The Birth of an Anti-Kerry Ad," *The New York Times*, August 20, 2004: http://www.nytimes.com/2004/08/20/politics/campaign/20swift.html?ex=1250913600&en=9b6f27de16c97265&ei=5090&partner=rssuserland&src=pm&pagewanted=3 (September 14, 2014).

16   A fully detailed account of Kerry's position on Iraq can be found at FactCheck.org: http://www.factcheck.org/2013/09/kerry-spins-his-record-on-iraq/ (September 14, 2014). The Kerry quotation can be found at http://www.cbsnews.com/news/kerrys-top-ten-flip-flops/ (September 15, 2014).

17   Congressional testimony of Leah Hodges in *The United States Since 1945: A Documentary Reader*, edited by Robert P. Ingalls and David K. Johnson (Malden, MA: Wiley-Blackwell, 2009), 220.

18   The foregoing discussion is based on Cullen, *Short History of the Modern Media*, 210–211.

19   http://www.publishersweekly.com/pw/by-topic/digital/retailing/article/54609-e-books-market-share-at-22-amazon-has-27.html (September 16, 2014).

20 Cullen, *Short History of the Modern Media*, 169–170.
21 Much of the following is based on Cullen, *Short History of the Modern Media*, 263–266.
22 Casey B. Mulligan, "Welfare Benefits for Big Business," *The New York Times*, December 25, 2013: http://economix.blogs.nytimes.com/2013/12/25/welfare-benefits-for-big-business/?_r=0 (June 23, 2015).
23 Smith, 11, 133.
24 Smith, xv, 137.
25 Smith, 76.
26 Smith, 75, 63. On the acceleration of robots in the workplace, see Martin Ford, *Rise of the Robots: Technology and the Threat of a Jobless Future* (New York: Basic Books, 2015).
27 Stiglitz, 102; Smith, 95.
28 Smith, 220.
29 Freeman, 478.
30 Stiglitz, 28.
31 Andrew Ross Sorkin, "JP Morgan Pays $2 a Share for Bear Stearns, *The New York Times*, March 17, 2008: http://www.nytimes.com/2008/03/17/business/17bear.html?_r=0 (September, 20, 2014); "Stiglitz, 29.
32 "Transcript: Illinois Senate Candidate Barack Obama," *The Washington Post*, July 27, 2004; http://www.washingtonpost.com/wp-dyn/articles/A19751-2004Jul27.html (September 21, 2014).
33 Smith, 322.
34 Stiglitz, 123.
35 Jesse Eisinger, "Why Only One Top Executive Went to Jail for the Financial Crisis," *The New York Times Magazine*, April 30, 2014: http://www.nytimes.com/2014/05/04/magazine/only-one-top-banker-jail-financial-crisis.html?_r=0 (September 25, 2014).
36 Clip available here: https://www.youtube.com/watch?v=WKzGZj32LYc (September 21, 2014).
37 http://www.politifact.com/truth-o-meter/statements/2012/sep/18/mitt-romney/romney-says-47-percent-americans-pay-no-income-tax/ (September 21, 2014).

Postlude:
The Ends of the American Century

YOU ARE A CHILD OF EMPIRE. You probably don't think of yourself that way, and there are some good reasons for that. However, the fact of the matter is that you are, and, at some point in the not-so-distant future, you may well have to reckon with it.

If and when that happens, it will no longer do to say that that you don't think of yourself that way. No, *you* did not invade any countries or steal any wealth. Not only was empire not waged in your name, you were opposed to such things when they were happening, and you reject them now. Besides, you hardly got anywhere near any of the benefits of those who did pursue empire (and, for that matter, many of those who didn't). You're just a person who happened to live in a particular place and a particular time. You have your affection for your home, like anyone would. But that hardly makes you an imperialist.

You may be right—now, and later. But don't be surprised if this argument holds little weight with those who challenge you. You *did* reap the benefits, such people will say. Principal among them was the liberty to ignore the wages of empire, small as they may have been, and having the luxury to focus on matters closer to that home. Americans have always been deeply invested in their own innocence, and their fervency on this point (*I'm* not a racist!) has intensified in direct proportion to their insulation. But there are no innocent victims, your adversary will say. There is a price to living in such a land, and someone must pay it. You may be unlucky, but you're not undeserving of such a fate.

Such a person may be wrong—now, and later. The question at hand is how you will deal with such accusations when your protestations of innocence are rejected and you are faced with the prospect of losing that which you hold dear. Neither of us knows—can possibly know—the answer to that question. Fight? Flight? Something else? The decision you make will likely be instinctive, and perhaps beyond your control.

Actually, that's true of a lot of things we do. But an important premise of our educations involves the idea that we can *inform* our instincts—that, by dint of preparation, practice, and reflection, we can train ourselves to do the right thing

Democratic Empire: The United States Since 1945, First Edition. Jim Cullen.
© 2017 Jim Cullen. Published 2017 by John Wiley & Sons, Inc.

without thinking about it—the way a wide receiver catches a ball over the middle knowing he's going to be hit by the safeties; or the way a nurse plunges in the needle as fast and sure and painlessly as possible; or how a distracted teacher strokes a young child's head and provides the needed reassurance without even realizing she's doing it.

Who are you? What do you care most about? What is it that you most want to do? These are big questions, the answers to which no book, let alone this one, can offer definitive answers. The goal here has been to provide you with information—not for its own sake, but to be a part of that process by which those instincts of yours become informed. More specifically, the goal has been to provide you with a rudimentary sense of your heritage—how and why the land you inhabit has taken on the contours it has, where it has succeeded, and where it has failed. The portrait may or may not be recognizable to you; if it's not, perhaps it can clarify where you might seek a better one.

And so now it's time to ask: What do you think of this story? Is it one you like? Does it have characters to whom you can relate? Toward whom do you feel some loyalty, or even love, despite their undoubted flaws? If not, where instead might you choose to cast your lot? Your answers, to the extent that you can even begin to articulate them at this point in your life, are likely to be provisional. But it is the faith of the historian—faith, because our notions of the past keep changing, and facts are useless until you try to do something with them on the basis of educated guesses—that history can become an instrument by which we can live better lives and make better choices with the finite freedom that defines the human condition.

Index

Democratic Empire: The United States Since 1945, First Edition. Jim Cullen.
© 2017 Jim Cullen. Published 2017 by John Wiley & Sons, Inc.